The Unitary Patent and the Unified Patent Court

Second Edition

The Unitary Patent and the Unified Patent Court

Second Edition

by

Pieter Callens

Sam Granata

Published by:
Kluwer Law International B.V.
PO Box 316
2400 AH Alphen aan den Rijn
The Netherlands
E-mail: lrs-sales@wolterskluwer.com
Website: www.wolterskluwer.com/en/solutions/kluwerlawinternational

Sold and distributed by:
Wolters Kluwer Legal & Regulatory U.S.
920 Links Avenue
Landisville, PA 17538
United States of America
E-mail: customer.service@wolterskluwer.com

Printed on acid-free paper.

ISBN: 978-94-035-2467-2

e-ISBN: 978-94-035-2477-1
Web PDF ISBN: 978-94-035-2487-0

© 2024 Pieter Callens and Sam Granata

All rights reserved. No part of this publication may be reproduced, stored in a retrieval system, or transmitted in any form or by any means, electronic, mechanical, photocopying, recording, or otherwise, without written permission from the publisher.

Permission to use this content must be obtained from the copyright owner. More information can be found at: www.wolterskluwer.com/en/solutions/legal-regulatory/permissions-reprints-and-licensing.

Printed in the Netherlands.

About the Authors

Pieter Callens (1980) is an attorney-at-law specialising in intellectual property law and ICT within the Belgian law firm Eubelius. He obtained a Master in Law at the Catholic University of Louvain (Belgium) and a Master in Economic Law at the Université Libre de Bruxelles (Belgium). During his law education, Pieter studied as an exchange student US patent law at Duke University (North Carolina, USA). He was admitted to the bar in Belgium in 2004.

Between 2008 and 2010 Pieter was advisor to the Belgian Minister of Economy with respect to intellectual property matters. Pieter advised the Belgian Presidency of the European Union in 2010 when the EU Council reached a political compromise on the language regime of the Unitary Patent.

Pieter is a member of AIPPI, INTA and LES and was appointed by the Belgian government as permanent member of the Advisory Board for Intellectual Property. He has written several publications on intellectual property law and is a frequent speaker regarding IP and ICT topics. Pieter is one of the authors of the Kluwer Patent Blog. Together with Sam Granata he published in 2013 the book *Introduction to the Unitary Patent and the Unified Patent Court* (Kluwer Law International).

Sam Granata (1970) is a judge at the Court of Appeal Antwerp (Belgium), Benelux Court of Justice (Luxembourg), part-time UPC judge (Court of First Instance UPC – Presiding Judge Local Division Brussels (Belgium)), member of the Advisory Board for Intellectual Property Rights to the Federal Belgian Ministry of Economy and member of the of the *Conseil Benelux de la Propriété Intellectuelle*. He was a member of the Legal Framework Group UPC (Subgroup 1: Rules of Procedures of the Court and Subgroup 6: Rules on Mediation and Arbitration). Throughout his academic and professional career, Sam has proven to have a strong interest in patent law. He obtained a Master in Law at the Catholic University of Louvain (Louvain, Belgium), a Master in Intellectual Property Law at Franklin Pierce Law Center (now University of New Hampshire, New Hampshire, US) and a Master of Arts in Interactive Multimedia at the University of London (London, UK).

In his previous professional life, Sam was a research fellow at the Center for Intellectual Property of the Catholic University of Louvain (Louvain, Belgium), worked as an attorney-at-law specialising in intellectual property law and mediator in Brussels and Antwerp (Belgium) and was judge at the Commercial Court of Antwerp dealing with patent cases. He is a frequent speaker at IP related events.

Table of Contents

About the Authors v
Introduction 1

PART ONE: THE UNITARY PATENT

Chapter I
History of the EU Patent Title 5
A. The Community Patent Convention 5
B. Proposal for Council Regulation on the Community Patent 6
C. Communication "Enhancing the patent system in Europe" 7
D. Council conclusions under the Swedish presidency 8
E. Failure to reach unanimity on the language regime 9
F. Enhanced cooperation 11
G. Opposition to the enhanced cooperation 13

Chapter II
Legal Instruments for Unitary Patent Protection 19

Chapter III
Legal Challenges against the Unitary Patent Regulation and the Translation Regulation 21
A. First judgment 22
  1. First plea: infringement of the rule of law 22
  2. Second plea: lack of a legal basis for the Unitary Patent Regulation 23
  3. Third plea: misuse of powers 23
  4. Fourth and fifth pleas: infringement of Article 291(2) TFEU and of the principles laid down in the judgment in *Meroni v. High Authority* 24
  5. Sixth and seventh pleas: infringement of the principles of autonomy and uniformity of EU law 25
B. Second judgment 27
  1. First plea: infringement of the principle of non-discrimination on the ground of language 27
  2. The second plea: infringement of the principles set out in the *Meroni* judgment 29

	3.	Third plea: lack of a legal basis for Article 4 of the Translation Regulation	29
	4.	Fourth plea: infringement of the principle of legal certainty	30
	5.	The fifth plea: infringement of the principle of the autonomy of EU law	31
C.		Consequence of the dismissals	31

Chapter IV
Accession of Italy to the Enhanced Cooperation 33

A.	Accession of Italy	33
B.	Accession by Spain?	33
C.	Brexit	34

Chapter V
The Unitary Patent 35

A.	Legal status of the Unitary Patent Regulation		35
B.	Additional layer of patent protection		37
C.	Granting procedure: request for unitary effect after EPO procedure		38
	1. EPO checks formal and substantive requirements		38
	2. Consequences if requirements are not met		40
D.	Equal claims		41
E.	Unitary character		42
	1. Scope of the unitary character determined by the date of publication of the patent		43
	2. Revocation or limitation of the European Patent		43
	3. Transfer/licence		43
	4. Impact of opposition		44
F.	Date of effect		44
G.	Effect		45
	1. Initial plan: effect and consequences included in the Unitary Patent Regulation		45
	2. Compromise: reference to the law of the Participating Member States		47
	3. Damages		48
H.	Exhaustion		49
I.	Unfair competition and competition law		49
J.	Register for Unitary Patent Protection		49
K.	Object of property		52
	1. Applicable law		52
	2. Offer of licences with 15% renewal fee reduction		53
		a. Offer of licences	53
		b. Withdrawal of the licence statement	54
		c. Appropriate consideration	54

		d. Registration of licence statements	54
	3.	Compulsory licences	56
	4.	Procedure for entering transfers, licences and other rights and any legal means of execution	56
L.	Publications regarding Unitary Patents		58
M.	Inclusion of decisions of the Unified Patent Court in the files of the EPO		59
N.	Lapse		60
O.	Role of the EPO		60
P.	Select Committee		61
Q.	Rules relating to Unitary Patent Protection		63
R.	Implementing Rules of the EPC applying *mutatis mutandis* to Unitary Patent Protection		63
S.	Oral proceedings		66
T.	Re-establishment of rights		67
U.	Renewal fees		68
	1.	General	68
	2.	Level of renewal fees	68
	3.	Distribution of renewal fees	71
	4.	Administration by the EPO	73
	5.	Rules relating to Fees for Unitary Patent Protection	76
V.	Budgetary and Financial Rules		77
W.	Follow-up		79
X.	Entry into force and application		79

Chapter VI
Language Regime of the Unitary Patent — 81

A.	Reimbursement of translation costs for patent application		81
	1.	Who benefits from the compensation?	82
	2.	Transfer	83
	3.	Procedure for acquiring compensation	83
	4.	Revision of the decision to grant compensation	84
	5.	Amount of compensation	84
B.	General principle: no translations		85
C.	First exception: translation in the event of a dispute		85
D.	Second exception: the transitional period		86
	1.	German and French into English	87
	2.	English to other official languages	87
	3.	Publication by the EPO	87
	4.	For information purposes only	87
E.	Entry into force		87

PART TWO: THE UNIFIED PATENT COURT

Chapter I
Legal Status of the UPCA and the Unified Patent Court   91

A. Treaty between EU Member States   91
B. CJEU Opinion on the conformity with EU treaties   91
    1. Primacy of Union law   92
    2. Preliminary rulings of the CJEU   94
    3. Liability for infringements of Union law   95
C. Opposition to the Unified Patent Court   97
D. Legal capacity of the Court   98

Chapter II
Structure of the Court   99

A. Court of First Instance   99
    1. Central division   100
    2. Local division   101
    3. Regional division   103
    4. Discontinuance of a local or regional division   103
B. Court of Appeal   104
C. No instance of legal review – preliminary rulings of the Court of Justice   105
D. The Registry   106
E. Administrative bodies   107
    1. The Preparatory Committee   107
        a. Legal Framework Group   108
        b. Financial aspects   109
        c. IT   110
        d. Facilities   110
        e. Human resources and training   110
    2. The Administrative Committee   110
    3. The Budget Committee   111
    4. The Advisory Committee   111
    5. The Presidium   112
F. Patent Mediation and Arbitration Centre   113
    1. Introduction   113
    2. The UPC as a one-stop shop dispute resolution system   114
    3. Rules of Operation of the Mediation and Arbitration Centre of the UPC   115
        a. Framework in which the Rules of Operation were discussed 115
        b. The Centre: name, status, seat and aims   116
        c. Languages   118
        d. Finances   118
        e. Organisational structure of the Centre   118
        f. List of arbitrators and mediators   120

		g. Start of operations	121
	4.	Issues	121
		a. Competence of the Centre	122
		b. Enforceability of settlements	123
		c. Revoking and limiting patents	125
	5.	Conclusion	125

Chapter III
Composition of the Different Divisions of the Court 127

A.	Court of First Instance	127
	1. Local division	127
	2. Regional division	128
	3. Addition of a technical judge before local or regional divisions	129
	4. Central division	130
	5. One or three judges?	130
	6. Panels	131
B.	The Court of Appeal	131

Chapter IV
The Judges of the Court 135

A.	Requirements	135
B.	Appointment of judges	136
	1. Preselection by the Preparatory Committee	136
	2. Appointment procedure by the Administrative Committee	137
	3. Actual first appointment procedure of the first appointed legally qualified judges to the UPC	139
	4. Working conditions	140
	a. Full-time judges and part-time judges	141
	b. Remuneration, allowances and reimbursement of expenses	142
	c. Leave	143
	d. Social security benefits	143
	e. Disciplinary measures	143
	f. Appeals	144
C.	Judicial independence and impartiality – conflicts of interest	144
D.	Immunity of judges	151
E.	End of the duties of the judge	152
F.	Pool of Judges	153
G.	Training framework for judges	153
H.	Staff and judicial vacations	155

Chapter V
Jurisdiction and Competence 157

A.	International jurisdiction	157

B.	Substantive competence of the Court	161
	1. Patents for which the Court is competent	161
	2. Actions for which the Court is competent	162
C.	Territorial competence of the first instance divisions	163
	1. Infringement actions	163
	2. Provisional protection – prior use – provisional and protective measures	164
	3. Actions regarding compensation for licences of Unitary Patents	165
	4. Conflicts of jurisdiction	165
	5. Counterclaim for revocation – bifurcation	166
	6. Independent revocation action	168
	7. Non-infringement actions	169
	8. Actions against Unitary Patent tasks of the EPO	170
	9. General exception: choice of the parties	170
	10. Relation between EPO oppositions and revocation actions	170
D.	Territorial scope of the decisions of the Court	170

Chapter VI
Sources of Law and Substantive Law — 173

A.	Sources of law	173
B.	Substantive patent law	175
	1. Direct use of the invention	175
	2. Indirect use of the invention	176
	3. Limitations	176
	4. Prior use	178
	5. Exhaustion of the rights conferred by a European Patent	179
	6. Effects of supplementary protection certificates	179

Chapter VII
Organisation of Proceedings — 181

A.	Statute and Rules of Procedure	181
B.	Procedural principles	182
C.	Parties and representation	183
	1. Parties	183
	2. Representation	184
	a. General	184
	b. Rules on the European Patent Litigation Certificate and appropriate qualifications	186
	c. Draft Code of Conduct for representatives	189
D.	Language of the proceedings	192
	1. Court of First Instance	192
	a. Local divisions	192
	b. Regional divisions	194
	c. Central division	194

		d. General exception: use of the language in which the patent was granted	195
	2.	Court of Appeal	196
	3.	Translation and interpretation arrangements	197
E.	Proceedings before the Court		198
	1.	Written, interim and oral procedure	198
	2.	Means of evidence and burden of proof	198
F.	Powers of the Court		200
	1.	General powers	200
	2.	Order to preserve evidence and to inspect premises	200
	3.	Freezing orders	202
	4.	Provisional and protective measures	202
	5.	Order to produce evidence	204
	6.	Court experts	204
	7.	Power to order the communication of information	205
	8.	Permanent injunctions in case of infringement	206
	9.	Corrective measures in infringement proceedings	207
	10.	Decision on the validity of a patent	208
	11.	Powers of the Court concerning decisions of the EPO	209
	12.	Award of damages	210
		a. Determination of the damages	210
		b. Period of limitation	212
	13.	Recoverable legal costs	212
G.	Court fees and legal aid		217
	1.	Court fees	217
	2.	Legal aid	218
H.	Appeal proceedings		218
	1.	Appeal	218
	2.	Effects of an appeal	220
	3.	Decision on appeal and referral back	221
I.	Decisions		222
	1.	Basis for decisions	222
	2.	Formal requirements of decisions	222
	3.	Decisions and dissenting opinions	222
		a. Decision making process	222
		b. Dissenting opinions	223
		c. Decisions by default	223
	4.	Settlement decisions	224
	5.	Publication of decisions	224
	6.	Rehearing	224
	7.	Enforcement of decisions and orders	225

Chapter VIII
Finance of the Court   227

A. Budget of the Court   227

B. Financing of the Court 227
C. Operating the budget 228

Chapter IX
Implementation and Operation of the UPCA 231

A. Transitional regime and opt-out 231
   1. Immediate and exclusive jurisdiction for Unitary Patents 231
   2. European Patents: national courts or Unified Patent Court 231
   3. Opt-out for European Patents 232
   4. National proceedings: in or out? 233
   5. National proceedings: application of the UPCA? 234
B. Ratification and entry into force 236
   1. Signature, ratification and accession 236
   2. Revision 237
   3. Authentic languages of the UPCA 238
   4. Entry into force 238
   5. Brexit 239
   6. Provisional application 241

Chapter X
Unified Patent Court Website and Case Management System 243

PART THREE: THE RULES OF PROCEDURE OF THE UNIFIED PATENT COURT

Chapter I
Introduction 247

A. Framework 247
B. Legal history of the Rules 247
C. Templates and guidances 249

Chapter II
Preamble 251

Chapter III
Application and Interpretation of the Rules of Procedure 253

A. Introduction 253
B. Application of the Rules and general principles of interpretation 253
C. Supplementary protection certificates 254
D. Power of the staff of the Registry and sub-registry to perform functions of the Registry 254
E. Lodging of documents 254

Table of Contents

F.	Service and supply of orders, decisions and written pleadings and other documents by the Registry	255
G.	Introduction to language regime	255
H.	Representation, communication with the Court and proprietorship of a patent	259
I.	Powers of the Court	260
J.	Application to opt-out and withdrawal of opt-out	261

Chapter IV
(Part 1) Procedures before the Court of First Instance (Rules 10–159): Stages of the Proceeding (inter partes proceedings) 271

A.	Birds' eye view	271
	1. Examination as to formal requirements	272
	2. Preliminary Objection	277
	3. Value-based fee for the infringement action	279
	4. Distribution of actions	282
B.	(Chapter 1) Written procedure (Rules 12–96)	283
	1. Infringement action (Rules 12–41)	283
	2. Revocation action (Rules 42–60)	289
	3. Action for declaration of non-infringement (Rules 61–74)	289
	4. Actions within Article 33(5) and (6) UPCA (Rules 75–77)	292
	5. Actions for compensation for licences on the basis of Article 8 of the Unitary Patent Regulation (Rule 80)	293
	6. Actions against a decision of the EPO in carrying out the tasks referred to in Article 9 Unitary Patent Regulation (Rules 85–98)	296
C.	(Chapter 2) Interim procedure (Rules 101–110)	298
D.	(Chapter 3) Oral procedure (Rules 111–119)	301
	1. The actual oral procedure (Rules 111–119)	301
	2. The decision on the merits (Rules 118–119)	305
E.	(Chapter 4) Procedure for the determination of damages and compensation (Rules 125–144)	307
	1. Application for the determination of damages (Rules 131–140)	307
	2. Request to lay open books (Rules 141–144)	310
F.	(Chapter 5) Procedure for cost orders (Rules 150–157)	311
G.	(Chapter 6) Security for costs (Rules 158–159)	312

Chapter V
(Part 2) Evidence (Rules 170–201) 313

A.	(Chapter 1) Witnesses and experts of the parties (Rules 175–181)	314
B.	(Chapter 2) Court experts (Rules 185–188)	317
C.	(Chapter 3) Order to produce evidence and communicate information (Rules 190–191)	318
	1. Order to produce evidence (Rule 190)	318

	2. Order to communicate information (R. 191)	319
D.	(Chapter 4) Order to preserve evidence (*saisie*) and order for inspection (Rules 192–199)	319
	1. Order to preserve evidence (*saisie*) (Rules 192–198)	321
	2. Order for Inspection (Rule 199)	324
E.	(Chapter 5) Other evidence (Rules 200–204)	324
	1. Order to freeze assets (Rule 200)	324
	2. Experiments ordered by the Court (Rule 201)	325

Chapter VI
(Part 3) Provisional Measures (*summary proceedings*) (Rules 205–213) — 327

A.	Overview of the proceedings (Rules 205–213)	327
B.	Protective letter (Rule 207)	329

Chapter VII
(Part 4) Procedures before the Court of Appeal (Rules 220–254) — 333

A.	Introductory and Basis Rules (Rules 220–223)	333
	1. Appealable decisions (Rule 220)	333
	2. Application for leave of appeal against cost decisions (Rule 221)	336
	3. Subject matter before the Court of Appeal (Rule 222)	337
	4. Application for suspensive effect (Rule 223)	338
B.	(Chapter 1) Written procedure (Rules 224–238A)	338
C.	(Chapter 2) Interim procedure (Rule 239)	343
D.	(Chapter 3) Oral procedure (Rules 240–241)	344
E.	(Chapter 4) Decisions and effects of decisions (Rules 242–243)	345
F.	(Chapter 5) Procedure for application for rehearing (Rules 245–254)	346
G.	(Chapter 6) Procedure for application for rehearing (Rules 295–304)	348

Chapter VIII
(Part 5) General Provisions — 349

A.	(Chapter 1) General procedural provisions (Rules 260–266)	349
	1. Examination by the Registry of its own motion (Rule 260)	349
	2. Date of pleadings (Rule 261)	349
	3. Public access to the Register (Rule 262)	350
	4. Protection of Confidential Information (Rule 262A)	352
	5. Leave to change claim or amend case (Rule 263)	353
	6. An opportunity to be heard (Rule 264)	353
	7. Withdrawal (Rule 265)	354
	8. Preliminary references to the CJEU (Rule 266)	354
	9. Actions pursuant to Article 22 UPCA (Rule 267)	355
B.	(Chapter 2) Service (Rules 270–279)	355
	1. Service within the Contracting Member States or by agreement (Rules 270–272)	355

		a. Scope of this section (Rule 270)	355
		b. Service of the Statement of claim (Rule 271)	355
		c. Notice of the service and non-service of the Statement of claim (Rule 272)	358
	2.	Service outside the Contracting Member States (Rules 273–274)	358
	3.	Service by an alternative method (Rule 275)	358
	4.	Service of Orders, Decisions and Written Pleadings (Rules 276–279)	359
		a. Service of orders and decisions (Rule 276)	359
		b. Decisions by default under Part 5, Chapter 11 (Rule 277)	359
		c. Service of written pleadings and other document (Rule 278)	360
		d. Change of electronic address for service (Rule 279)	360
C.	(Chapter 3) Rights and Obligations of Representatives (Rules 284–293)		360
	1.	Duty of representatives not to misrepresent facts or cases (Rule 284)	360
	2.	Powers of Attorney (Rule 285)	361
	3.	Certificate that a representative is authorised to practise before the Court (Rule 286)	361
	4.	Attorney-client privilege (Rule 287)	361
	5.	Litigation privilege (Rule 288)	362
	6.	Privileges, immunities and facilities (Rule 289)	363
	7.	Powers of the Court as regards representatives (Rule 290)	363
	8.	Exclusion from the proceedings (Rule 291)	363
	9.	Patent attorneys' right of audience (Rule 292)	364
	10.	Change of a representative (Rule 293)	364
	11.	Removal from the register of representatives (Rule 294)	364
D.	(Chapter 4) Stay of Proceedings (Rules 295–298)		365
	1.	Stay of proceedings (Rule 295)	365
	2.	Duration and effects of a stay of proceedings (Rule 296)	366
	3.	Resumption of proceedings (Rule 297)	366
	4.	Accelerated proceedings before the EPO (Rule 298)	366
E.	(Chapter 5) Time periods (Rules 300–301)		366
	1.	Calculation of periods (Rule 300)	366
	2.	Automatic extension of periods (Rule 301)	367
F.	(Chapter 6) Parties to proceedings (Rules 302–320)		367
	1.	Plurality of parties (Rules 302–303)	367
		a. Plurality of claimants or patents (Rule 302)	367
		b. Plurality of defendants (Rule 303)	368
	2.	Change in Parties (Rules 305–306)	369
		a. Change in parties (Rule 305)	369
		b. Consequences for the proceedings (Rule 306)	369
	3.	Death, Demise or Insolvency of a Party (Rules 310–311)	369
		a. Death or demise of a party (Rule 310)	369
		b. Insolvency of a party (Rule 311)	369
	4.	Transfer of patent (Rule 312)	370
	5.	Intervention (Rules 313–317)	370
	6.	Re-establishment of Rights (Rules 320)	373
G.	(Chapter 7) Miscellaneous provisions on languages (Rules 321–324)		373

	1.	Change of language in general	373
	2.	Application by both parties to use the language in which the patent was granted as language of the proceedings (Rule 321)	375
	3.	Proposal from the Judge-Rapporteur to use of the language in which the patent was granted as language of the proceedings (Rule 322)	375
	4.	Application by one party to use the language in which the patent was granted as language of the proceedings (Rule 323)	376
	5.	Consequences where the language of the proceedings is changed in the course of the proceedings (Rule 324)	376
H.	(Chapter 8) Case management (Rules 331–340)		376
	1.	Responsibility for case management (Rule 331)	376
	2.	General principles of case management (Rule 332)	377
	3.	Review of case management orders (Rule 333)	377
	4.	Case management powers (Rule 334)	378
	5.	Varying or revoking orders (Rule 335)	378
	6.	Exercise of managing powers (Rule 336)	378
	7.	Orders of the Court's own motion (Rule 337)	378
	8.	Connection – Joinder (Rule 340)	378
I.	(Chapter 9) Rules relating to the organisation of the Court (Rules 341–346)		379
	1.	Precedence (Rule 341)	379
	2.	Dates, times and place of the sittings of the Court (Rule 342)	379
	3.	Order in which actions are to be dealt with (Rule 343)	380
	4.	Deliberations (Rule 344)	380
	5.	Composition of panels and assignment of actions (Rule 345)	380
	6.	Application of Article 7 Statute (Rule 346)	381
J.	(Chapter 10) Decisions and orders (Rules 350–354)		383
	1.	Decisions (Rule 350)	383
	2.	Orders (Rule 351)	384
	3.	Binding effect of decisions or orders subject to security (Rule 352)	384
	4.	Rectification of decisions and orders (Rule 353)	384
	5.	Enforcement (Rule 354)	385
K.	(Chapter 11) Decision by default (Rules 355–357)		386
	1.	Court of First Instance (Rules 355–356)	386
	2.	Court of Appeal (Rule 357)	388
L.	(Chapter 12) Actions bound to fail or manifestly inadmissible (Rules 360–363)		388
	1.	No need to adjudicate (Rule 360)	388
	2.	Action manifestly bound to fail (Rule 361)	388
	3.	Absolute bar to proceeding with an action (Rule 362)	388
	4.	Orders dismissing manifestly inadmissible claims (Rule 363)	388
M.	(Chapter 13) Settlement (Rule 365)		389

Chapter IX
(Part 6) Fees and Legal Aid (Rules 370–382)   391

A. Court fees (Rules 370–372)   391
    1. Court fees (Rule 370)   391
       a. General   391
       b. No opt-out fee   392
       c. Fixed Fees   392
       d. Value-based fees   393
       e. Fixed fees for other actions   394
       f. Court of Appeal fees   395
       g. Guidelines for assessment of the value of the action   396
       h. Multiple claimants or defendants   397
       i. Small and micro-enterprises   398
       j. Reimbursement of Court fees   398
    2. Time period for paying fees (Rule 371)   399

B. Legal aid (Rules 375–382)   400
    1. Aim and scope (Rule 375)   400
    2. Costs eligible for legal aid (Rule 376)   402
    3. Maximum amount to be paid for representation (Rule 376A)   402
    4. Conditions for granting legal aid (Rule 377)   402
    5. Conditions regarding the financial situation of the applicant (Rule 377A)   403
    6. Appeal   404

Index   405

Introduction

The call from industry for a harmonised European patent system, consisting of an EU-wide patent title and a unified court system, is something most patent practitioners in Europe (irrespective of their period of service) have been hearing for a very long time. This is no surprise when one considers that ever since the Treaty of Rome establishing the European Economic Community was signed in 1957 and entered into force on 1 January 1958, there have been numerous attempts and propositions to create a unified European patent system.

But in 2012, finally, twenty-five EU Member States – Spain and Italy initially did not take part for language reasons – agreed to get started with a unified patent system on their territories. Two European Regulations of 17 December 2012 created the European patent with unitary effect (the *"Unitary Patent"*). One Regulation concerns the Unitary Patent itself, while the second Regulation relates to the translation regime of the Unitary Patent.

Since the 1970s, a European application procedure for patents exists, covering currently thirty-nine European Member States resulting in the so-called *"European Patent"*. The European Patent Office (the *"EPO"*), with its headquarters in Munich, examines European applications and decides whether or not to grant a patent. However, the disadvantage of the classic European Patent is that, after approval, the patent proprietor only obtains a bundle of national patents. To have effect in some or all of the thirty-eight participating European countries, the patent proprietor has to *"validate"* the European Patent in the different countries. This means that the patent proprietor needs to pay the renewal fees of the countries where patent protection is wanted and, if required, translate the patent into the official language(s) of the countries concerned. Therefore, obtaining patent protection for an invention in a great number of European countries (e.g. all EU countries) is very costly.

The new Unitary Patent intends to get rid of the disadvantages of the classic European Patent. As soon as the two European Regulations regarding Unitary Patent protection come into operation, a Unitary Patent proprietor shall only have to pay one renewal fee and translate the text of the patent into at most one additional language (other than the language of the EPO procedure), for its invention to be protected in the participating EU Member States (starting with seventeen on 1 June 2023).

Another disadvantage of the current system is the parallel litigation. Today, after the deadline for the opposition proceedings before the EPO has expired, it is not possible for an alleged infringer to revoke with a single court decision a European Patent in all Member States where the patent is valid. On the other hand, the current system can cause conflicting decisions on the validity and/or infringement of a patent. Parallel litigation is again very costly and certainly not effective. The participating EU Member States wanted a complete reform of the current patent system and therefore choose to also deal with these disadvantages. On 19 February 2013, the participating EU Member States signed a treaty – the Agreement on the Unified Patent Court ("*UPCA*") – to establish a Unified Patent Court. The Unified Patent Court (hereafter referred to as the "*Court*") installs a patent jurisdiction with effect in all Participating Member States (starting with seventeen as of 1 June 2023). This will, amongst other things, enable a Unitary Patent proprietor to obtain a cease-and-desist order or a preliminary injunction effective in all Participating Member States. It will also enable a defendant to obtain revocation of a Unitary Patent with effect in the Participating Member States.

The implementation phase of both the Unitary Patent and the Unified Patent Court was a bumpy ride: actions before the European Court of Justice, an action before the German Constitutional Court (*Bundesverfassungsgericht*), the UK leaving the system because of Brexit, a lot of work for setting up the Rules of Procedure of the Unified Patent Court, political issues hindering a smooth ratification of the legal instruments in the different participating EU Member States, etc. However, in 2022–2023, we finally saw the light at the end of the tunnel with a decision from the German Constitutional Court and subsequently Germany voting the new system with the required parliamentary quorum. The Unified Patent Court and the Unitary Patent became operational on 1 June 2023.

In this publication we shall describe all provisions of the two Regulations regarding the Unitary Patent, and the legal texts regarding the Unified Patent Court. As in the previous edition of this book, it is not our intention to take up any positive or negative position regarding the new system but rather provide interested parties with an introduction to the new patent and litigation system.

In the first place these interested parties are patent practitioners (patent attorneys, IP lawyers, researchers, judges, members of the national patent offices and the EPO, etc.). But this book is equally intended to be read and used by entrepreneurs, tech transfer officers, engineers, legal counsels, public servants and all other persons interested in the new system.

We hope you enjoy using the book.

PART ONE:

THE UNITARY PATENT

Chapter I
History of the EU Patent Title

A. THE COMMUNITY PATENT CONVENTION

The proposition of the French Senator Henri Longchambon to the Council of Europe in 1949 (known as the *"Longchambon plan"*)[1] was the beginning of discussions on a European Patent law system. After the entry into force of the Treaty of Rome in 1958 a lot of people feared that patent rights would replace the prohibited quantitative restrictions, since Article 36 of the Rome Treaty had mentioned *"the protection of industrial and commercial property"* as a prohibition or restriction that was still possible under the Treaty. Some critics claimed that instead of custom authorities, bailiffs would be present at the borders to block goods from other countries based on industrial property rights.[2] For this reason, the Court of Justice developed in those years the first jurisprudence on the Community exhaustion of rights.

This fear led in 1960 to the creation of three Working Parties with the intention of seeking solutions in the field of patents, trade marks and design rights. In 1962 the Working Party on patents put together a preliminary draft convention, which contained the substance of the future European Patent Convention and the Community Patent Convention. But due to political crisis this project was put on hold for several years.

The patent activities resumed in 1969 on the initiative of France, which suggested splitting the project up in two parts: the European Patent Convention (*"EPC"*) and the Community Patent Convention (*"CPC"*). The entry to the EPC would be open for all European countries (including non-EEC Member States). The entry to the CPC would only be open for EEC Member States. The EPC intended to install a centralised granting procedure for patent rights in the Contracting Member States, while the CPC wanted to create a unified patent title for the common market. The Community Patent Convention built further on the basis of the European Patent Convention.

Two preparatory Conferences were convened in Luxembourg in the beginning of the 1970s, which led to the conclusion of the EPC in Munich in October 1973[3] and the CPC in Luxembourg in December 1975.[4]

---

1. H. Longchambon, "Creation of a European Patents Office", Report of the Committee on Economic Affairs and Development of the Council of Europe, 6 September 1949, Doc 75, http://assembly.coe.int.
2. B. Schwab, "The Community Patent" in P. Vancraesbeeck (ed.), *Problems of Patent Law*, (Kluwer, Diegem, 1994), 245.
3. Convention on the grant of European Patents, 5 October 1973.
4. Convention for the European patent for the common market (Community Patent Convention) of 15 December 1975, *OJ* L 17/27, 26 January 1976.

Everyone expected the two Conventions to enter into force more or less simultaneously. In reality the EPC entered into force on 7 October 1977, but the CPC never entered into force. To enter into force, the CPC had to be ratified by all nine signing ECC Member States. However, Denmark and Ireland came across national obstacles during the ratification process.

While awaiting the entry into force of the CPC, the interim Committee in charge of the preparatory work, drafted three Protocols. One of them was the draft Protocol on litigation. This Protocol formed the first step towards unified patent litigation.

In order to finalise and adopt the Protocols and find a solution to the deadlock on the ratification of the CPC, a second Conference was convened in Luxembourg in December 1985. The Conference wanted to explore the possibility of putting the CPC into force progressively by a smaller number of ratifications than all signing parties. The Conference adopted the Protocol on litigation,[5] but failed to reach a solution to the problem of entry into force of the CPC.

Finally, in 1989 a third Conference in Luxembourg found an agreement on the entry into force concerning Community patents. Article 10 of the Agreement concerning Community patents[6] provides that the Agreement would enter into force upon ratification of twelve Member States. But at the same time a separate Protocol was agreed which provided that if the ratification by the twelve Member States had not taken place on 31 December 1991,[7] a new Conference would be convened. This Conference would then be able to amend the number of ratifications. The entry into force of the Protocol was again subject to twelve ratifications.[8] If the Protocol had not entered into force on 31 December 1991, the EEC Member States declared that "*a Conference of Representatives of the Governments of the Member States of the European Economic Community shall be convened by the Presidency of the Council of the European Communities in order to find unanimously the means of ensuring that the Community patent system is implemented at the time of the completion of the Internal Market*".[9]

Despite all efforts, neither the CPC, nor the Agreement concerning Community Patents or the Protocol of 1989 ever entered into force.

B. PROPOSAL FOR COUNCIL REGULATION ON THE COMMUNITY PATENT

After the many difficulties the CPC had encountered, the European Commission gave new impetus to the matter by presenting a proposal for a Council Regulation

---

5. Protocol on the settlement of litigation concerning the infringement and validity of Community Patents (Protocol on litigation), *OJ* L 401/4, 30 December 1989.
6. The Agreement 89/695/EEC relating to Community patents of 15 December 1989, *OJ* L 401/01, 30 December 1989.
7. Article 1 of the Protocol on a possible modification of the conditions of entry into force of the UPCA relating to Community patents, *OJ* L 401/51, 30 December 1989.
8. Article 4 of the Protocol on a possible modification of the conditions of entry into force of the UPCA relating to Community patents, *OJ* L 401/51, 30 December 1989.
9. "Declaration on a possible modification of the conditions of entry into force of the UPCA" in the Joint Declaration UPCA relating to Community patents, *OJ* L 401/57, 30 December 1989.

on the Community Patent[10] on 1 August 2000. In the accompanying press release[11] the Commission gave a comparison of the costs of a US patent, a Japanese patent and a patent delivered under the EPC. The comparison showed that the costs of an EPC patent amounted to EUR 49,900, while a US patent would only cost EUR 10,330 and a Japanese patent EUR 16,450.

In 2001 the Belgian presidency tried to find an agreement within the European Council on the Community Patent Regulation, but failed.[12] In the following years, further attempts were made, but at the Council meeting of 11 March 2004 it became clear that there was little immediate prospect of a Community patent. Commissioner Bolkestein stated: *"I can only hope that one day the vested, protectionist interests that stand in the way of agreement on this vital measure will be sidelined by the over-riding importance and interests of European manufacturing industry and Europe's competitiveness. That day has not yet come."*[13]

One of the major obstacles to finding a compromise was the translation requirements for the Community patent.

C. COMMUNICATION "ENHANCING THE PATENT SYSTEM IN EUROPE"

In recent history the patent file re-appeared on the European radar in 2007 with a Communication from the Commission regarding the European Patent system.[14] In the Communication the Commission pointed out that it strongly believed that an improved patent system was vital if Europe were to fulfil its potential for innovation. The purpose of the Communication was to revitalise the debate on the patent system in Europe to encourage Member States to work towards consensus and real progress on the issue.

Making the Community patent a reality (the Commission calls it *"a key objective for Europe"*)[15] and at the same time improving the existing fragmented patent litigation system would, according to the Commission, make the patent system significantly more accessible and bring cost savings for all who have a stake in the patent system. In parallel, supporting measures to maintain and, where necessary, improve the quality and efficiency of the current system, together with targeted measures to improve SME access, should ensure that Europe's patent system will play its role in boosting innovation and competitiveness in Europe.

---

10. Proposal for a Council Regulation on the Community Patent, COM/2000/0412, *OJ* C 337E 28 November 2000.
11. Press release of 5 July 2000, "Commission proposes the creation of a Community Patent", http://europa.eu/rapid/press-release_IP-00-714_en.htm.
12. Press release of 20 December 2001, "Results of the Internal Market Council on the Community Patent", http://europa.eu/rapid/press-release_MEMO-01-451_en.htm.
13. Press release of 11 March 2004, "Results of the Competitiveness Council of Ministers, Brussels, 11 March 2004 Internal Market, Enterprise and Consumer Protection issues", http://europa.eu/rapid/press-release_MEMO-04-58_en.htm?locale=fr.
14. Communication from the Commission to the European Parliament and the Council, "Enhancing the patent system in Europe", 3 April 2007, COM/2007/0165.
15. Communication from the Commission to the European Parliament and the Council, "Enhancing the patent system in Europe", 3 April 2007, COM/2007/0165, p. 4.

Annex I of the Communication gave an overview of the cost structure of direct patent filings and maintenance in 2003. It calculated the costs of a European Patent validated in three and in thirteen Member States and compared it to US and Japanese patents. The procedural cost with translation for a European Patent validated in thirteen countries would amount to EUR 20,175, while a US patent cost only EUR 1,856 and a Japanese patent EUR 1,541.[16] If the costs for maintaining the patent were included, the difference in costs became even more striking: EUR 129,183 for a European Patent maintained for twenty years in thirteen Member States, against EUR 14,556 for a US patent and EUR 17,341 for a Japanese patent.

Annex IV of the Communication compared patent litigation costs in France, UK, Germany and the Netherlands in 2003. The costs for first instance proceedings would amount to EUR 150,000 to 1,500,000 in the UK, EUR 50,000 to 200,000 in France, EUR 60,000 to 200,000 in the Netherlands and EUR 50,000 in Germany. Appeal proceedings in the UK would cost between EUR 150,000 and 1,000,000, EUR 40,000 to 150,000 in France and the Netherlands, and EUR 90,000 in Germany.[17]

D. COUNCIL CONCLUSIONS UNDER THE SWEDISH PRESIDENCY

After the Communication from the Commission, the Council under Swedish presidency in December 2009 approved a number of political conclusions with respect to the patent litigation system and the Unitary Patent title. At this stage, the name of the Unitary Patent title was changed from *"Community patent"* to *"EU patent,"* due to the entry into force of the Lisbon Treaty on 1 December 2009.

Regarding the translation arrangements, the Council concluded that:

"the EU Patent Regulation should be accompanied by a separate regulation, which should govern the translation arrangements for the EU patent adopted by the Council with unanimity in accordance with Article 118 second subparagraph of the Treaty on the Functioning of the European Union. The EU Patent Regulation should come into force together with the separate regulation on the translation arrangements for the EU patent."[18]

Meanwhile, the Council had requested an opinion of the European Court of Justice[19] on the compatibility of the envisaged agreement on a European and Community Patents Court in July 2009[20] This did not prevent the Council from paying a lot of attention to the creation of an *"integrated specialized and unified jurisdiction for*

---

16. Communication from the Commission to the European Parliament and the Council, "Enhancing the patent system in Europe", 3 April 2007, COM/2007/0165, Annex I.
17. Communication from the Commission to the European Parliament and the Council, "Enhancing the patent system in Europe", 3 April 2007, COM/2007/0165, Annex IV.
18. Council of the European Union "Enhanced patent system in Europe – Council conclusions", Doc 17229/09, 7 December 2008, point 36.
19. Request for an opinion submitted by the Council of the European Union pursuant to Article 300(6) EC, Opinion 1/09, 2009/C 220/15, *OJ* 12 September 2009.
20. Council Working Document on a revised Presidency text of the Draft UPCA on the European and Community Patents Court and Draft Statute, Doc 7928/09 of 23 March 2009.

patent related disputes"[21] in the Council conclusions of December 2009. The Council took decisions on the composition of the panels,[22] jurisdiction in respect of actions or counterclaims for revocation,[23] languages of the proceedings,[24] transitional period,[25] principles on the financing[26] and accession.[27]

With these conclusions, the Swedish presidency had the clear intention of reaching an agreement on the non-sensitive issues of the EU patent.

E. FAILURE TO REACH UNANIMITY ON THE LANGUAGE REGIME

In the second half of 2010 the Belgian presidency took on the difficult task of finding a compromise on the language regime for the EU patent. Article 118, §2 of the Treaty on the functioning of the European Union (hereinafter *"TFEU"*), as amended and renamed by the Treaty of Lisbon of 13 December 2007, provides that for regulations establishing language arrangements for European intellectual property rights, the Council should act unanimously after consulting the European Parliament.

In the past it appeared impossible to find unanimity for a language regime which would enhance the patent system. The reason for that is quite simple. The EPO has three official languages of proceedings: French, German and English. But because of the system of the European Patent Convention, patent proprietors needed (and for some Member States currently still need) to translate their patent in the official languages of the Member States in which they wish to validate their patent rights. One of the objectives of an EU patent title has always been to abolish, as far as possible, the costly translation requirements.

Traditionally most of industry was in favour of using only one official language, being English. The Scandinavian countries and some Eastern European countries were of the same opinion. After all, English is nowadays the language which is customary in the field of international technological research and publications. However, for France and Germany it was difficult to give up their national language, which made it equally difficult for other countries such as Spain and Italy to see French and German as an official patent language and Spanish and Italian not. Positions were much more nuanced and differentiated than that, but in a nutshell this was the challenge for the Council to overcome. Behind these language arguments economical and protectionist

---

21. Council of the European Union "Enhanced patent system in Europe – Council conclusions", Doc 17229/09, 7 December 2008, second recital.
22. Council of the European Union "Enhanced patent system in Europe – Council conclusions", Doc 17229/09, 7 December 2008, points 13–19.
23. Council of the European Union "Enhanced patent system in Europe – Council conclusions", Doc 17229/09, 7 December 2008, point 20.
24. Council of the European Union "Enhanced patent system in Europe – Council conclusions", Doc 17229/09, 7 December 2008, points 21–23.
25. Council of the European Union "Enhanced patent system in Europe – Council conclusions", Doc 17229/09, 7 December 2008, points 24–26.
26. Council of the European Union "Enhanced patent system in Europe – Council conclusions", Doc 17229/09, 7 December 2008, points 29–34.
27. Council of the European Union "Enhanced patent system in Europe – Council conclusions", Doc 17229/09, 7 December 2008, point 35.

arguments were also hidden. In Spain, for example, translation activities of patent attorneys for non-EU applicants were considered of great economic value.

As a starting point for negotiations under the Belgian presidency of 2010, the Commission presented a proposal in June 2010 for a Council Regulation on the translation arrangements for the European Union patent.[28] This proposal started from the existing official languages for granting European Patents (French, German and English),[29] but added two elements. First, a system of machine translations for EU patent specifications into all official EU languages would be put in place by the time the Regulation applies. Such machine translations would serve for information purposes only and would not have any legal effect. Secondly, applicants filing a European Patent application in an official EU language other than French, German or English,[30] would be entitled to a full reimbursement of their translation costs.

One of the problems with the proposal of the Commission was that automatic machine translations were not yet operational for all languages and their quality could not yet be guaranteed.

The Belgian presidency added the following compromise elements to the Commission proposal in order to obtain unanimity:

(i) speeding up the development of automatic machine translations by the EPO: In October 2010, the EPO's Administrative Council gave the green light to accelerate, together with the European Commission, the creation of patent-specific machine translation services from and into English for all the languages of the Member States of the EPO. German and French would follow at a later stage.[31] On 30 November 2012 the EPO and Google signed a Memorandum of Understanding to use Google's machine translation technology to translate patents into the languages of the 38 countries that it serves.[32] The EPO puts technical texts in the various languages at Google's disposal, and Google then uses these texts to "train" its machine translation software.
(ii) translation costs for European Patent applications submitted in other than the three official EPO languages, should be reimbursed immediately and not by way of a fee reduction;
(iii) granting EU patents by means of the existing EPC procedure:
If the choice between a classic European Patent or an EU patent were to be placed at the end of the EPO granting procedure, the use of the three existing official EPO languages for the EU patent would be better justified.

---

28. Proposal for a Council Regulation on the translation arrangements for the European Union patent, COM 2010/350, 2010/0198 (CNS), 30 June 2010.
29. Article 3 of the Commission proposal: "*After the publication of the EU patent specification in accordance with Article 14, paragraph 6, of the Convention on the Grant of the European Patents of 5 October 1973, as amended (hereinafter referred to as the 'EPC'), no further translations are required.*"
30. Article 14(2) EPC.
31. EPO, Patent Information News Issue 4/2010, www.epo.org.
32. EPO Press release, "European Patent Office and Google sign memorandum on translation of patents", 30 November 2010, www.epo.org.

(iv) during a transitional period the applicant should provide a full English translation of patents where the language of the proceedings was French or German.

In the Competitiveness Council of 10 November 2010 the presidency added two extra elements for compromise:

(i) in addition to the English translation, the applicant of patents for which the language of the proceedings is English should provide a full translation of the specification of the patent into any other official language of the Union;
(ii) protection of third parties acting in good faith:
In the event of a dispute concerning a claim for damages, the competent court should be able to take into consideration whether the alleged infringer acted without knowing or without reasonable grounds for knowing, that he was infringing the European patent with unitary effect before having been provided with a translation into an official language of either the Member State in which the alleged infringement took place or the Member State in which the alleged infringer is domiciled.

Both elements were a clear concession to Spain and Italy. The Spanish delegation kept insisting on Spanish as an official language and granting more than one language legal value. The first element would have made it possible to have Spanish translations of patents granted in English. For the calculation of damages the second element would allow a judge to take into account whether or not an infringer was provided with a translation in his own language.[33]

Despite all efforts to find a unanimous compromise between the (then) twenty-seven Member States of the European Union, the Council of 10 November 2010 established that the objectives of the EU patent could not be attained within a reasonable period by the Union as a whole.

F.   ENHANCED COOPERATION

Ironically, the conclusion of the Council of 10 November 2010 was not the end of the EU patent title, but the real starting point for political compromise.

If Member States cannot reach unanimous agreement on a particular subject within a reasonable period, the European Treaties provide, as a last resort, the possibility of entering into *"enhanced cooperation"* with a group of at least nine Member States. The principle of enhanced cooperation is laid down in Article 20 of the Treaty on the European Union (hereinafter the *"TEU"*).

According to Article 20 TEU, enhanced cooperation should aim to further the objectives of the Union, protect its interests and reinforce its integration process. Such cooperation shall be open at any time to all Member States. Acts adopted in the framework of enhanced cooperation shall bind only participating Member States and

---

33. Throughout the book we use male pronouns, which should be taken to include male and female.

shall not be regarded as part of the acquis which has to be accepted by candidate states for accession to the Union.[34]

The decision authorising enhanced cooperation can only be adopted by the Council as a last resort, when it has established that the objectives of such cooperation cannot be attained within a reasonable period by the Union as a whole, and provided that at least nine Member States participate in it.[35]

The details of enhanced cooperation are elaborated in Articles 326-334 TFEU. Article 326 TFEU states that enhanced cooperation may not undermine the internal market or economic, social and territorial cohesion, and shall not constitute a barrier to or discrimination in trade between Member States, nor shall it distort competition between them.

Article 329(1) TFEU describes the procedure that needs to be followed by Member States which intend to start with enhanced cooperation:

"Member States which wish to establish enhanced cooperation between themselves in one of the areas covered by the Treaties, with the exception of fields of exclusive competence and the common foreign and security policy, shall address a request to the Commission, specifying the scope and objectives of the enhanced cooperation proposed. The Commission may submit a proposal to the Council to that effect. In the event of the Commission not submitting a proposal, it shall inform the Member States concerned of the reasons for not doing so.

Authorization to proceed with the enhanced cooperation referred to in the first subparagraph shall be granted by the Council, on a proposal from the Commission and after obtaining the consent of the European Parliament."

Following this procedure, twelve Member States (Denmark, Estonia, Finland, France, Germany, Lithuania, Luxembourg, the Netherlands, Poland, Slovenia, Sweden and the United Kingdom) addressed requests to the Commission by letters dated 7, 8 and 13 December 2010 indicating that they wished to establish enhanced cooperation between themselves in the area of the creation of unitary patent protection, on the basis of the existing proposals supported by these Member States during the negotiations. The Member States requested the Commission to submit a proposal to the Council to that end. It was important that France, Germany and UK were part of the initial group of Member States requesting enhanced cooperation to ensure the strength of the enhanced cooperation.

The requests were confirmed at the meeting of the Council on 10 December 2010. Afterwards 13 more Member States, namely Austria, Belgium, Bulgaria, the Czech Republic, Ireland, Greece, Cyprus, Latvia, Hungary, Malta, Portugal, Romania and Slovakia wrote to the Commission indicating that they also wished to participate in the envisaged enhanced cooperation. A total of twenty-five Member States therefore requested enhanced cooperation. Only Spain and Italy did not take part.

On 14 December 2010, the Commission presented its proposal for a Council decision authorising enhanced cooperation in the area of the creation of unitary patent

---

34. Article 20(4) TEU.
35. Article 20(2) TEU.

protection.[36] The proposal was accompanied with an *"explanatory memorandum"* which recalled the history of the EU patent proposals, key elements that should ideally form part of the envisaged implementing measures, assessment of the legal conditions for enhanced cooperation and an impact assessment of the enhanced cooperation.

Finally, on 10 March 2011 the European Council gave the green light to the enhanced cooperation,[37] authorising the twenty-five Member States to establish enhanced cooperation between themselves in the area of the creation of unitary patent protection, by applying the relevant provisions of the Treaties. By deciding that the conditions laid down in Article 20 TEU and in Articles 326 and 329 TFEU were fulfilled, the long-standing opponents to the new patent system (namely Spain and Italy) were sidelined.

G. OPPOSITION TO THE ENHANCED COOPERATION

Spain and Italy did not leave it at that, and on 8[38] and 17 June 2011[39] respectively initiated an action before the European Court of Justice (the *"CJEU"*) for annulment of the Council decision of 10 March 2011 authorising enhanced cooperation in the area of the creation of unitary patent protection. Article 263 TFEU stipulates that the CJEU can review the legality of acts of the Council on grounds of lack of competence, infringement of an essential procedural requirement, infringement of the Treaties or of any rule of law relating to their application, or misuse of powers. If the action is well founded, the CJEU can declare the act concerned to be void.[40]

In the annulment cases (which were joined by the CJEU),[41] Spain claimed, principally, that the contested decision would be vitiated by misuse of powers and failure to have due regard for the judicial system of the Union. In addition, it alleged breach of the conditions set forth in Article 20 TEU and in Articles 326 TFEU and 327 TFEU, especially the conditions relating to the non-exclusive character of the competences whose exercise is authorised in respect of enhanced cooperation, to the requirement that enhanced cooperation can only be used as a last resort and on condition that enhanced cooperation may not undermine the internal market.[42]

Italy claimed that the contested decision would be marred, first of all, by the fact that the Council has no competence to establish enhanced cooperation in order to create protection by a unitary patent (*"the enhanced cooperation in question"*), next, by misuse of powers and breach of essential procedural requirements, namely, and in particular, failure to give reasons and breach of the condition laid down in Article 20(2) TEU, that the decision authorising enhanced cooperation must be

---

36. Proposal for a Council decision authorising enhanced cooperation in the area of the creation of unitary patent protection, COM(2010) 790, 2010/0384, 14 December 2010.
37. Council decision of 10 March 2011 authorising enhanced cooperation in the area of the creation of unitary patent protection, 2011/167/EU, OJ L 76/53, 22 March 2011.
38. CJEU, case C-274/11, *Kingdom of Spain v. the Council of the European Union*.
39. CJEU, case C-295/11, *Italian Republic v. the Council of the European Union*.
40. Article 264 TFEU.
41. Order of the President of the Court of Justice of 10 July 2012 to join the cases C-274/11 and C-295/11.
42. CJEU 16 April 2013, *Spain & Italy v. the Council of the European Union*, C-274/11 and C-295/11, §1.

adopted as a last resort and, lastly, various infringements of Article 20 TEU and of Articles 118 TFEU and 326 TFEU.

On 11 December 2012, the Advocate-General proposed the CJEU dismiss the actions of Spain and Italy.[43] Eventually, the CJEU dismissed the Spanish and Italian challenges by a judgment of 16 April 2013.[44]

The CJEU ruled that the arguments put forward in support of the two actions could be rearranged in five pleas in law: first, that the Council lacked competence to establish the enhanced cooperation in question; secondly, misuse of powers; thirdly, breach of the condition that the decision authorising enhanced cooperation must be adopted as a last resort; fourthly, infringements of Articles 20(1) TEU, 118 TEU, 326 TFEU and 327 TFEU, and fifthly, disregard for the judicial system of the Union.

For the plea regarding the alleged lack of competence of the Council to establish the enhanced cooperation in question, Spain and Italy essentially argued that the creation of a European intellectual property right with uniform protection (referred to in Article 118 TFEU) would be an exclusive competence of the Union (as provided for in Article 3(1)(b) TFEU, concerning *"the establishing of the competition rules necessary for the functioning of the internal market"*), and not one of the competences shared by the Member States and the Union. According to Spain and Italy, the Council had, therefore, no competence to authorise the enhanced cooperation in question since Article 20(1) TFEU excludes any enhanced cooperation within the ambit of the Union's exclusive competences. The CJEU concluded that the competences conferred by Article 118 TFEU do fall within an area of competences shared by the Member States and the Union for the purpose of Article 4(2) TFEU and are, in consequence, non-exclusive for the purpose of the first paragraph of Article 20(1) TEU. The CJEU ruled that the creation of European intellectual property rights and the closely bound competence to adopt the language arrangements of such rights, fall within the sphere of the functioning of the internal market, which is a non-exclusive competence.[45]

Secondly, Spain and Italy claimed that the true object of the contested decision would not be to achieve integration but to exclude them from the negotiations about the issue of the language arrangements for the Unitary Patent and so to deprive them from their right, conferred by the second paragraph of Article 118 TFEU, to oppose language arrangements. Spain and Italy claimed, in essence, that the Council, by authorising the enhanced cooperation in question, circumvented the requirement of unanimity laid down by the second paragraph of Article 118 TFEU and brushed aside those two Member States' objections to the Commission's proposal on the language arrangements for the Unitary Patent. The Court ruled that as a consequence of the existence of the articles on enhanced cooperation and the conditions laid down in those articles, the application of the enhanced cooperation is never by itself a misuse of power. The decision regarding enhanced cooperation, provided that it is compatible

---

43. Opinion of Advocate-General Bot, 11 December 2012, joined cases C-274/11 and C-295/11, *Kingdom of Spain and Italian Republic v. Council of the European Union*, www.curia.europe.eu.
44. CJEU 16 April 2013, *Spain & Italy v. the Council of the European Union*, C-274/11 and C-295/11.
45. CJEU 16 April 2013, *Spain & Italy v. the Council of the European Union*, C-274/11 and C-295/11, §§16–26.

with the conditions laid down in Article 20 TEU and in Article 326 et seq. TFEU (cf. *infra*), does not amount to misuse of powers, but rather, having regard to it being impossible to reach common arrangements for the whole Union within a reasonable period, contributes to the process of integration. Moreover, the Court pointed out that nothing in Article 20 TEU or in Articles 326 to 334 TFEU forbids the Member States from establishing between themselves enhanced cooperation within the ambit of those competences that must, according to the Treaties, be exercised unanimously. On the contrary, it follows from Article 333(1) TFEU that, when the conditions laid down in Article 20 TEU and in Articles 326 to 334 TFEU have been satisfied, those powers may be used in enhanced cooperation and that, in that case, provided that the Council has not decided to act by qualified majority, it is the votes of only those Member States taking part that constitute unanimity. In other words, since the decisions within the application of the enhanced cooperation need to be taken by unanimity, i.e. by all Member States participating in the enhanced cooperation, the participating Member States do not circumvent the unanimity rule.[46]

For the remaining pleas, the Court ruled that the conditions for enhanced cooperation and other articles of the EU treaties had been respected.

For the third plea, Italy and Spain maintained that the condition laid down in Article 20(2) TEU, concerning the adoption of a decision authorising enhanced cooperation as a last resort, had not been respected. They considered that the possibilities for negotiations among all the Member States on the language arrangements had by no means been exhausted. The Court referred to the several stages of the legislative process (which had started in the year 2000) and to the considerable number of different language arrangements for the Unitary Patent that had been discussed among all the Member States within the Council, without leading to a compromise. Additionally, the Court ruled that Spain and Italy did not adduce specific evidence that could disprove the Council's assertion that when the requests for enhanced cooperation were made, and when the proposal for authorisation was sent by the Commission to the Council, and at the date on which the contested decision was adopted, there was still insufficient support for any of the language arrangements proposed or possible to contemplate. Therefore, the Court held the condition of *"last resort"* to be met.[47]

For the fourth plea, the Court did not agree with Spain and Italy that creating a Unitary Patent covering only part of the Union would lead to a higher integration of the national laws, compared to the current situation of European Patents. The Court ruled that European Patents do not confer uniform protection in the Contracting States to the EPC but rather, in every one of those States, guarantee protection whose extent is defined by national law. In contrast, the Unitary Patent contemplated by the contested decision would confer uniform protection in the territory of all the Member States taking part in the enhanced cooperation.[48]

---

46. CJEU 16 April 2013, *Spain & Italy v. the Council of the European Union*, C-274/11 and C-295/11, §§33–40.
47. CJEU 16 April 2013, *Spain & Italy v. the Council of the European Union*, C-274/11 and C-295/11, §§47–59.
48. CJEU 16 April 2013, *Spain & Italy v. the Council of the European Union*, C-274/11 and C-295/11, §§60–63.

Furthermore, the Court did not agree with Italy that the Unitary Patent does not provide uniform protection *"throughout the Union"* (as provided in Article 118 TFEU). The Court held that it is inherent in the fact that the competence conferred by Article 118 TFEU is, in this instance, exercised within the ambit of enhanced cooperation that the European intellectual property right so created, the uniform protection given by it and the arrangements attaching to it will be in force, not in the Union in its entirety, but only in the territory of the Member States participating in the enhanced cooperation.[49]

The Court did not find the enhanced cooperation contrary to the condition that enhanced cooperation *"shall not undermine the internal market or economic, social and territorial cohesion [and] shall not constitute a barrier to or discrimination in trade between Member States, nor shall it distort competition between them"* (Article 326 TFEU), nor the condition that it has to *"respect the rights of the Member States not participating in it"* (Article 327 TFEU). According to the Court, it cannot validly be maintained that, by having it in view to create a Unitary Patent applicable in the participating Member States and not in the Union, the enhanced cooperation damages the internal market or the economic, social and territorial cohesion of the Union. In order to demonstrate such damage to the internal market and discrimination and distortion of competition as well, Spain and Italy also made reference to the language arrangements, the Court ruled that compatibility of those arrangements with Union law may not be examined in actions against the decision for enhanced cooperation and therefore inadmissible. With respect to Article 327 TFEU, the Court ruled that nothing in the decision for enhanced cooperation prejudiced any competence, right or obligation of Spain and Italy. While it is, admittedly, essential for enhanced cooperation not to lead to the adoption of measures that might prevent the non-participating Member States from exercising their competences and rights or shouldering their obligations, it is, in contrast, permissible for those taking part in this cooperation to prescribe rules with which those non-participating States would not agree if they did take part in it.[50]

For the fifth plea, Spain observed that the judicial system of the Union is composed of a whole body of means of obtaining redress and of procedures, designed to ensure review of the lawfulness of the acts of the institutions of the Union. It considered that the Council disregarded that system by authorising enhanced cooperation without specifying what the judicial system envisaged was. While it is true that it is not necessary to create, in every measure of secondary legislation, a set of judicial rules for that measure, Spain took the view that the judicial rules applicable must nevertheless be specified in a measure authorising the creation of a new European intellectual property right. The Court ruled that the Council was not obliged to provide, in the contested decision for enhanced cooperation, further information with regard to the possible content of the system adopted by the participants in the enhanced cooperation in question. The sole purpose of that decision was to authorise the requesting Member States to establish that cooperation. It was thereafter for

---

49. CJEU 16 April 2013, *Spain & Italy v. the Council of the European Union*, C-274/11 and C-295/11, §§64–69.
50. CJEU 16 April 2013, *Spain & Italy v. the Council of the European Union*, C-274/11 and C-295/11, §§70–86.

those States to set up the Unitary Patent and to lay down the rules attaching to it, including, if necessary, specific rules in the judicial sphere.[51]

In 2013, the judgment of the CJEU did not come as a surprise to most observers.[52] At the time of the judgment, the Member States of the enhanced cooperation had already made big steps forward into the direction of harmonisation, as we will describe in the following chapters. The arguments of Spain and Italy were not such that it was to be expected that the Court would block this long-standing harmonisation attempt.

---

51. CJEU 16 April 2013, *Spain & Italy v. the Council of the European Union*, C-274/11 and C-295/11, §§87–93.
52. IPKat blog post of 16 April 20113, "Surprise, surprise! CJEU dismisses Italian and Spanish challenges on enhanced cooperation", www.ipkat.com.

Chapter II
Legal Instruments for Unitary Patent Protection

For the establishment of the enhanced cooperation in the area of the creation of Unitary Patent protection within the initially twenty-five participating Member States (hereinafter referred to as *"Participating Member States"*) two legal instruments were adopted.

All substantive provisions regarding the European patent with unitary effect were included in Council Regulation No. 1257/2012 of 17 December 2012 of the European Parliament and of the Council implementing enhanced cooperation in the area of the creation of Unitary Patent protection (hereinafter referred to as the *"Unitary Patent Regulation"*). This Regulation was adopted by means of the EU co-decision procedure. Since the Lisbon Treaty that took effect on 1 December 2009, this renamed ordinary legislative procedure became the main legislative procedure of the EU's decision making system. The co-decision procedure gives the same weight to the European Parliament and the Council of the European Union, which both have to adopt the Regulation.[53] Article 118(1) TFEU provides that the ordinary legislative procedure needs to be followed for establishing measures for the creation of European intellectual property rights to provide uniform protection of intellectual property rights throughout the Union.

However, Article 118(2) TFEU provides that for establishing language arrangements for the European intellectual property rights, a special legislative procedure needs to be followed. For such measures, the Council shall act unanimously after consulting the European Parliament. As mentioned earlier, this was the main reason why the language arrangements for the Unitary Patent protection were included in a different Regulation.

On 17 December 2012 the Council adopted Regulation No. 1260/2012 implementing enhanced cooperation in the area of the creation of unitary patent protection with regard to the applicable translation arrangements (hereinafter referred to as the *"Translation Regulation"*).

---

53. Article 289 and 294 TFEU.

Chapter III
Legal Challenges against the Unitary Patent Regulation and the Translation Regulation

After the unsuccessful challenges by Spain and Italy to the decision for enhanced cooperation, Italy buried the hatchet. Italy had already signed the UPCA on a Unified Patent Court on 19 February 2013 (cf. *infra*). However, Spain did not immediately give up its battle against the Unitary Patent package. On the contrary, one month before the judgment of the CJEU in the annulment case against the decision for enhanced cooperation, i.e. on 22 March 2013, Spain filed two actions (C-146/13 and C-147/13) against the Council and the European Parliament to annul the Unitary Patent Regulation and the Translation Regulation, i.e. the results of the enhanced cooperation. Spain launched seven pleas against the Unitary Patent Regulation and five pleas against the Translation Regulation.

On 18 November 2014, the two Opinions of the Advocate General Yves Bot regarding the actions of Spain were published.[54] In his Opinions, the Advocate General proposed the CJEU to dismiss the respective actions.[55] Probably the most discussed position of the Advocate General in his Opinions was that *"by refraining from ratifying the Agreement on a Unified Patent Court, the Participating Member States would infringe the principle of sincere cooperation in that they would be jeopardizing the attainment of the Union's harmonization and uniform protection objectives."*[56] With this statement, the Advocate General responded in his Opinion to the argument by Spain that the Member States decide when the contested regulations enter into force, because the entry into force is linked to the ratification by thirteen Member States of the UPCA. The Unitary Patent Regulation states that jurisdiction in respect of Unitary Patents should be established and governed by an instrument setting up a unified patent litigation system for European and Unitary Patents.[57] According to the Unitary Patent Regulation, the establishment of such jurisdiction is essential in order to ensure the proper functioning of the EU, consistency of case law and hence

---

54. Opinion of Advocate General Bot, 18 November 2014, C-146/13, www.curia.europa.eu; Opinion of Advocate General Bot, 18 November 2014, C-147/13, www.curia.europa.eu.
55. See for a summary of the Advocate-General's opinions: Pieter Callens, "Advocate General proposes CJEU to dismiss Spain's actions against the Unitary Patent Regulations, 19 November 2014, kluwerpatentblog.com; Audrey Horton & Wouter Pors, "Advocate General's Opinion recommends dismissal of Spain's actions against the EU Regulations on Unitary Patent protection and translation arrangements and urges countries to ratify the UPC Agreement", 19 November 2014, www.eplawpatentblog.com.
56. Opinion of Advocate General Bot, 18 November 2014, C-146/13, www.curia.europa.eu, §180.
57. Recital 24 Unitary Patent Regulation.

legal certainty.⁵⁸ The Advocate General did not agree with Spain that the Member States decide when the contested Regulation enters into force, because he considered that, pursuant to the principle of sincere cooperation laid down in Article 4(3) TEU, the Participating Member States must take all appropriate measures to implement enhanced cooperation, including ratification of the UPCA, as such ratification is necessary for its implementation. Under that provision, the Member States are to take any appropriate measure, general or particular, to ensure fulfilment of the obligations arising out of the Treaties or resulting from the acts of the institutions of the European Union.⁵⁹

On 5 May 2015, the Court of Justice dismissed in two judgments⁶⁰ the actions of Spain against the Unitary Patent Regulation and the Translation Regulation.

A. FIRST JUDGMENT

In the judgment regarding the Unitary Patent Regulation, the CJEU had to respond to seven pleas in law:

1. First plea: infringement of the rule of law

Spain claimed that the Unitary Patent Regulation should be annulled on the ground that it disregards the values of the rule of law set out in Article 2 TEU. It argued that the Unitary Patent Regulation provides for protection based on the European Patent, although the administrative procedure preceding the grant of such a patent is not subject to judicial review to ensure the correct and uniform application of EU law and the protection of fundamental rights, which undermines the principle of effective judicial protection. Basically, Spain argued that the rule of law was not respected because the administrative pre-grant phase of the Unitary Patent was not subject to EU judicial review.

The CJEU ruled that it necessarily follows from the characterisation of the contested regulation as "*a special agreement within the meaning of Article 142 of the EPC*" (cf. *infra*) – a characterisation which was not contested by Spain – that that regulation merely (i) establishes the conditions under which a European Patent previously granted by the EPO pursuant to the provisions of the EPC may, at the request of the patent proprietor, benefit from unitary effect and (ii) provides a definition of that unitary effect. In other words, the referral to the EPC administrative procedure does not result in this procedure becoming part of EU law.⁶¹ It is actually the other way around: the Unitary Patent is a special sort of European Patent, as is foreseen in Article 142 of the EPC, which is possible since all Participating Member States are members of the European Patent Organisation.

---

58. Recital 25 Unitary Patent Regulation.
59. Opinion of Advocate General Bot, 18 November 2014, C-146/13, www.curia.europa.eu, §176–179.
60. CJEU 5 May 2015, C-146/13, www.curia.europa.eu; CJEU 5 May 2015, C-147/13, www.curia.europa.eu.
61. CJEU 5 May 2015, C-146/13, www.curia.europa.eu, §31.

2. Second plea: lack of a legal basis for the Unitary Patent Regulation

Spain claimed that the first paragraph of Article 118 TFEU was not an adequate legal basis for adopting the Unitary Patent Regulation. Article 118 TFEU provides that the European Parliament and the Council shall establish measures for the creation of European intellectual property rights *"to provide uniform protection of intellectual property rights throughout the Union and for the setting up of centralised Union-wide authorisation, coordination and supervision arrangements"*. Spain held that the Unitary Patent did not create such a uniform protection because it was not a comprehensive package of patent law provisions. Spain found the Unitary Patent Regulation to be an *"empty shell"* (*"devoid of substantial content"*) which itself did not provide for uniform protection. To this extent, Spain referred to the fact that the Regulation itself does not specify the acts against which the Unitary Patent provides protection, the Regulation refers to the applicable national law and the Regulation refers to the UPCA (an international treaty) for the effects of the Unitary Patent. The position of Spain was that the Regulation had been rendered devoid of content, since the *"approximation of laws"* had been transferred to the UPCA.

The Court ruled that Article 118 TFEU does not necessarily require the EU legislature to harmonise completely and exhaustively all aspects of intellectual property law. Notwithstanding the fact that the contested regulation contains no list of the acts against which a Unitary Patent provides protection, that protection remains uniform in so far as, under Article 7 of the Unitary Patent Regulation, that protection will apply in the territory of all the Participating Member States in which that patent has unitary effect. In other words, the protection remains uniform since, irrespective of the national law used to define the effects, the protection is the same in all Participating Member States.

3. Third plea: misuse of powers

Spain had submitted that the Parliament and the Council had misused their powers, since the Unitary Patent Regulation, which according to Spain is an "empty shell", does not establish any judicial system capable of ensuring uniform protection of intellectual property rights throughout the European Union.

The Court recalled its case law regarding misuse of powers,[62] which states that a measure is vitiated by misuse of powers only if it appears, on the basis of objective, relevant and consistent evidence, to have been taken solely, or at the very least chiefly, for ends other than those for which the power in question was conferred or with the aim of evading a procedure specifically prescribed by the TFEU for dealing with the circumstances of the case. The Court ruled that Spain did not show that the Unitary Patent Regulation was adopted either with the sole or chief aim of achieving ends other than those for which the power in question was conferred as listed in Article 1(1) of that Regulation or with the aim of evading a procedure specifically prescribed by the TFEU for dealing with the circumstances of the case.

---

62. CJEU 13 November 1999, *Fedesa and Others*, C-331/88, §24; CJEU 16 April 2013, *Spain and Italy v. Council*, C-274/11 and C-295/11, paragraph 33 and the case law cited.

4. Fourth and fifth pleas: infringement of Article 291(2) TFEU and of the principles laid down in the judgment in *Meroni v. High Authority*

These pleas concerned the argument by Spain that there was an unauthorised delegation of powers. In the fourth plea Spain claimed that the assignment of the power to set the level of renewal fees and to determine the distribution key to the Participating Member States acting in a select committee of the Administrative Council of the European Patent Organisation, as laid down in Article 9(2) of the Unitary Patent Regulation, constitutes an infringement of Article 291 TFEU and of the principles laid down in the judgment in *Meroni v. High Authority*.[63] In the fifth plea, Spain claimed that Article 9(1) of the Unitary Patent Regulation, which delegates certain administrative tasks to the EPO, disregards the principles laid down in the judgment in *Meroni v. High Authority*.

In the *Meroni* judgment in 1958, the Court had ruled, inter alia, that the delegation by an EU institution to a private entity of a discretionary power implying a wide margin of discretion and capable, according to the use which is made of it, of making possible the execution of actual economic policy, was not compatible with the (then applicable) Treaty of Rome establishing the European Economic Community.

The Court ruled that the setting of the level of renewal fees and the share of distribution of those fees constitutes the implementation of a legally binding Union act for the purposes of Article 291(1) TFEU. According to this provision, it is for the Member States to adopt all measures of national law necessary to implement legally binding Union acts. Under Article 291(2) TFEU, it is only where uniform conditions for implementing legally binding Union acts are needed that those acts are to confer implementing powers on the Commission, or on the Council. The Court found that Spain did not explain why those uniform conditions are needed for the purposes of implementing Article 9(2) of the Unitary Patent Regulation. The Court did not accept the argument that it follows from the provisions of the Unitary Patent Regulation and from the setting of a single fee for the Unitary Patent (rather than a fee for each Member State) that such conditions are needed. Although Article 9(1)(e) of the Unitary Patent Regulation provides that the Participating Member States are to give the EPO the task of *"collect[ing] and administer[ing] renewal fees"*, there is nothing in that Regulation stating that the amount of those renewal fees should be uniform for all the Participating Member States.

With respect to the *Meroni* judgment, the Court ruled that *Meroni* did not apply as it was not an EU institution which was delegating powers to the EPO but the Participating Member States. As regards Article 9(1) of the Unitary Patent Regulation, it can be seen from the wording of that provision that it is the Participating Member States, within the meaning of Article 143 of the EPC, that give the EPO the tasks listed in that provision.

---

63. CJEU 13 June 1958, *Meroni v. High Authority*, C-9/56.

Chapter III – Legal Challenges against the Unitary Patent and Translation Regulations

5. Sixth and seventh pleas: infringement of the principles of autonomy and uniformity of EU law

By its sixth plea in law, Spain held that preservation of the autonomy of the EU legal order requires that the essential character of the powers of the European Union and of its institutions should not be altered by any international treaty. Spain argued that there is no substantial difference between the UPCA and the draft agreement creating a court with jurisdiction to hear actions related to European and Community patents, which the Court held to be incompatible with the provisions of the EU and FEU Treaties (Opinion 1/09, cf. *supra*). First, the Unified Patent Court (the *"Court"*) does not form part of the institutional and judicial system of the European Union. Secondly, the UPCA does not lay down any guarantees for the preservation of EU law. The direct attribution of actions of the Court to the Contracting Member States individually and collectively – including for the purposes of Articles 258, 259 and 260 TFEU – provided for in Article 23 UPCA, even assuming that it is compatible with the Treaties, is insufficient in that regard.

By the second part of the sixth plea, Spain submitted that, in acceding to the UPCA, the Participating Member States are exercising a competence which is now a competence of the European Union, in breach of the principles of sincere cooperation and autonomy of EU law. Since the entry into force of the Treaty of Lisbon, the European Union has the exclusive competence to conclude international agreements in so far as their conclusion may affect common rules or alter their scope. The UPCA both affects and alters the scope of Regulation No. 1215/2012 and the Lugano Convention on jurisdiction and the recognition and enforcement of judgments in civil and commercial matters.

By the third part of the sixth plea, Spain submitted that it would follow from the first subparagraph of Article 18(2) of the Unitary Patent Regulation that the application of that Regulation is absolutely dependent on the entry into force of the UPCA. Article 89 UPCA makes the entry into force of that agreement conditional upon the deposit of the thirteenth instrument of ratification or accession, including by the three Member States in which the highest number of European Patents had effect in the year preceding the year in which the UPCA was signed. Spain concludes that it follows that the effectiveness of the competence exercised by the European Union through the Unitary Patent Regulation depends on the will of the Member States which are party to the UPCA.

The Court ruled that the first two parts of the sixth plea were intended to establish, first, that the provisions of the UPCA are not compatible with EU law and, secondly, that ratification by the Participating Member States of the UPCA is impossible unless they disregard their obligations under EU law. The Court found that it does not have jurisdiction to rule on the lawfulness of an international agreement concluded by Member States, nor does it have jurisdiction to rule on the lawfulness of a measure adopted by a national authority. Therefore, the Court rejected the first two parts of the sixth plea as being inadmissible.

With respect to the argument that the effectiveness of the competence exercised by the European Union through the Unitary Patent Regulation depends on the will of the Member States which are party to the UPCA, the Court ruled that according to its case law, the direct application of a regulation, provided for in the second paragraph of Article 288 TFEU, means that its entry into force and its application in favour of or against those subject to it are independent of any measure of reception into national law, unless the regulation in question leaves it to the Member States themselves to adopt the necessary legislative, regulatory, administrative and financial measures to ensure the application of the provisions of that regulation. The Court found that that was the situation in the present case, as the EU legislature had left it to the Member States, for the purposes of ensuring the application of the provisions of the Unitary Patent Regulation, to adopt several measures within the legal framework established by the EPC and to establish the Court, which – as is stated in Recitals 24 and 25 of that Regulation – is essential in order to ensure the proper functioning of the Unitary Patent, consistency of case law and hence legal certainty, and cost-effectiveness for patent proprietors.

By its seventh plea, Spain held that the second subparagraph of Article 18(2) of the Unitary Patent Regulation gives the Member States the capacity to decide unilaterally whether that Regulation is to apply to them. Thus, if a Member State were to decide not to ratify the UPCA, the Unitary Patent Regulation would not be applicable to that Member State and the Court would not acquire exclusive jurisdiction over its territory to decide on Unitary Patent cases, with the result that Unitary Patents would not have unitary effect as regards that Member State. Accordingly, that provision infringes the principles of autonomy and the uniform application of EU law.

The Court ruled that the seventh plea was based on a false premise, given that Article 18(2) of the Unitary Patent Regulation in question allows for derogation only from Article 3(1) and (2) and Article 4(1) of the Unitary Patent Regulation, to the exclusion of all other provisions of that Regulation.

It was with respect to the sixth and seventh plea that the Advocate General in his Opinion had argued that Participating Member States were obliged to ratify the UPCA. If not, they would infringe the principle of sincere cooperation. The reasoning of the Advocate General was the following:

> *"179. I consider that, pursuant to the principle of sincere cooperation laid down in Article 4(3) TEU, the participating Member States must take all appropriate measures to implement enhanced cooperation, including ratification of the UPCA, as such ratification is necessary for its implementation. Under that provision, the Member States are to take any appropriate measure, general or particular, to ensure fulfilment of the obligations arising out of the Treaties or resulting from the acts of the institutions of the European Union.*
>
> *180. By refraining from ratifying the UPCA, the participating Member States would infringe the principle of sincere cooperation in that they would be jeopardising the attainment of the Union's harmonisation and uniform protection objectives.*
>
> *181. It was with this in mind that, in recital 25 in the Preamble to the contested regulation, the EU legislature stated that it was 'therefore of paramount importance that the participating Member States ratify the UPCA in accordance with their national constitutional and parliamentary procedures and take the necessary steps for that Court to become operational as soon as possible'.*
>
> *182. The said recital 25 explains why, in Article 18(2) of the contested regulation, the EU legislature makes the applicability of the regulation conditional on the entry into force of the UPCA if this occurs after 1 January 2014.*

Chapter III – Legal Challenges against the Unitary Patent and Translation Regulations

> *183. If it were accepted that certain national courts could continue to have jurisdiction in certain participating Member States where the unitary effect of the European Patent is recognised, the harmonisation and uniform protection objectives which the unitary effect of the European Patents is designed to achieve would be jeopardised."*

The CJEU remained silent in its judgment about the aforementioned reasoning of the Advocate General. However, this does not necessarily mean that the CJEU did not agree with the reasoning. All Participating Member States have (as required) unanimously agreed to the Unitary Patent Regulation. The Regulation provides in Article 18(2) that the entry into force shall be the date of entry into force of the UPCA. Recital 25 of the Unitary Patent Regulation provides that the Court is essential in order to ensure the proper functioning of that patent, consistency of case law and hence legal certainty, and cost-effectiveness for patent proprietors. Furthermore, the same Recital provides that it is therefore of paramount importance that the Participating Member States ratify the UPCA in accordance with their national constitutional and parliamentary procedures and take the necessary steps for the Court to become operational as soon as possible. By agreeing to the Unified Patent Regulation, the Participating Member States implicitly (but certainly) agreed to ratify the UPCA, which is necessary to attain the harmonisation purposes of the Unitary Patent Regulation. It would be difficult to reconcile with the principle of sincere cooperation if a Member State would first agree to the Unitary Patent Regulation and its goals, but then block the same harmonisation goals by not ratifying the UPCA.

This reasoning of the Advocate General may become important for Poland in the near future. Poland has participated in the enhanced cooperation for the establishment of the Unitary Patent. However, Poland eventually did not sign the UPCA. One could argue that it follows from Poland's participation in the enhanced cooperation that Poland should sign and ratify the UPCA. If not, this could be considered as a breach of Poland's EU obligations concerning sincere cooperation. We will have to see what the EU Commission does about this.

B. SECOND JUDGMENT

In a second judgment of 5 May 2015, the CJEU dismissed five pleas in law by Spain against the Translation Regulation. The Court roughly followed the Opinion of Advocate General Bot in dismissing all pleas.

1. First plea: infringement of the principle of non-discrimination on the ground of language

Spain claimed that the Council, by adopting the Translation Regulation, disregarded the principle of non-discrimination, provided in Article 2 TEU, since it establishes, with respect to the Unitary Patent, a language arrangement which is prejudicial to individuals whose language is not one of the official languages of the EPO. The effect of that arrangement would be an unequal treatment of, on the one hand, European Union citizens and undertakings who have the means of understanding, to a certain level of competence, texts written in those languages, and, on the other hand, those who do not have such means and would have to produce translations at their own expense. Any restriction on the use of all the official languages of the European Union should be properly justified, with due regard to the principle of proportionality.

In its assessment of this plea, the Court first pointed out that it is not a general principle of EU law that *"anything that might affect the interests of a European Union citizen should be drawn up in his language in all circumstances"*. Regarding the translation arrangements for the Unitary Patent, the Court ruled that the Regulation differentiates between the official languages of the EU. In case of a difference in treatment on the grounds of language, such difference must observe the principle of proportionality, that is to say, it must be appropriate for attaining the objective pursued and must not go beyond what is necessary to achieve it.

The Court found that the objective of the Translation Regulation is the creation of a uniform and simple translation regime for the Unitary Patent. Recitals 4 and 5 of the Translation Regulation add that, in accordance with the decision on enhanced cooperation, the translation arrangements for Unitary Patents should be simple and cost-effective. They should moreover ensure legal certainty, stimulate innovation and benefit, in particular, small and medium-sized enterprises, so as to make access to the Unitary Patent and to the patent system as a whole easier, less costly and legally secure. It follows from the above that the aim of the Translation Regulation is to facilitate access to patent protection, particularly for small and medium-sized enterprises. With reference to the current complex and costly European Patent protection system which constitutes an obstacle to patent protection within the European Union, the Court argued that there can be no doubt that the language arrangements established by the contested regulation are capable of making access to the Unitary Patent and the patent system as a whole easier, less costly and legally more secure, compared to the rules under the current patent protection system created by the EPC.

In order to assess whether the Translation Regulation is appropriate to achieve the legitimate objective of facilitating access to patent protection, the Court pointed out that since the EPO is responsible for the issue of European Patents, the Translation Regulation is based on the translation arrangements in force at the EPO, which provide for the use of English, French and German, there being no requirement for a translation of the specification of the European Patent, or at least its claims, into the official language of each state in which the Unitary Patent is to be effective, as is the case for the European Patent. Consequently, the Court rules that the arrangement established by the Translation Regulation does indeed make it possible to facilitate access to patent protection by reducing the costs associated with translation requirements.

Regarding proportionality, the Court ruled that while the Union is committed to the preservation of multilingualism, the high costs attached to the issue of a European Patent covering the territory of all Member States constitute an obstacle to patent protection within the European Union, and consequently it was essential that the translation arrangements for the Unitary Patent should be demonstrably cost-effective. Additionally, the Court found that the Regulation provides a number of mechanisms designed to secure the necessary balance between the interests of applicants and the interests of other economic operators with regard to access to translations of texts which confer rights, or proceedings involving more than one economic operator. Such mechanisms are the reimbursement of translation costs for applications, the arrangements during the transitional period and the language arrangements in case of a dispute. Based on the foregoing, the Court concluded that the Translation Regulation maintains the necessary balance between the various interests and, therefore, does not go beyond what is necessary to achieve the legitimate objective pursued.

2. The second plea: infringement of the principles set out in the *Meroni* judgment

Spain claimed that the Council, by delegating to the EPO (in Articles 5 and 6(2) of the Translation Regulation) the administration of the compensation scheme for the reimbursement of translation costs and the task of publication of translations under the transitional rules, infringed the principles set out in the *Meroni* judgment (cf. *supra*).

The Court ruled that the fact that the EPO is given additional tasks is a consequence of the fact that the Participating Member States, as contracting parties to the EPC, entered into a special agreement within the meaning of Article 142 of the EPC. Under Articles 143 and 145 of the EPC, a group of Contracting States using the provisions in Part IX of the EPC may give tasks to the EPO. In order to implement the provisions regarding special agreements, Article 9(1)(d) and (f) of the Unitary Patent Regulation provide that Participating Member States are to give to the EPO the tasks, first, to publish the translations referred to in Article 6 of the contested regulation during the transitional period referred to in that Article and, secondly, to administer the compensation scheme for the reimbursement of translation costs referred to in Article 5 of the contested regulation. The Court found that those tasks are intrinsically linked to the implementation of the Unitary Patent protection created by the Unitary Patent Regulation.

Since not the Council but the Member States had delegated powers, the Court found that the principles set out by the Court in the *Meroni* judgment did not apply.

3. Third plea: lack of a legal basis for Article 4 of the Translation Regulation

In its third plea, Spain again refers to Article 118 TFEU, but this time to argue that paragraph 2 of this Article (which deals with the *"language arrangement"* for European intellectual property rights) is not the correct legal basis to introduce Article 4 into the Translation Regulation, since this Article would merely incorporate some procedural safeguards in the context of legal proceedings, which – according to Spain – has nothing to do with language arrangements.

The Court ruled that Article 4 directly forms part of the language arrangements for the Unitary Patent, since it sets out the special rules governing the translation of the Unitary Patent in the specific context of a dispute. Since the language arrangements for the Unitary Patent are defined by all the provisions of the contested Regulation and more specifically Articles 3, 4 and 6, which are intended to apply to different situations, Article 4 of the Translation Regulation cannot be detached, with respect to the legal basis, from the remainder of the provisions of the Translation Regulation.

With respect to the third plea, the Court added that the second paragraph of Article 118 TFEU does not preclude, when the language arrangements for European intellectual property rights are being determined, reference being made to the language arrangements of the EPO. It is moreover of no relevance that the Translation Regulation does not establish an exhaustive body of rules for the language arrangements applicable to the Unitary Patent. The second paragraph of Article 118 TFEU imposes no requirement on the Council to approximate all aspects of the language arrangements for intellectual property rights established on the basis of the first paragraph of Article 118 TFEU.

4. Fourth plea: infringement of the principle of legal certainty

In this plea, Spain groups a number of objections which in Spain's view all boil down to a lack of legal certainty of the Translation Regulation.

First, the Translation Regulation would limit access to information for economic operators, since the specification of the Unitary Patent is published only in the language of the proceedings, to the exclusion of other official languages of the EPO. The Court found that this argument is in effect a challenge to the language arrangements established by that Regulation on the ground that there is no provision for the translation of the Unitary Patent into all the official languages of the European Union. The Court had already rejected this argument in the context of the first plea in law.

Next, the Translation Regulation would not specify the arrangements, pertaining to language or otherwise, for the grant of the Unitary Patent. The Court ruled that a reading of the relevant provisions of that Regulation together with those of the Unitary Patent Regulation precludes any infringement of the principle of legal certainty. Article 3(2) of the Translation Regulation provides that any request for unitary effect is to be submitted in the language of the proceedings. In that regard, the language of the proceedings is defined in Article 2(b) of the Translation Regulation as being the language used in the proceedings before the EPO, as defined in Article 14(3) of the EPC. Under Article 3(1) of the Unitary Patent Regulation, the unitary effect must be registered in the Register for Unitary Patent Protection, such a Register constituting, under Article 2(e) of that Regulation, part of the European Patent Register, which is kept by the EPO. Yet entries in the European Patent Register are to be made in the three official languages of the EPO, in accordance with Article 14(8) of the EPC.

Further, the Translation Regulation would not indicate, in the context of administration of the compensation scheme, either the costs ceiling or how compensation is to be determined. Since a decision on the costs ceiling or the method of establishing the compensation scheme are matters which fall to the Participating Member States through a select committee of the Administration Council of the European Patent Organisation, within the meaning of Article 145 of the EPC, the Court found that it cannot be held that there has been an infringement of the principle of legal certainty.

Moreover, the provisions of Article 4 of the Translation Regulation would not be sufficient to offset the lack of information relating to the Unitary Patent. A translation of the Unitary Patent provided in the event of a dispute has no legal value and Article 4 would not set out the specific consequences of the possibility that an infringer of a patent has acted in good faith. The Court ruled that the fact that it is only the patent in the language in which it has been issued which produces legal effect and not the translation which, under Article 4 of the contested regulation, is to be provided in the event of a dispute, does not create any legal uncertainty, since it enables the operators involved to know with certainty which language is authentic in order to assess the extent of the protection conferred by the Unitary Patent. Nor does the omission to indicate the specific consequences of the possibility that an alleged patent infringer acted in good faith infringe the principle of legal certainty. On the contrary, according to the Court, as is stated in Recital 9 in the Preamble to the Translation Regulation, that circumstance enables the court with jurisdiction to undertake a case-by-case basis analysis by examining, inter alia, whether the alleged patent infringer is a small or medium-sized enterprise operating only at local level and taking into account the language of the proceedings before the EPO and, during the transitional period, the translation submitted together with the request for unitary effect.

Last, a machine translation system did not exist when the Translation Regulation was adopted and therefore there would be no guarantee that such a system could function in an area where accurate translation is of fundamental importance. While the Court agrees that there is no guarantee that such system, which is to be operational at the end of a transitional period, will function properly, the Court found this not sufficient ground to decide that the principle of legal certainty would be infringed.

5. The fifth plea: infringement of the principle of the autonomy of EU law

The fifth plea concerned once again the reference to the UPCA for the entry into force of the Translation Regulation. Article 7(2) of the Translation Regulation provides that the entry into force shall be 1 January 2014 or the date of entry into force of the UPCA, whichever is the later. Spain claimed that through such reference the contracting parties to the UPCA were given the power to determine the date when provisions of EU law (i.e. the Regulations) would become applicable, and consequently when the powers of the European Union are exercised. In line with the judgment regarding the Unitary Patent Regulation, the Court ruled that it was possible to make the entry into force of a regulation dependent on legislative arrangements to be made by the Member States.

C. CONSEQUENCE OF THE DISMISSALS

The dismissal by the CJEU of the two actions of Spain against the Unitary Patent Regulation and the Translation Regulation gave a boost to the progress of the Unitary Patent package (cf. *infra*). Although most observers agreed that chances of successful opposition by Spain against the Regulations were rather limited, the cases before the CJEU kept hanging during 2014 and the first half of 2015 as Damocles' sword above the activities of the Preparatory Committee and the Select Committee.

The reasons why most observers expected the Court to dismiss were partly caused by the context of the actions and partly by the pleas themselves. When reading the pleas by Spain, one could not avoid the impression that Spain did not launch its actions for the greater cause of respecting European law, but rather to knock down the Unitary Patent package for purely national reasons. Moreover, the pleas put forward by Spain were in most cases a recycling of arguments it had already used in its (lost) annulment action against the decision for enhanced cooperation.

Chapter IV
Accession of Italy to the Enhanced Cooperation

A. ACCESSION OF ITALY

After the dismissal by the CJEU of the actions by Spain against the Unitary Patent Regulation and the Translation Regulation, on 13 May 2015 the Italian Ministry of Economic Development published a press release on its website in which it declared that *"the Unitary Patent is a priority for the Ministry of Economic Development"*. According to the press release, Italy had found confirmation in the CJEU's decision of 5 May 2015 that the Unitary Patent Package's legal framework was not under discussion. In July 2015 the Italian government formalised its intention to be part of the Member States of the Unitary Patent Regulation by means of an official notification to the European Commission and the Council pursuant to Article 331(1) of the TFEU. Article 331(1) TFEU provides that any Member State which wishes to participate in enhanced cooperation shall notify its intention to the Council and the Commission. The Commission shall, within four months of the date of receipt of the notification, confirm the participation of the Member State concerned. It shall note where necessary that the conditions of participation have been fulfilled and shall adopt any transitional measures necessary with regard to the application of the acts already adopted within the framework of enhanced cooperation.

The European Commission accepted the Italian request on 30 September 2015. This means that the Unitary Patent Regulation and the Translation Regulation at that time had twenty-six Participating Member States.

B. ACCESSION BY SPAIN?

Despite the decisions of the CJEU and the accession by Italy in 2015, it was not expected that Spain would become a Participating Member State within the short term. National and/or protectionist arguments (e.g. Spanish patent agencies benefiting more from translations of patents than from drafting and registering European Patents) seemed to remain.

However, on 7 March 2017, the parliamentary committee for economics, industry and competitiveness adopted a motion requesting the government of Spain to reconsider joining the Unitary Patent system. Only the Partido Popular, which at the time of the motion ran the Spanish minority government, voted against the motion.⁶⁴ Although this motion appeared to provide a first opening in Spain towards the Unitary Patent package, Luis de Guindos, Minister of Economy and Competitiveness, declared in the Spanish parliament on 22 March 2017 that the government did not agree with this motion. He made it clear that there was little chance of Spain joining the system in the near future. In answer to a question by the author of the parliamentary motion (MP Patricia Blanquer), the Minister referred to Spain's classic political objections to the Unitary Patent package, i.e. the linguistic regime and the legal uncertainty the system would offer.⁶⁵

Also more recently, when it became clear in 2022–2023 that the system would indeed kick off, no signals were given or received from Spain that it would join the new system.

C. BREXIT

During the wait for the ratifications of the UPCA, the United Kingdom decided to leave the European Union after a referendum on 23 June 2016. Although the UK long sought to stay within the Unified Patent Court system (as this was an international treaty and not an EU legislative document) and even still intended to ratify the UPCA,⁶⁶ it became rapidly clear that the UK could no longer be part of the enhanced cooperation with respect to the Unitary Patent as a non-member of the EU.

Eventually, the UK decided to withdraw from the European Union invoking Article 50 of the Treaty on the European Union in March 2017. The actual withdrawal happened on 31 January 2020, and took full effect on 31 December 2020, at the end of the transition period provided for by the Agreement on the Withdrawal of the United Kingdom of Great Britain and Northern Ireland from the European Union. Since then, it is no longer a Participating Member State. At that moment the Unitary Patent Regulation and the Translation Regulation dropped back to twenty-five Participating Member States. As a consequence, the UK also withdrew its ratification instrument for the UPCA on 20 July 2020.

---

64. Kluwer patent blog, 7 March 2017: "Parliament votes in favour of Spain joining Unitary Patent system", http://kluwerpatentblog.com/2017/03/07/spanish-parliament-votes-on-motion-to-reconsider-joining-up-system/.
65. Kluwer patent blog, 22 March 2017: "Minister De Guindos says Spain will not join Unitary Patent system", http://kluwerpatentblog.com/2017/03/22/minister-de-guindos-says-spain-will-not-join-unitary-patent-system/.
66. Kluwer patent blog, 28 November 2016: "UK intends to ratify the Unified Patent Court Agreement", http://patentblog.kluweriplaw.com/2016/11/28/uk-will-ratify-%C2%ADunified-patent-court-agreement/

Chapter V
The Unitary Patent

A. LEGAL STATUS OF THE UNITARY PATENT REGULATION

The Unitary Patent Regulation is not only an instrument of Union law, but at the same time it constitutes a special agreement within the meaning of Article 142 of the EPC.[67]

Article 142 EPC stipulates that any group of Contracting States of the EPC, which has provided by a special agreement that a European Patent granted for those States has a unitary character throughout their territories, may provide that a European Patent may only be granted jointly in respect of all those states. By means of such *"special agreement"*, the Participating Member States can avoid a revision of the EPC and/or (in an earlier stage where all EU Member States participated) the accession of the EU to the EPC. The special agreement enables a group of Contracting States of the EPC to give additional tasks to the EPO[68] and to set up a special department within the EPO for that purpose.[69]

The designation of the Unitary Patent Regulation as a special agreement within the meaning of Article 142 EPC appeared to be very important in the assessment by the CJEU of the annulment action Spain raised against the Unitary Patent Regulation.

Spain had argued in the first plea of its nullity action against the Unitary Patent Regulation that this Regulation disregards the rule of law because the (i) protection is based on European Patents (for which the granting procedure is not subject to judicial EU law review) and (ii) the Regulation would *"incorporate"* the EPC procedure into EU law. According to the Court, the accessory nature of the Unitary Patent Regulation is due to the fact that the Regulation qualifies itself as a special agreement within the meaning of Article 142 of the EPC. It follows from the qualification of the Uniform Patent Regulation as a special agreement that that Regulation merely (i) establishes the conditions under which a European Patent previously granted by the EPO pursuant to the provisions of the EPC may, at the request of the patentee, benefit from unitary effect, and (ii) provides a definition of that unitary effect. The Court implies in this reasoning that all EU Member States have adopted the EPC and the provisions regarding the so-called special agreements regarding the unitary character of a European Patent. Therefore, according to the CJEU, the Unitary Patent Regulation cannot be considered to *"incorporate"* the procedure for granting European Patents laid down by the EPC into EU law. The Unitary Patent Regulation does not

---

67. Article 1(2) Unitary Patent Regulation.
68. Article 143(1) EPC.
69. Article 143(2) EPC.

intervene in the granting procedure for European Patents, but merely establishes and defines as a special agreement the unitary effect.

With respect to the fourth and fifth plea of Spain, the CJEU also referred to the qualification of the Unitary Patent Regulation as a special agreement within the meaning of Article 142 EPC. Spain contested in its fourth and fifth plea the assignment, in Article 9(2) of the Unitary Patent Regulation, to the Participating Member States acting in a select committee of the Administrative Council of the European Patent Organisation of the power to set the level of renewal fees and to determine the distribution key for those fees.

The CJEU ruled that it follows from the characterisation of the Unitary Patent Regulation as a special agreement that the Participating Member States may give tasks to the EPO and set up a select committee of the Administrative Council of the EPO. After all, the Member States have to apply the other provisions regarding special agreements, i.e. Articles 142 to 149 EPC. Since neither the Commission nor the Council of the EU are party to the EPC, they cannot apply these provisions and only the Member States themselves can. Therefore, the Court ruled that Spain was wrong to claim that the Member States may not delegate such powers to the EPO.

In the judgment (C-147/13) regarding the nullity action of Spain against the Translation Regulation, Spain repeated the argument of the unauthorised delegation of EU powers to the EPO. The Court ruled in the same way by providing that *"the fact that the EPO is given additional tasks is a consequence of the fact that the participating Member States, as contracting parties to the EPC, entered into a special agreement within the meaning of Article 142 of the EPC"* (§61) and summarised that *"the Council did not, contrary to what is asserted by the Kingdom of Spain, delegate to the participating Member States or to the EPO implementing powers which are uniquely its own under EU law"* (§62).

The judgments of the CJEU in the two annulment cases clearly show that the CJEU attached great importance to the characterisation of the Unitary Patent Regulation as a special agreement between Contracting Member States of the EPC. Such characterisation leaves the EU Member States a safe harbour for a number of powers that fall outside the exclusive control of EU law.

Besides a special agreement under the EPC, the Unitary Patent Regulation is also to be considered as a regional patent treaty within the meaning of Article 45(1) of the Patent Cooperation Treaty (PCT) of 19 June 1970 (as last modified on 3 February 2001) and a special agreement within the meaning of Article 19 of the Convention for the Protection of Industrial Property, signed in Paris on 20 March 1883 (and last amended on 28 September 1979).[70]

Article 45(1) of the PCT provides that any treaty providing for the grant of regional patents and giving to all persons who are entitled to file international applications the right to file applications for such patents, may provide that international applications designating or electing a state party to both the regional patent treaty and the PCT may be filed as applications for such patents. Although the Unitary Patent Regulation is technically not a treaty, the reference to Article 45(1) PCT is included in the Unitary Patent Regulation to ensure that patent applicants can, as is

---

70. Recital 6 of the Preamble to the Unitary Patent Regulation.

currently the case for European Patents, keep using the international (PCT) application procedure to obtain a Unitary Patent.

In Article 19 of the Paris Convention for the Protection of Industrial Property, the countries of the Paris Union reserve the right to make special agreements separately between themselves for the protection of industrial property, in so far as these agreements do not contravene the provisions of the Paris Convention.

B. ADDITIONAL LAYER OF PATENT PROTECTION

Recital 26 of the Preamble to the Unitary Patent Regulation stipulates that the Regulation should be without prejudice to the right of the Participating Member States to grant national patents and should not replace the Participating Member States' laws on patents.

This means that after the entry into force of the Unitary Patent Regulation, patent applicants shall have the choice to obtain in Europe:

- a national patent;
- a European Patent taking effect in one or more of the Contracting States to the EPC;
- a Unitary Patent; or
- a Unitary Patent which at the same time remains a European Patent for one or more of the Contracting States of the European Patent Organisation that are not among the Member States to which the Unitary Patent Regulation applies, if the patent is also validated in one or more of those EPO Contracting States.

The last situation shall occur when a patentee chooses to have a Unitary Patent in the Participating Member States, but additionally also validates its European Patent in other countries of the European Patent Organisation which are not Unitary Patent Member States (Spain, Croatia), did not yet ratify the UPCA (e.g. Ireland) or are simply not EU member states (e.g. UK, Switzerland, Turkey, Iceland). The patentee shall then acquire a Unitary Patent for the Participating Member States and a classic European Patent for the non-Participating Member States and for the Participating Member States that did not yet ratify the UPCA.

The Unitary Patent does not replace the existing European Patent. It is an additional patent protection system, which can only be *"activated"* once the EPC patent application procedure has been successfully completed. After grant, the patentee has to choose the Participating Member States that have ratified the UPCA to either obtain a European Patent (i.e. a bundle of national patents) or a Unitary Patent (i.e. one patent title with immediate effect in all Participating Member States that have ratified the UPCA). Since there are more countries participating in the EPC than in the Unitary Patent Regulation, the patent proprietor can still validate its European Patent in non-unitary patent countries. There will then be a co-existence of a European and Unitary Patent. The invention shall be protected in, for example, France and Germany by a Unitary Patent, while (if validated) the same invention shall be protected in, for example, Switzerland by a classic European Patent.

As is the case today for classic European Patents, Unitary Patents shall be available to applicants from anywhere in the world, including all Member States of the EU. Applicants from both Participating and non-Participating Member States shall have the opportunity to obtain Unitary Patent protection for their inventions.[71]

The additional layer of patent protection is considered positive by some as it offers (potential) patentees the opportunity to better adapt their patent strategies to their business models. Others consider the multitude of options for patent protection in Europe as being too complex.

C. GRANTING PROCEDURE: REQUEST FOR UNITARY EFFECT AFTER EPO PROCEDURE

To obtain a Unitary Patent title for all Participating Member States, the known procedure laid down in the EPC should first be completed. A classic European Patent is needed before a Unitary Patent can be opted for.

Hence, the task of examining applications which eventually lead to Unitary Patents shall be solely carried out by the European Patent Office. National patent offices shall have no role to play in the granting procedure of Unitary Patents.

The unitary effect can only be requested for European Patents that are granted on or after the date of application of the Regulations. The request for unitary effect can only be submitted in the post-grant phase, i.e. after the grant of the European Patent.

The patent proprietor can submit the request for Unitary Patent protection, at the latest one month after the publication of the mention of grant of the European Patent in the European Patent Bulletin.[72] Such request shall be submitted in the language of the proceedings[73] in which the European Patent application is filed or into which it is translated.[74] During the transitional period (*infra*), the request for Unitary Patent protection should be submitted together with the translations required by Article 6 of the Translation Regulation (*infra*, Part One, Chapter VI).[75]

When such a request is submitted to the EPO together with the necessary translation within the one month deadline and the formal and substantive requirements are met, the applicant shall obtain a European patent with unitary effect – the Unitary Patent.[76] The name *"European patent with unitary effect"* has been used ever since the enhanced cooperation procedure was initiated by the first twenty-five EU Member States. The name *"EU patent"* could not be maintained because not all of the EU Member States participate in the enhanced cooperation.[77]

1. EPO checks formal and substantive requirements

The EPO shall administer the requests for unitary effect by proprietors of European Patents and ensure that the unitary effect is indicated in the Register for Unitary

---

71. Recital 4 of the Preamble to the Unitary Patent Regulation.
72. Article 9(1)(g) Unitary Patent Regulation.
73. Article 14(1) EPC.
74. Article 14(3) EPC.
75. Article 9(1)(h) Unitary Patent Regulation.
76. Article 2(c) Unitary Patent Regulation.
77. Currently Spain and Croatia do not participate.

Chapter V – The Unitary Patent

Patent Protection.[78] Consequently, the EPO shall examine the request as to formal and substantive requirements.

The two *substantive requirements* are the designation of all the Participating Member States in the European Patent and the same set of claims for all these Member States (see Part One, Chapter V D, *infra*).[79]

The *formal requirements* are the filing within the one month time limit[80] and the content of the request for unitary effect.[81]

The request for unitary effect shall be filed in writing in the language of the proceedings and shall contain:[82]

(a) particulars of the proprietor of the European Patent making the request (hereinafter *"the Requester"*) as provided for in Rule 41, paragraph 2(c), EPC;
(b) the number of the European Patent to which unitary effect shall be attributed;
(c) where the Requester has appointed a representative, particulars of the representative as provided for in Rule 41, paragraph 2(d), EPC;
(d) a translation of the European Patent as required under Article 6(1) of the Translation Regulation (*infra*), as follows:
 – where the language of the proceedings is French or German, a full translation of the specification of the European Patent into English; or
 – where the language of the proceedings is English, a full translation of the specification of the European Patent into any other official language of the European Union.

Requirement (d) shall be deleted as soon as the transitional period is terminated.

In order to avoid any formal deficiencies, the EPO provides an appropriate (electronic) form for filing the request for unitary effect, which is currently EPO Form 7000 and is available on the website of the European Patent Office.[83] The form contains checkboxes alerting the patent proprietor to all the relevant formal requirements.

The request should preferably be filed online. The European Patent Office offers three ways to file Form 7000 online: Online Filing, Online Filing 2.0 and Web-Form Filing. In Online Filing and Online Filing 2.0, Form 7000 is integrated, enabling the entry of the information required for the request via several tabs. When using Web-Form Filing, an already completed PDF version of Form 7000 can be uploaded.

The request must be duly signed. It may be signed by the representative if one has been appointed. If there is more than one proprietor, the request for unitary effect should preferably appoint one proprietor or representative as common representative. If it does not name a common representative, the first-named Requester will be deemed to be the common representative. However, if one of the Requesters is obliged to appoint a professional representative, that representative is deemed to be the common representative unless the first-named Requester has appointed a

---

78. Article 9(1)(h) Unitary Patent Regulation.
79. Rule 5(2) of the Rules relating to the Unitary Patent Protection.
80. Rule 6(1) of the Rules relating to the Unitary Patent Protection.
81. Rule 6(2) of the Rules relating to the Unitary Patent Protection.
82. Rule 6(2) of the Rules relating to Unitary Patent Protection.
83. http://www.epo.org/applying/forms.html

professional representative.[84] Only, however, if the request for unitary effect has been duly signed by all the proprietors (or their representative(s)) is their common representative entitled to act for them all. Multiple proprietors need not be listed in the request for unitary effect in the same order as in the request for grant (EPO Form 1001) or in the European Patent specification. A co-proprietor of a European Patent who owns that patent exclusively in respect of one or more EPC Contracting States not territorially covered by the Unitary Patent scheme cannot request unitary effect or be designated as common representative. For instance, this will apply where the European Patent is granted to a co-proprietor either exclusively for one or more EPC Contracting States that are not participating Member States (e.g. Switzerland or the United Kingdom) or exclusively for one or more participating Member States in which the UPCA has not taken effect. Such a co-proprietor should therefore not be listed in the request for unitary effect.[85]

Where the request is signed on behalf of a legal person, the signatory's position within that legal entity must also be indicated. If it is filed using Online Filing, the signature may be in the form of a facsimile, text string or enhanced electronic signature. If it is filed using Online Filing 2.0 or the Web-Form Filing service, the signature may take the form of a facsimile signature or a text string signature. If it is filed on paper, it may be a handwritten signature or a reproduction of the filer's signature (on faxes). Where the request for unitary effect is filed on paper, one copy of the request itself must be filed. The receipt for documents must however be filed in triplicate. If it is filed online, no additional copies are necessary.

After the check of the substantive and formal requirements, the EPO shall register the unitary effect or reject the request, which in either case shall be communicated to the patent proprietor.

In case of registration, the EPO shall communicate the date of registration to the patent proprietor.[86] The Register for Unitary Patent Protection shall be included within the European Patent Register.[87]

No fee shall be due when requesting Unitary Patent protection.[88]

2. Consequences if requirements are not met

Should the patent proprietor omit to file a request for unitary effect, i.e. file no request for unitary effect with the EPO, he may obtain re-establishment of rights. The request for re-establishment must however be filed within two months of expiry of the aforementioned period, by analogy with the re-establishment of rights for the priority period under Article 87(1) EPC (see Rule 22(2) relating to Unitary Patent Protection) and the omitted act, i.e. the filing of the request for unitary effect must

---

84. Rule 151(1) EPC, which applies *mutatis mutandis* under Rule 20(2)(l) of the Rules relating to Unitary Patent Protection
85. Unitary Patent Guide, www.epo.org
86. Rule 7(1) of the Rules relating to Unitary Patent Protection.
87. Article 9(1)(h) Unitary Patent Regulation.
88. Explanatory remark 5 with respect to Rule 5 of the Rules relating to Unitary Patent Protection.

also be completed in this two-month period (Rule 22(3) relating to Unitary Patent Protection).[89]

Rule 7(2) of the rules regarding the implementation at the EPO of the Unitary Patent Regulation and the Translation Regulation (hereinafter *"Rules relating to Unitary Patent Protection"*, cf. *infra*) provides that if the substantive and formal requirements are not met, the EPO shall reject the request.

Rule 7(2) governs three scenarios: (a) the request is filed within the one-month period but the substantive requirements are not met; (b) the substantive requirements are met, but the request is filed after the expiry of the one-month period; (c) the request is filed after the expiry of the one-month period and the substantive requirements are not met.

In cases (a) to (c), the EPO will reject the request for unitary effect without setting a further time limit for correcting deficiencies. Before it does so, it will have to give the patentee the opportunity to comment, i.e. send out at least one communication inviting the Requester to comment under Article 113(1) EPC.

However, it is proposed in the explanatory note to Rule 7(2) of the Rules relating to Unitary Patent Protection that in case (b) the Requester should be given the possibility to request re-establishment of rights in respect of the one-month period within two months of expiry of that period. Procedurally speaking, the EPO may then, together with the rejection of the request, inform the patent proprietor that he may still request re-establishment of rights in respect of the one-month period within two months of the expiry of that period.[90]

Rule 7(3) of the Rules relating to Unitary Patent Protection governs the case where the one-month period and the substantive requirements are met but where any of the formal requirements set out in Rule 6(2) of the Rules relating to Unitary Patent Protection have not been fulfilled. In such a case, the EPO would – as usual in proceedings before the EPO – give the Requester the opportunity to remedy the deficiency within a non-extendable period of one month. If the Requester fails to observe this period, re-establishment of rights is ruled out, no other legal remedy is available and the request for unitary effect shall be rejected, i.e. the EPO takes a final decision against which an action can be brought before the Court.[91]

D. EQUAL CLAIMS

A Unitary Patent can only be obtained if the European Patent is granted with the same set of claims in respect of *all* the Participating Member States. Please be aware that *"Participating Member States"* refers to the EU Member States that participate in the enhanced cooperation regarding the Unitary Patent protection, which are currently 25 (after the departure of the UK but the joining of Italy). This will not mean that all of these Member States will also have ratified the UPCA. In other words, it does not matter if the Unitary Patent package is operational or not in a Member State

---

89. Explanatory remark 4 with respect to Rule 6 of the Rules relating to Unitary Patent Protection.
90. Explanatory remark 4 with respect to Rule 7 of the Rules relating to Unitary Patent Protection.
91. Article 32(1)(i) in conjunction with Article 66 UPCA.

for the requirement of equal claims. For example, Poland is a Member State that is a Participating Member State of the enhanced cooperation, but did not sign the UPCA. For the substantive requirement of equal claims in all Participating Member States, this means that Poland should always be appointed in the European Patent (even though Poland shall most likely not participate in the Unitary Patent package in the short term).

A European Patent granted with different sets of claims for different Participating Member States cannot benefit from unitary effect.[92]

The condition of equal claims actually embeds two joint requirements, i.e. designation of all the Participating Member States in the granted European Patent and the European Patent having the same set of claims for all these Member States. If one or both of these requirements are not fulfilled, unitary effect cannot be registered by the EPO.[93]

In practice, unitary effect can thus not be obtained if, for example, one or more designations of the twenty-five Participating Member States have been withdrawn during the granting procedure or if the European Patent was granted with a different set of claims for any of the twenty-five Participating Member States. Although a pretty hypothetical situation, one should take into account that if the European Patent application was filed before 1 March 2007, unitary effect is in any event excluded because this was the date Malta joined the European Patent Convention. Since Malta is one of the Participating Member States, the application should include Malta.

Therefore, the patentee shall have to make sure that all Participating Member States have been designated when applying for its (initial) European Patent. Withdrawal of designations or limitations of claims for certain Participating Member States shall lead to the impossibility to obtain a Unitary Patent.

Unitary effect can also be requested where a European Patent was granted to multiple proprietors in respect of the same or different Participating Member States as long as said European Patent has been granted with the same set of claims in respect of all the Participating Member States. Procedurally, the request will then have to be filed via the common representative referred to in Rule 151 EPC.[94]

The European Patent with the same set of claims in all Participating Member States benefits from unitary effect only if its unitary effect has been registered in the Register for Unitary Patent Protection.[95]

E. UNITARY CHARACTER

A Unitary Patent shall have a unitary character, which means that it shall provide uniform protection and shall have equal effect in all of the Participating Member States.[96]

---

92. Article 3(1) Unitary Patent Regulation.
93. Rule 5 of the Rules relating to Unitary Patent Protection.
94. Explanatory remark 6 with respect to Rule 5 of the Rules relating to Unitary Patent Protection.
95. Article 3(1) Unitary Patent Regulation.
96. Article 3(2) Unitary Patent Regulation.

Chapter V – The Unitary Patent

1. **Scope of the unitary character determined by the date of publication of the patent**

It is important to note that during a first phase the unitary character and effect shall only occur in those Participating Member States for which the UPCA has entered into force at the date of publication of mention of the grant of the European Patent.

Consequently, the unitary character and effect shall depend on the ratification of the UPCA and shall therefore gradually occur for the Participating Member States.[97] At the launch of the Court and the Unitary Patent on 1 June 2023 there were seventeen Participating Member States, which means that the unitary character and effect of a Unitary Patent registered at that time shall only apply to these seventeen Participating Member States that have ratified the UPCA at the date of publication of the European Patent. The scope of the seventeen Participating Member States shall remain for the whole lifespan of the Unitary Patent. If hypothetically after a few months nineteen Member States would have ratified the UPCA, this will not affect the scope of the specific Unitary Patent which was registered at the time there were seventeen Participating Member States. However, a European Patent that was published at the time there are nineteen Participating Member States shall have a unitary character and effect in those nineteen Participating Member States.

In order to easily follow up on the scope of the unitary character, the Register for Unitary Patent Protection shall mention the Participating Member States in which the Unitary Patent has unitary effect (see *infra*, Part One, Chapter V J).

2. **Revocation or limitation of the European Patent**

The unitary effect of a European Patent shall be deemed not to have arisen to the extent that the European Patent has been revoked or limited.[98] If an opposition procedure against a granted European Patent (for which a request for unitary effect has been submitted and registered) leads to the revocation or limitation of the patent, the Unitary Patent shall be deemed to never have existed in case of revocation and deemed to be equally limited in case of limitation. This is called the accessory nature of the unitary effect, meaning that the effect should be deemed not to have arisen to the extent that the basic European Patent has been revoked or limited.[99]

3. **Transfer/licence**

A major point of discussion during the negotiations over the Unitary Patent Regulation was whether the unitary character should mean that Unitary Patents can only be transferred or licensed as a whole, or whether it should be possible for example to split up the ownership per Member State and/or grant licences limited to certain territories. As a matter of compromise, it was decided that Unitary Patents should always be transferred (and limited) as a whole, but licences to certain (parts of the)

---

97. Article 18(2) Unitary Patent Regulation.
98. Article 3(3) Unitary Patent Regulation.
99. Point 7 of the Preamble to the Unitary Patent Regulation.

territories of the Participating Member States should remain possible. In this respect, Article 3(2) of the Unitary Patent Regulation clearly stipulates that a Unitary Patent may only be limited, transferred or revoked, or may only lapse, in respect of *all* the Participating Member States, but may be licensed in respect of the *whole or part of the territories* of the Participating Member States.[100]

4. Impact of opposition

The post-grant procedures under the EPC remain unchanged. This means that if, for example, opposition procedures are initiated against a European Patent which is at the same time a European patent with unitary effect, the opposition is directed against the European Patent. The same applies to requests for limitation or revocation before the EPO. The Opposition Division or the Examining Division shall examine the opposition or the request under the rules and procedures of the European Patent Convention.

If the Examining Division or the Opposition Division decide to revoke the European Patent, then both the European Patent validated in Member States that are not part of the Unitary Patent Participating Member States (e.g. UK, Switzerland, Turkey, Norway) as well as the Unitary Patent for the seventeen Participating Member States, shall both be immediately revoked (*ex tunc*) and will disappear. The same applies for limitations of the patent: both the European Patent and the Unitary Patent will be limited at the same time.

F. DATE OF EFFECT

According to Article 4(1) of the Unitary Patent Regulation, a Unitary Patent shall take effect (retroactively) in the Participating Member States on the date of publication by the EPO of the mention of the grant of the European Patent in the European Patent Bulletin. This Article is the equivalent of Article 64(1) EPC by which a European Patent confers on its proprietor from the date on which the mention of its grant is published in the European Patent Bulletin, in each Contracting State in respect of which it is granted, the same rights as would be conferred by a national patent granted in that State.

There is no "*unitary*" provisional protection, since the Unitary Patent Regulation does not include any arrangements regarding provisional protection. It shall remain an aspect of national law to determine the provisional protection of published European Patent applications.[101] Today, many EPC Member States provide provisional protection for patent applications. Such protection shall of course remain to apply and extend to European Patent applications which eventually lead to Unitary Patents.

When the unitary effect of a European Patent has been registered and extends to the territory of the Participating Member States, the Participating Member States should ensure that the European Patent is deemed not to have taken effect on their territory as a national patent on the date of publication of the mention of the grant in

---

100. Article 3(2) Unitary Patent Regulation.
101. Article 67 EPC.

the European Patent Bulletin, so as to avoid any duplication of patent protection.[102] In other words, the Unitary Patent Regulation prohibits the combination of national patent protection and protection by the Unitary Patent in the Participating Member States. Therefore, the Participating Member States have amended their national patent legislation to ensure the absence of effect of the European Patent as a national patent, once the Unitary Patent takes effect.

G. EFFECT

1. Initial plan: effect and consequences included in the Unitary Patent Regulation

The draft versions of the Unitary Patent Regulation included three articles dealing with the effect and the consequences of Unitary Patent protection. The fact that the right for the patent proprietor to prevent direct use of the invention (ex. Article 6), the right to prevent indirect use of the invention (ex. Article 7) and the limitations of the effects of the patent (ex. Article 8), formed part of an EU Regulation was heavily criticised by practitioners and patent judges. Patent judges from countries already having specialised courts with expertise in patent litigation were especially reluctant to include provisions of substantial patent law in EU legal instruments. Judges from different EU Member States pleaded for the deletion of Articles 6-8 in the draft Regulation.

The reason for this criticism was that by introducing these patent rights and limitations in EU law, the CJEU would become competent to interpret these provisions of material patent law and render preliminary rulings regarding these articles. The judges not only feared that extensive preliminary rulings would slow down proceedings, they also argued that provisions identical to Articles 6-8 in the Regulation were contained in the UPCA for classic European bundle patents with respect to which no preliminary references were possible. Hence, they feared the risk of a divergence of jurisprudence concerning the same provisions for Unitary Patents and classic European Patents by the CJEU and the Unified Patent Court, which could create confusion. On 2 November 2011, the General Assembly of the Intellectual Property Judges Association (IPJA) in San Servelo called on the European Council to delete Articles 6-8 from the draft Regulation. The call was supported by judges from twenty-four EU Member States.

Nevertheless, in a first phase the European Council upheld Articles 6-8 of the draft Regulation. The legal reason for this was that the legislation procedure stipulated in Article 118(1) TFEU can only be followed for the *"creation of European intellectual property rights to provide uniform protection of intellectual property rights throughout the Union"*. Therefore, Article 118(1) TFEU can only be used as a legal basis for a Unitary Patent regulation if the regulation contains a minimum set of *"uniform protection"*. The German Professor Dr Winfried Tilmann explained that in his opinion the regulation should at least include one sanction, the injunction claim,

---

102. Article 4(2) Unitary Patent Regulation; point 8 of the Preamble.

in order to fulfil the requirement of *"uniform protection".*[103] Professor Tilmann even went a step further and advocated the inclusion of an autonomous and harmonised damage-sanction in the regulation. Because of the very diverse national rules on damages, it would be difficult for the Court to apply the national rules to grant damages.[104]

Other authors, such as Professor Dr Rudolf Krasser, contested this thesis. According to Krasser, it is sufficient that Union law creates an intellectual property right which is unitary for all (Participating) Member States in order to apply Article 118(1) TFEU. If the invention is identical in all Participating Member States and the invention is in all Participating Member States exclusively attributed to a specific legal subject and accordingly this legal subject can forbid the use of the subject matter of the right without his consent in all these Member States, there is a uniform protection.[105]

---

103. W. Tilmann, "Moving towards completing the European Patent System – Overview of the draft UPCA on a European and EU Patents Court (EEUPC)": *"This Lisbon article provides the legal basis for (I quote) 'measures for the creation of European intellectual property rights to provide uniform protection of intellectual property rights'. In order to be based on art. 118 TFEU the Regulation must contain, as it does, at least one sanction, one measure to provide 'uniform protection', the injunction claim. The Regulation cannot leave the uniform protection to the UPCA. That would mean risking a decision of the CJEU that the Regulation cannot be based on art. 118."*
104. *"This small degree of involvement of the CJEU is unavoidable, because, as I said, art. 118 TFEU may be used as a legal basis for the Regulation only if the Regulation contains a minimum set of 'uniform protection'. I would go even further than the draft Regulation and the draft UPCA and advocate an inclusion also of an autonomous and harmonized damage-sanction in the Regulation. Despite the existence of art. 13 of the Enforcement Directive and its repetition in art. 41 of the draft UPCA it would be difficult for the Patent Court to apply the still widely differing or not even existent national civil laws on damages of the participating member states."*
105. R. Krasser, "Effects of an inclusion of regulations concerning the content and limits of the patent holder's rights to prohibit in an EU regulation for the creation of unitary European patent protection", Munich, 18 October 2011, www.eplawpatentblog.com: *"The minimum requirement for the application of the authorization is, according to Art. 118 Para. 1 of the TFEU, merely that an intellectual property right is created by Union law. This itself achieves the necessary minimum harmonization at least if the subject matter and core effect of the right in question is established identically in the law of the (participating) Member States. In the case of patents, the subject matter of the law consists of a technical invention, the core effect in the fact that the invention is exclusively attributed to a specific legal subject and accordingly this legal subject can forbid the use of the subject matter of the right without his consent. For this reason, the proposed Regulation can be restricted to creating the basis for the grant of unitary patents for the participating Member States. Thanks to the granting act under Union law, which is unitary for all participating states, a bond based on Union law is established with respect to the invention – as defined in the patent claims – to which it relates, which is closer than in the case of the grant of a ('bundle') patent based only on the European Patent Convention (EPC). This is reflected in the fact that the patent can only be limited, licensed or transferred or can only be cancelled uniformly for all participating states, as laid down in Art. 3(2) of the proposed Regulation. As we have already said, it is sufficient for the uniform protection required by Art. 118 Para. 1 of the TFEU and the 'same effect' of Art. 3(2) of the proposed Regulation that the aforesaid core effect is unitary."*

Because of the cases Italy and Spain had initiated against the enhanced cooperation in the field of Unitary Patent protection, many Member States found it dangerous to open legal discussions regarding the application of Article 118(1) if Articles 6-8 would be deleted from the project.

Despite this threat, the UK stressed the practical importance of the deletion during the negotiations preceding the Council of 29 June 2012. In the end, the Council of 29 June 2012[106] agreed to *"suggest"* that Articles 6-8 of the regulation to be adopted by the Council and the European Parliament would be deleted. The European Parliament was not happy with this decision and immediately postponed its vote of the patent package to further negotiate this aspect.

2. Compromise: reference to the law of the Participating Member States

On 19 November 2012 Council and Parliament agreed on a compromise text. The compromise consisted of removing the former Articles 6-8 from the draft Regulation and inserting them in the UPCA.[107] The current Article 5 of the Unitary Patent Regulation provides that the Unitary Patent shall confer on its proprietor the right to prevent any third party from committing acts against which the patent provides protection throughout the territories of the Participating Member States in which the patent has unitary effect, subject to applicable limitations.[108] The scope of this right and its limitations shall be uniform in all Participating Member States in which the patent has unitary effect.[109]

Paragraphs 1 and 2 of Article 5 provide a cease and desist claim open for all proprietors of Unitary Patents in all Participating Member States.

To determine which acts specifically can be prohibited, Article 5(3) provides that the acts against which the Unitary Patent provides protection and the applicable limitations shall be those defined by the law applied to Unitary Patents in the Participating Member State whose national law is applicable to the Unitary Patent as an object of property in accordance with Article 7 Unitary Patent Regulation.

At first sight, one could believe that the prohibited acts would be those provided by the national law applicable to the Unitary Patent as an object of property. In practice, Article 5(3) Unitary Patent Regulation is simply a reference to the UPCA. The Court is a court common to the Contracting Member States and thus part of their judicial system.[110] Irrespective of the national law indicated by Article 7 of the Unitary Patent Regulation, the articles of the UPCA regarding the right to prevent direct and indirect use of the invention[111] and limitations[112] shall be applicable as the law common to all jurisdictions. Instead of directly referring to the UPCA, the Regulation first refers to a national law of which the articles of the UPCA form part.

---

106. Conclusions of the European Council of 28 and 29 June 2012, EUCO 76/12, p.2, http://www.consilium.europa.eu/uedocs/cms_data/docs/pressdata/en/ec/131388.pdf.
107. Articles 25-28 UPCA.
108. Article 5(1) Unitary Patent Regulation.
109. Article 5(2) Unitary Patent Regulation.
110. Recital 7 of the Preamble to the UPCA.
111. Articles 25-26 UPCA.
112. Article 27 UPCA

The intention was to avoid preliminary references to the CJEU concerning the relevant provisions in the Unitary Patent Regulation and the development of divergent jurisprudence of the CJEU and the Unified Patent Court concerning the same provisions for Unitary and European Patents. Because the articles regarding the rights of the patent proprietor and the limitations thereof are included in a treaty, which is not an instrument of European Union law, the CJEU would have no competence. However, the question remains as to whether this goal is delivered with the new Article 5 of the Unitary Patent Regulation.

During an ERA conference on 29–30 November 2012 in Paris[113] Professor Tilmann questioned whether it could be fully assured that Article 5 of the Unitary Patent Regulation fully excludes any competence of the CJEU to interpret the Articles of the UPCA regarding direct and indirect use and limitations. It all depends on how the CJEU copes with the referral by Article 5. In a formalistic or *"international"* interpretation, the construction can be seen as a clear split between the articles of Union law (which are to be found in the Regulation) and the articles of international law (which are to be found in the UPCA). However, in an *"incorporating"* interpretation, the referral by Article 5 of the Unitary Patent Regulation to the UPCA can be seen as incorporating the application of the articles of the UPCA into the Unitary Patent Regulation, which would mean that they become part of Union law.[114] Following the *"incorporating"* interpretation, there is still a chance that the CJEU would declare itself competent to interpret Articles 25 and following UPCA.

Paragraph 4 of Article 5 Unitary Patent Regulation provides that the Commission shall evaluate the functioning of the applicable limitations in the report the Commission shall present to the European Parliament and the Council no later than three years from the date on which the first Unitary Patent takes effect, and every five years thereafter,[115] and, where necessary, shall make appropriate proposals for amending it.[116] According to Recital 11 of the Preamble to the Unitary Patent Regulation, the proposals from the Commission shall take into account the contribution of the patent system to innovation and technological progress, the legitimate interests of third parties or overriding interests of society.

To avoid any interference to this competence of the Commission, Recital 11 states that the UPCA does not preclude the European Union from exercising its powers in this field.

3. Damages

Recital 13 of the Preamble to the Unitary Patent Regulation provides that the regime applicable to damages shall be governed by the laws of the Participating Member States, in particular the provisions implementing Article 13 of Directive 2004/48/EC of the European Parliament and of the Council of 29 April 2004 on the enforcement

---

113. "The Creation of Unitary Patent Protection in the European Union", organised by ERA (Europäische Rechtsakademie), Paris, 29–30 November 2012.
114. "Overview of the Regulation on unitary patent protection and the applicable translation arrangements", lecture by Professor Dr W. Tilmann at the ERA conference in Paris.
115. Article 16(1) Unitary Patent Regulation.
116. Article 5 Unitary Patent Regulation.

of intellectual property rights. Consequently, the Court shall apply national law in cases where it has to decide on damages incurred by the patent proprietor for patent infringement or damages incurred by a defendant in case of a non-valid patent right.

H. EXHAUSTION

The rights conferred by a Unitary Patent shall not extend to acts concerning a product covered by that patent which are carried out within the Participating Member States in which that patent has unitary effect after that product has been placed on the market in the Union by, or with the consent of, the patent proprietor, unless there are legitimate grounds for the patent proprietor to oppose further commercialisation of the product.[117]

The principle of exhaustion laid down in the Unitary Patent Regulation is a codification of the case law of the CJEU regarding exhaustion.[118]

I. UNFAIR COMPETITION AND COMPETITION LAW

Article 15 of the Unitary Patent Regulation provides that the Regulation shall be without prejudice to the application of competition law and the law relating to unfair competition. This means that besides claims based on the infringements of the Unitary Patent Regulation, it remains possible to invoke parallel actions regarding competition law or unfair competition. Such actions shall be subject to EU law and/or the national laws of the Participating Member States.

J. REGISTER FOR UNITARY PATENT PROTECTION

The EPO shall set up and administer a special Register for Unitary Patent Protection which shall be included within the European Patent Register.[119] Article 2(e) of the Unitary Patent Regulation specifies that the *"Register for unitary patent protection means the register constituting part of the European Patent Register in which the unitary effect and any limitation, licence, transfer, revocation or lapse of a European Patent with unitary effect are registered."*

The Register for Unitary Patent Protection shall be an integral but special, i.e. dedicated,[120] part of the European Patent Register kept by the EPO under Article 127 EPC.[121] Entries in the Register for Unitary Patent Protection shall be made in the three official languages of the EPO. In case of doubt, the entry in the language of the proceedings shall be authentic.[122]

Explanatory remark 4 with respect to Rule 16 of the Rules relating to Unitary Patent Protection provides that for reasons of legal certainty and transparency for

---

117. Article 6 Unitary Patent Regulation.
118. Recital 12 of the Preamble to the Unitary Patent Regulation.
119. Article 9(1)(b) Unitary Patent Regulation.
120. Explanatory remark 2 with respect to Rule 16 of the Rules relating to Unitary Patent Protection.
121. Rule 15(1) of the Rules relating to Unitary Patent Protection.
122. Rule 15(2) of the Rules relating to Unitary Patent Protection.

the users, the Register for Unitary Patent Protection will be set up as a separate part of the European Patent Register covering all entries required for the Unitary Patent. This would be adequately reflected in the online architecture of the Register for Unitary Patent Protection. Strong interaction between the classic European Patent Register and the Register for Unitary Patent Protection (e.g. by interlinking) will ensure a smooth handling by the users. Appropriate links can also be envisaged to the Register of the Unified Patent Court.

The Register for Unitary Patent Protection shall contain the following entries:[123]

(a) date of publication of the mention of the grant of the European Patent;
(b) date of filing of the request for unitary effect for the European Patent;
(c) particulars of the representative of the proprietor of the European Patent as provided in Rule 41, paragraph 2(d), EPC; in the case of several representatives, only the particulars of the representative first named, followed by the words "*and others*" and, in the case of an association referred to in Rule 152, paragraph 11, EPC, only the name and address of the association;
(d) date and purport of the decision on the registration of unitary effect for the European Patent;
(e) date of registration of the unitary effect of the European Patent;
(f) date of effect of the Unitary Patent pursuant to Article 4, paragraph 1, of the Unitary Patent Regulation;
(g) Participating Member States in which the European patent with unitary effect has unitary effect pursuant to Article 18, paragraph 2, of the Unitary Patent Regulation;
(h) particulars of the proprietor of the European patent with unitary effect as provided for in Rule 41, paragraph 2(c), EPC;
(i) family name, given names and address of the inventor designated by the applicant for or proprietor of the patent, unless he has waived his right to be mentioned under Rule 20 paragraph 1 EPC;
(j) rights and transfer of such rights relating to the Unitary Patent where the Rules relating to Unitary Patent Protection provide that they shall be recorded at the request of an interested party;
(k) licensing commitments undertaken by the proprietor of the Unitary Patent in international standardisation bodies pursuant to Article 9, paragraph 1(c), of the Unitary Patent Regulation, where the proprietor requested their registration;
(l) date of filing and date of withdrawal of the statement provided for in Rule 12 of the Rules relating to Unitary Patent Protection;
(m) date of lapse of the Unitary Patent;
(n) data as to the payment of renewal fees for the Unitary Patent including, where applicable, data on the payment of an additional fee pursuant to Rule 13(3) of the Rules relating to Unitary Patent Protection;
(o) a record of the information communicated to the EPO concerning proceedings before the Court;

---

123. Rule 16(1) of the Rules relating to Unitary Patent Protection.

Chapter V – The Unitary Patent

(p) a record of the information communicated to the EPO by the central industrial property offices, courts and other competent authorities of the Participating Member States;
(q) date and purport of the decision on the validity of a Unitary Patent taken by the Court;
(r) date of receipt of request for re-establishment of rights;
(s) refusal of request for re-establishment of rights;
(t) date of re-establishment of rights;
(u) dates of interruption and resumption of proceedings;
(v) date of issuance, date of expiry and date and purport of the decision on the validity of a supplementary protection certificate for a product protected by the Unitary Patent as well as the Participating Member State issuing it;
(w) information regarding the place of business of the applicant on the date of filing of the application for the European Patent pursuant to Article 7, paragraph 1(b), of the Unitary Patent Regulation provided by the proprietor of the Unitary Patent.

For the sake of efficiency, Rule 16(2) was included in the Rules relating to Unitary Patent Protection. The President of the EPO may decide that entries additional to those referred to above shall be made in the Register for Unitary Patent Protection. This provision is equivalent to Rule 143(2) EPC allowing the President of the EPO to decide that entries additional to those referred to in Rule 16(1) relating to Unitary Patent Protection be made in the Register for Unitary Patent Protection. This implies that the entries referred to in paragraph 1 of Rule 16 may not be amended nor deleted by the President of the EPO, but additional entries can be decided by the President. Explanatory remarks 20 and 21 with respect to Rule 16 relating to Unitary Patent Protection explain that, in the interest of good patent information policy, there is a need to constantly improve and upgrade the European Patent Register including its future special part, i.e. the Register for Unitary Patent Protection, so as to adapt the Register to the evolving needs of its users. It would moreover be burdensome and inefficient to ask the Select Committee for each and every minor additional Register entry to amend the Rules relating to Unitary Patent Protection. This is also the ratio of Rule 143(2) EPC which gives the President the possibility to add entries to the European Patent Register. The President decided, for instance, to add via a decision some procedural occurrences such as the date of despatch of a supplementary European search report, new documents coming to light after the European search report was drawn up, or the date of a request for limitation or revocation of the European Patent. For the purpose of the Rules relating to Unitary Patent Protection, these additional entries could for example include entries which are required by the relevant national law applicable to the Unitary Patent as an object of property under Article 7 of the Unitary Patent Regulation.

Explanatory remark 18 with respect to Rule 16 of the Rules relating to Unitary Patent Protection explains that users have pointed out the practical usefulness of having an indication, in the Register for Unitary Patent Protection, of the place of business of the applicant on the date of filing of the application for the European Patent pursuant to Article 7, paragraph 1(b), of the Unitary Patent Regulation which governs the Unitary Patent as an object of property. This indication is considered useful in cases where the applicant of an international application under the PCT designating or electing the EPO (Euro-PCT application) or of a European Patent application does not have a principal place of business on the date of filing of the application in one of the Participating Member States pursuant to Article 7(1)(a) of the Unitary Patent Regulation. In such cases, the proprietor of a Unitary Patent may, on a purely voluntary basis, provide information to the EPO regarding the place of business of the applicant pursuant to Article 7(1)(b) of the Unitary Patent Regulation. The display of the place of business in the Register for Unitary Patent Protection shall have no legal effect with respect to the applicable law under Article 7 Regulation (EU) No. 1257/2012 and shall be for information only.

K. OBJECT OF PROPERTY

1. Applicable law

As an object of property, a Unitary Patent shall be treated in its entirety and in all the Participating Member States as a national patent of the Participating Member State in which that patent has unitary effect and in which, according to the European Patent Register:

(a) the applicant had his residence or principal place of business on the date of filing of the application for the European Patent; or
(b) where point (a) does not apply, the applicant had a place of business on the date of filing of the application for the European Patent.[124]

Where two or more persons are entered in the European Patent Register as joint applicants, point (a) shall apply to the joint applicant indicated first. Where this is not possible, point (a) shall apply to the next joint applicant indicated in the order of entry. Where point (a) does not apply to any of the joint applicants, point (b) shall apply accordingly.[125] Consequently, it shall become more and more important for patent applicants to make arrangements on who shall be mentioned first as the applicant. If a Dutch company and a French based researcher jointly apply for European Patent protection (which can become a Unitary Patent), the law governing the licences to such patent shall be determined by French law, if the researcher is mentioned first in the application, or by Dutch law if the company is mentioned first.

Where no applicant had his residence, principal place of business or place of business in a Participating Member State in which that patent has unitary effect, Article 7(3) Unitary Patent Regulation stipulates that the Unitary Patent as an object of property shall be treated in its entirety and in all the Participating Member States as a national patent of the State where the European Patent Organisation has its headquarters. The headquarters of the European Patent Organisation and the EPO is of course located in Munich. This Article has ensured Germany of a certain amount of patent litigation since all disputes regarding transfers and licences of Unitary Patents applied for by companies not having any place of business in the Participating Member States shall fall under German law. This rule shall not only apply for example to

---

124. Article 7(1) Unitary Patent Regulation.
125. Article 7(2) Unitary Patent Regulation.

US and Chinese applicants, but also to Spanish and Croatian applicants. Spain and Croatia do not participate in the enhanced cooperation, but their residents can of course apply for a Unitary Patent with effect in the Participating EU Member States.

Article 7(4) Unitary Patent Regulation provides that the acquisition of a right may not be dependent on any entry in a national patent register. This Article is designed to prevent Participating Member States still being able to have control over the rights conferred by the Unitary Patent on their territory by imposing an obligation to register the Unitary Patent in a national patent register. Imposing national requirements would be contrary to the intentions of the Unitary Patent.

The EPO shall be informed of any limitations, licences, transfers or revocations of Unitary Patents.[126]

Previous draft versions of the Unitary Patent Regulation contained provisions regarding minimum requirements for the transfer of Unitary Patents,[127] rights *in rem*[128] (e.g. Unitary Patent as a security), levy of execution,[129] insolvency proceedings,[130] contractual licensing[131] and compulsory licences,[132] but the Participating Member States eventually agreed to delete these articles and leave all these aspects of property to national law.

2. Offer of licences with 15% renewal fee reduction

a. *Offer of licences*

In order to promote and facilitate the economic exploitation of an invention protected by a Unitary Patent,[133] Article 8 of the Unitary Patent Regulation sets up a system for licence offers.

The proprietor of a Unitary Patent shall be able to file a statement at the EPO notifying that the proprietor is prepared to grant a licence. Such statement should preferably be filed with the EPO using dedicated Form 7001. To some extent the patent proprietor makes a licence offer public through the EPO. Article 8(1) Unitary Patent Regulation provides that the proprietor of a European patent with unitary effect may file a statement with the EPO to the effect that the proprietor is prepared to allow any person to use the invention as a licensee in return for appropriate consideration.

---

126. Article 9(1)(h) Unitary Patent Regulation.
127. Article 15 of the proposal for a Council Regulation on the Community patent, Working Document 13706/09 of 29 September 2009.
128. Article 16 of the proposal for a Council Regulation on the Community patent, Working Document 13706/09 of 29 September 2009.
129. Article 17 of the proposal for a Council Regulation on the Community patent, Working Document 13706/09 of 29 September 2009.
130. Article 18 of the proposal for a Council Regulation on the Community patent, Working Document 13706/09 of 29 September 2009.
131. Article 19 of the proposal for a Council Regulation on the Community patent, Working Document 13706/09 of 29 September 2009.
132. Articles 21–22 of the proposal for a Council Regulation on the Community patent, Working Document 13706/09 of 29 September 2009.
133. Recital 15 of the Preamble to the Unitary Patent Regulation.

The statement may not be filed as long as an exclusive licence is recorded in the Register for Unitary Patent Protection or a request for the recording of such a licence is pending before the EPO.[134]

No request for recording an exclusive licence in the Register for Unitary Patent Protection shall be admissible after the statement has been filed, unless that statement is withdrawn.[135]

Rule 12 of the Rules relating to Unitary Patent Protection further implements Article 8(1) of the Unitary Patent Regulation. If the proprietor of a Unitary Patent files a statement with the EPO that he is prepared to allow any person to use the invention as a licensee in return for appropriate compensation, the renewal fees for the European patent with unitary effect which fall due after receipt of the statement shall be reduced.

Article 3 of the Rules relating to Fees for Unitary Patent Protection (hereinafter "*RFeesUPP*") provides that this reduction of the renewal fees shall be 15%.

The statement shall be entered in the Register for Unitary Patent Protection.[136]

b.   *Withdrawal of the licence statement*

The statement may be withdrawn at any time by a communication to this effect to the EPO. Such withdrawal shall not take effect until the amount by which the renewal fees were reduced is paid back to the EPO.[137]

c.   *Appropriate consideration*

The compensation shall remain a matter for negotiation between the parties, the only requirement the Unitary Patent Regulation sets is that the consideration should be "*appropriate*".[138] The term "*consideration*" makes it clear that not only financial compensation can be granted for the licence, but also other forms of consideration, such as a cross-licence. Pursuant to Article 32(1)(h) UPCA, the Court will have exclusive competence in respect of actions for compensation for licences on the basis of Article 8 Unitary Patent Regulation. Therefore, in the case of dispute, the Court will have to determine the amount of the appropriate compensation if a request is made by one of the contracting parties to the licence agreement.[139]

d.   *Registration of licence statements*

The EPO shall make sure that statements on licensing are registered.[140] Pursuant to Article 9(1)(c) of the Unitary Patent Regulation the Participating Member States

---

134. Rule 12(3) of the Rules relating to Unitary Patent Protection.
135. Rule 12(4) of the Rules relating to Unitary Patent Protection.
136. Rule 12(1) of the Rules relating to Unitary Patent Protection.
137. Rule 12(2) of the Rules relating to Unitary Patent Protection.
138. Article 8(1) Unitary Patent Regulation.
139. Explanatory remark 15 with respect to Rule 12 of the Rules relating to Unitary Patent Protection.
140. Article 9(1)(c) Unitary Patent Regulation.

shall give the EPO the task of receiving and registering licensing commitments and their withdrawal, and of licensing the commitments undertaken by the proprietor of the Unitary Patent in international standardisation bodies.[141] The latter shall be the case if agreement is reached within a specific sector on the use of the invention as an international standard. Publishing the licensing commitments in the Register for Unitary Patent Protection can give parties interested in implementing a certain standard an overview of the patent number, patent claims, the proprietor to address for licensing and the type of licence commitment. Explanatory remarks 15 and 16 with respect to Rule 16 of the Rules relating to Unitary Patent Protection explain that this can facilitate the bilateral licensing negotiations necessary for the successful widespread adoption of a standard and to provide assurances to implementers of the standard that the patented technologies will be available to parties seeking to license them. Therefore, it may be of interest for the holder of a standard essential patent to have the licensing commitment made public not only within the standard association but also to the outside world via the publication in the Register for Unitary Patent Protection.

The entry in the Register for Unitary Patent Protection of a licence statement is voluntary, not subject to the payment of an administrative fee and takes place only upon express request by the patent proprietor. Additional information will be published by the EPO as to which precise information is to be filed by the patent proprietor for the purpose of registering a licence statement undertaken in European and international standardisation bodies.[142]

Once a licence has been granted by the proprietor of the Unitary Patent as a result of the licensing offer, this licence can be registered in the Register for Unitary Patent Protection.

A licence obtained by means of this system shall be treated as a contractual licence.[143]

Recital 15 of the Preamble and Article 11(3) of the Unitary Patent Regulation provide that in case the patent proprietor files a licensing statement, the patent proprietor should benefit from a reduction of the renewal fees as from the EPO's receipt of such statement. In our understanding, the patent proprietor remains free after submitting a licensing statement to grant a licence or not (for example, depending on the appropriate consideration). Neither the Unitary Patent Regulation, nor the Rules relating to Unitary Patent Protection provide a sanction or consequence for the situation in which a patent proprietor files a statement for the sole purpose of receiving a renewal fee reduction and never actually concludes licences with third parties.

The Court shall have competence over disputes regarding the compensation of the licences granted following a statement to the EPO (Part Two, Chapter V B.2 *infra*).

---

141. Article 9(1)(c) Unitary Patent Regulation.
142. Explanatory remark 16 with respect to Rule 16 of the Rules relating to Unitary Patent Protection.
143. Article 8(2) Unitary Patent Regulation.

Part One – The Unitary Patent

3. Compulsory licences

Compulsory licences for Unitary Patents shall be governed by the laws of the Participating Member States as regards their respective territories.[144]

4. Procedure for entering transfers, licences and other rights and any legal means of execution

The Unitary Patent Regulation contains no provisions as regards the procedure for registering transfers, licences and other rights (such as rights *in rem*, pledges and security interests) and any legal means of execution, in particular as to the required request, documentary evidence and administrative fee. Rule 20(2)(b) of the Rules relating to Unitary Patent Protection therefore provides that Rules 22 to 24 EPC apply *mutatis mutandis* to entries made in the Register for Unitary Patent Protection. This ensures full alignment with the current EPO practice.

Accordingly, Rule 16(1)(j) of the Rules relating to Unitary Patent Protection sets out that rights and transfer of such rights relating to the Unitary Patent shall be registered where the Rules relating to Unitary Patent Protection (which include Rules 22 to 24 EPC applying *mutatis mutandis* pursuant to Rule 20(2)(b)) provide that they shall be recorded at the request of an interested party. Rule 16(1)(j) and Rule 20(2)(b) are to be broadly interpreted so as to ensure that all types of national rights and legal means of execution can be registered in the Register for Unitary Patent Protection.[145]

A Unitary Patent may only be transferred in respect of all the Participating Member States. Therefore, the transfer of a European patent with unitary effect is recorded in the Register for Unitary Patent Protection at the request of an interested party and on production of documents satisfying the EPO that such transfer has taken place. The request is deemed not to have been filed until such time as the prescribed administrative fee has been paid.[146]

The administrative fee for registration of a transfer of a Unitary Patent shall be the same as the fee for the transfer of a European Patent. In this regard, Article 5 of the RFeesUPP provides that the administrative fees provided for in the Rules relating to Unitary Patent Protection and the fees and expenses charged for any services rendered by the EPO other than those specified in the present Rules shall be payable in the amounts laid down by the President of the EPO pursuant to Article 3 of the Rules relating to Fees under the EPC (hereinafter *"RFeesEPC"*). The latest decision of the President of the EPO revising the EPO's fees and expenses dates from 17 January 2023.[147] Said decision of the President contains, for example, the amounts of the administrative fees for the registering of a transfer (Rule 22(2) EPC), for the registering of a licence and other rights (Rule 23(1) EPC) and for the communication

---

144 Recital 10 of the Preamble to the Unitary Patent Regulation.
145. Explanatory remark 6 with respect to Rule 16 of the Rules relating to Unitary Patent Protection.
146. Explanatory remark 7 with respect to Rule 16 of the Rules relating to Unitary Patent Protection.
147. OJ EPO January 2023, A3.

of information contained in the files of a European Patent application (see Rule 146 EPC). Since under the Rules relating to Unitary Patent Protection, the aforementioned provisions of the EPC Implementing Regulations apply *mutatis mutandis* (see Rule 20(2) UPR), the same amounts of fees as set out in the decision of the President of the EPO revising the Office's fees and expenses, as amended, will apply pursuant to Article 5.

Any kind of written evidence suitable to prove the transfer is admissible. This includes formal documentary proof such as the instrument of transfer itself (original or a copy thereof) or other official documents or extracts thereof, provided that they directly verify the transfer. In case of doubt, the EPO may ask for a certified copy of the document. Where the original document is not in one of the three official languages of the EPO, the EPO may require a certified translation into one of the official languages. A declaration signed by both parties to the contract verifying the transfer is also sufficient.[148]

The above principles on standards of proof also apply to the registration of licences and rights *in rem*. The registration of legal means of execution, however, requires the filing of the instrument (original or copy) itself.[149]

If the evidence presented is found to be unsatisfactory, the EPO informs the party requesting the transfer accordingly and invites it to remedy the stated deficiencies. If the request complies with the requirements of Rule 22(1) EPC, the transfer is registered with the date on which the request, the required evidence or the fee has been received by the EPO, whichever is the latest. The competent department for decisions regarding entries in the Register for Unitary Patent Protection is the Unitary Patent Protection Division of the EPO.[150]

Pursuant to Article 3(2) of the Unitary Patent Regulation, a Unitary Patent may be licensed in respect of the whole or part of the territories of the Participating Member States. Pursuant to Article 7 of the Unitary Patent Regulation, a Unitary Patent may, in respect of all the Participating Member States, give rise to rights *in rem* and may be the subject of legal means of execution. Moreover, compulsory licences for Unitary Patents are governed by the laws of the Participating Member States as regards their respective territories. Rule 22(1) and (2) EPC also apply to the registration of the grant, establishment or transfer of such rights and any legal means of execution affecting a Unitary Patent.[151]

A licence will be recorded in the Register for Unitary Patent Protection as an exclusive licence if the applicant and the licensee so require. A licence will be recorded as a sub-licence where it is granted by a licensee whose licence is recorded in the Register for Unitary Patent Protection.[152]

---

148. Explanatory remark 8 with respect to Rule 16 of the Rules relating to Unitary Patent Protection.
149. Explanatory remark 9 with respect to Rule 16 of the Rules relating to Unitary Patent Protection.
150. Explanatory remark 10 with respect to Rule 16 of the Rules relating to Unitary Patent Protection.
151. Explanatory remark 11 with respect to Rule 16 of the Rules relating to Unitary Patent Protection.
152. Explanatory remark 12 with respect to Rule 16 of the Rules relating to Unitary Patent Protection.

Upon request and subject to the payment of the prescribed administrative fee (equal to the fee for registration of licences of European Patents), registration of a licence or other right shall be cancelled on production of documents satisfying the EPO that the right has lapsed or has been declared invalid, or of a declaration of the proprietor of the right that he consents to the cancellation pursuant to Rule 23(2) EPC.[153]

L.   PUBLICATIONS REGARDING UNITARY PATENTS

Article 129(a) EPC provides that the EPO will periodically publish a European Patent Bulletin containing the particulars the publication of which is prescribed by the EPC, the Implementing Regulations to the EPC, the Chairperson of the Select Committee or the President of the EPO.

Since no reference was made in Article 129(a) EPC to the Rules relating to Unitary Patent Protection, a special provision appeared necessary which would expressly make that reference and thereby ensure publication of all particulars set out in the Rules relating to Unitary Patent Protection in the European Patent Bulletin (which contains bibliographic data as well as data laid down in Rule 143 EPC). Therefore, Rule 17(1) provides that the European Patent Bulletin referred to in Article 129(a) EPC shall contain, as a special part, the particulars the publication of which is prescribed by the Rules relating to Unitary Patent Protection, the Chairperson of the Select Committee or the President of the EPO. The Official Journal referred to in Article 129(b) EPC shall contain, as a special part, notices and information of a general character issued by the Select Committee or by the President of the EPO, as well as any other information relevant to the implementation of Unitary Patent protection.[154]

Rule 18 of the Rules relating to Unitary Patent Protection concerns the publication of translations. Over a transitional period of a maximum of twelve years starting from the date of application of the Translation Regulation, a request for unitary effect will have to be submitted together with translations of the specification. Under Article 6(2) Translation Regulation, the Participating Member States will give the EPO the task of publishing the translations as soon as possible after the date on which a request for unitary effect is filed. The text of such translations will have no legal value and shall be for information purposes only. Rule 18 of the Rules relating to Unitary Patent Protection provides that the President of the EPO shall determine the form of the publication of the translations and the data to be included.

Article 2(e) of the Unitary Patent Regulation specifies that *"Register for unitary patent protection"* means the register constituting part of the European Patent Register in which the unitary effect and any limitation, licence, transfer, revocation or lapse of a European patent with unitary effect are registered. A Register for Unitary Patent Protection has therefore been set up as an integral but special part of the European Patent Register already kept by the EPO under Article 127 EPC. For reasons of legal certainty and transparency for users, the Register for Unitary Patent Protection has the same basic structure and functionality as the European Patent Register. The Register for Unitary Patent Protection contains all the entries that are expressly but

---

153. Explanatory remark 13 with respect to Rule 16 of the Rules relating to Unitary Patent Protection.
154. Rule 17(2) of the Rules relating to Unitary Patent Protection.

not exhaustively listed in the Unitary Patent Regulation, in particular the fact that unitary effect has been registered and the date of that registration.

The Register for Unitary Patent Protection comprises procedural information such as the date of filing of the request for unitary effect for the European Patent, the participating Member States in which the Unitary Patent has effect pursuant to Article 18(2) of the Unitary Patent Regulation and the date of filing – and, if applicable, the date of any withdrawal – of a statement on licences of rights. It also contains data as to the payment of renewal fees for Unitary Patents and information on decisions on the validity of Unitary Patents taken by the Court. The files relating to Unitary Patents are available for online inspection on the EPO website under "European Patent Register", in the chapter "Unitary Patent" under the panel view "UP All documents". On request and subject to payment of a fee, copies of the files can be made available for inspection.[155]

No additional documents beyond the European Patent specification published by the EPO under the EPC will be published for a Unitary Patent. Unitary Patent proprietors will be sent a certificate once unitary effect has been registered. Unitary Patents will be assigned a specific identifier (the identifier "C0") in the Register for Unitary Patent Protection, the European Patent Bulletin and in the data sets provided by the EPO, making it easier to identify them through the EPO's patent information products and services, such as Espacenet and Global Patent Index.[156]

M. INCLUSION OF DECISIONS OF THE UNIFIED PATENT COURT IN THE FILES OF THE EPO

In order to inform the public, Rule 19 of the Rules relating to Unitary Patent Protection provides that the EPO shall include a copy of any decision of the Court forwarded to the EPO by the Court and relating to Unitary Patents, in the files relating to the Unitary Patent, where it shall be open to inspection.

Explanatory remark 2 with respect to this Rule 19 explains that the Rule is worded as a blanket clause and allows inclusion in the files of any decision relating to the Unitary Patent, including decisions handed down by the Court in actions brought under in Article 32(1)(i) UPCA.

Based on this framework, any decision of the Court can be included in the files of the EPO in accordance with the UPCA and the Rules of Procedure of the Unified Patent Court. For instance, Article 65(5) UPCA sets out that, where the Court, in a final decision, has revoked a patent, either entirely or partly, it will send a copy of the decision to the EPO. The EPO will include said copy in the files relating to the Unitary Patent. The EPO will not publish a new specification where the European patent with unitary effect is partly revoked.[157]

---

155. Unitary Patent Guide of the European Patent Office (www.epo.org)
156. Unitary Patent Guide of the European Patent Office (www.epo.org)
157. Explanatory remark 3 with respect to Rule 19 of the Rules relating to Unitary Patent Protection.

Part One – The Unitary Patent

N. LAPSE

Rule 14 of the Rules relating to Unitary Patent Protection summarises the situations in which the Unitary Patent lapses.[158]

Paragraph 1(a) of Rule 14 reflects Article 63(1) EPC which provides that the term of the Unitary Patent is twenty years from the date of filing of the application.

Paragraph 1(b) covers the case of non-payment in due time of a renewal fee and, where applicable, any additional fee.

The lapse of a Unitary Patent for failure to pay a renewal fee and any additional fee within the due period shall be deemed to have occurred on the date on which the renewal fee was due.[159]

O. ROLE OF THE EPO

Within the framework of the Unitary Patent system, the European Patent Organisation and the EPO play an important administrative role.

The EPO shall have the following tasks with respect to the Unitary Patent:[160]

- administer requests for unitary effect by proprietors of European Patents;
- set up the Register for Unitary Patent Protection within the European Patent Register and administer the Register for Unitary Patent Protection;
- receive and register statements on licensing referred to in Article 8 Unitary Patent Regulation, their withdrawal and licensing commitments undertaken by the proprietor of the Unitary Patent in international standardisation bodies;
- publish the translations referred to in Article 6 Translation Regulation during the transitional period referred to in that Article;
- collect and administer renewal fees for Unitary Patents, in respect of the years following the year in which the mention of the grant is published in the European Patent Bulletin;
- collect and administer additional fees for late payment of renewal fees where such late payment is made within six months of the due date, as well as to distribute part of the collected renewal fees to the Participating Member States;
- administer the compensation scheme for the reimbursement of translation costs in case of applications submitted in an official language other than French, German and English;
- ensure that a request for unitary effect by a proprietor of a European Patent is submitted in the language of the proceedings no later than one month after the mention of the grant is published in the European Patent Bulletin; and
- ensure that the unitary effect is indicated in the Register for Unitary Patent Protection, where a request for unitary effect has been filed and, during

---

158. Explanatory remark 1 with respect to Rule 14 of the Rules relating to Unitary Patent Protection.
159. Rule 14(2) of the Rules relating to Unitary Patent Protection.
160. Article 9(1) Unitary Patent Regulation.

Chapter V – The Unitary Patent

the transitional period, has been submitted together with the translations referred to in Article 6 Translation Regulation, and that the EPO is informed of any limitations, licences, transfers or revocations of European patents with unitary effect.

In fact, the EPO shall act as a centralised one-stop shop for administrating Unitary Patents. The Participating Member States shall ensure effective legal protection before a competent court of one or several Participating Member States against the decisions of the EPO in carrying out the aforementioned tasks.[161] This role shall be taken up by the Unified Patent Court.

Decisions of the EPO against which actions can be brought before the Unified Patent Court (in accordance with Article 32, paragraph 1(i) UPCA) shall be reasoned and shall be accompanied by a communication pointing out the possibility of bringing an action before the Court.[162] However, if they are not accompanied by such communication, the parties may not invoke the omission of the communication.

Actions concerning decisions of the EPO in carrying out the tasks referred to in Article 9 of the Unitary Patent Regulation are to be brought before the Unified Patent Court within two months of service of the decision of the EPO.[163] The Unified Patent Court then makes an admissibility check (and the applicant can correct deficiencies where applicable). If the application is admissible, the Court will forward it to the EPO.[164] Under Rule 91 Rules of Procedure of the Unified Patent Court, the EPO has a period of two months from the date of receipt of the Application to rectify in accordance with the order or remedy sought by the claimant the contested decision and to inform the Court that the decision has been rectified.[165]

Explanatory note 5 with respect to Rule 24 of the Rules relating to Unitary Patent Protection proposes to establish, in the framework of the implementation, an EPO internal procedure (e.g. internal Guidelines) which will ensure that in cases where an adverse decision is likely to be issued (e.g. rejection of a request) or where the case involves complex legal questions, a legally qualified member of the Unitary Patent Protection Division is involved before the issuance of the decision. This would guarantee that EPO decisions against which an action can be brought before the Unified Patent Court are legally sound. Rule 97 Rules of Procedure provides an expedited action against a decision of the EPO rejecting a request for unitary effect. The proprietor whose request for unitary effect has been rejected by the EPO shall lodge an application at the Registry to reverse the decision of the EPO, in the language in which the patent was granted, within three weeks of service of the decision of the EPO.

P. SELECT COMMITTEE

To ensure the governance and supervision of the EPO tasks, the Participating Member States have set up a select committee of the Administrative Council of the European

---

161. Article 9(3) Unitary Patent Regulation.
162. Rule 23 of the Rules relating to Unitary Patent Protection.
163. Article 32(1)(i) UPCA and Rule 88 Rules of Procedure.
164. Rule 90 Rules of Procedure.
165. Rule 24 of the Rules relating to Unitary Patent Protection.

Patent Organisation (hereinafter *"Select Committee"*).[166] The possibility to set up a select committee of the Administrative Council by members of the European Patent Organisation is stipulated in Article 145 EPC. Article 145 EPC clarifies that the EPO places at the disposal of such a select committee the staff, premises and equipment as may be necessary for the performance of its duties.

The Select Committee consists of representatives of the Participating Member States and a representative of the Commission as an observer, as well as alternates who will represent them in their absence.[167] The members of the Select Committee may be assisted by advisers or experts. Decisions of the Select Committee shall be taken with due regard for the position of the Commission and with a majority of three-quarters of the votes.[168]

The tasks of the Select Committee are essentially (i) ensuring the governance and supervision of the activities related to the special tasks of the EPO, and (ii) setting the level of the renewal fees and the share of distribution of these fees in accordance with Articles 12 and 13 of Unitary Patent Regulation.

The Select Committee held its first meeting in Munich on 20 March 2013 and adopted internal rules of procedure for the Select Committee on 25 June 2013.

The Chairman and the Deputy Chairman are elected for a period of three years, after which they can be re-elected.[169] Currently, Jérôme Debrulle of the Belgian Intellectual Property is the Chairman and Simona Marozetti from Italy is the Deputy Chairman. The members of the Select Committee are representatives of the Participating Member States, the President of the EPO, the Board of Auditors of the EPO and the EPO staff committee. The Participating Member States may appoint one representative and one alternate representative.[170] These representatives may vote on behalf of their Member State.[171] The right to vote in the Select Committee is restricted to the Participating Member States, who each have one vote.[172] Member States can be assisted by advisers or experts.[173]

A representative of the European Commission participates as an observer to the meetings of the Select Committee. Furthermore, the Select Committee invited as additional observers the European Patent Institute and BusinessEurope, and representatives of the following *"observer states"*: Albania, Croatia, Iceland, Italy, Monaco, Norway, San Marino, Serbia, Spain, Switzerland and Turkey.

At its 11th meeting on 9 December 2014 the Select Committee approved in principle the draft Rules relating to Unitary Patent Protection.[174] At the 15th meeting on 23–24 June 2015 the Select Committee decided on the EPO's renewal fees for Unitary Patents (cf. *infra*).

---

166. Article 9(2), §2 Unitary Patent Regulation.
167. Article 9(2), §3 Unitary Patent Regulation.
168. Article 9(2), §4 Unitary Patent Regulation with reference to Article 35(2) EPC.
169. Article 3(2) of the Rules of Procedure of the Select Committee of the Administrative Council.
170. Article 1(1) of the Rules of Procedure of the Select Committee of the Administrative Council.
171. Article 1(5) of the Rules of Procedure of the Select Committee of the Administrative Council.
172. Article 9(1) and (2) of the Rules of Procedure of the Select Committee of the Administrative Council.
173. Article 2(1) of the Rules of Procedure of the Select Committee of the Administrative Council.
174. http://www.epo.org/about-us/organisation/select-committee/documentation.html.

Chapter V – The Unitary Patent

On 15 December 2015, the Select Committee adopted the Rules relating to Unitary Patent Protection, the Rules relating to Fees for Unitary Patent Protection and the Budgetary and Financial Rules (BFR). At the same meeting, the Select Committee agreed on the distribution key between the Participating Member States of the renewal fees for Unitary Patents. However, given the sensitivity of the distribution key, the different percentages of the renewal fees each Participating Member State shall receive (laid down in the Rules relating the Distribution of Fees), remain confidential.

Q. RULES RELATING TO UNITARY PATENT PROTECTION

The Rules relating to Unitary Patent Protection are intended to provide rules for the EPO in carrying out its tasks referred to in Article 9(1) of the Unitary Patent Regulation. In case of conflict between the provisions of the Rules and Union law, including the Unitary Patent and Translation Regulations, the provisions of Union law shall prevail.[175]

Mirroring the competences of the Administrative Council as provided for in the EPC,[176] Rule 2 provides that the Select Committee should be competent to amend the Rules relating to Unitary Patent Protection, the Rules relating to Fees, other rules or decisions of a financial or budgetary nature and the Rules of Procedure of the Select Committee.

R. IMPLEMENTING RULES OF THE EPC APPLYING *MUTATIS MUTANDIS* TO UNITARY PATENT PROTECTION

Rule 20(1) provides a list of provisions of the EPC that shall apply *mutatis mutandis* to Unitary Patent Protection, and Rule 20(2) provides a list of provisions of the Implementing Rules of the EPC that shall apply *mutatis mutandis* to Unitary Patent Protection. When applying these provisions *mutatis mutandis*, the term *"Contracting States"* shall be understood as meaning the Contracting States to the EPC, except for Article 125 EPC where it shall be understood as meaning the Participating Member States.[177]

Where the Rules relating to Unitary Patent Protection, including the provisions of the EPC applicable *mutatis mutandis*, refer to *"a period to be specified"*, this period shall be specified by the EPO. Unless otherwise provided, a period specified by the EPO shall be neither less than one month nor more than four months.[178] As regards the calculation of periods, Rule 131 EPC also applies *mutatis mutandis*. For the purpose of legal certainty, and in order to keep the overall duration of the procedure for requesting unitary effect reasonably short, in line with the Unitary Patent Regulation, some modifications to the periods of the EPC apply. Rule 20(4) of the Rules relating to Unitary Protection takes over the substance of Rule 132 EPC but shortens the minimum period to one month instead of two. The reason for this shortening is that the procedure for requesting unitary effect differs significantly from

---

175. Rule 1(2) of the Rules relating to Unitary Patent Protection.
176. Articles 33(1)(2) and 46 EPC.
177. Rule 20(3) of the Rules relating to Unitary Patent Protection.
178. Rule 20(4) of the Rules relating to Unitary Patent Protection.

the patent grant procedure insofar as it exclusively relates to the fulfilment of purely formal requirements. In particular it does not require the preparation of substantive replies from the Requester which would justify longer periods.[179] Furthermore, the content of Rule 133(1) EPC is set out separately in Rule 20(1)(g) of the Rules relating to Unitary Patent Protection with the proviso that the document referred to therein must have been received no later than one month after expiry of the relevant period. This is to be in line with the one-month period for filing the request for unitary effect, given the fact that the main documents to be filed with the EPO will in fact be the request for unitary effect and the translations.[180]

Explanatory remark 1 with respect to Rule 20 of the Rules relating to Unitary Patent Protection explains that the Unitary Patent Regulation sets out that the Participating Member States will give the EPO some additional tasks to be carried out in accordance with the *"internal rules"* of the EPO. For the sake of clarity and definiteness, i.e. legal certainty, and since not all procedural rules of the EPC are of relevance in the present context, Rule 20 provides a list of the procedural rules of the EPC (both from the Convention and the Implementing Regulations) that apply. As a result, with respect to the purely procedural aspects of the tasks entrusted to the EPO, only the EPC provisions enumerated in Rule 20 and those referred to in some other of the Rules relating to Unitary Patent Protection (see for example Rule 13(6) referring to Rule 51(4) and (5) EPC) will apply. The legislative technique chosen, i.e. a dynamic reference to the relevant EPC provisions, allows automatic and full alignment to the current EPO procedures and related practice. It thereby provides legal certainty and clarity for the users acquainted with the classic EPO procedures. In terms of legislation, the dynamic reference ensures that whenever EPC procedural rules are being amended by the Administrative Council so as to improve the EPO procedures, these changes will automatically be applicable without necessitating adoption by the Select Committee.[181]

Only in exceptional cases have some EPC provisions been reworded and adapted to the needs of the procedures relating to Unitary Patent protection. This is in particular the case for all the time limits which have been kept short in line with the aim of the Regulation which is to keep the overall duration of the procedure for requesting unitary effect reasonably short for the sake of legal certainty.[182]

The applicability of some EPC provisions will sometimes imply a delegation of powers to the President of the EPO for implementing this rule. For example, with respect to the implementation of Rule 144(d) EPC which deals with *"Parts of the file to be excluded from file inspection"*, the President of the EPO took a decision excluding documents from inspection if their inspection would for example be prejudicial to personal or economic interests. This decision would for instance also apply since

---

179. Explanatory remark 15 with respect to Rule 20 of the Rules relating to Unitary Patent Protection.
180. Explanatory remark 16 with respect to Rule 20 of the Rules relating to Unitary Patent Protection.
181. Explanatory remark 2 with respect to Rule 20 of the Rules relating to Unitary Patent Protection.
182. Explanatory remark 3 with respect to Rule 20 of the Rules relating to Unitary Patent Protection.

it was taken under the relevant EPC rule applying *mutatis mutandis*. Again, the objective is to have a full alignment to the EPO procedure in order to avoid parallel procedures and higher costs arising therefrom and to obtain legal certainty and simplicity for the users acquainted with the EPO procedures.[183]

Article 14(1) EPC determines the official languages of the EPO, and Article 14(3) EPC defines the term *"language of proceedings"*. Both provisions are applicable *mutatis mutandis* as laid down in Rule 20(1) of the Rules relating to Unitary Patent Protection. However, the request for unitary effect has to be filed in the language of proceedings. This deviates from the EPC regime, where any of the three EPO official languages may be used as a matter of principle in written proceedings. It is therefore proposed that unless otherwise provided, Rule 3(1), first sentence, EPC (as well as Rule 3(3) EPC) should apply *mutatis mutandis*. As a consequence, as regards the language in written proceedings before the EPO, any party may use any official language of the EPO except for the request for unitary effect itself, which has to be filed in the language of the proceedings. In practice, users will complete a dedicated form when requesting unitary effect which will inter alia contain the request in the three official languages of the EPO.[184]

In order to avoid delays in the straightforward procedure for requesting unitary effect, the EPC provisions allowing documents to be filed within a time limit in an admissible non-EPO language provided that a translation is filed within a month are not applicable (Article 14(4) EPC; Rule 3(1), second sentence, EPC; and Rule 6(2) EPC). As a result, it will for instance not be possible to file a request for re-establishment of rights in an admissible non-EPO language and to file a translation within a month. This is in contrast to the proceedings governed by the EPC. In practice, however, this possibility is almost never used when it comes to requests for re-establishment of rights or replying to an invitation from the EPO to rectify a deficiency within a certain period.[185]

Documents relating to the procedure for the registration of unitary effect as well as any document relating to the Unitary Patent will have to be open to public file inspection. It is therefore proposed that a special part be created in the existing electronic file relating to the European Patent application and the resulting European Patents. For that purpose, Rule 20 provides that Article 128(4) EPC should apply *mutatis mutandis* to Unitary Patents. As a result, the files relating to a Unitary Patent could be inspected on request, subject to the modalities and restrictions laid down in Rules 144 to 146 EPC, which also apply *mutatis mutandis*.[186] As regards the constitution, maintenance and preservation of files, it is proposed that Rule 147 EPC should apply *mutatis mutandis*.[187]

---

183. Explanatory remark 4 with respect to Rule 20 of the Rules relating to Unitary Patent Protection.
184. Explanatory remarks 6 and 7 with respect to Rule 20 of the Rules relating to Unitary Patent Protection.
185. Explanatory remark 8 with respect to Rule 20 of the Rules relating to Unitary Patent Protection.
186. Explanatory remarks 9 and 10 with respect to Rule 20 of the Rules relating to Unitary Patent Protection.
187. Explanatory remark 11 with respect to Rule 20 of the Rules relating to Unitary Patent Protection.

With respect to representation, Rule 20 provides that Articles 133 and 134 paragraphs 1, 5 and 8 EPC, as well as Rules 151 to 153 EPC apply *mutatis mutandis*. In other words, almost the entire, unaltered EPO regime applies, except for some provisions on the list of professional representatives which are not relevant in the present context.[188] This means that for example a Spanish firm having its place of business in Spain is not subject to compulsory representation by a professional representative for the purpose of filing a request for unitary effect and all the other procedures regarding a Unitary Patent. Where a legal person does not have its place of business in an EPC Contracting State, however, it will need to be represented by a professional representative and act through him in all proceedings regarding the Unitary Patent, including for the act of filing of the request for unitary effect.[189]

Part VII, Chapters III (oral proceedings and taking of evidence) and IV (notifications) of the Implementing Regulations to the EPC apply *mutatis mutandis*.[190]

S. ORAL PROCEEDINGS

Article 116(1) EPC provides the fundamental right to oral proceedings. In accordance with this Article, Rule 21(1) of the Rules relating to Unitary Patent Protection provides that oral proceedings take place either at the instance of the Unitary Patent Protection Division of the EPO if it considers this to be expedient or at the request of any party to the proceedings. The Unitary Patent Protection Division may reject a request for further oral proceedings before it where the parties and the subject of the proceedings are the same.[191]

However, in the interest of procedural economy, Rule 21(2) of the Rules relating to Unitary Patent Protection provides that the principle under which oral proceedings are to be held upon request of any party to the proceedings should be expressly restricted in proceedings concerning the request for unitary effect. Thus, oral proceedings in proceedings concerning the request for unitary effect will normally be excluded and should take place only if the Unified Patent Protection Division considers this to be expedient. Only in exceptional cases where face-to-face dialogue is likely to result in a speedier resolution of the issues relevant to the registration of unitary effect will the EPO deem oral proceedings to be expedient.[192]

The procedure for registering unitary effect should be kept as expeditious as possible for reasons of legal certainty. The Select Committee considered that holding oral proceedings at the request of the proprietor where the EPO intends to refuse the request for unitary effect would as a rule considerably delay the whole proceedings

---

188. Explanatory remark 12 with respect to Rule 20 of the Rules relating to Unitary Patent Protection.
189. Explanatory remark 13 with respect to Rule 20 of the Rules relating to Unitary Patent Protection.
190. Explanatory remark 14 with respect to Rule 20 of the Rules relating to Unitary Patent Protection.
191. Explanatory remark 1 with respect to Rule 21 of the Rules relating to Unitary Patent Protection.
192. Explanatory remark 2 with respect to Rule 21 of the Rules relating to Unitary Patent Protection.

because the EPO would need to duly prepare oral proceedings (proprietor to be summoned with at least two months' notice of the summons according to Rule 115(1) EPC which applies *mutatis mutandis*, see Rule 20(2)(e)). This would also be very cost-intensive (communication accompanying the summons to be issued, translations to be provided, minutes to be taken). Oral proceedings would moreover not produce any further clarity, because the possible formal defects cannot usually be removed and the legal situation will be clear cut and simple in the majority of cases.[193]

Oral proceedings with respect to other procedures, such as the procedure for re-establishment of rights with regard to the time limit for paying renewal fees or with regard to the time limit for filing the request for unitary effect, are unaffected by this restriction and are to be held on request in accordance with Rule 21(1).[194]

Oral proceedings before the Unitary Patent Protection Division shall not be public.[195]

T. RE-ESTABLISHMENT OF RIGHTS

A proprietor of a European Patent or of a Unitary Patent who, in spite of all due care required by the circumstances having been taken, was unable to observe a time limit vis-à-vis the EPO shall have his rights re-established upon request if the non-observance of this time limit has the direct consequence of causing the Unitary Patent to lapse because a renewal fee and, where applicable, any additional fee have not been paid in due time, or the loss of any other right or means of redress.[196]

Any request for re-establishment of rights shall be filed in writing within two months of the removal of the cause of non-compliance with the period, but at the latest within one year of expiry of the unobserved time limit. However, a request for re-establishment of rights in respect of the one-month period to request unitary effect shall be filed within two months of expiry of that period.

The request for re-establishment of rights shall not be deemed to have been filed until the prescribed fee has been paid.[197] Article 2(2) RFeesUPP provides that the amount of the fee for re-establishment of rights shall correspond to the amount of the equivalent fee laid down in the RFeesEPC. This ensures full alignment with the fee for re-establishment of rights to be paid under the EPC. A biennial adjustment of the fees to be paid under the EPC shall thereby also apply to the fee for re-establishment of rights for Unitary Patents.

The request shall state the grounds on which it is based and shall set out the facts on which it relies. The omitted act shall be completed within the relevant period for filing the request.[198] The EPO shall grant the request, provided that the

---

193. Explanatory remark 3 with respect to Rule 21 of the Rules relating to Unitary Patent Protection.
194. Explanatory remark 4 with respect to Rule 21 of the Rules relating to Unitary Patent Protection.
195. Rule 21(3) of the Rules relating to Unitary Patent Protection.
196. Rule 22(1) of the Rules relating to Unitary Patent Protection.
197. Rule 22(2) of the Rules relating to Unitary Patent Protection.
198. Rule 22(3) of the Rules relating to Unitary Patent Protection.

conditions are met. Otherwise, it shall reject the request.[199] If the request is granted, the legal consequences of the failure to observe the time limit shall be deemed not to have ensued.[200]

Re-establishment of rights shall be ruled out in respect of the time limit for requesting re-establishment of rights and in respect of the one-month period referred to in Rule 7(3) of the Rules relating to Unitary Protection, i.e. the one-month period in which the formal deficiencies need to be corrected.[201]

Any person who, in one or several Participating Member States, has in good faith used or made effective any serious preparations for using an invention which is the subject of a Unitary Patent in the period between the loss of rights and publication in the Register for Unitary Patent Protection of the mention of re-establishment of those rights, may without payment continue such use in the course of his business or for the needs thereof.[202]

U. RENEWAL FEES

1. General

Instead of paying renewal fees in every Participating Member State (as for classic European Patents), patent proprietors shall only pay one single annual renewal fee for a Unitary Patent.

Renewal fees for Unitary Patents and additional fees for their late payment shall be paid to the European Patent Organisation by the patent proprietor. Those fees shall be due in respect of the years following the year in which the mention of the grant of the European Patent which benefits from unitary effect is published in the European Patent Bulletin.[203]

Following the general rules on renewal fees, a Unitary Patent shall lapse if a renewal fee and, where applicable, any additional fee have not been paid in due time.[204]

2. Level of renewal fees

The Regulation itself does not set the level of renewal fees. Setting the level of renewal fees is the responsibility of the Select Committee of the EPO. But the Unitary Patent Regulation does provide a number of requirements which have to be respected by the Select Committee when determining the renewal fees.

The renewal fees for Unitary Patents should be:

– progressive throughout the term of the Unitary Patent protection;

---

199. Rule 22(4) of the Rules relating to Unitary Patent Protection.
200. Rule 22(5) of the Rules relating to Unitary Patent Protection.
201. Rule 22(6) of the Rules relating to Unitary Patent Protection.
202. Rule 22(7) of the Rules relating to Unitary Patent Protection.
203. Article 11(1) Unitary Patent Regulation.
204. Article 11(2) Unitary Patent Regulation.

- sufficient to cover all costs associated with the grant of the European Patent and the administration of the Unitary Patent protection; and
- sufficient, together with the fees to be paid to the European Patent Organisation during the pre-grant stage, to ensure a balanced budget of the European Patent Organisation.[205]

The Unitary Patent Regulation provides that the level of the renewal fees shall be set, taking into account, among other things, the situation of specific entities such as small and medium-sized enterprises, with the aim of:

- facilitating innovation and fostering the competitiveness of European businesses;
- reflecting the size of the market covered by the patent; and
- being similar to the level of the national renewal fees for an average European Patent taking effect in the Participating Member States at the time the level of the renewal fees is first set.[206]

With respect to the first objective of facilitating innovation and fostering competitiveness, Recital 19 of the Preamble to the Unitary Patent Regulation explicitly states that the situation of specific entities such as small and medium-sized enterprises should be taken into account, for example in the form of lower fees.

In order to attain the aforementioned objectives, Article 12(3) Unitary Patent Regulation provides that the level of renewal fees shall be set at a level that:

- is equivalent to the level of the renewal fee to be paid for the average geographical coverage of current European Patents;
- reflects the renewal rate of current European Patents; and
- reflects the number of requests for unitary effect.

Based on the aforementioned principles the Select Committee started its negotiations regarding the level of renewal fees in 2014. In March 2015 the EPO presented two proposals to the Select Committee. The proposals were presented as the "Top 4" and "Top 5" models, i.e. renewal fees equivalent to the national renewal fees of respectively the four and five Member States where European Patents are most frequently validated. At that time, these Member States were Germany, France, the UK, the Netherlands and Sweden. The Top 5 model contained a 25% fee reduction for SMEs during the first ten years.

However, the two models only corresponded to the actual renewal fees in the Top 4 and Top 5 Member States after year 10. For years 3–5, the EPO had proposed setting the renewal fees of the Unitary Patent at the level of the EPO's internal renewal fees (IRF). For years 6–9, the level would be a transitional level between the IRF level and the year 10 level of the Top 4 or Top 5. Business Europe calculated that because of the taking into account of the IRF level, the renewal fees would amount to the equivalent of the Top 10 countries for years 2 to 4, Top 9 in year 5, Top 8 in year 6, close to Top 6 (year 7), close to Top 5 (year 8) and around Top 4 in years 9 and 10. This would mean that, certainly for the first ten years, the level of renewal

---

205. Article 12(1) Unitary Patent Regulation.
206. Article 15(2) Unitary Patent Regulation.

fees would be much higher than applicants paid at that time for average European Patents (validated in three or four countries). Business Europe also criticised the prospective models estimating the penetration rate of Unitary Patents.

Not only the first ten years, but also the total amount of renewal fees for the full twenty years were considered rather expensive. The total cost for twenty years of renewal fees would be EUR 37,995 in the Top 4 model and EUR 43,625 in the (non-SME) Top 5 model. SMEs would pay EUR 41,655 in the Top 5 model. These total costs were higher than the costs for a European Patent validated in Germany, France, UK and Italy (EUR 32,603) and even more than for a European Patent validated in the same countries plus Spain (EUR 37,613).

The criticism regarding the use of the IRF levels for the first ten years was shared by a large number of Member States in the Select Committee. If the renewal fees are high in the first years, this could discourage applicants from opting for Unitary Patents rather than for traditional European Patents validated in a small number of Member States or even for national patents. On 7 May 2015, the EPO adjusted its proposals and presented a *"true"* Top 4 and 5 level of renewal fees. The model of the IRF levels during the first years was abandoned and to the estimates of the penetration rates the EPO added a new model, i.e. the Upper + assumption, as well as the Business Europe assumption. These penetration rates were important for the national patent offices to be able to calculate their estimated *"income"*.

In June 2015 the Select Committee came to a preliminary agreement on the level of renewal fees. A compromise was found in the *"true"* Top 4 model. This means that the level of renewal fees for the Unitary Patent shall be equal to the fees paid for validation of a European Patent in the four most popular Member States (currently Germany, France, the UK and the Netherlands). On 24 June 2015 the EPO published a grid with the agreed renewal fees for the Unitary Patent and compared these with the renewal fees to be paid for European Patents validated in twenty-five Member States (since Italy at that time had not yet entered the enhanced cooperation). The renewal fees were incorporated in the RFeesUPP. The RFeesUPP were adopted by the Select Committee on 15 December 2015.

The renewal fees (in EUR) for the Unitary Patent are as follows:[207]

Year	Unitary Patent	European Patent validated in 25 Member States
2	35	0
3	105	1,298
4	145	1,874
5	315	2,545
6	475	3,271
7	630	3,886
8	815	4,625
9	990	5,513

---

207. Article 2(1) of the RFeesUPP.

Chapter V – The Unitary Patent

Year	Unitary Patent	European Patent validated in 25 Member States
10	1,175	6,416
11	1,460	7,424
12	1,775	8,473
13	2,105	9,594
14	2,455	10,741
15	2,830	11,917
16	3,240	13,369
17	3,640	14,753
18	4,055	16,065
19	4,455	17,660
20	4,855	19,197
Total	35,555	158,621

The renewal fees will be less than EUR 5,000 during the first ten years of the Unitary Patent. The cumulative total to be paid over the full 20-year term will be EUR 35,555. At the time of this decision, the total amount of renewal fees for a European Patent validated in twenty-five Member States is EUR 29,500 during the first ten years and EUR 158,621 in total. In other words, the *"true"* Top 4 decision corresponds to a reduction of 78% compared to a fully validated European Patent.

The level of renewal fees was not renegotiated after 2015. Although one could consider that because of inflation and increased costs, these renewal fees could be open for discussion at the start of the system in 2023, this was not the case. The Select Committee decided to keep the renewal fees at the same level as was decided in 2015 in order to keep the system attractive for companies and SMEs and not to re-open political discussions.

3. **Distribution of renewal fees**

The EPO shall retain an amount of 50% of the renewal fees to cover the expenses generated at the EPO in carrying out tasks in relation to the Unitary Patents.[208] In this respect, Article 146 EPC provides that where additional tasks have been given to the EPO, the group of Contracting States shall bear the expenses incurred by the European Patent Organisation in carrying out these tasks. Where special departments have been set up in the EPO to carry out these additional tasks, the group of Contracting States shall bear the expenditure on staff, premises and equipment chargeable in respect of these departments.

After the EPO retains 50%, the remaining amount of renewal fees shall be distributed among the Participating Member States[209] and should be used for

---

208. Article 10 Unitary Patent Regulation.
209. Article 13(1) Unitary Patent Regulation.

patent-related purposes.[210] One of the possibilities could be that Participating Member States use the share of renewal fees to finance the costs of their local division of the Court. Hence, during the first seven years the facilities and administrative support staff for the local division need to be financed by the Member States where the local division is located.[211]

Recital 20 of the Preamble to the Unitary Patent Regulation provides that the appropriate level and distribution of renewal fees shall be determined in order to ensure that, in relation to the Unitary Patent protection, all costs of the tasks entrusted to the EPO are fully covered by the resources generated by the Unitary Patents and that, together with the fees to be paid to the European Patent Organisation during the pre-grant stage, the revenues from the renewal fees ensure a balanced budget for the European Patent Organisation.[212]

The setting of the distribution key for the renewal fees between the Participating Member States is the competence of the Select Committee of the EPO.[213] The distribution key for renewal fees to be set by the Select Committee is to be based on the following fair, equitable and relevant criteria:[214]

(a) the number of patent applications;
(b) the size of the market, while ensuring a minimum amount to be distributed to each Participating Member State;
(c) compensation for Participating Member States which have:
   (i) an official language other than one of the official languages of the EPO,
   (ii) a disproportionately low level of patenting activity, and/or
   (iii) acquired membership of the European Patent Organisation relatively recently.

On 17 November 2015 the Select Committee agreed on the distribution key for the 50% of the renewal fee revenues that need to be allocated to the Participating Member States. The decision was not taken unanimously, but only two Member States voted against the agreement. The agreement was announced on 18 November 2015 in press releases by the European Commission[215] and the EPO.[216] The European Commission stressed in its press release that a balance had to be achieved between ensuring competitiveness for companies, setting fees that would encourage people, particularly SMEs, to undertake innovation on the one hand, and ensuring the financing of high-quality administrative structures (the EPO and national patent offices) on the other.

The exact distribution key per Member State and the Rules relating to the Distribution of Fees have not been disclosed by the Select Committee. Given the sensitive nature of the distribution key, the Select Committee decided to keep the specific distribution percentage per Member State confidential.

---

210. Recital 21 of the Preamble to the Unitary Patent Regulation.
211. Article 15 UPCA.
212. Recital 20 of the Preamble to the Unitary Patent Regulation.
213. Article 9(2) Unitary Patent Regulation.
214. Article 13(2) Unitary Patent Regulation.
215. http://ec.europa.eu/growth/tools-databases/newsroom/cf/itemdetail.cfm?item_id=8561&lang=en&title=Unitary-patent%3A-26-countries-agree-on-distribution-key.
216. https://www.epo.org/news-issues/news/2015/20151118.html.

Chapter V – The Unitary Patent

The agreement of the Select Committee fixes the distribution key for an initial period of operation: 50% of fees will be retained by the EPO while the remainder (minus an administrative charge) will be distributed among the participating countries according to a formula that takes account of the GDP and the number of applications filed from that country.

No later than five years from the date of application of the Unitary Patent Regulation and every five years thereafter, the EPO shall submit a report to the Select Committee of the Administrative Council assessing the financial impact of the Unitary Patent on the budget of the EPO and on the renewal fee income of the Participating Member States and, where necessary, make an appropriate proposal for adjusting the level of renewal fees.[217] This report is without prejudice to the reports of the Commission to the Council and the European Parliament regarding the operation of the Unitary Patent Regulation and on the functioning of the renewal fees.[218]

Within the same five-year period the EPO shall, after consultation with the European Commission, submit a report to the Select Committee of the Administrative Council on the use of the Unitary Patent by specific entities, such as small and medium-sized enterprises, and, where necessary, make proposals with a view to improving their access to the Unitary Patent.[219]

4. Administration by the EPO

The EPO shall be responsible for the collection and administration of the renewal fees for Unitary Patents, in respect of the years following the year in which the mention of the grant is published in the European Patent Bulletin, and for the distribution of the part of the collected renewal fees to the Participating Member States. The EPO shall also collect and administer additional fees for late payment of renewal fees where such late payment is made within six months of the due date.[220]

Rule 13(1) of the Rules relating to Unitary Patent Protection provides that the renewal fees and additional fees for late payment shall be paid to the EPO. Those fees shall be due in respect of the years following the year in which the mention of the grant of the European Patent which benefits from unitary effect is published in the European Patent Bulletin. A renewal fee for Unitary Patents in respect of the coming year shall be due on the last day of the month containing the anniversary of the date of filing of the European Patent application which led to the Unitary Patent. Renewal fees may not be validly paid more than three months before they fall due.[221] This arrangement is almost identical to the wording of Rule 51(1) EPC.

If a renewal fee is not paid in due time, the fee may still be paid within six months of the due date, provided that an additional fee for late payment is also paid within that period.[222]

---

217. Article 7(a) RFeesUPP.
218. Article 16(1) and (2) Unitary Patent Regulation.
219. Article 7(b) RFeesUPP.
220. Article 9(1)(e) Unitary Patent Regulation.
221. Rule 13(2) of the Rules relating to Unitary Patent Protection.
222. Rule 13(3) of the Rules relating to Unitary Patent Protection.

If the renewal fee has not been paid on the due date, the EPO will inform, as a courtesy service (and as is the current practice with respect to renewal fees to be paid for the European Patent application under Article 86 EPC), the proprietor of the Unitary Patent as soon as possible of the option of paying the fee, plus an additional fee, in the six months following the due date, that period having already begun.[223]

Article 2(1), item 2, RFeesUPP lays down the amount of the additional fee for belated payment of a renewal fee. The additional fee for belated payment of a renewal fee is 50% of the renewal fee. Where a renewal fee is reduced in accordance with Article 3 RFeesUPP, the 50% additional fee is to be calculated on the basis of the reduced renewal fee.

If the renewal fee is not paid within the additional six-month period, the EPO will send a communication under Rule 112(1) EPC, notifying the proprietor of the Unitary Patent of the loss of rights. The communication does not constitute a decision within the meaning of Article 32(1)(i) UPCA, so an action cannot be brought against it before the Court.[224] Failure to pay the renewal fee within the additional six-month period can be redressed using re-establishment of rights under Rule 22 of the Rules relating to Unitary Patent Protection. Alternatively, if the finding of the EPO causing the loss of rights is inaccurate, a review of the finding can be requested by applying for a decision under Rule 112(2) EPC, said Rule applying *mutatis mutandis*. An action against that decision can then be brought before the Court.[225]

The calculation of time limits is to be effected under Rules 131 and 134 EPC in accordance with the current EPO practice: when the due date falls on a date on which the EPO cannot receive mail within the meaning of Rule 134(1) EPC (which applies *mutatis mutandis*), the due date is not changed since it does not constitute a period which can be extended. Instead, the last day for valid payment is deferred to the first working day thereafter.[226] Furthermore, the six-month additional period for late payment starts on the last day of the month referred to in Rule 13(2), even if the EPO cannot receive mail on that date because of holidays, mail interruption or strike. However, Rule 134(1) EPC is to be applied to the expiry of the six-month additional period, deferring the last day for valid payment to the first working day thereafter.[227]

Article 9(1)(e) of the Unitary Patent Regulation provides that the EPO, when collecting and administering renewal fees as well as additional fees for late payment, shall perform these tasks in accordance with the internal rules of the EPO. The purpose of the application of these internal rules of the EPO is the full alignment between EPO procedures relating to European Patent applications and European Patents on the one hand and the procedures relating to the European patent with unitary effect on the other. Therefore, when calculating the additional six-month period, the internal

---

223. Explanatory remark 3 with respect to Rule 13 of the Rules relating to Unitary Patent Protection.
224. Explanatory remark 4 with respect to Rule 13 of the Rules relating to Unitary Patent Protection.
225. Explanatory remark 5 with respect to Rule 13 of the Rules relating to Unitary Patent Protection.
226. Explanatory remark 6 with respect to Rule 13 of the Rules relating to Unitary Patent Protection.
227. Explanatory remark 7 with respect to Rule 13 of the Rules relating to Unitary Patent Protection.

rules of the EPO, as resulting from Decision J 4/91 of the Legal Board of Appeal[228] are to be applied. It follows that the six-month period for the payment of a renewal fee with an additional fee expires on the last day of the sixth month after the due date and not on the day of that month corresponding in number to the due date (see Rule 131(4) EPC applying *mutatis mutandis*). Thus, the calculation is to be made from the last day of the month to the last day of the month (*"de ultimo ad ultimo"*).[229] For example, if the due date is 28 February, then the end of the six-month period will be 31 August and not 28 August.

The consequence of non-payment of the renewal fee, and where applicable of the additional fee, is the lapse of the European patent with unitary effect in accordance with Article 11(2) of the Unitary Patent Regulation. The lapse takes effect on the due date.[230]

A renewal fee falling due within three months of the notification of the communication of unitary protection referred to in Rule 7(1) relating to Unitary Patent Protection may still be paid within that period without the additional fee for late payment.[231] Rule 13(4) of the Rules relating to Unitary Patent Protection is similar to the content of Article 141(2) EPC and extends the two-month safety period to three months. A renewal fee in respect of a Unitary Patent falling due within three months of the notification of the communication may still be paid within that period without the additional fee. In case the Court overturns a decision of the EPO and orders the EPO to register unitary effect, the EPO will notify the patent proprietor with a communication under Rule 7(1) informing him of the date of registration of unitary effect in the Register for Unitary Patent Protection. This will trigger the three-month period for paying the renewal fee without an additional fee. The course of the six-month period under Rule 13(3) is unaffected: it starts running from the due date. However, Rule 13(4) has the effect that an additional fee under Rule 13(3) does not have to be paid where the renewal fee is paid within the three-month safety period.[232]

A renewal fee for a Unitary Patent which would have fallen due in the period starting on the date of publication of the mention of the grant of the European Patent in the European Patent Bulletin up to and including the date of the notification of the communication by the EPO referred to in Rule 7(1) shall be due on that latter date. This fee may still be paid within three months of that latter date without the additional fee for late payment.[233] This covers the case where a renewal fee falls due after the grant of the European Patent but before the unitary effect is registered. This could in particular occur where the procedure for registering unitary effect takes a long time owing, for example, to a request for re-establishment of rights or the involvement of the Court. If, at the end of such a procedure, the decision to register unitary effect is finally notified to the patent proprietor by the EPO, the Unitary Patent

---

228. See Official Journal 1992, 402.
229. Explanatory remark 8 with respect to Rule 13 of the Rules relating to Unitary Patent Protection.
230. Explanatory remark 9 with respect to Rule 13 of the Rules relating to Unitary Patent Protection.
231. Rule 13(4) of the Rules relating to Unitary Patent Protection.
232. Explanatory remark 10 with respect to Rule 13 of the Rules relating to Unitary Patent Protection.
233. Rule 13(5) of the Rules relating to Unitary Patent Protection.

takes effect on the date of publication of the mention of the grant of the European Patent in the European Patent Bulletin. Owing to this retroactive effect (see Recital 8 Unitary Patent Regulation), renewal fees would have fallen due for the period starting on the date of publication of the mention of the grant of the European Patent in the European Patent Bulletin and up to and including the date of the notification of the communication referred to in Rule 7(1). Rule 13(5) shifts the due date to the date of said notification and allows the payment of renewal fees within three months of this notification without any additional fee. If not paid within this period, Rule 13(3) applies, i.e. the fee(s) can still be paid with an additional fee within six months, starting from the date of notification.[234]

Rule 51(4) and (5) EPC shall apply *mutatis mutandis* to the renewal fees for a Unitary Patent.[235] Rule 51(4) EPC refers to the case where a Unitary Patent lapses due to the non-payment of renewal fees and a request for re-establishment of rights is successful. Rule 51(5) governs the analogous situation where a petition for review or a rehearing under Article 81 UPCA is successful.

The European Commission shall establish a close cooperation through a working agreement with the EPO in the fields covered by the Unitary Patent Regulation.[236] This cooperation shall include regular exchanges of views on the functioning of the working agreement and, in particular, on the issue of renewal fees and their impact on the budget of the European Patent Organisation.

5. Rules relating to Fees for Unitary Patent Protection

On 15 December 2015, the Select Committee of the Administrative Council of the EPO adopted the RFeesUPP. These Rules consist of seven articles and mainly concern the level of renewal fees, the additional fee for late payment, the fee for re-establishment of rights, the discount for licence commitments (cf. *supra*) and the compensation for translation costs (cf. *infra*).

Besides the setting of a number of fees specific to the Unitary Patent, Article 5 of the RFeesUPP provides that the administrative fees provided for in the Rules relating to Unitary Patent Protection and the fees and expenses charged for any services rendered by the EPO other than those specified in these Rules shall be payable in the amounts laid down by the President of the EPO pursuant to Article 3 of the Rules relating to Fees under the EPC. Pursuant to Article 3(1) RFeesEPC, the President of the EPO shall lay down the amount of the administrative fees provided for in the Implementing Regulations to the EPC and, where appropriate, the amount of the fees and expenses payable by the patent proprietor for any services rendered by the EPO other than those specified in Article 2 RFeesEPC. The latest decision of the President of the EPO revising the EPO's fees and expenses dates from 17 January 2023. Said decision of the President contains, for example, the amounts of the administrative fees for the registering of a transfer (Rule 22(2) EPC), for the registering of a licence and other rights (Rule 23(1) EPC) and for the communication

---

234. Explanatory remark 11 with respect to Rule 13 of the Rules relating to Unitary Patent Protection.
235. Rule 13(6) of the Rules relating to Unitary Patent Protection.
236. Article 14 Unitary Patent Regulation.

of information contained in the files of a European Patent application (see Rule 146 EPC). Since under the Rules relating to Unitary Patent Protection, the above cited provisions of the EPC Implementing Regulations apply *mutatis mutandis* (see Rule 20(2) UPR), the same amounts of fees as set out in the decision of the President of the EPO revising the EPO's fees and expenses, as amended, will apply. Moreover, the decision of the President of the EPO revising the EPO's fees and expenses lays down some fees for services rendered by the EPO other than those specified in the present Rules, for example a fee for obtaining extracts from the European Patent Register, which includes the Register for Unitary Patent Protection. Article 5 RFeesUPP thus ensures full alignment with the EPO's already applicable schedule of fees as regards both administrative fees and fees or expenses for any services rendered by the EPO.

Article 6 RFeesUPP sets out that some of the provisions of the RFeesEPC, as amended, shall apply *mutatis mutandis*. The legislative technique chosen, i.e. a dynamic reference to the relevant provisions, allows automatic and full alignment with the current EPO procedures and related practice.

The following provisions of the RFeesEPC, as amended, shall apply *mutatis mutandis*: Article 4 (*"Due date for fees"*), Article 5 (*"Payment of fees"*), Article 6 (*"Particulars concerning payments"*), Article 7 (*"Date to be considered as the date on which payment is made"*), Article 8 (*"Insufficiency of the amount paid"*), Article 12 (*"Refund of insignificant amounts"*) and Article 13 (*"Termination of financial obligations"*).

The applicability of some of the provisions of the RFeesEPC will imply a delegation of powers to the President of the EPO for the implementation of said Rules. For example, under Article 5(2) RFeesEPC, the President of the EPO may allow methods of paying fees other than those set out in Article 5(1) RFeesEPC. This means in particular that for the purpose of paying any fee under the present Rules, the arrangements for deposit accounts, as amended, will apply.[237]

V. BUDGETARY AND FINANCIAL RULES

On 15 December 2015, the Select Committee of the Administrative Council of the EPO also adopted the Budgetary and Financial Rules (hereinafter "*BFR*").[238] These Rules contain five Articles dealing with the way the EPO will handle its budget regarding its tasks for the Unitary Patents.

Article 1 BFR provides that the income and expenditure with regard to the implementation of the tasks relating to Unitary Patent Protection shall be an integral part of the budget of the European Patent Organisation. The Financial Regulations of the European Patent Organisation and the rules for their implementation, as amended, shall apply except where the BFR provide otherwise.

The President of the EPO shall submit to the Select Committee of the Administrative Council a draft statement of income and expenditure. The Select Committee of the Administrative Council shall give an opinion on this draft statement before the corresponding income and expenditure, along with the necessary explanations, are

---

237. Arrangements for deposit accounts (ADA) and their annexes, OJ EPO 3/2015, valid as from 1 April 2015.
238. http://www.epo.org/about-us/organisation/select-committee/documentation.html.

integrated into the overall draft budget of the European Patent Organisation, which is submitted to the Budget and Finance Committee and the Administrative Council of the European Patent Organisation by the President of the EPO. The Budget and Finance Committee and the Administrative Council of the European Patent Organisation shall be informed of the opinion of the Select Committee of the Administrative Council and of the response of the EPO.[239]

The President of the EPO shall quarterly draw up and submit to the Select Committee of the Administrative Council a budget implementation statement on the income and expenditure during the preceding quarter.[240]

If the actual expenditure exceeds the budget estimates, the budget implementation statement shall be accompanied by an extraordinary report. This report shall provide detailed explanations as to why the estimated costs have been exceeded and propose, where necessary, possible corrective measures. An extraordinary meeting of the Select Committee of the Administrative Council shall be convened by its Chairman in order to discuss the extraordinary report.[241]

Regarding the establishment of overall fee income and of overall costs, Article 2 BFR provides that the EPO shall, on a quarterly basis, establish the overall income from the fees paid to the EPO under the Rules relating to Fees for Unitary Patent Protection.[242] The EPO shall, on a quarterly basis, provide an estimate of the overall actual costs incurred by the European Patent Organisation for the additional tasks relating to Unitary Patent Protection, including the costs of compensation for translation costs.[243] The income and costs shall be accounted for under the relevant articles of the European Patent Organisation's budget.[244]

Article 3 BFR provides that the EPO shall determine the amounts of renewal fees to be distributed to the Participating Member States, in accordance with the agreed distribution key laid down in Article 2 of the Rules relating to the Distribution of Fees (which is currently still confidential), from the overall income after first deducting its 50% share of the renewal fees and of any additional fees for their belated payment, and secondly deducting the overall costs.

The payment to the individual Participating Member States shall be made before the end of the month following the quarter in question.[245] Where the determination of the amount to be distributed leads to a negative result which would amount to a payment obligation by the Participating Member States in a given quarter, the negative amount shall be withheld from the next quarterly remittance for a period not exceeding twelve consecutive quarters. Article 39(4) EPC and Article 17(1) of the Financial Regulations of the European Patent Organisation shall apply *mutatis mutandis*.[246]

---

239. Article 1(2) BFR.
240. Article 1(3) BFR.
241. Article 1(4) BFR.
242. Article 2(1) BFR.
243. Article 2(2) BFR.
244. Article 2(3) BFR.
245. Article 4(1) BFR.
246. Article 4(2) BFR.

Chapter V – The Unitary Patent

A yearly liquidation of the income and expenditure shall be made upon approval by the Administrative Council of the European Patent Organisation of the annual accounts. Any ensuing final payment to the Participating Member States shall be made before the end of the month following the date of this approval.[247]

If the payment is not effected fully by the due date, the EPO shall pay interest from said due date on the amount remaining unpaid. Article 17(1) of the Financial Regulations of the European Patent Organisation shall apply *mutatis mutandis*.[248]

Article 5 BFR provides for an enabling clause allowing the President of the EPO to adopt administrative instructions with respect to the implementation of Articles 1 to 4 BFR after consultation with the Select Committee. The purpose of such administrative instructions is to regulate any details required for the implementation of Articles 1 to 4 BFR, in particular with respect to technical issues such as refunds, liquidation procedures or bank payments.

W. FOLLOW-UP

Not later than three years from the date on which the first Unitary Patent takes effect, and every five years thereafter, the Commission shall present to the European Parliament and the Council a report on the operation of the Unitary Patent Regulation and, where necessary, make appropriate proposals for amending it.[249]

Besides this report, the European Commission shall regularly submit to the European Parliament and the Council reports on the functioning of the renewal fees, with particular emphasis on compliance with Article 12 of the Unitary Patent Regulation.[250] It is to be seen in practice how the term *"regularly"* shall be interpreted by the European Commission.

X. ENTRY INTO FORCE AND APPLICATION

The entry into force of the Unitary Patent Regulation takes place on the twentieth day following that of its publication in the Official Journal of the European Union.[251]

But the Unitary Patent Regulation shall only apply from the date of entry into force of the UPCA.[252] The territorial scope of the Unitary Patent protection shall in a first phase be limited to the first seventeen Member States that have ratified the UPCA. A European Patent for which unitary effect is registered in the Register for Unitary Patent Protection shall have unitary effect only in those Participating Member States in which the Court has exclusive jurisdiction with regard to Unitary Patents.[253] Consequently, the territory of the Unitary Patent protection shall in the beginning be limited to those seventeen Member States where such patent can be litigated before the Court. In this respect, Recital 25 of the Preamble to the Unitary

---

247. Article 4(3) BFR.
248. Article 4(4) BFR.
249. Article 16(1) Unitary Patent Regulation.
250. Article 16(2) Unitary Patent Regulation.
251. Article 18(1) Unitary Patent Regulation.
252. Article 18(2), §1 Unitary Patent Regulation.
253. Article 18(2), §2 Unitary Patent Regulation.

Patent Regulation states that establishing a Court to hear cases concerning the Unitary Patent is essential in order to ensure the proper functioning of that patent, consistency of case law and hence legal certainty, and cost-effectiveness for patent proprietors. According to the Preamble, it is therefore of paramount importance that the Participating Member States ratify the UPCA and take the necessary steps for that Court to become operational as soon as possible.

Each Participating Member State needs to notify the Commission of its ratification of the UPCA. The Commission needs to publish in the Official Journal of the European Union the date of entry into force of the UPCA and a list of the Member States who have ratified the UPCA at the date of entry into force. The Commission shall thereafter regularly update the list of the Participating Member States which have ratified the UPCA and shall publish such updated list in the Official Journal of the European Union.[254] The Participating Member States that have ratified the UPCA are listed on the website of the Court (www.unified-patent-court.org).

Before the Unitary Patent Regulation applies to a Member State, the Member State has two important tasks to fulfil. The first task is to ensure that the measures referred to in Article 9 Unitary Patent Regulation are in place by the date of application of this Regulation.[255] Therefore, the Member State shall need to grant the EPO its new tasks regarding Unitary Patents. The second task is an individual task for the Member State, namely to ensure that, where the unitary effect of a European Patent has been registered and extends to its territory, that European Patent is deemed not to have taken effect as a national patent in its territory on the date of publication of the mention of the grant in the European Patent Bulletin.[256] In other words, the Member State has to adapt its national law to ensure that the national effect of a European Patent is reversed as soon as the unitary effect has been registered. In the case of a Participating Member State in which the Court does not have exclusive jurisdiction with regard to Unitary Patents on the date of application of this Regulation, the national law should be modified by the date from which the Court has such exclusive jurisdiction in that Participating Member State.

Unitary Patent protection may be requested for any European Patent granted on or after the date of application of the Regulation.[257] However the EPO has provided two transitional measures to support users in an early uptake of the Unitary Patent. These two transitional measures were available from 1 January 2023 until 31 May 2023.

First of all, applicants could file early requests for unitary effect before the start of the system (1 June 2023).[258] Secondly, applicants could request a delay in issuing the decision to grant a European Patent.[259]

---

254. Article 18(3) Unitary Patent Regulation.
255. Article 18(4) Unitary Patent Regulation.
256. Article 18(5) Unitary Patent Regulation.
257. Article 18(6) Unitary Patent Regulation.
258. EPO Notice 11 November 2022 on the possibility to file early requests for unitary effect, *OJ* 2022, A105.
259. Decision of the President of the EPO dated 11 November 2022 on the possibility of requesting a delay in issuing the decision to grant a European patent in response to a communication under Rule 71(3) EPC, *OJ EPO* 2022, A102

Chapter VI
Language Regime of the Unitary Patent

A. REIMBURSEMENT OF TRANSLATION COSTS FOR PATENT APPLICATION

As mentioned above, in order to receive a Unitary Patent, the applicant first has to obtain a European Patent. Therefore, the same granting procedure before the EPO needs to be followed.

Currently, the applicant can file a European Patent application in one of the official languages of the EPO (i.e. French, German or English).[260] But natural or legal persons having their residence or principal place of business within an EPC Member State having a language other than English, French or German as an official language, and nationals of that Member State who are resident abroad, may file their patent application in an official language of that Member State.[261] However, a translation in an official language of the EPO needs to be filed within two months of filing the European Patent application.[262] Such persons filing in a language other than the three languages of the EPO, are entitled to a reduction of the filing fee.[263]

For Unitary Patents, the Translation Regulation goes a step further. If SMEs, natural persons, non-profit organisations, universities or public research organisations having their residence or principal place of business within a Participating Member State, file a European Patent application at the EPO in one of the official languages of the EU that is not an official language of the EPO (namely, all official EU languages other than French, German and English), these applicants shall be entitled to a reimbursement of all translation costs up to a ceiling.[264] For many Participating Member States it was important that patent applicants would still be able to file their European applications (leading to Unitary Patents) in their national language without any additional cost.

The EPO has the task of administering a compensation scheme for the reimbursement of all translation costs, up to a ceiling, for applicants filing patent applications[265] at the EPO in an official language of the Union other than French, English or German.[266]

---

260. Article 14(2) EPC.
261. Article 14(4) EPC.
262. Article 14(2) EPC *juncto* Rule 6.1 of the Implementing Regulations to the EPC.
263. Rule 6.3 of the Implementing Regulations to the EPC.
264. Article 5(1) Translation Regulation.
265. Article 14(2) EPC.
266. Article 5(1) Translation Regulation.

The compensation scheme shall also apply to Euro-PCT applications originally filed at a receiving office in an official language of the European Union other than English, French or German.[267] This means that the compensation scheme applies to Euro-direct patent applications filed at the EPO and also to Euro-PCT applications.

The compensation scheme shall be funded through the renewal fees for Unitary Patents and additional fees for their late payment.[268]

1. Who benefits from the compensation?

Such reimbursement shall only be available for SMEs, natural persons, non-profit organisations, universities and public research organisations having their residence or principal place of business within a Member State.

SMEs are to be understood as SMEs as defined in European Commission Recommendation 2003/361/EC of 6 May 2003.[269] The category of micro enterprises and SMEs is made up of enterprises which employ fewer than 250 persons, which have an annual turnover not exceeding EUR 50 million or an annual balance-sheet total not exceeding EUR 43 million, and for which no more than 25% of the capital is held directly or indirectly by another company which is itself not an SME.[270]

The definition of non-profit organisations is that set out in Article 2, paragraph 1(14) of Regulation (EU) No. 1290/2013 laying down the rules for participation in the framework programme for research and innovation, i.e. a *"non-profit legal entity"* means a legal entity which by its legal form is non-profitmaking or which has a legal or statutory obligation not to distribute profits to its shareholders or individual members.[271]

Universities and public research organisations are not expressly defined in EU texts. Therefore, Explanatory remark 5 with respect to Rule 8 of the Rules relating to Unitary Patent Protection provides that details will be presented in an EPO notice, reflecting these bodies' definitions with a view to the amendment of the scope of application of Rule 6 EPC.[272]

If the patent has multiple proprietors, compensation will be granted only if each proprietor is an entity or a natural person to which the compensation is available.[273] This is provided to prevent abuse, such as making a natural person or SME a co-proprietor of the patent in order to qualify for the scheme.[274]

---

267. Rule 8(5) of the Rules relating to Unitary Patent Protection.
268. Article 5(2) Translation Regulation.
269. Rule 8(2)(a) of the Rules relating to Unitary Patent Protection.
270. Explanatory remark 3 with respect to Rule 8 of the Rules relating to Unitary Patent Protection.
271. Explanatory remark 4 with respect to Rule 8 of the Rules relating to Unitary Patent Protection.
272. Cf. CA/97/13 Rev. 1 and the notice from the EPO dated 10 January 2014, OJ EPO 2014, A23.
273. Rule 8(3) of the Rules relating to Unitary Patent Protection.
274. Explanatory remark 6 with respect to Rule 8 of the Rules relating to Unitary Patent Protection.

2. Transfer

Rule 8(1) relating to Unitary Patent Protection governs compensation requests submitted by the same entity that filed the patent application. In such cases the eligibility criteria must be fulfilled when the European Patent application is filed.

However, if the European Patent application or the European Patent was transferred before a request for unitary effect was filed, compensation will be granted only if both the initial applicant and the proprietor of the patent fulfil the conditions.[275]

3. Procedure for acquiring compensation

The request for compensation is to be submitted together with the request for unitary effect, i.e. no later than one month after publication of the mention of grant of the European Patent in the European Patent Bulletin.[276] Although translation costs will then be reimbursed some time (three to four years) after they were actually incurred, this possibility of subsequent reimbursement shall be seen as an incentive for SMEs to opt for unitary protection.[277]

The request Form 7000 for unitary effect also includes a box where the proprietor can fill in the account to which the compensation can be wired. [278]

Together with the request for compensation the proprietor must submit a solemn declaration that he (and the initial applicant, if a transfer of ownership has occurred) fulfils the eligibility requirements. He must make this declaration on an EPO form. The EPO does not require him to provide supporting documents about his status, and will normally not verify the veracity of the declaration. It may however conduct spot checks before granting compensation.[279]

According to Rule 10(1) of the Rules relating to Unitary Patent Protection, the EPO will quickly examine requests for compensation to make sure that the request for unitary effect has indeed been filed, that all proprietors have made the necessary declaration, and that there are no doubts as to the declaration's veracity. After these simple checks, the EPO will notify the proprietor that it is granting compensation and pay it to him.

Compensation cannot be paid until the European Patent's unitary effect has been entered in the Register for Unitary Patent Protection. This compensation is to be covered by the renewal fees for European patents with unitary effect, which means that it cannot be granted until unitary effect is registered, as opposed to merely requested.[280]

---

275. Rule 8(4) of the Rules relating to Unitary Patent Protection.
276. Recital 10 Translation Regulation.
277. Explanatory remark 1 with respect to Rule 9 of the Rules relating to Unitary Patent Protection.
278. Explanatory remark 2 with respect to Rule 9 of the Rules relating to Unitary Patent Protection.
279. Explanatory remark 3 with respect to Rule 9 of the Rules relating to Unitary Patent Protection.
280. Explanatory remark 1 with respect to Rule 10 of the Rules relating to Unitary Patent Protection.

4. Revision of the decision to grant compensation

Once compensation is granted, the proprietor will keep it, whatever happens to his status, for example if he no longer fulfils the SME criteria or assigns his Unitary Patent to a new proprietor who does not meet the eligibility requirements.[281]

However, if the EPO has serious doubts about the veracity of the declaration filed with the compensation request, for example because of information received from a third party, under Rule 10(3) of the Rules relating to Unitary Patent Protection it could exceptionally review its grant of the compensation, and ask the beneficiary to provide evidence (such as a copy of his balance sheet or a declaration about how many person he employs) that he fulfils the eligibility criteria. Proceedings under Articles 113(1) and 114 EPC would then ensue. If, at the end of these proceedings, the EPO believes that a false declaration has been made, it will inform the beneficiary in accordance with Rule 10(4) of the Rules relating to Unitary Patent Protection that it has revised its decision to grant the compensation, and require him to refund the sum paid, in the form of an additional fee when paying the next renewal fee for his Unitary Patent (possibly within the six-month grace period).

This additional fee will be equal to the translation costs paid, plus an administrative fee to cover processing costs. Article 4(2) RFeesUPP provides that the aforementioned administrative fee shall be 50% of the amount of compensation paid. If this additional fee is not paid in due time, the Unitary Patent will lapse in accordance with Rule 14(1) of the Rules relating to Unitary Patent Protection. Decisions taken by the EPO in administering the compensation scheme procedures described above are appealable before the Court.[282]

5. Amount of compensation

Reimbursement of translation costs shall be made up to a ceiling and paid in the form of a lump sum. The reimbursement ceiling shall be fixed on the basis of the average length of European Patent specifications, the average cost of translating a text from one of the twenty-one EU but non-EPO official languages into English, French or German and the reductions granted on filing and during examination, under Rule 6 EPC and Article 14 Rules relating to Fees (EPC), for the same categories of applicant.[283]

Article 4(1) RFeesUPP provides that the amount of the lump sum shall be EUR 500. This means that the reimbursement shall always be EUR 500. The explanatory note accompanying Rule 11 of the Rules relating to Unitary Patent Protection admits that for real translation costs below this ceiling, the scheme will thus bring Requesters financial advantages which go beyond what is foreseen in Article 5 of the Translation Regulation. The compensation can also be combined with the reduction in filing and examination fees already available.[284]

---

281. Rule 10(2) of the Rules relating to Unitary Patent Protection.
282. Explanatory remark 5 with respect to Rule 10 of the Rules relating to Unitary Patent Protection.
283. Explanatory remarks 2 and 3 with respect to Rule 11 of the Rules relating to Unitary Patent Protection.
284. Rule 6 (3) to 6 (7) EPC.

The lump sum of EUR 500 will be reviewed periodically as further technical progress in machine translation enables applicants to obtain translations more cheaply.[285]

B. GENERAL PRINCIPLE: NO TRANSLATIONS

As a general principle, Article 3 Translation Regulation provides that where the specification of a European Patent, which benefits from unitary effect, has been published in the three official languages of proceedings of the EPO, no further translations shall be required.

Article 14(6) EPC provides that for European Patents the specification shall be published in the language of the proceedings and shall include a translation of the claims in the other two official languages of the EPO. If this is done well, as a general rule, no additional translations are required if the patent proprietor decides to file a request for unitary effect. A request for unitary effect[286] shall be submitted in the language of the proceedings before the EPO.[287]

There are two exceptions to this general rule: the translations in case of a dispute and translations during a transitional period.

C. FIRST EXCEPTION: TRANSLATION IN THE EVENT OF A DISPUTE

In case of an infringement dispute, the Translation Regulation provides two different sorts of protection for the defendant. At any time during the dispute the defendant can request a full translation of the Unitary Patent into an official language of either the Participating Member State in which the alleged infringement took place or the Participating Member State in which the alleged infringer is domiciled.[288] Consequently, the defendant can request a full translation when he receives a cease-and-desist letter.

Secondly, when legal proceedings have commenced, the competent court for disputes concerning Unitary Patents (which shall be the Court) can demand a full translation of the patent into the language used in the proceedings of that court.[289]

The cost of translations in case of a dispute shall be borne by the patent proprietor.[290] To avoid the patent proprietor using the automatic translation software of the EPO, Recital 8 of the Preamble to the Translation Regulation stipulates that such translations may not be carried out by automated means.

One of the very important elements in finding a compromise for the language regime was that certain Member States which do not have an official language of the EPO in their country, sought to protect alleged infringers who were not aware of the patent claims. Therefore, Article 4(4) of the Translation Regulation provides that in the event of a dispute concerning a claim for damages, the court hearing

---

285. Explanatory remark 4 with respect to Rule 11 of the Rules relating to Unitary Patent Protection.
286. Article 9 Unitary Patent Regulation.
287. Article 3(2) Translation Regulation.
288. Article 4(1) Translation Regulation.
289. Article 4(2) Translation Regulation.
290. Article 4(3) Translation Regulation.

the dispute shall assess and take into consideration, in particular where the alleged infringer is an SME, a natural person or a non-profit organisation, a university or a public research organisation, whether the alleged infringer acted without knowing or without reasonable grounds for knowing, that he was infringing the Unitary Patent before having been provided with the translation that can be requested by the alleged infringer in case of dispute.[291]

D. SECOND EXCEPTION: THE TRANSITIONAL PERIOD

The key to the political compromise regarding the language regime was the setting up of a transitional regime. The reason for the transitional regime is that the software for machine translations was not yet available for all official languages of the European Union. For as long as automated translations could not provide alleged infringers with the necessary information regarding patents, the Participating Member States felt that during a transitional period manual translations still had to be available.

The transitional period shall start on the date of application of the Translation Regulation.[292]

Six years after the date of application of the Translation Regulation and every two years thereafter, an independent expert committee shall carry out an objective evaluation of the availability of high quality machine translations of patent applications and specifications into all the official languages of the Union, as developed by the EPO.[293] This expert committee shall be established by the Participating Member States in the framework of the European Patent Organisation and shall be composed of representatives of the EPO and of the non-governmental organisations representing users of the European Patent system invited by the Administrative Council of the European Patent Organisation as observers.[294]

On the basis of the first of the evaluations and every two years thereafter on the basis of the subsequent evaluations, the European Commission shall present a report to the Council and, if appropriate, make proposals for terminating the transitional period.[295]

If the transitional period is not terminated on the basis of a proposal of the Commission, it shall lapse twelve years from the date of application of the Translation Regulation.[296] In practice, chances are small that the transitional period shall be terminated earlier than twelve years from the date of application because the Participating Member States have to take an unanimous decision to terminate the transitional period.

---

291. Article 4(4) Translation Regulation.
292. Article 6(1) Translation Regulation.
293. Article 6(3) Translation Regulation.
294. Article 30(3) EPC.
295. Article 6(4) Translation Regulation.
296. Article 6(5) Translation Regulation.

1. German and French into English

During the transitional period a request for unitary effect shall be submitted together with a full translation of the specification of the European Patent into English, where the language of the proceedings before the EPO is French or German.[297]

Recital 12 of the Preamble to the Translation Regulation explains that this should ensure that during a transitional period all Unitary Patents are made available in English which is the language customarily used in the field of international technological research and publications.

2. English to other official languages

Where the language of the proceedings is English, a full translation of the specification of the European Patent into any other official language of the Union shall have to be submitted together with the request for unitary effect.[298]

This would ensure that with respect to Unitary Patents, translations would be published in other official languages of the Participating Member States.[299]

3. Publication by the EPO

During the transitional period, the EPO shall have the task of publishing the translations as soon as possible after the date of the submission of a request for unitary effect as referred to in Article 9 of the Unitary Patent Regulation.[300]

4. For information purposes only

Just as is the case for automated machine translations, the text of the (human) translations during the transitional regime shall have no legal effect and shall be for information purposes only.[301] Only the specification of the patent in the language of the proceeding shall have legal effect.

In this respect, the effect of translation is different from the effect of translations necessary for national validations of European Patents, for which under the EPC the Member States may provide a limited legal effect and for which the patent holder bears the risk of errors in translations.[302]

E. ENTRY INTO FORCE

The arrangements for the entry into force and application of the Translation Regulation are of course the same as for the entry into force of the Unitary Patent Regulation. The

---

297. Article 6(1)(a) Translation Regulation.
298. Article 6(1)(b) Translation Regulation.
299. Recital 12 of the Preamble to the Translation Regulation.
300. Article 6(2) Translation Regulation.
301. Article 6(2) Translation Regulation.
302. Article 73(3) European Patent Convention

Regulation shall enter into force on the twentieth day following that of its publication in the Official Journal of the European Union.[303]

The Translation Regulation shall apply from the date of entry into force of the UPCA.[304]

To overcome the current shortcomings of the whole of the European Patent system, the Member States participating in the enhanced cooperation felt that it was not enough to install a new patent system with lower translation costs and a one-stop shop for renewal fees. The Participating Member States decided that to improve the patent system it was necessary to also install a pan-European patent court. Because the Participating Member States see the Court as an integral part of the Unitary Patent package, they linked the application of the Unitary Patent Regulation and the Translation Regulation to the application of the Court.

---

303. Article 7(1) Translation Regulation.
304. Article 7(2) Translation Regulation.

PART TWO:

THE UNIFIED PATENT COURT

Chapter I
Legal Status of the UPCA and the Unified Patent Court

A. TREATY BETWEEN EU MEMBER STATES

On 18 February 2013, twenty-five EU Member States signed the Agreement on a Unified Patent Court. The club of EU Member States that signed the UPCA were not the same as the twenty-five Member States that started the enhanced cooperation. Poland joined the enhanced cooperation that led to the Unitary Patent Regulation and the Translation Regulation, but (for political reasons) eventually did not sign the UPCA. For Italy, the situation was at first the opposite: Italy was not a member of the enhanced cooperation but did sign the UPCA. Meanwhile, Italy has also entered the group of Member States of the enhanced cooperation (cf. *supra*).

This means that the enhanced cooperation for the Unitary Patent at a certain stage numbered twenty-six EU Member States (including Italy and Poland but excluding Croatia and Spain), dropping back to twenty-five in 2020 after UK retracted due to Brexit. The UPCA was signed by twenty-five EU Member States (including Italy, but excluding Croatia, Spain and Poland). The UPCA is nothing more or less than a treaty between Austria, Belgium, Bulgaria, Cyprus, the Czech Republic, Denmark, Estonia, Finland, France, Germany, Greece, Hungary, Ireland, Italy, Latvia, Lithuania, Luxembourg, Malta, the Netherlands, Portugal, Romania, Slovakia, Slovenia, Sweden and the United Kingdom (the *"Contracting Member States"*). Since Brexit, the UK withdrew its ratification instrument on 20 July 2020 (see *infra*). Unlike the two Regulations regarding the Unitary Patent, the UPCA is not an instrument of Union law. It is not a European Union treaty, but merely an international agreement between countries which are also Member States of the European Union.

B. CJEU OPINION ON THE CONFORMITY WITH EU TREATIES

The legal status of the UPCA and the Court were a major issue during the negotiations over the UPCA. The Member States were looking for a way to fit the new litigation system into the existing legal order of Union law and determine its position with respect to national law and to other international treaties (e.g. the EPC). The biggest difficulty appeared to be the match with Union law. Therefore, on 6 July 2009 the Council requested an opinion of the CJEU on the question of whether *"the envisaged agreement creating a Unified Patent Litigation System*[305] *is compatible with the*

---

305. At the time of the request named *"European and Community Patents Court"*.

provisions of the Treaty establishing the European Community".

The CJEU took two years to form its opinion. However, this did not paralyse the negotiations on the draft UPCA which continued. The time was used by the Council to find a political comprise on the language regime for the Unitary Patent (*supra*, Part One, Chapter I E-F).

The opinion of the CJEU was delivered on 8 March 2011 (the *"Opinion"*),[306] but was negative. According to the full Court of Justice, the envisaged agreement creating a unified patent litigation system was not compatible with the provisions of the TEU and TFEU.

The CJEU had major concerns about the respect for some basic principles of Union law, such as the primacy of Union law and the liability of the Member States in case of infringement of Union law. Luckily, the CJEU itself gave some guidance in its Opinion on how the basic principles of Union law could be respected by an international court system by giving the example of the Benelux Court of Justice.[307] Based on the CJEU Opinion, the Council amended the UPCA.

1. Primacy of Union law

In its Opinion, the CJEU stressed that the founding treaties of the European Union had established a new legal order, for the benefit of which the Member States have limited their sovereign rights. The essential characteristics of the European Union legal order are in particular its primacy over the laws of the Member States and the direct effect of a whole series of provisions which are applicable to the Member States themselves and to their nationals.[308]

The Member States are obliged, inter alia, by the principle of sincere cooperation,[309] to ensure, in their respective territories, the application of and respect for European Union law.[310] The national court, in collaboration with the Court of Justice, fulfils a duty of ensuring that, in the interpretation and application of the Treaties, Union law is observed.[311]

The draft agreement as it was presented to the CJEU described a court system which was outside the institutional and judicial framework of the European Union, and to which even non-EU Member States could adhere. The patent court as it was first developed was an organisation with a distinct legal personality under international law. The problem for the CJEU was that through this system the courts of the EU Member States would be divested of certain powers with respect to patent law and the envisaged patent court would have the duty to interpret and apply EU law.[312]

According to the CJEU, the envisaged court would interpret and apply the future regulation on the Community patent (now the Unitary Patent) and other instruments of European Union law, in particular regulations and directives in conjunction with

---

306. Opinion 1/09 of the (full) Court of Justice, 8 March 2011, www.curia.europa.eu.
307. Opinion 1/09 of the (full) Court of Justice, 8 March 2011, www.curia.europa.eu, point 82.
308. Opinion 1/09 of the (full) Court of Justice, 8 March 2011, www.curia.europa.eu, point 65.
309. Article 4(3) TEU.
310. Opinion 1/09 of the (full) Court of Justice, 8 March 2011, www.curia.europa.eu, point 68.
311. Opinion 1/09 of the (full) Court of Justice, 8 March 2011, www.curia.europa.eu, point 69.
312. Opinion 1/09 of the (full) Court of Justice, 8 March 2011, www.curia.europa.eu, point 73.

which that regulation would, when necessary, have to be read, namely provisions relating to other bodies of rules on intellectual property, and rules of the TFEU concerning the internal market and competition law.

The CJEU earlier ruled that international agreements creating a court responsible for the interpretation of the provisions of its own agreement are not in principle incompatible with European Union law. An international agreement may even affect the own powers of the CJEU provided that the indispensable conditions for safeguarding the essential character of those powers are satisfied and, consequently, there is no adverse effect on the autonomy of the European Union legal order.[313]

As an example of an international agreement which respects the aforementioned principles, the CJEU referred to the Benelux Court of Justice. Since the Benelux Court is a court common to a number of Member States, situated, consequently, within the judicial system of the European Union, the CJEU was of the opinion that the decisions of the Benelux Court are subject to mechanisms capable of ensuring the full effectiveness of the rules of the European Union.[314]

Therefore, following the CJEU Opinion, the Commission re-designed the legal status of the Unified Patent Court in the image of the Benelux Court of Justice. The UPCA was set up by EU Member States only. Additionally, the current UPCA clarifies that the Unified Patent Court is a court *"common to the Contracting Member States"*.

In this respect, §7 of the Preamble to the UPCA states that *"the Unified Patent Court should be a court common to the Contracting Member States and thus part of their judicial system, with exclusive competence in respect of European Patents with unitary effect and European Patents granted under the provisions of the EPC"*. Under §9, the Preamble recalls that *"the obligations of the Contracting Member States under the Treaty on European Union (TEU) and the Treaty on the Functioning of the European Union (TFEU), including the obligation of sincere cooperation as set out in Article 4(3) TEU and the obligation to ensure through the Unified Patent Court the full application of, and respect for, Union law in their respective territories and the judicial protection of an individual's rights under that law"*.

In the UPCA itself, Article 1 clearly stipulates that the Unified Patent Court shall be a court common to the Contracting Member States and thus subject to the same obligations under Union law as any national court of the Contracting Member States. Article 20 confirms that the Court shall apply Union law in its entirety and shall respect its primacy.

§ 13 of the Preamble recalls that Union law includes the TEU, the TFEU, the Charter of Fundamental Rights of the European Union, the general principles of Union law as developed by the Court of Justice of the European Union (and in particular the right to an effective remedy before a tribunal and a fair and public hearing within a reasonable time by an independent and impartial tribunal), the case law of the Court of Justice of the European Union and secondary Union law. The Court shall always have to respect all these instruments of Union law in its decisions.

---

313. Opinion 1/09 of the (full) Court of Justice, 8 March 2011, www.curia.europa.eu, points 74–76.
314. Opinion 1/09 of the (full) Court of Justice, 8 March 2011, www.curia.europa.eu, point 82.

2. Preliminary rulings of the CJEU

The principle of primacy of Union law and the correct application of Union law have to be safeguarded by the courts of the Member States and the CJEU.

In its Opinion, the CJEU recalled that Article 267 TFEU (regarding preliminary rulings by the CJEU) aims to ensure that, in all circumstances, Union law has the same effect in all Member States. The preliminary ruling mechanism aims to avoid divergences in the interpretation of European Union law which the national courts have to apply and tends to ensure this application by making available to national judges a means of eliminating difficulties which may be occasioned by the requirement of giving European Union law its full effect within the framework of the judicial systems of the Member States.[315] The system set up by Article 267 TFEU therefore establishes direct cooperation between the Court of Justice and the national courts as part of which the latter are closely involved in the correct application and uniform interpretation of European Union law and also in the protection of individual rights conferred by that legal order.[316]

The CJEU concluded in its Opinion that the envisaged agreement:

> *"by conferring on an international court which is outside the institutional and judicial framework of the European Union an exclusive jurisdiction to hear a significant number of actions brought by individuals in the field of the Community patent and to interpret and apply European Union law in that field, would deprive courts of Member States of their powers in relation to the interpretation and application of European Union law and the Court of its powers to reply, by preliminary ruling, to questions referred by those courts and, consequently, would alter the essential character of the powers which the Treaties confer on the institutions of the European Union and on the Member States and which are indispensable to the preservation of the very nature of European Union law."*[317]

According to the CJEU, the power of the Court to apply and interpret the Unitary Patent Regulation and other EU legal instruments, results in depriving the national courts of doing so and of the CJEU ensuring the correct interpretation through preliminary rulings.

In response to the Opinion of the CJEU, the Preamble to the UPCA now considers under § 8 that the Court of Justice of the European Union must ensure the uniformity of the Union legal order and the primacy of European Union law. The Preamble further stresses under § 10 the parallel between the duty of the national courts and the duty of the Court. Like any national court, the Court must respect and apply Union law and, in collaboration with the Court of Justice of the European Union as guardian of Union law, ensure its correct application and uniform interpretation. The Court must in particular cooperate with the Court of Justice of the European Union in properly interpreting Union law by relying on the latter's case law and by requesting preliminary rulings in accordance with Article 267 TFEU.[318]

---

315. Opinion 1/09 of the (full) Court of Justice, 8 March 2011, www.curia.europa.eu, point 83.
316. Opinion 1/09 of the (full) Court of Justice, 8 March 2011, www.curia.europa.eu, point 83.
317. Opinion 1/09 of the (full) Court of Justice, 8 March 2011, www.curia.europa.eu, point 89.
318. §10 of the Preamble to the UPCA.

In the UPCA itself requests for preliminary rulings are laid down in Article 21. This Article provides that as a court common to the Contracting Member States and as part of their judicial system, the Court shall cooperate with the Court of Justice of the European Union to ensure the correct application and uniform interpretation of Union law, like any national court, in accordance with Article 267 TFEU in particular.

3. Liability for infringements of Union law

Another important remark made in the CJEU Opinion was that the submitted draft agreement could not ensure the liability of the Contracting (Member) States for the non-respect of Union law. This would not be the case if non-EU Member States could participate in the Court.

According to the CJEU, the principle that a Member State is obliged to make good damage caused to individuals as a result of breaches of European Union law for which it is responsible, also applies under specific conditions to judicial bodies of a Member State that infringes European Union law.[319] If Union law is infringed, the provisions of Articles 258 TFEU to 260 TFEU provide for the opportunity of bringing a case before the Court to obtain a declaration that the Member State concerned has failed to fulfil its obligations.

Under the draft agreement which was subject to the CJEU Opinion, a decision of the envisaged patent court which would be in breach of Union law could not be attacked by infringement proceedings nor could it give rise to any financial liability on the part of one or more Member States.[320]

To align itself to the CJEU Opinion, the UPCA now contains a liability system for the Contracting Member States in case of infringement of Union law.

§ 11 of the Preamble stipulates that in general the Contracting Member States should, in line with the case law of the Court of Justice of the European Union on non-contractual liability, be liable for damages caused by infringements of Union law by the Court, including the failure to request preliminary rulings from the Court of Justice of the European Union. Further, § 12 adds that infringements of Union law by the Court, including the failure to request preliminary rulings from the Court of Justice of the European Union, are directly attributable to the Contracting Member States and infringement proceedings can therefore be brought under Articles 258, 259 and 260 TFEU against any Contracting Member State to ensure the respect of the primacy and proper application of Union law.

The liability in case of a judgment of a national court is easily attributable to a Member State, but the question was what would happen if a court, which is common to all Member States, infringes the Union law. Article 22(1) UPCA provides that the Contracting Member States are jointly and severally liable for damage resulting from an infringement of Union law by the Court of Appeal, in accordance with Union law concerning non-contractual liability of Member States for damage caused by their national courts breaching Union law.

To avoid that in case of damages, the claimant should start proceedings in all Contracting Member States, Article 22(2) works out a procedure for obtaining

---

319. Opinion 1/09 of the (full) Court of Justice, 8 March 2011, www.curia.europa.eu, point 86.
320. Opinion 1/09 of the (full) Court of Justice, 8 March 2011, www.curia.europa.eu, point 88.

damages for infringement of Union law. An action for such damages shall be brought against the Contracting Member State where the claimant has its residence or principal place of business or, in the absence of residence or principal place of business, any place of business, before the competent authority of that Contracting Member State. Where the claimant does not have its residence, or principal place of business or, in the absence of residence or principal place of business, any place of business in a Contracting Member State, the claimant may bring such an action against the Contracting Member State where the Court of Appeal has its seat, before the competent authority of that Contracting Member State. This Article first determines against which Contracting Member State the action should be brought. Once the (defending) Contracting Member State has been determined, the claimant brings its action before the competent court of that Member State. This means that the national courts of the Contracting Member State against which the action is directed are competent to decide on the liability.

The competent authority shall apply the *lex fori*, with the exception of its private international law, to all questions not regulated by Union law or by the UPCA. The claimant shall be entitled to obtain the entire amount of damages awarded by the competent authority from the Contracting Member State against which the action was brought.[321]

With the aforementioned procedure, the claimant shall obtain the full amount of damages from one Contracting Member State. Given the joint and several liability of all Contracting Member States for infringement of Union law, the Contracting Member State that has paid damages is entitled to obtain proportional contribution from the other Contracting Member States.[322] The proportion of the Contracting Member States' contributions shall be calculated in the same way as the initial financial contributions the Contracting Member States need to pay for financing the Court. This means that during the transitional period of seven years, the number of European Patents having effect in the territory of that State on the date of entry into force of this UPCA and the number of European Patents with respect to which actions of infringement or for revocation have been brought before the national courts of that State in the three years preceding entry into force or ratification of the UPCA, shall be taken into account to determine the contribution key.[323] Afterwards, the contribution key shall be determined in accordance with the scale for the distribution of annual renewal fees for Unitary Patents applicable at the time of contribution.[324]

The detailed rules governing the Contracting Member States' contributions to the damages shall be determined by the Administrative Committee.[325]

Finally, Article 23 UPCA affirms that actions of the Court are directly attributable to each Contracting Member State individually, including for the purposes of Articles 258, 259 and 260 TFEU, and to all Contracting Member States collectively. These Articles deal with the infringement procedure the Commission or a Member State can initiate if one or more of the EU Member States fails to fulfil an obligation

---

321. Article 22(2) UPCA.
322. Article 22(3) UPCA.
323. Article 37(3) UPCA.
324. Article 37(4) UPCA.
325. Article 22(3) UPCA.

Chapter I – Legal Status of the UPCA and the Unified Patent Court

under the EU Treaties. Consequently, a decision or other action of the Court which would infringe an obligation under the EU Treaties shall be an infringement by all Participating Member States, for which all Participating Member States can be brought by the Commission or any other EU Member State before the CJEU.

C. OPPOSITION TO THE UNIFIED PATENT COURT

In March 2015 – a few months before the decision of the CJEU regarding the actions of Spain against the Unitary Patent Regulation and the Translation Regulation – a number of European academics published an English-French motion against the Unitary Patent package.[326] The signatories argued that the Unitary Patent package would be a dangerous precedent by which the Member States strip the Union of one of its powers, i.e. the power to establish measures for the creation of European intellectual property rights to provide uniform protection of intellectual property rights throughout the Union, as laid down in Article 118 TFEU. Irrespective of the argument used by the signatories – an argument which was finally dismissed by the CJEU in cases C-146/13 and C-147/13 – the signatories did not disguise the fact that they preferred a court system similar to that of the Community trade mark and design courts.[327] They believed that *"one could design an EU protection of inventions inspired by the regulations adopted for the Community trade marks and designs"* and thought *"it would be far less complex to institute a solution of that sort than the system discussed here"*. Wouter Pors reacted to the motion on the EPLAW patent blog by stating that certainly one could imagine other systems for harmonising patent litigation in Europe, but in this case the political history and difficulties in finding a compromise solution should be taken into account. Pors refers to the Court as the *"next best thing"*.[328]

We share the view of Pors that the objectives of harmonisation and the political difficulties peculiar to the European Union to achieve such objectives should be kept in mind when analysing the system. However, we are not convinced that a European litigation system based on the example of the Community trade mark/design courts would be more preferable than the Court. For sure, a system mirroring the Community trade mark or design courts would have had substantial advantages during the implementation track. Contracting Member States would not have to bother about drafting a new set of rules of procedure. Contracting Member States would not have to bother about recruiting and appointing judges for international panels. Contracting Member States would not even have to bother about negotiating the locations of central, regional or local divisions and the languages in which they will operate. All these things would have been available within the Member States and would have been paid for by the Member States. But the main question is whether

---

326. http://ipkitten.blogspot.nl/2015/03/the-eu-patent-package-dangerous.html.
327. Article 95 of the Council Regulation No. 207/2009 of 26 February 2009 on the Community trade mark; Article 80 of the Council Regulation No. 6/2002 of 12 December 2001 on Community designs.
328. W. Pors, "Comments on law professors petition against the Unitary Patent Package", http://www.eplawpatentblog.com/eplaw/2015/03/eu-comments-on-law-professors-petition-against-the-unitary-patent-package.html.

such *"Community patent courts"* would offer users a solution to the problems they have with the current enforcement system in Europe? We believe they would not.

The purpose of the Court was not only to have a court with EU-wide jurisdiction regarding validity and/or infringement of patents, but also to avoid as much as possible inconsistent case law and/or case law driven by national flavour in the proceedings. Such national flavour can originate from national procedural rules, from national judges or from other national traditions (e.g. lawyer usages). A court based on the trade mark or design courts would not achieve such harmonisation goals, but would remain stuck in national law traditions. The Court operates with a uniform set of Rules of Procedure in all Participating Member States. Each panel of the Court will be composed of judges of different nationalities. For most divisions of the Court, English will be one of the possible languages of the proceedings. Based on these elements, we believe that the Court will offer more guarantees to users to obtain high quality judgments and legal certainty, than *"Community patent courts"* would offer.[329]

D. LEGAL CAPACITY OF THE COURT

The Court shall have legal personality in each Contracting Member State and shall enjoy the most extensive legal capacity accorded to legal persons under the national law of that State.[330]

The President of the Court of Appeal shall be able to represent the Court before third parties.[331]

The contractual liability of the Court shall be governed by the law applicable to the contract in question in accordance with the Rome I Regulation,[332] where applicable, or in accordance with the law of the Member State of the court seized.[333]

The non-contractual liability of the Court in respect of any damage caused by it or its staff in the performance of their duties, to the extent that it is not a civil and commercial matter within the meaning of the Rome II Regulation,[334] shall be governed by the law of the Contracting Member State in which the damage occurred. The court with jurisdiction to settle disputes concerning non-contractual liability shall be a court of the Contracting Member State in which the damage occurred.[335]

---

329. P. Callens, "Does the EU patent package strip the Union of one of its legislative powers? An analysis of a recent motion against the EU patent package", http://kluwerpatentblog.com/2015/03/31/does-the-eu-patent-package-strip-the-union-of-one-of-its-legislative-powers-an-analysis-of-a-recent-motion-against-the-eu-patent-package/.
330. Article 4(1) UPCA.
331. Article 4(2) UPCA.
332. Regulation No. 593/2008 of 17 June 2008 on the law applicable to contractual obligations (Rome I), L177/6, 4 July 2008.
333. Article 5(1) UPCA.
334. Regulation No. 864/2007 of 11 July 2007 on the law applicable to non-contractual obligations (Rome II), L199/40, 31 July 2007.
335. Article 5(3) UPCA.

Chapter II
Structure of the Court

The Court has an atypical structure. Therefore, when analysing the functioning of the Court, it is important to first clearly understand the different institutions of the Court.

The Court shall comprise of two levels: the Court of First Instance and the Court of Appeal.

A. COURT OF FIRST INSTANCE

The Court of First Instance shall comprise three sorts of divisions: one central division and various local and regional divisions.[336]

Although the terminology ("*central*") could lead to a different conclusion, it is very important to understand that the central division and the local and regional divisions all act at the same level of jurisdiction. There is no hierarchy between the divisions. All divisions shall treat patent disputes as a first instance court. Nevertheless, each division has its own competence and in some cases there is exclusive jurisdiction for the central division.

The office of the President of the Court of First Instance shall be located in Paris. According to Article 14 of the Statute, the President of the Court of First Instance shall be elected by all full-time judges of the Court of First Instance from among their number, for a term of three years. The President may be re-elected twice. The election of the President shall be by secret ballot. A judge obtaining an absolute majority shall be elected. If no judge obtains an absolute majority, a second ballot shall be held and the judge obtaining the most votes shall be elected. If the office of the President falls vacant before the date of expiry of his term, a successor shall be elected for the remainder thereof.

However, in order to facilitate the practical setting up of the Court of First Instance (and also as result of a political compromise) it was decided that the first President of the Court of First Instance shall be a national of the Contracting Member State hosting the seat of the central division, which is France.[337] Florence Butin has been appointed as the President of the Court of First Instance. After the initial three-year period, the first French President of the Court of First Instance can be re-elected by all full-time judges of the Court of First Instance.

The President of the Court of First Instance shall direct the judicial activities and the administration of the Court of First Instance.[338] The President of the Court of First Instance shall amongst other things allocate technically qualified judges to the

---

336. Article 7 UPCA.
337. Article 14(2) Statute.
338. Article 14(3) Statute.

panel in case of a counterclaim for revocation,[339] reject actions against decisions of the EPO when formalities are not respected or fees are not paid,[340] order to change the language of proceedings to the language in which the patent was granted,[341] allocate the judges for the panels of the local and regional divisions[342] and designate the judges assigned to each division, the seat of the central division and each of its sections as standing judges for urgent actions.[343]

1. Central division

There will be one central division, but this central division is described in the UPCA as having three sections. Therefore, the name *"central"* division could be misleading. Central does not mean it will only have one location. This central division is the go-to division for independent revocation actions and actions for declaration of non-infringement, and also for defendants located outside the Member States or in a Member State without a local or regional division. As a result of a political comprise between Germany, France and the United Kingdom, the European Council of 29 June 2012 decided that the central division shall comprise three sections on three different locations. Article 7(2) UPCA explicitly provides that the Central Division of the Court of First Instance of the Court shall have *"its seat in Paris with sections in London and Munich"*. Moreover, Annex II UPCA explicitly provided that cases concerning patent sections (A) and (C) of the International Patent Classification (IPC) would be handled by the London section.

After Brexit, the question arose what would happen with the London section, as London was no longer an option. The legal problem was that London was clearly mentioned in the UPCA as a section of the central division. To appoint a new city for this section, the Participating Member States would normally amend the UPCA. Since it was considered too risky to re-open discussions about the content of the UPCA, the Participating Member States considered it not to be an option to do this before the actual start of the Court. Therefore, In its meeting of 8 May 2023, the Presidium of the Unified Patent Court decided that, as from 1 June 2023 and until a final decision was taken on the creation of another section of the Central Division, actions pending before the Central Division related to patents in IPC section (A) shall be assigned to the seat in Paris while actions related to patents in IPC section (C) shall be assigned to the section in Munich.

However, this solution was of course not ideal. Additionally, it was no secret that Italy was the strongest candidate to acquire the seat of the third section of the central division.

Finally, after the start of the Court, the Administrative Committee decided on 26 June 2023 to amend the UPCA. Article 87(2) UPCA provides that the Administrative Committee may amend the UPCA to bring it into line with an international treaty relating to patents or Union law. According to the decision of the Administrative

---

339. Rules 33–34 Rules of Procedure.
340. Rule 89.4 Rules of Procedure.
341. Rule 323 Rules of Procedure.
342. Rule 345.1 Rules of Procedure.
343. Rule 345.5 Rules of Procedure.

Committee, the withdrawal of the United Kingdom from the European Union and as a consequence from the UPCA constitutes a change in Union law which allows the recourse to such simplified revision procedure.

Article 87(3) UPCA provides that a decision of the Administrative Committee taken under Article 87(2) shall not take effect if, within twelve months from the date of the decision, a Contracting Member State declares on the basis of its relevant national decision-making procedures that it does not wish to be bound by the decision. In order to provide legal certainty, any change by way of the simplified procedure should therefore, only take effect twelve months after the decision.

Based on these provisions, the Administrative Committee decided to amend paragraph 2 of Article 7 as follows:

"The central division shall have its seat in Paris, with sections in London and Milan and Munich. The cases before the central division shall be distributed in accordance with Annex II, which shall form an integral part of this Agreement."

Annex II to the UPCA stipulates the types of cases each geographical section of the central division would handle. The parts in bold represent the amendments compared to the original version of Annex II:

Milan section	*Paris seat*	*Munich section*
(A) Human necessities, without Supplementary protection certificates	President's Office	(C) Chemistry, metallurgy, without Supplementary protection certificates
	(B) Performing operations, transporting	(F) Mechanical engineering, lighting, heating, weapons, blasting
	(D) Textiles and paper	
	(E) Fixed constructions	
	(G) Physics	
	(H) Electricity	
	Supplementary protection certificates	

Florence Butin was designated as presiding judge of the Paris seat and Ulrike Voß as presiding judge of the Munich section.

2. Local division

Each Contracting Member State can request the setting up of a local division of the Court of First Instance.[344] Such request shall be addressed to the Chairman of the Administrative Committee and indicate the seat of the local division. The decision for setting up a local division has to be taken by the Administrative Committee. The decision shall indicate the number of judges for the division and shall be made

---

344. Article 7(3) UPCA.

public.[345] The Administrative Committee shall be composed of one representative per Contracting Member State, each having one vote (*infra*, Part Two, Chapter II E.1). Decisions are taken with a majority of three-quarters of the Contracting Member States represented and voting.[346]

The UPCA does not include any thresholds for setting up a local division, which may indicate that each Member State (including Member States with only a few patent cases per year) is encouraged to set up a local division.

Upon request of the Contracting Member State, an additional local division can be set up in that Contracting Member State for every one hundred patent cases per calendar year that have been commenced in that Contracting Member State during three successive years prior to or subsequent to the date of entry into force of the UPCA.[347] The number of local divisions in one Contracting Member State may not exceed four. The maximum number of local divisions per Contracting Member State was originally three, but the Competitiveness Council of 6 December 2011 decided to extend this to four,[348] which primarily favours Germany. Currently, only Germany can be expected to reach more than 300 patent cases per year.

The following local divisions started on 1 June 2023 in the respective Contracting Member States:

Member State	*Location(s)*	*Language(s)*	*Presiding judge(s)*
Austria	Vienna	German and English	Walter Schober
Belgium	Brussels	Dutch, French, German and English*	Samuel Granata
Denmark	Copenhagen	Danish and English	Peter Agergaard
France	Paris	French and English*	Camille Lignieres
Finland	Helsinki	Finnish, Swedish and English	Petri Rinkinen
Germany	Hamburg, Munich, Mannheim, Düsseldorf	German and English*	Ronny Thomas (Düsseldorf) Sabine Klepsch (Hamburg) Peter Michael Tochtermann (Mannheim) Matthias Zigann (Munich)
Italy	Milan	Italian and English*	Pierluigi Perrotti
Netherlands	The Hague	Dutch and English	Edger Brinkman
Slovenia	Ljubljana	Slovenian and English	Mojca Mlakar

* with indication as to Rule 14.2(c) UPC Rules of Procedure regarding the use of the official language(s) as to Rule 14.1(a) UPC Rules of Procedure and/or the delivery of any order and any decision in the official language(s) as to Rule 14.1(a) UPC Rules of Procedure.

---

345. Article 18(1) and 18(2) Statute.
346. Article 12 UPCA.
347. Article 7(4) UPCA.
348. Council of the European Union, working document 18239/11, 6 December 2011.

3. Regional division

A regional division shall be set up for two or more Contracting Member States. The same procedure as for setting up a local division needs to be followed (request to the Chairman of the Administrative Committee and decision of the Administrative Committee).[349] The requesting Contracting Member States shall designate the seat of the division concerned. The regional division may hear cases in multiple locations.

The purpose of regional divisions is to offer Contracting Member States the opportunity to cooperate in patent litigation. Nothing in the UPCA and the Statute prohibits cooperation between non-neighbouring Contracting Member States. Therefore, a regional division between, for example, the Netherlands and Sweden would be theoretically possible. It is less clear if a regional division should cover the whole territory of a Contracting Member State and if a Contracting Member State can take part in several regional divisions.

Since a regional division can hear cases in different locations, it is perfectly possible for the Nordic and Baltic countries to form a regional division which has four or more locations in each of the Contracting Member States. Nothing in the UPCA prohibits a regional division with four Contracting Member States working with *"sub-divisions"* on different locations.

It is unclear if Contracting Member States can participate in a regional division, while having a local division at the same time. Nothing in the UPCA or Statute explicitly prohibits such combination.

The Court has started with only one regional division, i.e. the regional division formed by Estonia, Latvia, Lithuania and Sweden. On 4 March 2014 Estonia, Latvia, Lithuania and Sweden concluded an agreement on the creation of a regional Nordic Baltic division of the Court.

The Nordic Baltic division will have its seat in Stockholm but with additional places for hearings in Riga, Tallinn and Vilnius allowing for a flexible set-up when it comes to oral hearings. When it is justified, considering the nationalities of the parties, oral hearings can be held the other places of hearing. The language of this regional division is English. The presiding judge is Stefan Johansson.

At some point there were also rumours regarding a *"southeast"* regional division composed of Romania, Bulgaria, Greece and Cyprus, and a Czechoslovakian regional division composed of Czechia and Slovakia. But these plans were never realised.

4. Discontinuance of a local or regional division

The Administrative Committee shall decide to discontinue a local or regional division at the request of the Contracting Member State hosting the local division or the Contracting Member States participating in the regional division. The decision to discontinue a local or regional division shall mention the date after which no new cases may be brought before the division and the date on which the division will cease to exist.[350]

---

349. Article 7(5) UPCA.
350. Article 18(3) Statute.

As from the date on which a local or regional division ceases to exist, the judges assigned to that local or regional division shall be assigned to the central division, and cases still pending before that local or regional division together with the sub-registry and all of its documentation shall be transferred to the central division.[351]

B. COURT OF APPEAL

The Court of Appeal shall have its seat in one location, i.e. Luxembourg.[352]

The President of the Court of Appeal shall be elected by all judges of the Court of Appeal for a term of three years, from among their number. The President of the Court of Appeal may be re-elected twice and the elections take place in the same way as for the President of the Court of First Instance.[353]

Unlike for the President of the Court of First Instance, the first President of the Court of Appeal shall not necessarily originate from the hosting Contracting Member State (Luxembourg). Klaus Grabinski (Germany) has been appointed on 1 November 2022 as President of the Court of Appeal.

The President of the Court of Appeal shall direct the judicial activities and the administration of the Court of Appeal and chair the Court of Appeal sitting as a full court.[354] The President of the Court of Appeal shall assign, amongst other things:

- a request for a discretionary review to a panel of the Court of Appeal for a decision;[355]
- reject an appeal as inadmissible by a decision by default in case deficiencies are not corrected or fees are not paid;[356]
- appoint together with the Presidium the judges to the full Court of Appeal;[357]
- provide the competent authority of a Contracting Member State with copies of all pleadings, evidence, decisions and orders that are relevant to an action for damages against a Contracting Member State;[358]
- fix the duration of judicial vacations;[359]
- allocate the judges for the panels;[360] and
- designate the judges assigned as standing judges for urgent actions.[361]

When assessing the Unified Patent Court system, the importance of the Court of Appeal cannot be overlooked. One of the criticisms of the Court which is sometimes heard is that because it is a system in which the patentee can to a large extent choose the local or regional division before which he starts proceedings, the Court would

---

351. Article 18(4) Statute.
352. Article 9 UPCA.
353. Article 13(1) Statute.
354. Article 13(3) Statute.
355. Rule 220.4 Rules of Procedure.
356. Rule 229.4 Rules of Procedure.
357. Rule 238A.2 Rules of Procedure.
358. Rule 267 Rules of Procedure.
359. Rule 342.1 Rules of Procedure.
360. Rule 345.1 Rules of Procedure.
361. Rule 345.5 Rules of Procedure.

give rise to forum-shopping. Because in larger patent countries like Germany or the Netherlands, two national judges shall sit in the panel, it cannot be avoided that despite the efforts of the Contracting Member States there will remain important differences in the case law of the local and regional divisions. If this would be the case, it is up to the Court of Appeal to streamline the case law of the Court. Unlike the Court of First Instance within the Unified Patent Court system (which operates through different divisions), there will only be one Court of Appeal within the Court. Therefore the Court of Appeal will have an important task of providing uniform case law and uniform tests for assessing patent infringement and patent validity.

C. NO INSTANCE OF LEGAL REVIEW – PRELIMINARY RULINGS OF THE COURT OF JUSTICE

Unlike in several Contracting Member States, the Unified Patent Court system does not provide an instance which assesses the application of the Treaty provisions.[362]

However, since the Court shall be considered as a national court under EU law, the CJEU remains the guardian of the correct application and uniform interpretation of EU law. In practice, this means that the Court shall be obliged to rely on the case law of the CJEU in matters of Union law and request preliminary questions in accordance with Article 267 TFEU for matters of Union law.[363]

In practice, the application of Article 267 TFEU shall mean that if a question regarding the validity and interpretation of Union law is raised before the Court of First Instance (which is to be considered as a court of the Member States), the Court of First Instance may, if it considers that a decision on the question is necessary to enable it to give judgment, request the CJEU to give a ruling thereon. When a question is raised in a case pending before the Court of Appeal, the Court of Appeal is obliged to bring the matter before the CJEU. Decisions of the CJEU shall be binding on the Court.[364]

The procedures established by the CJEU for referrals for preliminary rulings within the European Union shall apply to the Court.[365]

Whenever the Court of First Instance or the Court of Appeal has decided to refer to the CJEU a question of interpretation of the Treaty on the Functioning of the European Union or of the Treaty on European Union or a question on the validity or interpretation of acts of the institutions of the European Union, it shall stay its proceedings.[366]

Although on many occasions during the negotiations for the UPCA, Member States tried to minimise the role of the CJEU in the new patent system, we believe that the CJEU shall play a bigger role in the Unified Patent Court system than some practitioners today expect. The reason for this is that for the enforcement of patent rights, the impact of EU Directive 2004/48/EC of 29 April 2004 on the enforcement

---

362. As for the *Cour de Cassation* in France and Belgium, the *Hoge Raad* in the Netherlands or the *Bundesgerichtshof* in Germany.
363. § 10 of the Preamble to the UPCA.
364. Article 21 UPCA.
365. Article 38(1) Statute.
366. Article 62(2) UPCA.

of intellectual property rights (hereinafter *"the Enforcement Directive"*) is not to be underestimated. The Enforcement Directive contains amongst other things a number of provisions regarding measures for preserving evidence, provisional and precautionary measures, corrective measures, injunctions and damages.

D. THE REGISTRY

Since the Court is a supranational court, it cannot rely on the registries of the national courts of the Contracting Member States for its functioning. Therefore, a Registry shall be set up at the seat of the Court of Appeal. The Register shall be managed by a Registrar and shall be public. Sub-registries shall be set up at all divisions of the Court of First Instance.[367]

The purpose of the Registry is to keep records of all cases before the Court. Upon filing, the sub-registry concerned shall notify the Registry of every case.

The Presidium shall appoint the Registrar for a (renewable) term of six years.[368] Alexander Ramsay has been appointed as the first Registrar of the Court. Before taking up his duties, the Registrar swears an oath before the Presidium to perform the duties of the Registrar impartially and conscientiously.

The Registrar may be removed from office only if the Registrar no longer meets the obligations arising from his office. Only the Presidium can take such decision after having heard the Registrar. If the office of the Registrar falls vacant before the date of expiry of the term thereof, the Presidium shall appoint a new Registrar for a term of six years.[369]

The Registrar assists the Court, the President of the Court of Appeal, the President of the Court of First Instance and the judges in the performance of their functions. The Registrar shall be responsible for the organisation and activities of the Registry under the authority of the President of the Court of Appeal.

The duties of the Registrar are laid down in Article 10 UPCA and Article 23 of the Statute. The Registrar shall not only be responsible for keeping the records of all cases before the Court, but also for keeping and administering the list of the Pool of Judges,[370] the list of European patent attorneys authorised to represent parties before the Court[371] and an indicative list of court experts.[372] The Registrar shall keep and publish a list of notifications and withdrawals of opt-outs from the exclusive jurisdiction of the Court by European Patent proprietors or applicants[373] and ensure that the information on opt-outs is notified to the EPO. The Registrar shall also publish the decisions of the Court (paying attention to the protection of confidential information) and the annual reports of the Court with statistical data. Up to now there is very little statistical information within the Contracting Member

---

367. Article 10 UPCA.
368. Article 22 Statute.
369. Article 22(5) Statute.
370. Article 18 UPCA.
371. Article 48(3) UPCA.
372. Article 57(2) UPCA.
373. Article 83 UPCA.

Chapter II – Structure of the Court

States regarding patent litigation. Therefore, an annual report of the Court shall be useful to monitor European patent litigation.

Rules governing the Registry shall be adopted by the Presidium. Such rules shall include detailed rules for keeping the Register of the Court. The rules on access to documents of the Registry are part of the Rules of Procedure (see Part Three, Chapter VIII A.3).[374]

The Registry shall also have a Deputy-Registrar responsible for the organisation and activities of sub-registries under the authority of the Registrar and the President of the Court of First Instance.[375] On 19 January 2023, the Administrative Committee appointed Axel Jacobi (Germany) as Deputy-Registrar. The Deputy-Registrar shall be appointed for a term of six years by the Presidium and may be re-appointed. The duties of the Deputy-Registrar shall in particular include keeping records of all cases before the Court of First Instance and notifying every case before the Court of First Instance to the Registry.[376] The Deputy-Registrar shall also provide administrative and secretarial assistance to the divisions of the Court of First Instance.

E.   ADMINISTRATIVE BODIES

In order to ensure the effective implementation and operation of the Court, the UPCA, the Statute and the minutes of the signing of the UPCA have set up a number of administrative bodies.

1.   The Preparatory Committee

On signing in 2013, the UPCA was accompanied by minutes of the signing. These minutes contained a declaration of the signing Member States (the *"Signatory States"*) regarding the coming into operation of the Court. In this declaration, the Signatory States announced their intention of setting up without delay a Preparatory Committee composed of their representatives. The Preparatory Committee would prepare the practical arrangements and set out a roadmap for the early establishment and coming into operation of the Court. It could establish subgroups as appropriate and make use of teams of experts.

According to the declaration, the Signatory States were determined to ensure that the Court achieves a high degree of efficiency and deliver expeditious and high quality decisions from the outset. With this in mind they thought it necessary that all practical arrangements for the proper functioning of the Court should already be in place or be duly prepared before the entry into force of the UPCA.

The declaration listed the following important tasks for the Preparatory Committee:

- organise training of future judges without delay;
- prepare Rules of Procedure for the Unified Patent Court;
- prepare the budget of the Court for the first financial year;

---

374. Article 24 Statute.
375. Article 25 Statute.
376. Article 25(3) Statute.

- make proposals for appropriate facilities for the divisions of the Court of First Instance and the Court of Appeal;
- prepare the setting-up of the Administrative Committee and the adoption of its Rules of Procedure;
- prepare the setting-up of the Budget Committee;
- prepare the election of the members of the Advisory Committee;
- prepare the election of judges;
- recruit administrative staff.

The Preparatory Committee was composed of representatives of all the Signatory Member States. It was chaired between 2013 and 2015 by Paul Van Beukering (Netherlands). In 2015 Van Beukering stepped down as chair and was replaced by Alexander Ramsay (Sweden) and current Registrar of the Court.

The work of the Preparatory Committee was divided into five major streams, each having a different working group and a coordinator.[377] The working groups were:

- legal framework;
- financial aspects;
- IT;
- facilities;
- human resources & training.

The major issues to be dealt with by each working group were as follows:

a.   *Legal Framework Group*

The main tasks of this working group were:

- Prepare the draft of the Rules of Procedure of the Unified Patent Court (hereinafter *"Rules of Procedure"*):
  - The first 16 drafts of the Rules of Procedure were prepared by an expert group, called the Drafting Committee, consisting of a number of senior patent judges and lawyers from Germany, the UK, France and the Netherlands. The Drafting Committee was composed of Kevin Mooney (UK, Chairman), Klaus Grabinski (Germany), Willem Hoyng (Netherlands), Winfried Tilmann (Germany), Pierre Véron (France), Alice Pezard (France) and Christopher Floyd (UK).
  - Based on the 15th draft of the Rules of Procedure, the Preparatory Committee held a public consultation in 2013. From 25 June 2013 until 1 October 2013 the draft Rules of Procedure were open to written comments from stakeholders or other interested parties. After the public consultation the Drafting Committee prepared a 16th draft which was provided to the Preparatory Committee on 31 January 2014. The legal working group then drafted subsequent 17th and 18th drafts of the Rules of Procedure. The 18th draft of the Rules of Procedure was adopted by

---

377. www.unified-patent-court.org.

the Preparatory Committee on 19 October 2015.[378] During 2015-2017 the Preparatory Committee made some final adjustments to the 18th draft. The last of these were adopted by the Preparatory Committee in their meeting of 15 March 2017. This draft shall be subject to formal adoption by the Administrative Committee of the Unified Patent Court.
- Prepare the rules governing the Registry and the Registrar service;
- Prepare the rules on legal aid;
- Prepare the schedule for Court fees and recoverable costs;
- Prepare the rules governing the Advisory, Budget and Administrative Committees: the legal group presented two proposals to the Preparatory Committee in March 2014, one on the Rules for the Administrative Committee of the Unified Patent Court and one on the Budget Committee of the Unified Patent Court. Consensus was reached on the contents of both proposals in July 2014;
- Prepare the rules regarding mediation and arbitration;
- Prepare the rules on the litigation certificate for patent attorneys.

On 3 September 2015, the Preparatory Committee agreed on the draft proposal for the Rules on the European Patent Litigation Certificate and other appropriate qualifications.

b. *Financial aspects*

The main issues which were prepared by this working group were the following:

- financial regulations;
- pension, social security and salary schemes: the Preparatory Committee considered that managing social security systems should not be a main task for the Court. These activities shall therefore be outsourced;[379]
- budgets and sustainability: the working group evaluated the operational costs that could be foreseen for the first seven years, taking into account that during this transitional period many costs will be borne by Contracting States hosting seats or divisions of the Court. Based on this evaluation and the provisions developed with regard to Court fees and legal aid, a budget for the first year was developed;
- determine the amount of Court fees;
- determine Member State's proportional contribution to a Member State that has paid damages.

The financial working group developed a schedule for Member States' proportional contributions to a Member State that has paid damages to a party in case of violation of Union law by the Court.

---

378. www.unified-patent-court.org.
379. Roadmap of the Preparatory Committee of the Unified Patent Court, as updated in September 2014, www.unified-patent-court.org.

c. IT

The main task of this working group was to develop an electronic filing and case management system which needs to be fully accessible online for judges and other staff of the Court, and enable a secure exchange of documents and information both internally (between seats, sections, divisions, panels, judges and staff of the Registry and sub-registries) and externally (between the Court and parties to proceedings, who should be able to file submissions and documents in electronic form).[380]

In addition, public online inspection of certain parts of the files needed to be included in the IT system.

d. Facilities

Because the Contracting Member States hosting a local, regional or the central division of the Court of First Instance or the Court of Appeal were to set up their own appropriate facilities in terms of premises, furniture, offices, IT equipment and administrative support staff, this issue was not to be tackled by the Preparatory Committee. However, the HR working group determined the required number and qualifications of local staff on the basis of which hosting countries shall be asked to provide these resources. Furthermore, this working group was to analyse and prepare headquarter agreements.[381]

e. Human resources and training

The main tasks of this working group were the organisation of the training of candidate judges, the preparation of the nomination of the first group of judges and the organisation of the initial Pool of Judges. This working group was assisted by an Advisory Panel, composed of former lawyers with recognised competence in patent litigation or experienced, active or former members of chambers of appeal or supreme courts, such as Sir Robin Jacob.

This working group had to:

- organise the pre-training of candidate judges;
- organise and prepare the nomination of judges (cf. *infra*);
- draw up a list of arbitrators and mediators and a list of court experts;
- plan the future permanent training framework for judges provided in Article 19 UPCA.

2. The Administrative Committee

The administration of the Court is into the hands of the Administrative Committee. Each Contracting Member State has one representative on the Administrative

---

380. Roadmap of the Preparatory Committee of the Unified Patent Court, as updated in September 2014, www.unified-patent-court.org.
381. Roadmap of the Preparatory Committee of the Unified Patent Court, as updated in September 2014, www.unified-patent-court.org.

Committee. The European Commission shall be represented at the meetings of the Administrative Committee as an observer.[382]

Each Contracting Member State shall have one vote on the Administrative Committee. The Administrative Committee shall adopt its decisions by a majority of three-quarters of the Contracting Member States represented and voting.[383] The Administrative Committee shall elect a chairperson from among its members for a term of three years. That term shall be renewable.[384]

The first decisions of the Administrative Committee concerned the adoption of the documents and decisions prepared by the Preparatory Committee, such as the adoption of the Rules of Procedure, the nomination of the judges and the approval of the IT system.

3. The Budget Committee

As for the Administrative Committee, the Budget Committee is composed of one representative of each Contracting Member State, each having one vote. The European Commission is neither a member nor an observer of the Budget Committee. Member States did not wish the European Commission to have any interference in the financial governance of the Court.[385]

The main task of the Budget Committee is of course adopting the budget. The budget shall be adopted by the Budget Committee on a proposal from the Presidium.[386]

The Budget Committee shall adopt its own set of rules of procedure and take its decisions by a simple majority of the representatives of the Contracting Member States. However, a majority of three-quarters of the representatives of Contracting Member States shall be required for the adoption of the budget.[387]

The Budget Committee shall elect a chairperson from among its members for a renewable term of three years.[388]

4. The Advisory Committee

The Advisory Committee can comprise patent judges and practitioners in patent law and patent litigation with the highest recognised competence.[389] They are appointed for a renewable term of six years. Each Contracting Member State proposed a member of the Advisory Committee who meets the aforementioned requirements. The members of the Advisory Committee are appointed by the Administrative Committee acting by common accord.[390]

---

382. Article 12(1) UPCA.
383. Article 12(2) and (3) UPCA.
384. Article 12(3) UPCA.
385. Article 13(1) and (2) UPCA.
386. Article 26 Statute.
387. Article 13(3) and 13(4) UPCA.
388. Article 13(5) UPCA.
389. Article 14(2) UPCA.
390. Article 5 Statute.

The current Advisory Committee is composed of Chairperson Willem Hoyng and Deputy Chairperson Sylvie Mandel and 18 other members and alternate members.

The duty of the Advisory Committee is to assist the Administrative Committee in the preparation of the appointment of judges of the Court, make proposals to the Presidium regarding guidelines for the training framework for judges and deliver opinions to the Administrative Committee concerning the requirements for qualifications of European patent attorneys to represent parties before the Court.[391]

The composition of the Advisory Committee shall ensure a broad range of relevant expertise and the representation of each of the Contracting Member States. The members of the Advisory Committee shall be completely independent in the performance of their duties and shall not be bound by any instructions.[392] The Advisory Committee shall adopt its own rules of procedure and shall elect a chairperson from among its members for a renewable term of three years.[393]

5. The Presidium

The Presidium is a body which is not set up by the UPCA but by the Statute. The Presidium needs to be composed of the President of the Court of Appeal, who shall act as chairperson, the President of the Court of First Instance, two judges of the Court of Appeal elected from among their number, three judges of the Court of First Instance who are full-time judges of the Court elected from among their number, and the Registrar as a non-voting member.[394] The voting members of the Presidium are all judges. Therefore, the Presidium can be considered as the *"managing judges"* of the Court.

The current Presidium consists of Klaus Grabinski (Germany), as President of the Court of Appeal, and Florence Butin (France), as President of the Court of First Instance. The Presidium is completed by two judges from the Court of Appeal: Rian Kalden (Netherland) and Ingeborg Simonsson (Sweden) and three judges from the Court of First Instance: Camille Lignieres (France), Ronny Thomas (Germany) and Peter Tochtermann (Germany).

The Presidium can take valid decisions only when all members are present or duly represented. Decisions shall be taken by a majority of the votes.[395]

The Presidium shall be responsible for the management of the Court and shall in particular draw up proposals for the amendment of the Rules of Procedure and proposals regarding the Financial Regulations of the Court; prepare the annual budget, the annual accounts and the annual report of the Court and submit them to the Budget Committee; establish the guidelines for the training program for judges and supervise the implementation thereof; take decisions on the appointment and removal of the Registrar and the Deputy-Registrar; lay down the rules governing the Registry including the sub-registries; and give an opinion after five years from the

---

391. Article 14(1) UPCA.
392. Article 14(3) UPCA.
393. Article 14(5) UPCA.
394. Article 15(1) Statute.
395. Article 15(5) Statute.

entry into force of the UPCA on the reasons and implications of actions based on European Patents that are still brought before national courts.[396]

In the Rules of Procedure the Presidium is given the following tasks:

- appoint the judges of the Court of Appeal who will be member of the full Court of Appeal;[397]
- determine the presiding judge on a panel;[398]
- make a proposal for the duration of the judicial vacations;[399]
- decide on objections to a judge taking part in proceedings pursuant to Article 7(4) of the Statute.[400]

F. PATENT MEDIATION AND ARBITRATION CENTRE

1. Introduction

By establishing an alternative dispute resolution (ADR) Centre, the UPCA follows a trend in line with the expanding importance of ADR systems settling intellectual property disputes, proven by the growing number of cases and the national regulations adopted in several European Member States in this area.[401]

Article 35 UPCA establishes a *"Patent Mediation and Arbitration Centre"* (hereinafter referred to as the *"Centre"*) with seats in Ljubljana (Slovenia) and Lisbon (Portugal). Article 35 UPCA further states that the Centre shall provide facilities for mediation and arbitration of patent disputes falling within the scope of the UPCA.[402]

The Centre shall establish the rules on mediation and on arbitration (hereinafter referred to as the *"Mediation Rules"* and the *"Arbitration Rules"*)[403] and will draw up a list of mediators and arbitrators to assist parties in the settlement of their dispute.[404]

This part provides an overview (i) explaining the unique position the UPC has created on the dispute resolution market (one-stop shop dispute resolution system), (ii) examining the Operational Rules and (iii) providing opposing views regarding legal uncertainties which could interfere with the functioning of the Centre.

It is not the objective to examine the draft Mediation Rules and Arbitration Rules, which, roughly stated, are in line with the existing systems offered by alternative ADR centres in the IP field. Although the Mediation Rules and Arbitration Rules have been drafted by the Patent Mediation and Arbitration Centre working group (Group 6 of

---

396. Article 83(5) UPCA.
397. Rule 238A Rules of Procedure.
398. Rule 341 Rules of Procedure
399. Rule 342 Rules of Procedure.
400. Rule 346 Rules of Procedure.
401. J. De Werra, "New Developments of IP Arbitration and Mediation in Europe: The Patent Mediation and Arbitration Center instituted by the Agreement on a Unified Patent Court", *Revista Brasiliera de Arbitragem (Special Edition)* (2014), 17–35.
402. Article 35(2) UPCA. Whether this Article should be read as limiting the competence of the Centre or as a minimum condition to make use of the facilities of the Centre was and is the subject of discussion (see *infra*).
403. Article 35(3) UPCA.
404. Article 35(4) UPCA.

the Legal Framework Group), they have not been communicated to the public. The draft Rules will be examined by an expert group after the Centre has been established and adopted by the Administrative Committee of the UPC. Therefore, any reference to a specific Mediation or Arbitration Rule is to be considered under reservation.

2. The UPC as a one-stop shop dispute resolution system

With the establishment of an ADR Centre, the UPC offers its users a one-stop shop dispute resolution system quite different to the set up of other ADR centres.[405] The UPC will comprise a Court (an *"above the parties"* dispute resolution entity) and an ADR Centre (an *"above and between the parties"* dispute resolution entity) which will work independently of each other but under the same legal roof.

The bridge-builder between the Court and the Centre is the Judge-Rapporteur.

It will be his task to seek settlements throughout the actions and especially during the interim proceedings.[406] The fields of the Court and the Centre have been brought somewhat closer to each other in the setting up of a procedural scheme where the damages and costs are (likely) to be decided after a decision on infringement or validity.[407] This might narrow the gap and make it possible for the Judge-Rapporteur to build a bridge between them.

Indeed, due to (i) the nature of disputes in the patent law field (linked mainly to infringements and validity), (ii) the impossibility of revoking or limiting a patent *erga omnes* in mediation and arbitration proceedings,[408] (iii) the consecutive nature of the damages proceedings, and (iv) the more stringent confidentiality warranties for the parties, it would seem likely that most cases to be dealt with by the Centre will be consecutive to actions on infringement and/or validity already decided by the Court, and more specifically by the mediation infrastructure offered by the Centre.

In this phase of the proceedings, it would seem indeed likely that *"mediation"* is proposed as, by introducing their action before the Court, parties have already made a decision to have it decided by an *"above the parties"* entity. The explicit choice to introduce an action before the Court implicitly implies the rejection of an alternative *"above the parties"* entity (arbitration).

Therefore, the Centre should not be viewed as an immediate competitor to existing ADR centres, but rather as an alternative system to resolve a patent dispute within the UPC structure.

If the Centre were given adequate attention by the Judge-Rapporteur of the Court, it might in the long run be beneficial for ADR in general. Providing means

---

405. Either there exists no formal connection between the Court and the ADR Centre, or, where a certain connection exists between the Court and the ADR entity, the alternative dispute resolver (e.g. mediator) is directly linked with the Court (as a judge) (cf. §278 section 5 of the German Rules of Civil procedure and applied regularly in patent cases by the High Court of Munich (Landgericht München I) or in another legal position (mediation services offered by the EUIPO)).
406. Cfr. Article 52(2) (last sentence) UPCA, Rule 11.1 and Rule 104(d).
407. Cf. Rule 125 and see also Part Three, Chapter IV E.1.
408. Article 35(2) UPCA.

Chapter II – Structure of the Court

for patent dispute settlements (either through the use of the Court or through the use of the Centre, or by a combination of them) should be the objective of the UPC.

3. Rules of Operation of the Mediation and Arbitration Centre of the UPC

a. Framework in which the Rules of Operation were discussed

The legal working group, preparing the Centre and one of the work streams set up by the Preparatory Committee, consisted of a specific sub-working group (Group 6). It was the task of this group to pre-draft the Mediation Rules and the Arbitration Rules as well as to set up an organisational and managerial structure for the Centre (expressed in the Rules of Operations of the Mediation and Arbitration Centre of the Unified Patent Court comprising fourteen articles) (hereinafter referred to as the "*Operational Rules*"). By decision from the Administrative Committee of 8 July 2022 the Operational Rules were adopted.[409]

As the UPCA does not provide outlined instructions regarding the organisational and managerial structure of the Centre and as the Centre was not the focus of the UPC, the working group aimed at designing a flexible organisation that could grow with the needs of the Court and its users.

It speaks per se that the focus of the UPCA is (the establishment of) the Court and not (the establishment of) the Centre.

Throughout the negotiations leading to the Operational Rules (and later the drafts of the Mediation Rules and the Arbitration Rules) the working group was confronted with several opposing points of view based on the multi-interpretational text of the UPCA related to the Centre and with the attitude of intellectual property practitioners that the Centre "*will never work*". Most probably this attitude was based on:

- bias regarding ADR in the intellectual property field (especially mediation) and its limited successful track record;
- protective reflex in favour of national and international ADR systems;
- financial constraints related to the establishment of the UPC.

Although the working group could understand these issues, it remained focused on designing an ADR structure which would secure the establishment of the Centre and leave the path open to develop this Centre based on the needs of its users while taking into consideration that the Centre could operate on a minimal budget.

A specific issue was whether the physical place of the administrative seats could have an impact on the operational structure. Proposals were made to include

---

409. In the explanatory notes to the decision by the Administrative Committee of 8 July 2022 reference is made to the discussions by the Preparatory Committee on various occasions. The draft Operational Rules were finally approved by this committee at its 15th meeting on 14 April 2016. The Operational Rules were not changed between 14 April 2016 and 8 July 2022 except for Article 17 which deals with the entry into force of the Rules. There are no Articles 15 and 16.

Portuguese and Slovenian as working languages and/or to oblige participation of a Portuguese and Slovenian expert in the Expert Committee. These issues were presented as options to the Preparatory Committee but not accepted.[410]

This decision by the Preparatory Committee seems in line with the status of the Centre. One should not compare the administrative seats of the Centre with local or regional divisions of the Court. Unlike a local or regional division of the Court (where the Contracting Member State hosting such a division is linked to this state itself, be it financially during the transitional phase, or in its internal operation by having one or two national judges in each panel and regarding the language(s) to be used), the seats of the Centre in Lisbon (Portugal) and Ljubljana (Slovenia) are to be considered purely administrative. They should be considered seats of an international organisation having no operational link with the national government hosting them. If a comparison should be made to an entity within the UPC, the Registry would come the closest.

The only proposal which was adopted relating to the national interests of Slovenia and Portugal was that, in the event that parties could not come to agree on a place of arbitration, arbitration should be organised either in Lisbon or in Ljubljana (to be decided by the Centre).[411]

b. *The Centre: name, status, seat and aims*

After defining the Centre in its first Rule, the second Rule of the Operational Rules explicitly states that, although the Centre is part of the UPC, it is an independent and impartial body.[412] It will carry out its tasks in close contact and cooperation with the committees/bodies of the UPC which will have to take decisions relating to the operation of the Centre. As a part of the UPC, the Centre will have the same legal status and liabilities.[413]

---

410. This was decided on the 15th Preparatory Committee meeting held in Luxembourg on 14 April 2016.
411. Article 16 (non-public draft) Arbitration Rules: such a principle is not foreseen in the (non-public draft) Mediation Rules (Article 9) where it is up to the Centre to decide on the place of mediation, but it can be that the Mediation Rules are aligned with this principle in the Arbitration Rules.
412. Rule 2 Operational Rules.
413. The Centre will have legal personality in each of the Member States of the European Union in which the UPCA has entered into force and shall enjoy the most extensive legal capacity accorded to legal persons under the national law of that state. The *contractual liability* of the Centre will be governed by the law applicable to the contract in question in accordance with Regulation (EC) No. 593/2008 (Rome I) where applicable or failing that in accordance with the international private law of the Member State where the arbitration or mediation procedure takes place. The *non-contractual liability* of the Centre in any respect of damages caused by it or its staff in performance of its duties will be governed by the law applicable in accordance with Regulation (EC) No. 864/2007 (Rome II) or failing that in accordance with the international private law of the contracting Member State in which the damage occurred.

Although the Centre will have a permanent address in each of its seats,[414] the actual arbitration and mediation proceedings can be organised elsewhere. For official communications the permanent address of the Centre should be used. Should the proceedings be held at the seats, appropriate facilities should be provided.[415] This principle was stipulated with the aim of attracting mediation and arbitration proceedings to Lisbon and Ljubljana. When parties make use of the Centre and an administrative fee is paid, the use of the facilities might be complementary.[416] This may be aided by the already mentioned Article in the Arbitrational Rules where proceedings should be held either in Lisbon or in Ljubljana if parties could not agree on the place for the arbitration proceedings.[417] Such a principle is not part of the Mediation Rules (Article 9) where it is up to the Centre to decide on the place of mediation.[418]

The objective of the Centre is to promote arbitration and mediation in cases falling, wholly or in part, within the competence of the Court. The promotion includes a wide variety of tools[419] including:

- to make available institutional support for the mediation and arbitration proceedings;
- to provide mediation and arbitration rules, fee schedules, model clauses for use in mediation and arbitration and other regulations;
- to provide facilities which the parties can use to carry out mediation and arbitration proceedings;
- to encourage, and to organise preferably in cooperation, the training of mediators and arbitrators.[420]

The Centre may conduct information events, maintain a website (which will be linked to the UPC website), develop and distribute publications in the field of patent arbitration and mediation.[421]

---

414. Rule 3 Operational Rules.
415. Rule 4 Operational Rules.
416. In earlier drafts, this idea was explicitly expressed. In the final draft, this option has not been excluded. It will be up to the Director (and the Administrative Committee) to decide on such a complementary use.
417. Article 16 (non-public draft) Arbitration Rules.
418. It may be foreseen that in the final Mediation Rules (to be adopted by the Administrative Committee) the same principle as mentioned in the Arbitration Rules will be introduced. The reason for this difference may lie in the fact that it was at the 15th Preparatory Committee meeting held on 14 April 2016, that the (non-public draft) Arbitration Rules were discussed while the (non-public draft) Mediation Rules already were the subject of the earlier discussions.
419. Rule 5 Operational Rules.
420. Regarding this last objective, considerable issues were raised as to whether the UPC itself would organise such trainings for mediators and arbitrators and whether it would be obligatory to make use of the Training Centre of the UPC for its judges. This resulted in a broad objective which would not limit the Centre but on the other had would allow it to seek cooperation with this training Centre. During 15th Preparatory Committee meeting held in Luxembourg on 14 April 2016 it was made clear that the training of the judges in ADR techniques in order to function as a Judge-Rapporteur would be organised at the Training Centre of the UPC in Budapest.
421. Rule 5.3 Operational Rules.

Finally, the general principle is expressed stating that the Centre may develop any other activities that will contribute to the efficiency and efficacy of the UPC.[422]

c. Languages

The working languages of the Centre are English, French and German.[423] The Centre shall communicate in the working language in which it is addressed.[424] As is proposed in the draft Mediation Rules and the Arbitration Rules, the language of the actual proceedings may be agreed upon between the parties.[425] Therefore, the working language should not be confused with the language of proceedings.

d. Finances

The budget of the Centre is part of the budget of the UPC in accordance with Article 39 UPCA.[426] The financial regulations of the UPC apply to the Centre. The Director is responsible for preparing the draft annual budget for approval by the Budget Committee of the UPC. The Centre will be financed by the budget of the UPC.[427]

The fees derived from conducting arbitration and mediation proceedings by the Centre and revenues from conducting events and the distribution of publications by the Centre will become part of the regular budget of the UPC.[428]

The Centre will provide an annual financial statement containing its income and expenses during the fiscal year[429].[430]

e. Organisational structure of the Centre

The organs of the Centre are:[431]

- a (single) **Director** (five-year renewable contract[432]) who represents the Centre and performs all duties not exclusively assigned to another organ.[433] These duties may be performed at the seats or where necessary or appropriate

---

422. Rule 5.4 Operational Rules.
423. Rule 6.1 Operational Rules.
424. Rule 6.2 Operational Rules.
425. This is expressed in the Mediation Rules (Article 12(1)) and the Arbitration Rules (Article 17). Where the Mediation Rules refer to the language in which the patent was granted if an agreement cannot be reached on the procedural language (Article 12(2)), the Arbitration Rules state that the tribunal will determine the language of arbitration (Article 17(1)).
426. Rule 7.1 Operational Rules.
427. Rule 7.2 Operational Rules.
428. Rule 7.3 Operational Rules.
429. Rule 7.4 Operational Rules.
430. The rules of the UPC on auditing the financial statement will most probably apply *mutatis mutandis*.
431. Rule 8 Operational Rules.
432. Rule 9.6 Operational Rules.
433. Rule 9.1 Operational Rules.

Chapter II – Structure of the Court

elsewhere.[434] He should function independently and will be responsible for the complete operational and organisational structure of the Centre including financial, secretarial and staffing issues.[435] The Operational Rules state specific responsibilities for the Director[436] including: to ensure that the facilities of the Centre are available, to distribute the workload of the Centre including fair distribution of cases to a specific seat; to take the necessary decisions attributed to the Centre by the arbitration and mediation rules, including the appointment and removal of arbitrators and mediators (after consulting the Expert Committee); to approve and maintain a list of arbitrators and mediators in cooperation with the Expert Committee; and to promote the Centre publicly. The Director will be employed by the UPC.[437] His competences should consist of experience in the field of intellectual property law, alternative dispute resolution and management.[438]

- an **Administrative Committee**. The Administrative Committee of the UPC should act as the Administrative Committee of the Centre.[439] The duties of the Administrative Committee include: adopting the Operational Rules, the Mediation Rules and the Arbitration Rules, the fee schedules and other important bylaws of the Centre; approving the annual report of the Centre; appointing the members of the Expert Committee on proposal by the Contracting States; appointing the Director on proposal of the Contracting States; and accepting the criteria and qualifications for arbitrators and mediators.[440]
- a **Budget Committee** and the **auditors**. Again the Budget Committee of the UPC will act as the Budget Committee of the Centre. It will decide the draft budget of the Centre and transfer such financial contributions necessary to instal, maintain and operate the Centre.[441] Also the auditors of the UPC will act as auditors of the Centre. They will evaluate the annual financial statement of the Director.[442]
- an **Expert Committee:** The Expert Committee is composed of 12 independent experts in the field of patent and arbitration and mediation law[443] [444] to be appointed by the Administrative Committee for a renewable term of six years on the proposal of the Contracting Member States.[445] The Expert Committee is independent and not bound by any considerations other than

---

434. By introducing this Rule (Rule 9.2) it is clear that it is not necessary that the Director performs his duties at the administrative seats.
435. Rule 9.3 Operational Rules.
436. Rule 9.4 Operational Rules.
437. Rule 7.4 Operational Rules.
438. Rule 7.5 Operational Rules.
439. Rule 10.1 Operational Rules.
440. Rule 10.2 Operational Rules.
441. Rule 11.1 Operational Rules.
442. Rule 11.2 Operational Rules.
443. Rule 12.1 and Rule 12.5 Operational Rules.
444. In the drafts presented to the members of the Preparatory Committee it was foreseen that one of the members of the committee should be Portuguese and another Slovenian. This was not accepted by the 15th Preparatory Committee meeting of 14 April 2016.
445. Rule 12.4 Operational Rules.

those provided for in these rules.[446] The Expert Committee has been attributed duties in line with its expertise: to cooperate with the Director in setting up a list of arbitrators and mediators; and to propose necessary or appropriate amendments changes of the Centre's Rules.[447] The Expert Committee will be convened by the Director at least once a year. The annual meetings will be held alternatively in the seats of the Centre: Lisbon (Portugal) and Ljubljana (Slovenia).[448] The Expert Committee will reach its decisions by a majority of votes of its members present at the meeting, with a quorum of eight.[449] Finally, it is important to note that the members of the Expert Committee will not be paid. They will get reimbursed for reasonable travel and accommodation costs and will receive a daily allowance from the Centre's budget.[450]

The staff of the Centre comprises following persons:[451]

- One **Director**.[452]
- **Case managerial assistance:** the case manager will administer arbitration and mediation proceedings and assist the Director.[453] In the Rules no specific number of case managers has been stipulated. Where the Preparatory Committee was asked to decide whether one or two case managers were necessary, it was felt that the exact number should not be mentioned in the Operational Rules as it may vary based on the development of case load. It may be expected that on establishment of the Centre two case managers might be appointed, be it each on a part-time basis. The case manager shall provide administrative support to any mediation and arbitration proceedings, as delegated by the Director.[454]
- **Secretarial assistance:** to help the management of the Centre with secretarial support.[455]

f. *List of arbitrators and mediators*

The Centre will establish and maintain a list of competent arbitrators and mediators in the field of patent law.[456] The Centre will strive to enlist mediators and arbitrators of each Contracting Member State on the list.[457]

---

446. Rule 12.3 Operational Rules.
447. Rule 12.3 Operational Rules.
448. Rule 12.6 Operational Rules.
449. Rule 12.7 Operational Rules.
450. Rule 12.8 Operational Rules.
451. Under Rule 13.1 it is stated that the staff should carry out its duties at the seats or, when necessary and appropriate, elsewhere.
452. Rule 13.1 Operational Rules.
453. Rule 13.1 Operational Rules.
454. Rule 13.2 Operational Rules.
455. Rule 13.1 Operational Rules.
456. Rule 14.1 Operational Rules. It was not decided whether this list should be made public or kept secret.
457. This does not seem to exclude mediators and arbitrators from non-Contracting Member States.

The criteria and qualifications for mediators and arbitrators to be admitted to the list will be determined by the Director and the Expert Committee.[458] These criteria and qualifications need to be accepted by the Administrative Committee[459] and will be published on the Centre's website together with the application form. Although not explicitly stipulated each mediator and arbitrator who fulfils the criteria and qualifications will be enlisted. It is not foreseen that the Centre should examine whether the information in the application is correct. The list will be updated.[460]

Most of the arbitrators and mediators will (most probably) appear on the (public or secret)[461] lists held by alternative ADR centres.

g. Start of operations

Where in earlier drafts a Rule covered the start of the operations,[462] the Preparatory Committee limited itself by referring to Article 35 UPCA stating that the Centre is established when the UPCA itself comes into force.

The timeframe within which the Centre will be able to initiate its actual activities upon establishment will depend on the (timely) appointment and the competences of the Director but also the importance the Administrative Committee attributes to the Centre.

Article 17 states that Operational Rules came into force on 1 August 2022.

4. Issues

The limited guidelines provided in the UPCA and most of all the interpretative problems gave rise to some important issues related to the actual framework within which the Centre has to develop its activities.[463]

Some of the problems are touched upon hereunder taking into consideration that it will be up to the Court or national court to take a more definite stance.

It is not the object of this overview to take a position but merely to list the main arguments in either direction and further explain the reasoning made by the working group and Preparatory Committee.

---

458. Rule 12.1 Operational Rules.
459. Rule 14.2 *juncto* Rule 10.2 Operational Rules.
460. Rule 14.3 Operational Rules.
461. The Preparatory Committee has not taken a position regarding this issue. It will be up to the Director to propose whether this list is open to the public or held secret (as part of its business secrets).
462. In an earlier version of the Operational Rules it was stated that Centre will start its operation one month after the Administrative Committee of the UPC has approved the Rules of Operation, the Arbitration Rules and the Mediation Rules and the bylaws, and has appointed the members of the advisory committee and the director.
463. See also J. de Werra, "New Developments of IP Arbitration and Mediation in Europe: The Patent Mediation and Arbitration Center Instituted by the Agreement on a Unified Patent Court", *Revista Brasileira de Arbitragem* (2014), 17–35.

a. Competence of the Centre

Although the Centre should provide facilities for mediation and arbitration regarding disputes *falling within the scope of the UPCA*,[464] the working group and (most of the members of) the Preparatory Committee seem of the opinion that the Centre should be competent to deal with global patent issues and other issues when at least one of these issues falls within the competences of the Court.

"Falling within the scope of the UPCA" should be read as a minimum condition to make use of the Centre (its rules and facilities). In other words: once a patent dispute falls within the scope of the UPCA, the Centre is competent to deal with all patent (and even other IP and contractual) issues related to the dispute. This is explicitly translated in the Operational Rules under Rule 5 stating that the objective of the Centre is to promote mediation and arbitration in cases which fall *wholly or in part* within the competence of the Court.

It is argued that the Centre would be unworkable should it only be competent to deal with those disputes falling within the scope of the UPCA. Two arguments are introduced to counter the literal and narrow understanding of Article 35(2) UPCA:

- A narrow approach seems to go against the objectives of ADR, and, specifically, the ADR system of mediation whose main objective is not only to solve the actual legal dispute but more importantly the underlying disagreement between parties of which the patent dispute may be the result. This underlying disagreement will most probably be of a different legal nature than the patent dispute. Limiting mediation to the patent dispute falling within the scope of the competence of the Court cannot be aligned with the objective of a mediation process.
- Based on the consecutive nature of proceedings (damages and costs to be decided after the infringement/validity issue – see *infra*), it would not be opportune to hinder parties if they would wish to have the damages issues decided on a territorially broader scale than the infringement issue.

Related to this issue is also the law to be applied in arbitration and mediation proceedings. In the Arbitration Rules[465] this is kept quite broad and not limited to the applicable law to be used by the Court when resolving a dispute.[466] It has been held that limiting the applicable law in such a way would lead to an indirect limitation of the competences of the Centre.

---

464. Cf. Article 35(2) UPCA.
465. Cf. Article 19(1) Arbitration Rules where the choice of law is left to agreement by the parties. Should parties not agree, the Tribunal shall apply the rules of law which it deems most appropriate after hearing the parties observations.
466. A specific reference could be made to the proposals of the Belgian delegation arguing that the Tribunal should in all circumstances and in full compliance with Article 20 UPCA base its decision on the sources of law as provided in Article 24 UPCA.

b.   Enforceability of settlements

An important issue pertains to the enforceability of settlements reached through the use of the facilities of the Centre, and more specifically whether, when a settlement is reached *"through the use of the facilities of the Centre (including through mediation)"*, the Centre can establish an enforceable title itself. This issue has been the subject of tense discussions within the working group and the Preparatory Committee.

Article 35 UPCA refers to Article 82 UPCA regarding the enforceability of the decisions stating that latter Article shall apply *"mutatis mutandis to any settlement reached through the use of the facilities of the Centre, including through mediation"*. Article 82(1) UPCA states that *"decisions (...) shall be enforceable in any Contracting Member State"*. When reading Article 35(2) UPCA one could assume that establishing an enforceable title by itself is possible. A settlement reached through the use of the facilities of the Centre is enforceable *as such* as reference is made to Article 82(1) UPCA (giving such settlement the same value (*"mutatis mutandis"*) as a decision by the Court).

However, this approach did not find its way in the Operational Rules, nor in the draft Mediation Rules, nor in the draft Arbitration Rules. The main argument for opposing to a strict interpretation of Article 35(2) UPCA was that the distinction regarding enforceability between an ad hoc settlement reached during the proceedings before the Court (where Article 79 UPCA applies, which states that the settlement should be confirmed by a decision of the Court and can only be enforceable after such confirmation) and the settlement reached through the use of the facilities of the Centre (where in a literal reading no confirmation by the Court is necessary to be enforceable) cannot depend on *how* the settlement is reached.

It seems that the option chosen was that *any* settlement should be confirmed in a decision by the Court in order to be enforceable based on Article 82 UPCA. This was given form by referring in the draft Mediation Rules in its Article 20[467] to the applicability of Rule 11.2.[468] Rule 11.2 itself refers to Rule 365 which states that where the parties have concluded their action by way of settlement, the Court shall confirm the settlement by decision of the Court and the decision may be enforced as a final decision of the Court. When reading Rule 11.2 (where the term *"settlement"* is made distinct from *"arbitral award by consent"*) one may deduce that Article 35(2) UPCA is not applicable when the settlement was confirmed in an arbitral award. Such distinction seems to be introduced because should the settlement, as mentioned under Article 35(2) UPCA, also include an arbitral award by consent, the enforceability based on Article 85 UPCA would go beyond the agreement reached in the Convention on the Recognition and Enforcement of Foreign Arbitral Awards (hereinafter referred to as the *"New York Convention"*). The New York Convention applies to the *recognition and enforcement of foreign arbitral awards* and the *referral by a court to arbitration*.

Finally, it is only in this interpretation of Article 35(2) UPCA that the broad competences of the Centre can be upheld. It would not be reasonable to, on the one hand, state that the Centre is competent for cases which wholly or in part lie within

---

467. For the enforcement of such settlement Rule 11.2 shall apply.
468. In the Arbitration Rules no reference was made to Rule 11.2.

the competence of the Court and, on the other hand, to hold that Centre can establish an enforceable title making reference (*mutatis mutandis*) to decisions of the Court (cf. Article 82 UPCA) which can only pertain to issues for which it is competent.

The counterarguments regarding the above seem to be the following:
- The main argument pertains to the interpretation given to the word "*settlement*" (understood as "*an agreement reached between parties*" and made distinct from the resolution of a dispute by court decision or arbitral award). The given interpretation is too narrow and the term "*settlement*" should be interpreted as the "*resolution of a dispute in general regardless whether it was reached by consent*". The argument used to back this broad interpretation is the following:
  - When an interpretative problem is encountered in an international treaty the interpretative principles as set out in the Vienna Convention on the law of treaties concluded at Vienna on 23 May 1969,[469] and more specifically Article 31(1) and Article 31(4), should be applied. The word "*settlement*" and its verb "*to settle*" are used throughout the UPCA to point to the resolution of the dispute (either by a decision[470] taken by the Court or the arbitral tribunal or by an agreement). It is only when interpreting the word "*settlement*" broadly and as intended by the Contracting Member States that Article 35(2) UPCA makes sense ("*settlement, (...), including through mediation*"). The introduction of the term "*including through mediation*" in this key Article, when referring to settlements "*reached through the use of the facilities of the Centre*" proves that the word "*settlement*" cannot be understood other than to include settlement in its textual meaning of "*resolution of a dispute*" and should therefore include "*arbitral award*" irrespective of whether it is reached by consent or not. After applying the mentioned interpretative principles and taking into consideration the ancillary nature of the Rules of Procedure, it should be held that Rule 11.2 is not in line with the

---

469. Article 31(1): "*A treaty shall be interpreted in good faith in accordance with the ordinary meaning to be given to the terms of the treaty in their context and in the light of its object and purpose.*" Article 31(4): "*A special meaning shall be given to a term if it is established that the parties so intended*".
470. Article 1 UPCA ("*A Unified Patent Court for the settlement of disputes relating to European patents and European patents with unitary effect is hereby established*"; Article 5(3) UPCA ("*The court with jurisdiction to settle disputes under paragraph 2 shall be a court of the Contracting Member State in which the damage occurred*"), Article 7(4) UPCA ("*Any difficulty arising as to the application of this Article shall be settled by decision of the Presidium, in accordance with the Rules of Procedure. (...)*"), Article 35(4) UPCA ("*The Centre shall draw up a list of mediators and arbitrators to assist the parties in the settlement of their dispute*"), Article 52(2) UPCA ("*That judge shall in particular explore with the parties the possibility for a settlement, including through mediation, and/or arbitration, by using the facilities of the Centre referred to in Article 35*") and mentioned Article 79 UPCA. This last Article seems to use the term "*settlement*" in its limitative view as an agreement reached between parties. But when examining this Article closer, it should be noted that Article 79 expressly mentions the settlement by the parties ("*The parties may, at any time in the course of proceedings, conclude their case by way of settlement, ...*"). As such the term "*settlement*" is in line with the use of the term in the previous Articles.

prevailing Article 35(2) UPCA. In this regard reference should be made to Article 41(1) UPCA where it is stated that the Rules of Procedure should comply with the UPCA. This principle is repeated in the Rules of Procedure themselves under Rule 1.1 which explicitly state that *"in the event of a conflict between the provisions of the Agreement (...) on the one hand and of the Rules on the other hand, the provisions of the Agreement (...) shall prevail."*
- The reference in Rule 11.2 to Rule 365 seems to imply that this rule can only be applicable if *"the parties have concluded their action"* which indicates that an action should have been commenced before the Court. How can Rule 365 (and Rule 11.2 as it also refers to this Rule) be applicable if the settlement is reached between parties without the introduction of an action before the Court?
- The option the Preparatory Committee backed (i.e. confirmation by the Court is always necessary regardless of how the settlement is reached) seems to make Article 35(2) purposeless. Why was Article 35(2) included if Article 79 would cover all settlements? The only option is to consider Article 35(2) as *lex specialis* when the settlement was reached through the use of the facilities of the Centre.

c. *Revoking and limiting patents*

A last important issue pertains to the (im)possibility of revoking or limiting a patent in mediation or arbitration proceedings.[471] It has been argued in the working group that this limitation regarding arbitration proceedings should be understood such that the impossibility pertains to limitations *erga omnes* and not *inter partes*. By understanding this Article as such and with regard to arbitral awards, parties have the possibility to revoke and limit a patent as long as there is no impact on the rights of third parties and, more generally, the public at large. In settlements it is clear that a party may accept to revoke or limit its patent. This approach can also be read in Rule 11.2 where it mentions that the Court can confirm by decision the terms of a settlement or arbitral award by consent, *"including a term which obliges the patent owner to limit, surrender or agree on the revocation of a patent or not to assert it against the other party and/or third parties"*. Should such term be made public (e.g. as part of a deal) it seems reasonable that third parties can refer to such acceptance and such is opposable to the patent holder.

5. **Conclusion**

The Centre offers several advantages to its users:
- It is built on the same fundaments as a specialised court in patent disputes.
- It will work independently of but on the fringes of the Court.

---

471. Article 35(2) (last sentence) UPCA but also Article 79 UPCA where generally the same principle is articulated regarding settlements in general.

- An ADR educational framework will be offered to the judges of the Court. This will mean that the judges handling a case are acquainted with ADR and the advantages it may offer for the parties.
- The judges, and more specifically the Judge-Rapporteurs, are offered tools to build a bridge between the Court and the Centre.
- The consecutive proceedings are such that these issues (such as damages and costs) are more acceptable as the subject of a settlement between parties with the aid of ADR (especially mediation) taking into consideration the confidentiality warranty within such proceedings.
- The freedom of parties to conduct ADR proceedings under the Mediation Rules and the Arbitration Rules in whichever language and where they want.
- A light and optimised organisational structure which can be developed based on the case load.

Whether the Centre will be a success remains to be seen and will depend largely on how the above advantages are used. On the other hand, some specific factors will play an important role on the successful development of the Centre:

- The success of the UPC and more specifically the Court. The Centre will, at least in the start-up years, only have a role to play if the Court is used sufficiently, and this will depend mainly on the confidence the Court can built with its users.
- Not only confidence in the Court as such is of importance but also specifically confidence in ADR for patent law disputes.
- The belief of the Administrative Committee in the Centre and related to this the (timely) appointment and qualities of the Director. The Director will play an important role in the development and promotion of the Centre.
- The expertise of the arbitrators and mediators who are enlisted. Although an important factor, most probably these will be the same names as on lists held by existing ADR centres.
- A court/Court decision regarding the competence of the Centre and the enforceability of the settlements reached and awards rendered through the use of the Centre and its rules.

There are important issues to overcome in order for the Centre to secure its place within the UPC and alongside existing ADR centres. However, if the potential users of the Centre and their representatives, the Administrative Committee of the UPC and most of all the judges of the Court are confident of the advantages of the one-stop shop resolution system which is offered, one might be optimistic regarding the future of the Centre.

Chapter III
Composition of the Different Divisions of the Court

A. COURT OF FIRST INSTANCE

Any panel of the Court of First Instance shall have a multinational composition, meaning that at least one foreign judge is part of the panel. In principle, each panel shall consist of three judges.[472] Under certain circumstances, a technically qualified judge can be added to the panel.

1. Local division

The number of patent cases per calendar year shall determine the number of national judges in the panel of a local division.

A local division in a Contracting Member State, where, during a period of three successive years prior or subsequent to the entry into force of the UPCA, fewer than 50 patent cases per calendar year on average have been commenced, shall sit in a composition of one legally qualified judge who is a national of the Contracting Member State hosting the local division concerned and two legally qualified judges who are not nationals of the Contracting Member State concerned and are allocated from a Pool of Judges on a case-by-case basis.[473]

The Pool of Judges shall be composed of all legally qualified judges and technically qualified judges from the Court of First Instance who are full-time or part-time judges of the Court.[474]

Any panel of a local division in a Contracting Member State where, during a period of three successive years prior or subsequent to the entry into force of the UPCA, 50 or more patent cases per calendar year on average have been commenced, shall sit in a composition of two legally qualified judges who are nationals of the Contracting Member State hosting the local division concerned and one legally qualified judge who is not a national of the Contracting Member State concerned allocated from the Pool of Judges. Such third judge shall serve at the local division on a long term basis, where this is necessary for the efficient functioning of divisions with a high work load.[475]

---

472. Article 8 Statute.
473. Article 8(2) UPCA.
474. Article 18 UPCA.
475. Article 8(3) UPCA.

Neither the UPCA nor the Statute provides any guidance on how the number of patent cases should be calculated to determine the composition of the panels. Does *"patent case"* mean any case regarding patents brought before a national judge, irrespective of the parties, the claim (interim measures or claims on the merits) or the instance (including appeal and cassation)? Or should the meaning of *"patent case"* be limited to the whole proceedings surrounding a particular patent? The verbatim text of the UPCA leads to the first interpretation, so that all proceedings regarding patents may be included in the calculation. This means for example that if a patent dispute started with a request by the plaintiff to the judge for inspection of the premises of the defendant, then interim measures were requested by the patent proprietor by summary proceedings, proceedings on the merits were initiated and finally decided by the Court of Appeal, four proceedings are to be taken into account for the calculation of the number of patent cases. Calculating only one patent case in the aforementioned example would mean that only very few Contracting Member States would have a local division with two national judges.

One can question whether in countries in which revocation and infringement claims are split up in different proceedings (e.g. Germany), each claim can be calculated as a separate *"patent case"*. If so, then it seems logical that in other countries which jointly decide upon infringement claims and counterclaims for revocation in one proceeding, such proceedings are calculated as two separate patent cases.

In a local division with 50 or more patent cases, the judge from the Pool of Judges can serve at the local division on a long term basis, but only when this is necessary for the efficient functioning of divisions with a high work load. Providing the possibility to serve for a long period in the same local division is laudable, but in our view this may not lead to the situation that the third judge remains in service for an indefinite period of time. An indefinite (or very long-lasting) service of the third judge could lead to the situation that small local divisions have a permanent rotation of pool judges, making it difficult to elaborate consistent case law, while large local divisions would always work with the same judges, giving them the opportunity to set out consistent case law which is considered to be of better quality.

At the start of the system, Germany, France, Italy and the Netherlands will be the local divisions having two national judges in the panel.

2. Regional division

Any panel of a regional division shall sit in a composition of two legally qualified judges chosen from a regional list of judges, who shall be nationals of the Contracting Member States concerned, and one legally qualified judge who shall not be a national of the Contracting Member States concerned and who shall be allocated from the Pool of Judges.[476] For the Nordic Baltic regional division, this will mean that two legally qualified judges shall always come from Estonia, Latvia, Lithuania or Sweden, and one legally qualified judge shall come from another Contracting Member State.

---

476. Article 8(4) UPCA.

3. Addition of a technical judge before local or regional divisions

The local and regional divisions shall request the President of the Court of First Instance to add a technically qualified judge (with qualifications and experience in the field of technology concerned) from the Pool of Judges if in an infringement case a counterclaim for revocation is initiated by the defendant and the local or regional division decides to proceed with both the action for infringement and with the counterclaim for revocation.[477]

But besides this specific situation, any panel of a local or regional division may, upon request of one of the parties, request the President of the Court of First Instance to allocate from the Pool of Judges an additional technically qualified judge with qualifications and experience in the field of technology concerned. The application by a party for allocating a technically qualified judge is governed by Rule 33 Rules of Procedure (see Part Three, Chapter IV B.1).

Moreover, any panel of a local or regional division may, after having heard the parties, submit such request on its own initiative, where it deems this appropriate.[478] In cases where such a technically qualified judge is already allocated, no further technically qualified judge may be allocated because of a counterclaim for revocation.[479]

Rule 34 Rules of Procedure describes the procedure to be followed in case of a request by the Judge-Rapporteur for allocating a technically qualified judge (see Part Three, Chapter IV B.1).

The addition of technically qualified judges opens up many possibilities for patent specialists. Today, in most Member States patent attorneys or other patent or technically qualified specialists assist the parties or are appointed by the courts as a court expert. But it is exceptional that patent specialists are involved in the rulings of the courts and/or can act as a judge in patent matters. Since the Pool of Judges shall have to include at least one technically qualified judge per field of technology,[480] in theory many technically qualified judges shall be needed by the Court.

The Administrative Committee has appointed eight technically qualified judges in the field of biotechnology, eight in the field of chemistry and pharmaceutics, nine in the field of electricity, sixteen in the field of mechanical engineering and eight in the field of physics.

According to the Statute, the decision of the Administrative Committee appointing technically qualified judges shall state the field(s) of technology for which a technically qualified judge is appointed.[481] To ensure that all fields of technology are covered, it shall be possible to appoint part-time technically qualified judges.[482]

---

477. Article 33(3)(a) UPCA.
478. Article 8(5) UPCA.
479. Article 8(5), §2 UPCA.
480. Article 18(2) UPCA.
481. Article 3(5) Statute.
482. Article 3(6) Statute.

4. Central division

Any panel of the central division shall sit in a composition of two legally qualified judges who are nationals of different Contracting Member States and one technically qualified judge allocated from the Pool of Judges with qualifications and experience in the field of technology concerned.[483] This means that parties before the central division shall be automatically confronted with technically qualified judges in all cases.

Only when the central division deals with actions concerning decisions of the EPO in carrying out the new tasks for Unitary Patents as mentioned in Article 9 of the Unitary Patent Regulation[484] shall the panel of the central division sit in a composition of three legally qualified judges who are nationals of different Contracting Member States.[485]

5. One or three judges?

As mentioned above, any panel of the different divisions of the Court shall sit in a composition of three judges, having a multinational composition.[486] Any panel of the Court shall be chaired by a legally qualified judge.[487] However, in accordance to Rule 345.6 Rules of Procedure, parties can agree to have their case heard by one single legally qualified judge.[488]

A standing judge for each division to hear urgent cases may be designated in accordance with Rule 345.4 Rules of Procedure.[489] Neither the UPCA nor the Rules of Procedure contain any criterion for urgency, which means that the Court shall have a great deal of discretion to determine whether a case is urgent.

In cases where parties agree to a single judge, or if a standing judge in urgent matters hears a case, that judge shall carry out all functions of a panel.[490]

It seems very unlikely that parties would often decide to agree to have only one single judge deciding their case. Furthermore, it is unclear from the UPCA which nationality the single legally qualified judge should have in cases before a local or regional division. Shall it be a national judge from the Pool of Judges or a judge from the Pool who comes from another Contracting Member State? Rule 345.4(a) Rules of Procedure merely provides that each panel (of three judges) may delegate to one of more judges on the panel the function of acting as a single judge. If the judge were a national, parties could choose to have only one judge to circumvent the interference of judges from other countries (appointed from the Pool of Judges). This would for example be interesting for the parties if they know that a certain national judge applies a specific national interpretation or other case law. However, it would be exceptional to have in a specific case all parties benefit from such *couleur locale*.

---

483. Article 8(6) UPCA.
484. Article 32(1)(i) UPCA.
485. Article 8(6) UPCA.
486. Article 8(1) UPCA.
487. Article 8(8) UPCA.
488. Article 8(7) UPCA.
489. Article 19(3) Statute.
490. Article 19(4) Statute.

Therefore, abuse based on the possibility of the parties agreeing on one judge seems unlikely to occur if both parties have to agree to this.

Rule 345.6 Rules of Procedure provides that if all parties agree to having the action heard by a single judge, the presiding judge on the panel to which the action is allocated shall assign the action to a legally qualified judge on the panel.

6. Panels

The allocation of judges and the assignment of cases to its panels within a division is governed by the Rules of Procedure.[491] Rule 345.1 provides that the President of the Court of First Instance or a judge to whom he has delegated this task in a division, the seat of the central division or one of its sections, shall allocate the judges to the panels of the local and regional divisions, the seat of the central division and its sections.

Actions pending in the division, the seat of the central division or one of its sections shall be assigned to the panels by the Registrar following an action-distribution scheme established by the presiding judge of each local or regional division, the seat of the central division and its sections (being the judge appointed by the Presidium as the presiding judge) for the duration of one calendar year, preferably distributing the actions according to the date of receipt of the actions at the division or section.[492]

Each panel may delegate to one or more judges on the panel (a) the function of acting as a single judge; or (b) the function of acting for the panel in the procedures for the Determination of Damages and Compensation, including the procedure for the laying open of books (Part 1 Chapter 4 Rules of Procedure) and the procedure for Cost Decisions (Chapter 5). These functions may be delegated to the Judge-Rapporteur who has prepared the action for the oral hearing.[493]

The President of the Court of First Instance or a judge to whom he has delegated this task in a division, the seat of the central division or one of its sections shall designate the judges assigned to each division, the seat of the central division and each of its sections as standing judges for urgent actions. The assignment may be limited to certain periods of time.[494]

In any event, one judge on the panel shall act as Rapporteur, in accordance with Rule 18 Rules of Procedure.[495]

B. THE COURT OF APPEAL

Any panel of the Court of Appeal shall sit in a multinational composition of five judges. It shall sit in a composition of three legally qualified judges who are nationals of different Contracting Member States and two technically qualified judges with qualifications and experience in the field of technology concerned. Those technically

---

491. Article 19(1) Statute.
492. Rule 345.3 Rules of Procedure.
493. Rule 345.4 Rules of Procedure.
494. Rule 345.5 Rules of Procedure.
495. Article 19(5) Statute.

qualified judges shall be assigned to the panel by the President of the Court of Appeal from the Pool of Judges.[496]

However, a panel dealing with actions concerning decisions of the EPO in carrying out the new tasks for Unitary Patents as mentioned in Article 9 of the Unitary Patent Regulation[497] shall sit in a composition of three legally qualified judges who are nationals of different Contracting Member States.

Any panel of the Court of Appeal shall be chaired by a legally qualified judge.[498] The allocation of judges and the assignment of cases to panels shall be done in the same way as in the Court of First Instance. Rule 345.8 Rules of Procedure provides that the rules regarding the allocation of judges and the assignment of cases to panels at first instance apply *mutatis mutandis* to the Court of Appeal. There, the President of the Court of Appeal shall of course exercise the respective functions.[499]

One judge on the panel shall be appointed as the presiding judge. Rule 341.4 Rules of Procedure provides that the Presidium may determine the presiding judge on a panel. In the absence of such a determination by the Presidium and unless otherwise agreed by the panel the most senior judge shall be the presiding judge.[500] The panel may delegate, in accordance with Rule 345.4 Rules of Procedure, certain functions to one or more of its judges.[501] One judge on the panel shall act as Rapporteur.[502]

When a case is of exceptional importance, and in particular when the decision may affect the unity and consistency of the case law of the Court, the Court of Appeal may decide, on the basis of a proposal from the presiding judge, to refer the case to the full Court.[503] The presiding judge on the panel shall request that the President of the Court of Appeal and the two judges of the Court of Appeal who are members of the Presidium appoint the judges of the Court of Appeal to the full Court. The appointees shall be the President of the Court of Appeal and not less than ten (legally and technically qualified) judges of the Court of Appeal to represent the initial two panels of the Court of Appeal. In the event that the Court of Appeal shall have more than two panels, the appointees to the full Court shall increase by five judges (legally and technically qualified) for each additional panel.[504] Decisions of the full Court shall be made by no less than a three-quarters majority of the judges of the full Court.[505]

The criterion of *"exceptional importance"* is vague, but originates from the similar criterion in the Statute of the European Court of Justice.[506] A difference between the competence of the full Court of Appeal of the Unified Patent Court and the European Court of Justice, is that in four Articles of the Treaty on the Functioning

---

496. Article 9(1) UPCA.
497. Article 32(1)(i) UPCA.
498. Article 9(3) UPCA.
499. Rule 345.8 Rules of Procedure.
500. Article 21(1) Statute.
501. Article 21(3) Statute.
502. Article 21(4) Statute.
503. Article 21(2) Statute.
504. Rule 238A(2) Rules of Procedure.
505. Rule 238A(3) Rules of Procedure.
506. Article 16 of the Statute of the European Court of Justice: *"Moreover, where it considers that a case before it is of exceptional importance, the Court may decide, after hearing the Advocate-General, to refer the case to the full Court."*

Chapter III – Composition of the Different Divisions of the Court

of the European Union, the full court of the CJEU has been provided with exclusive jurisdiction in certain specific cases.[507] No such specific exclusive jurisdiction is provided in the UPCA for the full Court of Appeal of the Unified Patent Court.

---

507. Articles 228, §2, 245, 247 and 286, §6 of the Treaty on the Functioning of the European Union.

Chapter IV
The Judges of the Court

A. REQUIREMENTS

The requirements for legally qualified judges and for technically qualified judges differ.

Legally qualified judges have to possess the qualifications required for appointment to judicial offices in a Contracting Member State.[508] A literal reading of this condition implies that to become a judge in the Court, it is sufficient to have the qualifications in Contracting Member State to become a judge. This means that it is not actually necessary to be or have been a judge in one of the Member States to be appointed as a judge of the Court, only to possess the qualifications required for appointment to judicial offices in a Contracting Member State.

Article 15 UPCA further specifies that judges should ensure the highest standards of competence and have proven experience in the field of patent litigation. Practising patent judges shall of course fulfil these conditions, but the wording of Article 15 does not for example seem to exclude lawyers who have a proven experience in the field of patent litigation and have acquired the qualifications required for appointment to judicial office in a Contracting Member State (such as having passed a national judge's examination). However, at the start of the Court, all newly appointed legally qualified judges were actual judges in the Contracting Member States.

Technically qualified judges need to have a university degree and proven expertise in a field of technology.[509] They shall also have proven knowledge of civil law and procedure relevant to patent litigation.

All judges need to have a good command of at least one official language of the EPO.[510] This means that the only obligatory language requirement for judges is a good command of English, French or German. Nevertheless, it is clear that the linguistic skills of the judge shall be taken into account when allocating a judge to a local or regional division.

Article 2 of the Statute specifies that experience with patent litigation may be acquired by training organised under the system of the Court. The training framework of the Court shall according to Article 11(4)(a) of the Statute ensure appropriate training for candidate judges and newly appointed judges of the Court. The facilities of the training framework of the Court shall be situated in Budapest.[511]

---

508. Article 15(2) UPCA.
509. Article 15(3) UPCA.
510. Article 2 Statute.
511. Article 19(1) UPCA.

B. APPOINTMENT OF JUDGES

1. Preselection by the Preparatory Committee

The UPCA provides that the Administrative Committee shall appoint the judges. However, during the preparations for the Court, it became clear that the Preparatory Committee needed to contribute to the nomination process of the first group of candidate judges and to ensure the organisation of the training of candidate judges in the preparatory phase. Therefore, on 20 September 2013 the Preparatory Committee launched a call for expression of interest of candidates, both on a part-time and on full-time basis, for legally qualified judge positions and technically qualified judge positions of the Court.

Paragraph 6 of the call for expression of interest provided that it was apparent from Article 15 UPCA, read in conjunction with Article 2 of the Statute of the Unified Patent Court, that candidates for the position of judge of the Court must satisfy the following conditions:

- the candidates must be nationals of a Contracting Member States; –
 they must have a good command of at least one official language of the EPO (German, English, French);
- they must be able to ensure the highest standards of competence and shall have proven experience in the field of patent litigation:
  - candidates for a legally qualified judge position must possess the qualifications required for appointment to judicial offices in a Contracting Member State;
  - candidates for a technically qualified judge position must have a university degree and proven expertise in a field of technology. They must also have proven knowledge of civil law and procedure relevant in patent ligation.

Regarding the proven experience in the field of patent litigation, the call for expression of interest drew candidates' attention to the fact that according to Article 2(3) of the Statute of the Unified Patent Court, experience with patent litigation which has to be proven for the appointment may be acquired by the training framework of the Court.

The Preparatory Committee received more than 1,300 applications for Court judges (both legally and technically qualified).

The pre-selection of candidate judges was a duty of the Preparatory Committee. However, an Advisory Panel comprising of five to seven persons chosen from among experienced, active or former members of Courts of Appeal or Supreme Courts or active or former lawyers with recognised competence in patent litigation was established (pursuant to Article 9 of the Organisational rules of the Preparatory Committee of the Unified Patent Court) to assist the Preparatory Committee and the human resources and training working group both in assessing the qualification and experience of candidates and in establishing the training requirements for the candidate judges.[512] This procedure was without prejudice to the formal appointment procedure.

---

512. Article 2 of the Rules on the pre-selection procedure of judge candidates of the future Unified Patent Court, www.unified-patent-court.org.

Following the receipt of all applications, the Advisory Panel provided the Preparatory Committee with an opinion assessing all applications received with a view to the suitability of candidates to perform the duties of a judge of the Court.

When assessing the applications, the Advisory Panel needed to ensure the best legal and technical expertise and a balanced composition of the Court on as broad a geographical basis as possible among nationals of the Contracting Member States. The prospective location of regional and local divisions and the requirements regarding the composition of their panels had to be taken into account.[513]

At its sixth meeting (8 July 2014), the Preparatory Committee approved a provisional list of suitable candidate judges who had the potential to become judges of the Court. Based on the assessment of the Advisory Panel, a provisional list of suitable candidates was developed by the human resources and training working group and approved by the Preparatory Committee, allowing the candidates where necessary to participate in the training program.[514]

Article 4 of the Rules on the pre-selection procedure of judge candidates of the future Court provided that while offering no guarantee of future appointment as judges of the Court, inclusion on the provisional list and, as necessary, participation in the training program of the preparatory phase means that candidates are identified as being among qualified judge candidates of the Court before the formal appointment procedure is launched. Preceding the formal appointment procedure, oral interviews may be held where appropriate.

2. Appointment procedure by the Administrative Committee

Vacant judicial posts should be publicly advertised for at least eight weeks before the deadline for applying for the post on the Court's website. The call should indicate the relevant eligibility criteria for the vacant post, in accordance with the UPCA and the Statute, and the necessary information on the appointment procedure. The deadline for applying for a post is set at no less than to eight weeks before the date fixed for appointing the judge in the judicial post.[515]

Advertisement of the post on the website
↓ (at least) 8 weeks
Application for the post
↓ 8 weeks
Date fixed for appointment

The shortlist adopted by the Preparatory Committee was of course without prejudice to the formal adoption of the judges. The judges indeed need to be appointed by

---

513. Article 2 of the Rules on the pre-selection procedure of judge candidates of the future Unified Patent Court, www.unified-patent-court.org.
514. Article 3 of the Rules on the pre-selection procedure of judge candidates of the future Unified Patent Court, www.unified-patent-court.org.
515. Article 15 UPCA, Articles 2 and 3 Statute *juncto* Article 20 Judges Regulations.

the Administrative Committee of the Court. Article 16(1) UPCA provides that the Advisory Committee shall establish a list of the most suitable candidates to be appointed as judges of the Court. The Advisory Committee shall give an opinion on candidates' suitability to perform the duties of a judge of the Court. The opinion shall comprise a list of most suitable candidates. The list shall contain at least twice as many candidates as there are vacancies. Where necessary, the Advisory Committee may recommend that, prior to the decision on the appointment, a candidate judge receives training in patent litigation.[516]

On the basis of the list established by the Advisory Committee, the Administrative Committee appointed the judges of the Court acting by common accord.[517] When appointing judges, the Administrative Committee ensured the best legal and technical expertise and a balanced composition of the Court on as broad a geographical basis as possible among nationals of the Contracting Member States.[518] The requirement of a balanced composition of the Court, created great opportunities for judges from smaller Member States. Even if the Member State does not have any specialised legally qualified patent judges and/or only a small number of technical specialists, the geographical spread of the judges should bring about vacancies for the Court.

The Administrative Committee appointed as many judges as were needed for the proper functioning of the Court. The Administrative Committee initially appointed the necessary number of judges for setting up at least one panel in each of the divisions of the Court of First Instance and at least two panels in the Court of Appeal.[519]

In a first phase 36 legally qualified judges and 50 technically qualified judges were appointed. Most of them will be part-time judges at the start of the Court. In the Administrative Committee on 2 June 2023, and on the basis of the opinion of the Advisory Committee, the Member States agreed unanimously on an additional list of most suitable candidates for appointment as technically qualified judge. In the future, altogether around 20 additional technically qualified judges will be offered a position as a part-time judge. Also, around two dozen legally qualified judges have been selected to further build the *"reserve list"* of the Court. Additions in both areas will be considered later in 2023 on an opinion by the Advisory Committee. These additions are intended to reinforce the capacity of the Court already from the early days of its work.

The decision of the Administrative Committee appointing full-time or part-time legally qualified judges and full-time technically qualified judges stated the instance of the Court and/or the division of the Court of First Instance for which each judge is appointed and the field(s) of technology for which a technically qualified judge is appointed.[520]

Part-time technically qualified judges were appointed as judges of the Court and were included in the Pool of Judges on the basis of their specific qualifications

---

516. Article 3(2) Statute.
517. Article 16(2) UPCA.
518. Article 3(3) Statute.
519. Article 3(4) Statute.
520. Article 3(5) Statute

and experience. The appointment of these judges to the Court ensured that all fields of technology are covered.[521]

Judges are appointed for a term of six years, beginning on the date laid down in the instrument of appointment. They may be re-appointed. In the absence of any provision regarding the date, the term shall begin on the date of the instrument of appointment.[522]

The appointment procedure can be summarised in the following scheme:

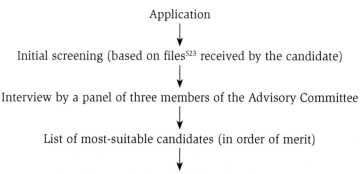

Appointment by the Administrative Committee
- giving due consideration to the opinion of the Advisory Committee;
- stating the instance of the Court and/or division of the Court of First Instance;
- stating the technical field (technically qualified judge);
- for six years.

3. Actual first appointment procedure of the first appointed legally qualified judges to the UPC

On 5 January 2022, the judges who applied for a position received an e-mail from the UPC secretariat informing them that 12 states had completed the ratification process of the Protocol on the Provisional Application of the UPCA ("PPA"), and that Austria, as thirteenth state, received the parliamentary approval to ratify the PPA which would be expected to be deposited in January 2022, leading to entering into force of the PPA and as such the period of provisional application. The applicants were informed that upon the setting-up of the governing bodies of the UPC the interviews of the selected judge candidates would be initiated. Applicants were requested to inform the UPC secretariat whether they wished to withdraw their application and this by 17 January 2022. On 7 March 2022 the applicants received a formal invitation for

---

521. Article 3(6) Statute.
522. Article 4 Statute.
523. Any personal data shall be dealt with in strict confidence and only legitimate persons will have access to the candidate's file.

an interview which would be organised either in Luxembourg (in English), Munich (in German or English) or Paris (in French or English) between 21 March 2022 and 13 May 2022 (divided between the different interview locations).

By e-mail of 1 July 2022 from the UPC secretariat, the interviewed applicants were informed that the opinion of the Advisory Committee and its list of most suitable candidates had been tabled for approval at the Administrative Committee's meeting to be held on 8 July 2022. If the list would be approved, the applicants were informed that it was expected that the Administrative Committee would start to offer positions to those candidates. Applicants were further informed that most positions at the UPC will be on a part-time basis.

By e-mail of 13 July 2022 from the UPC secretariat, the interviewed applicants were informed that during the meeting of 8 July 2022 the Advisory Committee was asked to advise on a further judge to be nominated at the Court of Appeal. A validation of this further advice by the Administrative Committee would be expected in the context of a written procedure (which would last fourteen days). The sending of the offers was therefore delayed and foreseen *"for end of July/early August"*.

Finally, by mail of 12 August 2022, the applicants received the offers detailing whether they were appointed as full-time or part-time judges and indicating whether they were appointed as a first instance judge (with indication of division) or Court of Appeal judge. The selected candidates were provided a time frame (two weeks) to reply to the offer. On acceptance of this offer, a further time frame was given (three weeks) to carry out a standard evaluation for medical fitness for office as per Article 19 of the Regulations governing the Condition of Service of Judges, the Registrar and the Deputy-Registrar of the Unified Patent Court (hereinafter *"Judges Regulations"*). At the end of this process, a formal letter was sent to the selected candidates.

4. Working conditions

The *Judges Regulations* set out the conditions of service and the rights, duties and obligations of judges of the Court.[524]

Hereafter an overview is provided regarding the position of the judges.[525] The judicial ethics as expressed in the Judges Regulations (judicial independence,[526] impartiality,[527] integrity,[528] diligence,[529] freedom of expression and association,[530] undertakings of judges after ceasing to hold office,[531] use of property and undertakings

---

524. Article 1 Judges Regulations. This Regulation was adopted by the Administrative Committee on its inaugural meeting of 22 February 2022, but was subject to amendments which were adopted by the Administrative Committee of 8 July 2022. The articles subject to amendments were Article 22, Article 27(4) and 48, Article 33(3), Article 39 and Article 40.
525. Most Articles are also applicable to Registrar and the Deputy-Registrar.
526. Article 6 Judges Regulations.
527. Article 7 Judges Regulations.
528. Article 8 Judges Regulations.
529. Article 9 Judges Regulations.
530. Article 10 Judges Regulations.
531. Article 11 Judges Regulations.

of the Court[532]) are not explained as they are common to most, if not all, of the Contracting Member States.[533]

It would go beyond the object of this book to detail the complete working conditions of the judges in great detail. Therefore only the most important working conditions are explained:

a. Full-time judges and part-time judges

The Judges Regulations provide information on the system of full-time[534] and part-time judges (applicable to both legally and technically qualified judges).[535]

Full-time and part-time judges are to be appointed by the Administrative Committee. Part-time judges may be appointed either on a case-by-case basis or for fixed[536] percentage of their working time.[537]

By Decision of the Administrative Committee a *"Concept for the remuneration and the procedure for remunerating case-by-case part-time judges of the Unified Patent Court"* was decided. This concept reiterates that part-time UPC judges will be employed in two ways:[538] either for a fixed percentage of their working time or on a case-by-case basis. For the judges employed on a case-by-case basis the details of the renumeration-procedure will have to be defined by the Presidium and this guided by two kinds of rules: *"general principles*[539] *for assessing the right amount of remuneration for case-by-case employment and specific rules*[540] *for determining the remuneration in individual, specific cases"*.

Further, the Judges Regulations foresee that a reserve list was established by the Administrative Committee.[541]

---

532. Article 12 Judges Regulations.
533. The Judges Regulations were in first instance from the Code of Conduct of the Court of Justice of the EU and the Code of Judicial Ethics of the International Criminal Court.
534. Article 26(2) Judges Regulations states that a full-time service of a judge consists of 220 working days.
535. Articles 26 and 27 Judges Regulations.
536. This percentage may be adjusted by the Presidium to reflect the Court's workload.
537. Article 27(2) Judges Regulations.
538. Cf. Article 27(2) of the Regulations Governing the Conditions of Service of Judges, the Registrar and the Deputy-Registrar of the UPC.
539. The General Principles stated in the adopted concept comprise that overcompensation should be avoided and that to calculate the remuneration a standard amount of time should be determined for typical situations, e.g. a Preliminary Objection, interim conference, each type of action, or expert involvement.
540. The Specific Principles stated in the adopted concept comprise that (inter alia) the remuneration should be calculated and paid on a monthly basis; the amount of remuneration for each respective month should be determined by multiplying a time factor by a money factor; and the Registrar or Deputy-Registrar will be involved in the procedure to approve the monthly amount of remuneration of case-by-case judges on the basis of the request and having due regard to the guidelines on the standard amount of time required to fulfil specific judicial tasks for specific procedural constellations.
541.

b. Remuneration, allowances and reimbursement of expenses

The Administrative Committee set out the remuneration of the judges and of the President of the Court of Appeal, the President of the Court of First Instance, the Registrar, the Deputy-Registrar and the staff.[542]

The basic monthly salary[543] of judges shall be the following:

Court of Appeal	EUR 20.062
Court of First Instance	EUR 18.089

The President of the Court of Appeal and the President of the Court of First Instance will earn a basic monthly salary equal to 105% of that of the judges in their respective grade.[544]

Besides the mentioned salary, the remuneration of judges will comprise family allowances,[545] dependent child's allowance,[546] disabled or severely disabled child allowance,[547] and an expatriation allowance.[548]

Further, it is stated that judges are entitled to reimbursement of expenses (including an installation allowance,[549] training costs[550] and mission expenses[551]).

Judges with part-time status will be entitled to a *pro rata* salary[552] in accordance with the remuneration conditions applicable to full-time judges of the Court to which they are appointed. The *pro rata* basis is also applicable for the allowances.[553]

Special attention should be given to the provision allowing legally qualified part-time judges from countries where national salaries are higher than the salary they are entitled to from the Court to choose between maintaining their national judges' salary and transferring the remuneration they are entitled to from the Court to their national government.[554]

---

542. In conformity with Article 12 Statute.
543. Article 32(1) Judges Regulations.
544. Article 32(2) Judges Regulations.
545. Article 34 Judges Regulations.
546. Article 35 Judges Regulations.
547. Article 36 Judges Regulations.
548. Article 37 Judges Regulations.
549. Article 38 Judges Regulations.
550. Article 39 Judges Regulations.
551. Article 22 Judges Regulations (as amended by the Administrative Committee on 8 July 2022).
552. Article 31(5) Judges Regulations.
553. The basic salary is the salary before deduction of internal taxes (Article 31(5) Judges Regulations). By Decision of the Administrative Committee of 8 July 2022 (on Annex III to the Regulations governing the conditions of service of judges, the registrar and the deputy-registrar of the unified patent court and to the staff regulations of the unified patent court) the internal taxes were set in the form of an upscaling percentage from 8% to 45%.
554. Article 31(7) Judges Regulations.

Chapter IV – The Judges of the Court

c. *Leave*

In Chapter 2 of the Judges Regulations the system of leave is detailed.
The Judges Regulations list several situations as constituting *"leave"*:

- annual leave (basic is 2½ days for each calendar month);[555]
- birth leave;[556]
- parental leave;[557]
- sick leave;[558]
- emergency or special leave;[559]
- official holidays (to be drawn up by the President of Court of Appeal).[560]

d. *Social security benefits*

Again, it would go beyond the scope of this book to go into too much detail regarding social security benefits. The Regulations refer to a Medical and Social Security Plan (Annex I) and Pension Plan (Annex II).[561]

Part-time judges are entitled to the benefits from the Court's Medical and Social Security Plan, inasmuch as they have been appointed for a fixed percentage at a rate of at least 50% and to the extent they have paid contributions to the Court's Medical and Social Security Plan.[562] It should be noted that in the earlier Judges Regulations[563] no difference was made between judges appointed for a fixed percentage (with no minimum) and on a case-by-case basis.

e. *Disciplinary measures*

Should a judge of the Court of First Instance during the term of office not respect the obligations arising from his office, pursuant to the UPCA, the Statute, the Judges Regulations and/or the Code of Conduct[564] the President of the Court of the First Instance, after hearing the person concerned, will formally in writing put the judge on notice of such failure. Should the judge continue not to fully respect the obligations of his office, the President of the Court of First Instance will ask the Presidium to decide on further disciplinary measures.[565] The same system is foreseen for judges of the Court of Appeal where the President of the Court of First Instance will be

---

555. Article 41 Judges Regulations.
556. Article 42 Judges Regulations.
557. Article 43 Judges Regulations.
558. Article 44 Judges Regulations.
559. Article 45 Judges Regulations.
560. Article 46 Judges Regulations.
561. Article 48 Judges Regulations.
562. Article 27(4) Judges Regulations.
563. 22 February 2022 (but amended on 8 July 2022).
564. Cf. Article 7 (3) Judges Regulations referring to a Code of Conduct to be adopted by the Administrative Committee drafted in cooperation with the Presidium and specifically focusing on avoiding a conflict of interest.
565. Article 49(1) Judges Regulations.

replaced by the President of the Court of Appeal.[566] Article 11 Judges Regulations state the undertakings of judges after ceasing to hold office. A disciplinary procedure is foreseen for judges not acting in accordance with this Article, which states that the Presidium is empowered to impose disciplinary measures.[567] The disciplinary measures may take the form of a written warning, a reprimand, a reduction of salary or removal from office.[568]

f. Appeals

A distinction is made between an appeal against a disciplinary decision,[569] an appeal against an administrative decision[570] and a revision of a recruitment decision for a judicial post.[571]

Complaints against administrative decisions of the Court, pertaining to the application of the Judges Regulations shall be filed with the Presidium. The decision of the Presidium may be appealed to the Administrative Committee.

In cases where a candidate for a judicial post at the Court considers that the merits of his candidacy have not been rightfully assessed, said candidate can file a petition for review to the Advisory Committee.[572]

C. JUDICIAL INDEPENDENCE AND IMPARTIALITY – CONFLICTS OF INTEREST

Article 17 UPCA repeats the general principles of independence and impartiality of judges. The Court, its judges and the Registrar shall enjoy judicial independence. In the performance of their duties, the judges shall not be bound by any instructions. Legally qualified judges, as well as technically qualified judges who are full-time judges of the Court, may not engage in any other occupation, whether gainful or not, unless an exception is granted by the Administrative Committee. Nevertheless, the exercise of the office of judges shall not exclude the exercise of other judicial functions at national level.[573] The combination of a function as a judge within the Court and a national judicial function offers the Contracting Member States the opportunity to let their national patent disputes be decided by the same judges. In a local or regional division of the Court with a limited case load, this can lead to the judge using his expertise built up at the local or regional division in national disputes.

---

566. Article 49(2) Judges Regulations.
567. Article 49(3) Judges Regulations.
568. Article 49(4) Judges Regulations.
569. Article 50 Judges Regulations.
570. Article 51 Judges Regulations.
571. Article 52 Judges Regulations.
572. Note that no similar provisions on the revision of recruitment decisions for judges in other Courts or Boards of Appeal were found.
573. Article 17(3) UPCA.

Before taking up their duties, judges shall, in open court, take an oath to perform their duties impartially and conscientiously and to preserve the secrecy of the deliberations of the Court.[574]

Immediately after taking their oath, judges shall sign a declaration by which they solemnly undertake that, both during and after their term of office, they shall respect the obligations arising therefrom, in particular the duty to behave with integrity and discretion as regards the acceptance, after they have ceased to hold office, of certain appointments or benefits.[575]

The exercise of the office of technically qualified judges who are part-time judges of the Court shall not exclude the exercise of other functions provided there is no conflict of interest.[576] In case of a conflict of interest, the judge concerned shall not take part in proceedings.

The conflict of interest rules for all types of judges are set out in Article 7 of the Statute. According to Article 7(2) of the Statute, judges may not take part in the proceedings of a case in which they:

(a) have taken part as adviser;
(b) have been a party or have acted for one of the parties;
(c) have been called upon to pronounce as a member of a court, tribunal, board of appeal, arbitration or mediation panel, a commission of inquiry or in any other capacity;
(d) have a personal or financial interest in the case or in relation to one of the parties; or
(e) are related to one of the parties or the representatives of the parties by family ties.

If, for some special reason, a judge considers that he should not take part in the judgment or examination of a particular case, that judge shall inform the President of the Court of Appeal accordingly or, in the case of judges of the Court of First Instance, the President of the Court of First Instance. If, for some special reason, the President of the Court of Appeal or, in the case of judges of the Court of First Instance, the President of the Court of First Instance considers that a judge should not sit or make submissions in a particular case, the President of the Court of Appeal or the President of the Court of First Instance shall justify this in writing and notify the judge concerned accordingly.[577]

Any party to an action may object to a judge taking part in the proceedings on any of the grounds listed above or where the judge is suspected, with good reason, of partiality.[578] If a party objects to a judge taking part in proceedings, the presiding judge of the local or regional division to which the judge is allocated or, if the action is pending before the seat of the central division or one of its sections, the respective presiding judge shall, after hearing the judge concerned, decide whether the

---

574. Article 6 Statute.
575. Article 7(1) Statute.
576. Article 17(4) UPCA.
577. Article 7(3) Statute.
578. Article 7(4) Statute.

objection is admissible having regard to Article 7(2) of the Statute.[579] If the objection is admissible, the respective presiding judge shall refer the action to the Presidium which shall hear the judge concerned and shall decide whether the objection shall stand or not.[580] The judge concerned shall be heard by the Presidium but shall not take part in the deliberations.[581] The same procedure shall apply to a judge of the Court of Appeal. The presiding judge on the panel at the Court of Appeal shall perform the functions attributed by Rule 346.1 and 346.2 Rules of Procedure to the presiding judge of the division, the seat of the central division or one of its sections in these paragraphs.[582]

The Administrative Committee has adopted (on proposal of the Advisory Committee) on 24 April 2023 the Code of Conduct for judges of the Unified Patent Court to provide guidance to judges on how to avoid situations which might be perceived by an informed observer as giving rise to a conflict of interest (hereafter "*Code of Conduct*").

The Code of Conduct applies to current judges, and where applicable former legally and technically qualified judges. Except where otherwise provided, all provisions of the Code of Conduct apply to legally qualified judges and to technically qualified judges, to full-time judges, and to part-time judges.[583]

A judge shall uphold the independence of his office and the authority of the Court and shall conduct himself accordingly in carrying out his judicial functions. He shall perform these functions with probity, integrity, impartiality, conscience, loyalty and discretion, in compliance with the Agreement, the Statute, the Regulations and this Code of Conduct, thereby respecting the dignity of his office and enhancing public confidence in the Court.[584]

A judge shall perform his duties solely on the basis of his own assessment of the merits of the case as presented by the parties, without taking account of any personal or national interest. He shall neither seek nor accept any instructions from any government, authority, organisation or person.[585]

A judge shall not directly or indirectly accept any gift, advantage, privilege or reward that can reasonably be perceived as being intended or having the capacity to influence the performance of his judicial functions. Any courtesy gift of minor value shall not be regarded as having such influence.[586]

A judge shall avoid being placed in any situation which might reasonably be perceived by an informed observer as giving rise to a conflict of interest.[587] Notwithstanding the judge's freedom of expression and association, a judge shall act and express himself, through whatever medium, with the constraint that the office requires and in such a manner that the performance of his judicial functions or the

---

579. Rule 346.1 Rules of Procedure.
580. Rule 346.2 Rules of Procedure.
581. Article 7(5) Statute.
582. Rule 346.3 Rules of Procedure.
583. Article 2 Code of Conduct.
584. Article 3(1) Code of Conduct.
585. Article 3(2) Code of Conduct.
586. Article 3(3) Code of Conduct.
587. Article 3(4) Code of Conduct.

confidence in his independence, integrity, impartiality, the dignity of his office or the authority of the Court may not be or appear to be adversely affected.[588]

A judge shall be independent of the parties to the dispute from the time he is allocated to the panel until the final decision or any other way of settlement of the proceedings he takes part in.[589] A judge may not refer to his position at the Court as means of promoting his business or interests. A judge shall prevent the firm he works for from using his position at the Court as means of promoting its business or interests. A judge may refer to his appointment as a judge of the Court, provided it is not used as a marketing tool.[590]

A judge shall take reasonable steps to maintain and enhance the knowledge and skills necessary for judicial office at a specialised patent court and shall endeavour to render his decisions carefully and as soon as possible.[591]

Confidential information acquired by a judge in his judicial capacity shall not be used or disclosed by him for any purpose not related to his judicial duties. A judge shall preserve the secrecy of everything discussed between judges in the course of performing their judicial duties, whether or not related to a specific case, and whether or not expressed during deliberations.[592]

Clearly, the technically qualified judges do have other professional activities besides being a judge. Therefore, Article 4 of the Code of Conduct gives guidance on how to deal with those other occupations activities. As a general principle, Article 4(1) provides that all types of judges shall comply with the obligation to be available so as to devote himself, to the extent of his appointment, fully to the performance of his duties. As per Article 17(2) of the Agreement, a legally qualified judge, as well as a technically qualified judge who is a full-time judge of the Court may not engage in any other occupation, whether gainful of not, unless an exception is granted by the Administrative Committee. As per Article 17(3) of the Agreement, the exercise of other judicial functions at national level does not require an exception pursuant to Article 17(2) of the Agreement.[593]

As per Article 17(4) of the Agreement, the exercise of the office of a technically qualified judge who is a part-time judge of the Court shall not exclude the exercise of other functions provided there is no conflict of interest. However, in order to maintain confidence in the independence and impartiality of the Court, to allow judges to work together in a spirit of mutual trust and to avoid potential conflicts of interest, Article 4(3) of the Code of Conduct provides that the judge may not act as a representative before the Court, as provided for in Article 48 of the Agreement, in any matter, and may not give legal or technical advice in any capacity on a case pending before the Court or after being instructed to prepare therefor. For some technically qualified judges, this was the reason to refuse their appointment, as they wanted to continue to act as a representative before the Court.

---

588. Article 3(5) Code of Conduct.
589. Article 3(6) Code of Conduct.
590. Article 3(7) Code of Conduct.
591. Article 3(8) Code of Conduct.
592. Article 3(9) Code of Conduct.
593. Article 4(2) Code of Conduct.

Activities closely related to his judicial functions, such as occasional participation in and occasional contributions to seminars, conferences, symposia, lectures or publications such as articles, commentaries and handbooks, shall not be regarded as *"other occupation"* which requires an exception granted by the Administrative Committee.[594] Assuming unremunerated managerial or administrative duties in non-profit organisations which carry out activities in the general interest in the legal, cultural, artistic, social, sporting or charitable fields and in teaching or research establishments shall not be regarded as holding a public office within the meaning of Article 8(4) of the Regulations.[595] A judge who intends to undertake such activities, shall be allowed to do so if, prior to doing so, he notifies the President of the Court of Appeal thereof, using a form provided by the President, and the President does not object thereto on the grounds that the activity may interfere with the judge's office or judicial functions. In case of an objection by the President, the judge may refer the issue to the Presidium for review.[596]

Whenever involved in external activities, the judge shall express himself orally or in writing in such a way that under the given circumstances it is clear that he only expresses his personal opinion and not that of the Court. A judge shall not comment on pending cases and shall avoid expressing views which may undermine the standing and integrity of the Court.[597]

If a judge engages in gainful activities or receives a remuneration for any external activities, he shall declare said activities to the President of his instance.[598] A judge may receive remuneration for any external activity only if he performs that activity while on leave or outside the working time for the Court.[599] A judge should be aware that activities which are sponsored by, or that target specific industry or interest groups, as well as participation in and contributions to in-house events, whether or not remuneration is paid, create an impression of dependence or partiality of the judge.[600]

When published, especially Article 5 of the Code of Conduct, which sets out the reasons for excluding participation in proceedings, was considered as very strict and causing issues for technically qualified judges who were part of a firm of patent attorneys. As per Article 7(2) of the Statute, a judge may not take part in the proceedings of a case in which he:

(a) has taken part as advisor;
(b) has been a party to the dispute or has acted for one of the parties to the dispute;
(c) has been called upon to pronounce as a member of a court, tribunal, board of appeal, arbitration or mediation panel, a commission of inquiry or in any other capacity;

---

594. Article 4(4) Code of Conduct.
595. Article 4(5) Code of Conduct.
596. Article 4(6) Code of Conduct.
597. Article 4(7) Code of Conduct.
598. Article 4(8) Code of Conduct.
599. Article 4(9) Code of Conduct.
600. Article 4(10) Code of Conduct.

(d) has a personal or financial interest in the case or in relation to one of the parties to the dispute; or
(e) is related to one of the parties to the dispute or one of the representatives of the parties to the dispute by family ties.

However, Article 5(2) of the Code of Conduct provides that a judge should always be aware, that, without prejudice to Article 7(2) of the Statute, any party to an action may object to a judge taking part in the proceedings where the judge is suspected, with good reason, of partiality (reason for recusal). Such a reason arises upon the occurrence of circumstances that, from the point of view of an informed and reasonable observer, would give rise to justifiable doubts as to the judge's impartiality or independence. Such doubts are justified if an informed and reasonable observer would conclude that there is a likelihood that the judge may be influenced in his decision by factors other than the merits of the case as presented by the parties. As far as possible, the judge should avoid conduct that gives rise to such reasonable doubt. However, since circumstances giving rise to reasonable doubt cannot always be avoided, especially for technically qualified judges who are part-time judges, immediate and comprehensive disclosure of those circumstances from which reasonable doubts about impartiality or independence might arise for the judge himself or for a party is particularly important in these cases. Article 5(3) of the Code of Conduct specifies that those doubts may in particular arise if:

(a) the judge is or has been within the past five years a member of the governing body or employee of a party to the dispute or is or was otherwise able to exert a perceptible influence on a party to the dispute either in a personal capacity or through a firm the judge works or has worked for;
(b) the judge or a close family member holds assets or has other financial or personal interests in a party to the dispute which, because of their scale, might reasonably be perceived as being capable of giving rise to a conflict of interest;
(c) the judge or a close family member is related to a party to the dispute or to a person having a controlling influence on a party or to one of the representatives of a party by close family ties;
(d) the judge has a close friendship or serious enmity with a party to the dispute or with a person having a controlling influence on a party or with one of the representatives of a party;
(e) the judge or the firm the judge works for is or was acting for or against a party to the dispute, in any other matter, in any capacity, within the last three years;
(f) the judge or the firm the judge works for is or was within the past year acting in an administrative capacity as the contact person for the patent in dispute;
(g) the judge or the firm the judge works for is or was within the past year mandated by a party to the dispute to provide an address of notification for the maintenance of intellectual property rights;
(h) the judge or the firm he works for advises or represents, on a regular or repeated basis, a competitor of a party to the dispute, in particular a competitor in a market where the patent interests of different groups of market

participants typically diverge (such as the interests of originator and generic producers or the interests of holders and users of standard-essential patents);
(i) the judge or a close family member or the firm the judge works for has a personal or financial interest in the matter in dispute;
(j) the judge or the firm the judge works for is or was involved in the dispute or the matter in dispute or does or did advise or represent a party to the dispute or a third party in the matter in dispute; or
(k) the judge has publicly stated an opinion on a matter specifically pertaining to the case, unless it is a general statement without a direct link to the matter.

Advising a third party in the technical field of the matter in dispute shall not per se give rise to apprehension of bias. The judge should nevertheless be aware that the more similarities there are between the subject matter of such an advice and the matter in dispute, the more significant the decision of the dispute could be for the subject matter of such an advice and the more similar the interests involved appear to be, the closer a possible concern of bias is.[601] For the purposes of situations provided in Article 5(3) of the Code of Conduct, a party to the dispute shall include, where appropriate, in case of a legal entity, any person or other legal entity having a controlling influence on the party, as well as any other legal entity the party has a controlling influence on.[602]

As per Article 7(3) of the Statute, when allocated to a panel, a judge shall make reasonable inquiries to identify any reason for not taking part in the proceedings and shall disclose any such reason without delay to the President of the relevant instance. If a judge is to be allocated to a panel, the judge shall, at the request of the President of the relevant instance, carry out such an inquiry and report about the result of his inquiry prior to his allocation to the panel. The judge shall ensure that the information provided by him when making the required inquiries shall be kept confidential, also by persons other than himself.[603] In a situation where there is a reason for not taking part in the proceedings concerning the President of the Court of Appeal or of the Court of First Instance, the President shall report to the Presidium for the purpose of excluding the respective President.[604] In considering whether any possible reason for not taking part in the proceedings is to be disclosed, a judge shall not give consideration to the status of the proceedings. Any doubt as to whether a judge should disclose certain facts or circumstances should be resolved in favour of disclosure which in itself does not indicate the existence of a conflict of interest.[605]

Article 7 of the Code of Conduct deals with the decision on recusal. As per Article 7(3) of the Statute, the President of the relevant instance shall, upon disclosure of any possible reason for recusal and having heard the judge concerned, decide whether or not the judge may take part in the proceedings. The President shall notify the judge in writing, giving reasons for the decision. As per Article 7(5) of the Statute, any difficulty arising as to the foregoing shall be settled by decision of the Presidium. In the situation where there is a reason for not taking part in the

---

601. Article 5(4) Code of Conduct.
602. Article 5(5) Code of Conduct.
603. Article 6(2) Code of Conduct.
604. Article 6(3) Code of Conduct.
605. Article 6(4) Code of Conduct.

proceedings concerning the President of the Court of Appeal or of the Court of First Instance, the Presidium shall replace the President in the decision on recusal. The judge concerned shall be heard. If he is a member of the Presidium, he may not take part in the decision or in the deliberations.[606]

Unless the President of the relevant instance or the Presidium has decided that the judge shall not take part in the proceedings, the President shall inform the parties of the existence of a possible reason for recusal. The procedure under Rule 346 of the Rules of Procedure shall apply *mutatis mutandis*.[607]

A reason for recusal shall be considered not to be present if the parties, having been informed or having otherwise acquired knowledge of said reason, accept the allocation of the judge to the panel or the continued participation of the judge to the proceedings or fail to notify an objection to the judge taking part in the proceedings as soon as reasonably practicable.[608]

Article 8 of the Code of Conduct provides a number of duties judges have to respect after they have left office. After leaving office, a judge shall continue to be bound by the duty of discretion.[609] A full-time judge shall, after leaving office, not become involved: (a) in any manner whatsoever in cases which were pending before the panel of which he was a member when he left office; (b) in any manner whatsoever in cases directly or clearly connected with cases, including concluded cases, which he has dealt with as a judge.[610] This will apply *mutatis mutandis* to a part-time judge after the proceedings he has taken part in have ended.[611] A judge shall not act as advisor to any of the parties to proceedings he has taken part in as a judge within a period of three years after the final decision in such proceedings.[612]

A judge who has been assigned to a panel at least once in the last two years before leaving office shall not act as a representative as provided for in Article 48 of the Agreement for a period of three years after leaving office before a division of the Court to which he was permanently assigned within the last three years, for a period of two years before a division to which he was assigned in individual cases within the last two years, and for a period of one year before all other divisions.[613] For the purposes of Article 8 of the Code of Conduct, the Court of Appeal shall be deemed to be a division and the sections of the central division shall be deemed to be different divisions.

D. IMMUNITY OF JUDGES

Similar to the immunity of the judges in the different Contracting Member States, the Statute provides an immunity rule for all judges of the Court. The judges shall be immune from legal proceedings. After they have ceased to hold office, they shall

---

606. Article 7(2) Code of Conduct.
607. Article 7(3) Code of Conduct.
608. Article 7(4) Code of Conduct.
609. Article 8(1) Code of Conduct.
610. Article 8(2) Code of Conduct.
611. Article 8(3) Code of Conduct.
612. Article 8(4) Code of Conduct.
613. Article 8(5) Code of Conduct.

continue to enjoy immunity in respect of acts performed by them in relation to their official capacity.[614]

Only the Presidium may waive the immunity. Where immunity has been waived and criminal proceedings are instituted against a judge, that judge shall be tried, in any of the Contracting Member States, only by the court competent to judge the members of the highest national judiciary.[615]

Without prejudice to the specific provisions of the Statute regarding immunity, the Protocol on the privileges and immunities of the European Union shall apply to the judges of the Court.[616]

E. END OF THE DUTIES OF THE JUDGE

The duties of the judge can end in four ways:[617]

(1) if after expiry of the six-year term, the judge is not re-appointed;
(2) by death;
(3) if the judge resigns;
(4) if the judge is removed from office by the Presidium.

In case of resignation, the letter of resignation of judges of the Court of Appeal shall be addressed to the President of the Court of Appeal or, in the case of judges of the Court of First Instance, to the President of the Court of First Instance for transmission to the Chairman of the Administrative Committee.[618]

In case of removal from office, a judge is deprived of his office or of other benefits in its stead only if the Presidium decides that that judge no longer fulfils the requisite conditions or meets the obligations arising from his office. The judge concerned shall be heard but shall not take part in the deliberations of the Presidium.[619] The decision of the Presidium shall be communicated to the Chairman of the Administrative Committee by the Registrar to inform the Administrative Committee of a vacancy.[620]

Except in case of removal from the office or death, a judge shall continue to hold office until that judge's successor takes up his duties.[621] Any vacancy shall by filled by the appointment of a new judge for the remainder of his predecessor's term.[622]

Important to note is that judges may retire at the age of 65 if requested. At the age of 70 the judges will have to retire automatically except if this limit is extended until the end of the term of the judge.[623] The age limit for an appointment as judge is 67.

---

614. Article 8(1) Statute.
615. Article 8(3) Statute.
616. Article 8(4) Statute.
617. Article 9(1) Statute.
618. Article 9(2) Statute.
619. Article 10(1) Statute.
620. Article 10(2) and 10(3) Statute.
621. Article 9(3) Statute.
622. Article 9(4) Statute.
623. Article 21 through 23 Judges Regulations.

F. POOL OF JUDGES

The Pool of Judges shall be composed of all legally qualified judges and technically qualified judges from the Court of First Instance who are full-time or part-time judges of the Court. The Pool of Judges shall include at least one technically qualified judge per field of technology with the relevant qualifications and experience. The technically qualified judges from the Pool of Judges shall also be available to the Court of Appeal.[624]

The judges from the Pool of Judges shall be allocated to the division concerned by the President of the Court of First Instance (see Rule 345 Rules of Procedure). The allocation of judges shall be based on their legal or technical expertise, linguistic skills and relevant experience. The allocation of judges shall guarantee the same high quality of work and the same high level of legal and technical expertise in all panels of the Court of First Instance.[625]

A request addressed to the President of the Court of First Instance by a division to assign a judge from the Pool of Judges shall indicate, in particular, the subject matter of the case, the official language of the EPO used by the judges on the panel, the language of the proceedings and the field of technology required.[626]

The Registrar is responsible for drawing up a list with the names of the judges included in the Pool of Judges. In relation to each judge, the list shall at least indicate the linguistic skills, the field of technology and experience of, as well as the cases previously handled by, that judge.[627] This means that the Court itself shall monitor the experience of the judge by keeping a record of the cases handled.

G. TRAINING FRAMEWORK FOR JUDGES

The UPCA and the Statute pay special attention to the training of judges. It was a clear choice of the legislator to ensure that each division of the Court guarantees a high quality of jurisprudence. Logically, the success of the Court shall mainly depend on the quality of the judgments and the skill of the legally and technically qualified judges. Certainly for smaller Contracting Member States, training of the permanent and part-time judges shall be very important. According to Article 19(1) UPCA, the function of the training framework is to improve and increase available patent litigation expertise and to ensure a broad geographic distribution of such specific knowledge and experience. The UPCA explicitly provides that facilities for the training framework shall be situated in Budapest.[628]

On 13 March 2014, the Training Centre for the Unified Patent Court was officially opened in Budapest. The Training Centre functions as a coordinating office for the training of judges and candidate judges of the new court system. The opening was followed by a two-day conference (13/14 March), where participants discussed the functions of the new Training Centre in relation to the European patent reform. In

---

624. Article 18 UPCA.
625. Article 18(3) UPCA.
626. Article 20(2) Statute.
627. Article 20(1) Statute.
628. Article 19(1) UPCA.

his keynote speech, Paul van Beukering, the former chairman of the Preparatory Committee said: *"If we want the Unified Patent Court to be amongst the best patent courts in the world, we need the best judges we can get. They are the most important asset of the court. To achieve that, training is essential."*[629]

Although the first training of the candidate Court judges should have started in 2014 according to the roadmap of the Preparatory Committee, the seventh meeting of the Preparatory Committee decided on 6 November 2014 that the first tranche of training for candidate judges would commence in early 2015. The first training was geared for judges with limited or no experience in the field of patent litigation (the so-called *"eligible upon training"*). The training consisted of courses on patent law and patent litigation. This training was not always at the Training Centre in Budapest itself. The European Patent Academy has developed a comprehensive set of learning modules covering a large number of topics. In addition to that, there has been a training program at the Budapest Training Centre.

The training not only consisted of theoretical courses but also included internships at specialised patent courts in the UK, Germany, France and the Netherlands.

The training framework shall of course continue once the Court is operational. The training shall always focus on internships in national patent courts or divisions of the Court of First Instance hearing a substantial number of patent litigation cases, improvement of linguistic skills, technical aspects of patent law, the dissemination of knowledge and experience in civil procedure for technically qualified judges and the preparation of candidate judges.[630] The internships in national patent courts or divisions with a great number of cases reflects the intention of the Contracting Member States to set up a system in which countries with little experience in patent litigation can learn from countries with a longer tradition in patent litigation. No internships at the EPO were envisaged in the training framework.

The training framework shall provide for continuous, appropriate and regular training. Regular meetings shall be organised between all judges of the Court in order to discuss developments in patent law and to ensure the consistency of the Court's case law.[631] The Presidium shall adopt Training Regulations ensuring the implementation and overall coherence of the training framework.[632]

The training framework shall provide a platform for the exchange of expertise and a forum for discussion, in particular by organising courses, conferences, seminars, workshops and symposia, cooperating with international organisations and education institutes in the field of intellectual property, and promoting and supporting further vocational training.[633]

An annual work program and training guidelines shall be drawn up, which shall include for each judge an annual training plan identifying that judge's main training needs in accordance with the Training Regulations,[634] so each judge shall have his own individual training path focused on his own needs.

---

629. www.unified-patent-court.org.
630. Article 19(2) UPCA.
631. Article 19(3) UPCA.
632. Article 11(1) Statute.
633. Article 11(2) Statute.
634. Article 11(3) Statute.

Chapter IV – The Judges of the Court

The training framework shall in addition ensure appropriate training for candidate judges and newly appointed judges of the Court, and support projects aimed at facilitating cooperation between representatives, patent attorneys and the Court.[635]

H.   STAFF AND JUDICIAL VACATIONS

The staff of the Court fall under the responsibility of the Registrar, but act under the authority of the President of the Court of Appeal and the President of the Court of First Instance.[636] The officials and other servants of the Court shall have the task of assisting the President of the Court of Appeal, the President of the Court of First Instance, the judges and the Registrar.

The Administrative Committee shall establish Staff Regulations for the officials and other servants of the Court.[637] A draft for Staff Regulations was drawn up by the Preparatory Committee. The Committee adopted the draft together with a medical and social security plan and pension plan of the Court.

The judicial vacations shall be determined by the President of the Court of Appeal. After consulting the Presidium, the President of the Court of Appeal shall establish the duration of judicial vacations and the rules on observing official holidays. During the period of judicial vacations, the functions of the President of the Court of Appeal and of the President of the Court of First Instance may be exercised by any judge invited by the respective President to that effect. In cases of urgency, the President of the Court of Appeal may convene the judges.[638]

---

635. Article 11(4) Statute.
636. Article 16(1) Statute.
637. Article 16(2) Statute.
638. Article 17(1) and 17(2) Statute.

Chapter V
Jurisdiction and Competence

A. INTERNATIONAL JURISDICTION

The international jurisdiction of the Court shall be established in accordance with the Brussels I Regulation, or where applicable, on the basis of the Lugano Convention on Jurisdiction and the recognition and enforcement of judgments in civil and commercial matters.[639] In its referral to the Brussels I Regulation, the UPCA indicates that this includes any subsequent amendments to this Regulation.

Further, the UPCA states as one of the conditions for the UPCA to enter into force the entry into force of the amendments to Regulation (EU) No. 1215/2012[640] [641] (hereinafter referred to as *"Brussels I (recast) Regulation"*). The amendments were necessary to insert the Court into the mechanics of the Brussels I (recast) Regulation.[642]

These amendments came into force on 10 January 2015 and are stipulated in Regulation (EU) No. 542/2014.[643]

Where the UPCA could regulate its competence regarding actions related to European Patents and Unitary Patents and exclude the competence of the national courts of the Contracting Member States, it could not touch on the international jurisdiction and recognition and enforcement of judgments concerning disputes falling within the competence of the Court. Indeed, the Brussels I Regulation[644] prevents Member States entering into an agreement relating to the international jurisdiction or recognition or enforcement of judgments. Therefore, the international jurisdiction

---

639. Article 31 UPCA.
640. Regulation No. 1215/2012 of the European Parliament and of the Council of 12 December 2012 on jurisdiction and the recognition and enforcement of judgments in civil and commercial matters, *OJ* L 351, 20 December 2012, p. 1.
641. Article 89 UPCA.
642. P. Véron, "Extent of the Long-Arm Jurisdiction Conferred upon the Unified Patent Court by Art. 71(b)(3) of the Brussels I Regulation as Amended by Regulation 542/2014 of 15 May 2014: Turkish Delight and a bit of Swiss Chocolate for the Unified Patent Court", EIPR 37:9 (2015), 589; and Gandia Selens, M.A.G., "The Relationship between the Brussels I Recast and the UPCA on a Unified Patent Court, specifically focusing on patent infringement: when reality exceeds fiction", in J.-S. Bergé, S. Francq and M. Gardenes Santiago (eds.), *Boundaries of European Private Law* (Bruylant, 2015), 619–635.
643. Regulation (EU) No. 542/2014 of the European Parliament and the Council of 15 May 2014, amending Regulation (EU) No. 1215/2012 as regards the rules to be applied with respect to the Unified Patent Court and the Benelux Court of Justice (2014 *OJ* L 163, p. 1.) (hereinafter referred to as "Regulation (EU) No. 542/2014"). References to the Benelux Court of Justice do not fall within the aim of this book and are therefore not mentioned.
644. Article 71 of Regulation No. 44/2001 (Brussels I Regulation).

and recognition and enforcement of judgments was to be established in accordance with Brussels I (recast) Regulation or the Lugano Convention.[645]

Regulation (EU) No. 542/2014 adapts Brussels I Regulation to ensure the compliance of the latter with the UPCA.

Regulation (EU) No. 542/2014 introduces four new Articles in Brussels I (recast) Regulation (Articles 71a to 71d) and establishes the rules that regulate the international jurisdiction of the Court, and the recognition and enforcement of decisions given by the Court in Non-Contracting Member States (Croatia, Poland and Spain).

Article 71a provides that for the purpose of the Brussels I (recast) Regulation "*a court common to several Member States (…) shall be deemed to be a court of a Member State, when pursuant to the instrument establishing it, such a common court exercises jurisdiction in matters falling within the scope of Brussels I (recast) Regulation*".[646]

Article 71b(1) provides that a common court has jurisdiction when a national court of a Contracting Member State would have jurisdiction based on the UPCA.

In other words, the Court is considered as a (national) court within the meaning of the Brussels I (recast) Regulation. This Article is specifically important should, for example, a defendant be sued before a regional division of the Court having its seat in another country of the division where the infringement took place and/or where the defendant has its domicile. Without the mentioned introduction of Article 71a *juncto* Article 71b(1), such regional division, considered as a national court of that state, would not be competent in view of Brussels I (recast) Regulation. By introducing the notion of a court common to the Member States, the court (regional division irrespective of its seat) is common to the Contracting Member States where the infringement was committed and/or where the defendant has its domicile.

It is important to note that the amendments made to the Brussels I (recast) Regulation are merely intended to establish the international jurisdiction of the Court and do not affect the internal allocation of proceedings among the divisions of the Court nor the arrangements laid down in the UPCA concerning the exercise of jurisdiction, including exclusive jurisdiction, during the transitional period provided in that Agreement.[647]

Article 71b(2) refers to the situation where the defendant is not domiciled in a Contracting Member State, stating that Chapter II (Jurisdiction) of the Brussels I (recast) Regulation is applicable. This provision was included because the general rule as stipulated under Article 6 of the Brussels I Regulation could not be applied since it is not suitable for a court common to the several states. Article 71b(2) introduces a uniform rule wherein it extends the jurisdictional rules of the Brussels I (recast) Regulation to disputes involving defendants domiciled in third states.

A jurisdictional novelty is introduced in Article 71b(3) which has been indicated as *"long-arm jurisdiction"* or referred to as *"asset-based competence"*.

Should the following conditions cumulatively be met, the Court *may* exercise jurisdiction in relation to damage arising outside the Union regarding the infringement

---

645. Convention on jurisdiction and the recognition and enforcement of judgements in civil and commercial matters, Lugano 30 October 2007, 2007, *OJ* L 339, p. 3.
646. Indeed in Article 71a(2) reference is made to the Unified Patent Court as such a common court.
647. Recital 5 Regulation (EU) 542/2014.

(object of the action brought before the Court[648]). The conditions to expand the jurisdiction are the following:

- the defendant, not domiciled in the European Union, is sued before the Court (i.e. jurisdiction determined based on Article 71b(2));
- the dispute involves an alleged infringement of a European Patent;
- the infringement gives rise to damage within the Union and damage outside the Union;[649]
- the defendant owns property located in any Contracting Member State;
- the action has sufficient connection with the state where the defendant owns this property.

If the conditions are met, the use of the wording *"may"* indicates that the Court has discretionary power to exercise its jurisdiction on acts of infringements[650] outside the territory of the Court.[651] However, this extra-territorial power is limited by the Lugano Convention applicable between the EU Member States and Iceland, Norway and Switzerland, more specifically if the defendant is domiciled in one of these countries.[652]

This long-arm jurisdiction, which may – if successful – find its way on alternative legal fields, has been the object of some critical legal doctrine.[653]

Article 71c provides rules on *lis pendens* and related issues. Article 71c(1) indicates that Articles 29 to 32 should apply where proceedings are brought in the Court and in a court of an EU non-Contracting Member State (e.g. Spain, Croatia or Poland).

Article 71c(2) provides the application of Articles 29 to 32 in the situation where a case is brought before the Court and in a court of a Contracting Member State during the transitional period. This Article will be very important in discussions regarding jurisdiction.

Applied in the context of the Court, Article 29 of the Brussels I (recast) Regulation means that if during the transitional period a same cause of action between the same parties is brought before a national court and before the Court, the court first seized has jurisdiction.[654] The court seized secondly shall decline jurisdiction. The conditions of *"same cause of action"* and *"same parties"* are important. For example, in the case of a European Patent which has not been opted out, a patent proprietor who has started an infringement action before a national court blocks an infringement

---

648. The extra-territorial jurisdiction constitutes an additional jurisdiction should the Court be competent to judge an action related to an infringement of a European Patent committed within the territory of the Union.
649. It would seem that the term *"Union"* should be understood as European Union.
650. Mr Véron takes the position that this does not confer powers to the Court to rule on validity of the patent at issue regarding territories outside the EU (Véron, P., *op. cit.*, p. 596). The Court will not have the power to revoke the patent.
651. Should it exercise its jurisdiction, this would mean that the Court could decide on infringements in Albania, Bosnia, the former Yugoslav Republic of Macedonia, Monaco, Montenegro, Serbia and Turkey.
652. Cf. Article 64(2) 2007 Lugano Convention.
653. P. Assensio, "Regulation (EU) No. 542/2014 and the International Jurisdiction of the Unified Patent Court", ICC *(IIC)* 45:8 (December 2014), 868–888.
654. Article 29(1) Brussels I (recast) Regulation.

action before the Court for that Member State. Conversely, a potential infringer can start a revocation action against a European Patent before the Court, which blocks the jurisdiction of the national courts of the Participating Member States for such action against the same patent.

Article 30 of the Brussels I (recast) Regulation provides that if *"related actions"* are pending in the courts of different Member States, any court other than the court first seized *may* stay its proceedings. For the purposes of this Article 30, actions are deemed to be related where they are so closely connected that it is expedient to hear and determine them together to avoid the risk of irreconcilable judgments resulting from separate proceedings.[655] Where the action in the court first seized is pending at first instance, any other court may also, on the application of one of the parties, decline jurisdiction if the court first seized has jurisdiction over the actions in question and its law permits the consolidation thereof.[656]

The practical implications of these *lis pendens* rules during the transitional period are not at all clear at this stage. The following examples demonstrate the blind spots:

1) If the Court is first seized for an infringement action based on a European Patent (which has not been opted out), the infringement action before the national court is blocked. However, it is unclear if a subsequent revocation action initiated before a national court shall be considered as a *"related action"* by the national courts and therefore shall stay its proceedings. One can even imagine that this question could be decided otherwise in Germany where there is a bifurcation rule (i.e. revocation and infringement actions are not treated in the same proceedings), compared to other Member States where revocation and infringement actions are treated in the same proceedings. The national courts of Germany can consider the revocation action as a non-related action. Other national courts can consider the revocation action as related.

2) If an infringement action based on a European Patent (which has not been opted out) has been commenced before a national court, the Court shall still have jurisdiction for infringement actions regarding the other Member States where no infringement action is pending before the national court. Will the Court in such case still have jurisdiction for a revocation action or will this be considered as a *"related action"*? One could even say that the Court only has jurisdiction for the revocation action which concerns all Member States other than the Member States in which the infringement action is pending.

3) If a revocation action against a European Patent which has not been opted out is initiated before the Court, does this block an infringement action before the national courts? Is this a related action or not?

4) If a revocation action against a European Patent which has not been opted out has been commenced before a national court of one of the Participating Member States, does this block a revocation action at the Court for the

---

655. Article 30(2) Brussels I (recast) Regulation.
656. Article 30(3) Brussels I (recast) Regulation.

remaining Member States? And does this block an infringement action at the Court?

The *lis pendens* rules of the Brussels I (recast) Regulation do not provide an answer to these situations. Notwithstanding the call of practitioners to clarify these matters, this has not been done up to now. It can be expected that in the first years this will evoke jurisdiction discussions at national courts and at the Court.

Finally, Article 71d provides that the Brussels I (recast) Regulation applies to the recognition and enforcement of (a) judgments given by the Court which need to be recognised and enforced in EU Member States which are not contracting parties to the Court;[657] and (b) judgments given by the courts of Member States which are not contracting parties to the Court and need to be recognised and enforced in a Contracting Member State.[658]

B. SUBSTANTIVE COMPETENCE OF THE COURT

1. Patents for which the Court is competent

The Court shall have competence with respect to any:

- Unitary Patent;
- supplementary protection certificate issued for a product protected by a European or Unitary Patent;
- European Patent which has not yet lapsed at the date of entry into force of the UPCA, or was granted after that date, without prejudice to the opt-out possibility; and
- European Patent application which is pending at the date of entry into force of the UPCA or which is filed after that date, without prejudice to the opt-out possibility.[659]

In principle, the Court shall immediately have competence to take decisions regarding classic European Patents, irrespective of whether they are already granted or only granted after the entry into force of the Court. The same goes for classic European Patent applications, the Court has competence whether they are pending at the date of entry into force, or are only filed afterwards.

Nevertheless, European Patent proprietors or applicants shall have the choice to either bring actions before the national courts or before the Court during a transitional period (*infra*). Furthermore, European Patent proprietors or applicants can always opt-out of the exclusive jurisdiction of the Court before the end of the transitional period. Such opt-out is not available for proprietors of a Unitary Patent.

---

657. Article 71d, §1, a) Brussels I (recast).
658. Article 71d, §1, b) Brussels I (recast).
659. Article 3 UPCA.

2. Actions for which the Court is competent

Article 32 UPCA provides a list of all actions for which the Court has exclusive competence. It concerns the following actions:

- actions for actual or threatened infringements of Unitary and European Patents and supplementary protection certificates and related defences, including counterclaims concerning licences;
- actions for declarations of non-infringement of Unitary and European patents and supplementary protection certificates;
- actions for provisional and protective measures and injunctions;
- actions for revocation of Unitary and European Patents and for declaration of invalidity of supplementary protection certificates;
- counterclaims for revocation of Unitary and European Patents and for declaration of invalidity of supplementary protection certificates;
- actions for damages or compensation derived from the provisional protection conferred by a published European Patent application;
- actions relating to the use of the invention prior to the granting of the European or Unitary Patent or to the right based on prior use of the invention;
- actions for compensation for licences on the basis of Article 8 of the Unitary Patent Regulation, which enables the proprietor of a Unitary Patent to file a statement with the EPO that he is prepared to allow any person to use the invention as a licensee in return for appropriate compensation;
- actions concerning decisions of the EPO in carrying out the tasks referred to in Article 9 of the Unitary Patent Regulation.

Article 9 of the Unitary Patent Regulation provides that the Participating Member States grant a number of tasks to the EPO. These tasks include the administration of requests for unitary effect by proprietors of European Patents, the inclusion and administration of a Register for Unitary Patent Protection within the European Patent Register, receiving and registering statements on licensing, withdrawal and licensing commitments undertaken in international standardisation bodies, the publication of translations during the transitional period, the collection and administration of renewal fees for Unitary Patents, the collection and administration of additional fees paid in cases of late payment of renewal fees and the administration of a compensation scheme of translation costs for applicants filing European Patent applications in one of the official languages of the Union that is not an official language of the EPO. To provide effective legal protection against the decisions of the EPO in carrying out these tasks, the Court is given exclusive competence for actions that concern such decisions of the EPO.

"*Patents*" are to be understood as both Unitary patents as European Patents.[660]

The competence of the Court is very broad. Nevertheless, the national courts of the Contracting Member States remain competent for example for compulsory licences, disputes regarding inventorship and disputes regarding Unitary or European Patents as object of property. Of course, the national courts also remain competent for all actions relating to national patents. Furthermore, during the transitional period the

---

660. Article 2(g) UPCA.

national courts shall be competent to decide all disputes regarding European Patents for which the proprietor has opted out of the exclusive competence of the Court.

C. TERRITORIAL COMPETENCE OF THE FIRST INSTANCE DIVISIONS

1. Infringement actions

Actions for actual or threatened infringement of patents and supplementary protection certificates and all *"related defences, including counterclaims concerning licences"*[661] can be brought before the following divisions:

- the local division hosted by the Contracting Member State *where the actual or threatened infringement has occurred or may occur*;
- the regional division in which the Contracting Member State *where the actual or threatened infringement has occurred or may occur* participates;
- the local division hosted by the Contracting Member State where the *defendant* or, in the case of multiple defendants, one of the defendants has its *residence*, or *principal place of business*, or in the absence of residence or principal place of business, its *place of business*;
- the regional division in which the Contracting Member State where the *defendant* or, in the case of multiple defendants, one of the defendants has its *residence*, or *principal place of business*, or in the absence of residence or principal place of business, its *place of business*, participates.[662]

When the competence is determined by the residence, principal place of business or place of business of the defendant, an action may be brought against multiple defendants only where the defendants have a commercial relationship and where the action relates to the same alleged infringement.[663]

Besides the possibility of bringing actions before the local or regional division of the Contracting Member State where the infringement has occurred or may occur, actions against defendants having their residence, or principal place of business or, in the absence of residence or principal place of business, their place of business, *outside* the territory of the Contracting Member States can also be brought before the central division.[664] For example, if the alleged infringing product is imported by a Chinese company in Denmark, an infringement action in which the Chinese company is (co-)defendant, can be brought before the Danish local division or before the central division.

If the Contracting Member State concerned does not host a local division and does not participate in a regional division, actions shall be brought before the central division.[665] If in the previous example Denmark had had no local division, the infringement action against the Chinese company could only be brought before the central division.

---

661. Article 32(1)(a) UPCA.
662. Article 33(1)(a) and (b) UPCA.
663. Article 33(1) (b) UPCA.
664. Article 33(4) UPCA.
665. Article 33(5) UPCA.

In view of the diversity of potential competent divisions, it is important to touch upon the issue of *"forum shopping"* at first instance and more specifically the option for the claimant to introduce his action before a local, regional or central division of the Court. Forum shopping as such is not an improper legal strategy, but rather natural, where a claimant seeks a court that serves his interests best. The Court provokes forum shopping to a certain extent as a patentee can sue in a division where the infringer is located or threatened infringement takes place.[666]

However, it should be borne in mind that the local, regional and central divisions are part of one Court of First Instance and the Court of Appeal overshadows all of them.

A local or regional division should not be considered as a national division or territorially regional division. It is possible that the judges sitting in a local division – because of the system of a Pool of Judges – are also at the same time part of a local division in another Member State. For example, when introducing a case in Germany (two German judges and one international judge) it is possible that two out of three of these judges are part of a panel in another local division.

In his *"forum shopping"*, the claimant can take into consideration the following elements:

- the speed of the proceedings at a specific local/regional division;
- territorial inconveniences for opposing party (long travel time, expensive lawyers or patent attorneys in that Member State, etc.);
- logistics of access to a local/regional division;
- language options of the specific local/regional division.[667]

2. Provisional protection – prior use – provisional and protective measures

The actions for damages or compensation derived from the provisional protection conferred by a published European Patent application,[668] actions for provisional and protective measures and injunctions[669] and actions relating to the use of the invention prior to the granting of the patent or to the right based on prior use of the invention,[670] can be brought before the same divisions which are competent for infringement actions.

The competence shall be determined by the place of the actual or threatened infringement or the residence, principal place of business or place of business of the defendant.[671] The rules for defendants outside the territory of the Contracting Member States and multiple defendants equally apply.

Consequently, preliminary injunctions can be granted by any territorially competent local or regional division with effect in the Contracting Member States.

---

666. Cf. Article 32(7) UPCA.
667. E.g. should a claimant prefer to introduce a case in German, he actually will only have three options regarding a local division: Germany, Austria and Belgium.
668. Article 32(1)(f) UPCA.
669. Article 32(1)(c) UPCA.
670. Article 32(1)(g) UPCA.
671. Article 33(1) UPCA.

Once the local or regional division has granted a preliminary injunction, it remains competent for subsequent actions on the merits.[672] It cannot be precluded that patent proprietors shall search in the beginning for patentee-friendly local or regional divisions to get a preliminary injunction granted. The centralised procedure of Protective letters (see Rule 207 Rules of Procedure) may prevent such a grant.

The actions for provisional protection and provisional/protective measures are strongly linked to the infringement actions, as the provisional and protective measures offer remedies to avoid further infringements. Therefore, it is obvious why such actions follow the competence of the infringement action. For actions based on the right of prior use, this is less obvious because the plaintiff can be the party using the invention. This means that in case of actions of prior use based on the competence of residence or (principal) place of business of the defendant, these actions shall be brought before the local or regional division of the patent proprietor and not the division of the alleged infringing party.

3. **Actions regarding compensation for licences of Unitary Patents**

In the absence of a *"place of infringement"*, the actions for compensation for licences on the basis of Article 8 of the Unitary Patent Regulation shall be brought before the local or regional division where the defendant or, in the case of multiple defendants, one of the defendants has its residence, or principal place of business, or in the absence of residence or principal place of business, its place of business.[673]

Such actions are intended to deal with any compensation discussion between a licensee who has obtained a licence through the new system of Article 8 Unitary Patent Regulation, and the patent proprietor.

4. **Conflicts of jurisdiction**

If any of the abovementioned actions for infringement, provisional and protective measures and injunctions, provisional protection, prior use or compensation for licences, is pending before a division of the Court of First Instance, any other action based on one of the mentioned grounds between the same parties and based on the same patent, may not be brought before any other division.

The local or regional division where the first action was initiated has exclusive jurisdiction for all the abovementioned actions. In case an action between the same parties based on the same patent is brought before different divisions, the division first seized shall be competent for the whole case and any division later seized shall declare the action inadmissible in accordance with the Rules of Procedure.[674] Rule 19 Rules of Procedure provides that a defendant may lodge a Preliminary Objection within one month of service of the Statement of claim. This Preliminary Objection can for example be an objection regarding the competence of the division indicated by the claimant. Rule 13.1(i) Rules of Procedure obliges the claimant to not only

---

672. Article 33(2) UPCA.
673. Article 33(1) UPCA.
674. Article 33(2) UPCA.

indicate in its Statement of claim the competent division, but also to explain why that division has competence.

This exclusive jurisdiction has its consequences. If a patent applicant for example starts an action for damages derived from the provisional protection of a patent application based on the residence of the alleged infringing party and the action is still pending at the time the patent is granted, it shall not then be possible for the patent proprietor to start proceedings before the local division of another Contracting Member State in which an infringement takes place. On the other hand, the defendant in an infringement discussion who wants to defend himself by invoking prior use, can first start proceedings before the local division of the Contracting Member State in which the alleged infringement takes place (which happens to be the local division of his residence), to avoid that the plaintiff first initiates an infringement action in another local division where the infringement also takes place, but is not the division of the residence of the defendant. The first party to initiate proceedings receives priority ("*first-to-litigate principle*").

Another consequence is that preliminary injunctions shall determine the further competence for infringement actions on the merits.

There is one very important exception to the first-to-litigate principle regarding infringement actions. If an infringement action is pending before a regional division and the infringement has occurred in the territories of three or more regional divisions, the regional division concerned shall, at the request of the defendant, refer the case to the central division.[675] This rule was included to ensure that very important (and wide-spread) infringement cases can be dealt with by the central division. However, strangely enough, this rule only applies to cases pending before a regional division. If an infringement action pending before a local division concerns an infringement which occurred in the territories of several local divisions, the defendant cannot request referral to the central division. In practice, during the first years of the Court this rule shall have no impact because at present there is only one planned regional division, i.e. the Nordic Baltic regional division.

5. Counterclaim for revocation – bifurcation

A counterclaim for revocation[676] may be brought in an infringement case, but it is not certain that the local or regional division shall proceed with both the infringement and revocation action. The division concerned shall have several options. The local or regional division concerned shall, after having heard the parties, have the discretion to either:

- proceed with both the action for infringement and with the counterclaim for revocation and request the President of the Court of First Instance to allocate from the Pool of Judges a technically qualified judge with qualifications and experience in the field of technology concerned;
- refer the counterclaim for revocation for decision to the central division and suspend the action for infringement;

---

675. Article 33(2), §2 UPCA.
676. Article 32(1)(e) UPCA.

- refer the counterclaim for revocation for decision to the central division and proceed with the action for infringement; or
- with the agreement of the parties, refer the whole case for decision to the central division.[677]

The article on the counterclaim for revocation has been subject to extensive debate between patent practitioners. The main reason for this is that it tries to combine the German *"bifurcation"* system – in which infringement actions and counterclaims for revocation can be separated in different proceedings – and the system of most other Contracting Member States by which counterclaims for revocation and infringement actions are combined in one procedure. The UPCA leaves it to the discretion of the local or regional division concerned to decide whether or not to combine both claims.

After the adoption of the UPCA, many interested parties feared that bifurcation would lead to the situation for defendants that the infringement action would be decided without investigating the validity of the patent. This could be potentially interesting for non-practising entities, for example, which was claimed by major companies (mainly from the telecom sector) to be a very big downside of the system. Although practitioners from Germany pointed out that even there bifurcation is not a general rule and does not cause substantial problems, the Preparatory Committee still wanted to reassure the patent proprietors.

The Preparatory Committee could of course not delete the bifurcation option from the UPCA. The option is there and shall remain there. Nevertheless, it is important to note that the local or regional divisions are never obliged to continue the infringement proceedings without a decision on the validity of the patent. It is only one of the four options the division has in case of a counterclaim for revocation. What the Preparatory Committee did was to try to mitigate possible negative effects of bifurcation in the Rules of Procedure. Three rules are specifically important here.

Rule 37.4 Rules of Procedure provides that where the panel refers only the revocation action to the central division, the panel of the local or regional division may stay the infringement proceedings pending a final decision in the revocation proceedings and *shall stay* the infringement proceedings where there is a *high likelihood* that the relevant claims of the patent will be held to be invalid on any ground by the final decision in the revocation proceedings. It will be up to the parties to defend such high likelihood of invalidity.

Rule 40 Rules of Procedure provides that the Judge-Rapporteur shall accelerate proceedings before the central division where the regional or local division has referred the counterclaim for revocation to the central division and where the infringement action has not been stayed. In such case, the Judge-Rapporteur of the panel of the central division shall endeavour to set a date for the oral hearing on the revocation action prior to the date of the oral hearing of the infringement action.

Rule 118.2 Rules of Procedure provides that if a revocation action is pending before the central division or an opposition is pending before the EPO, a local or regional division may (a) render its decision on the merits of the infringement claim, including its orders, under the *condition subsequent* that the patent is not held to be wholly or partially invalid by a final decision of the EPO or under any other term or condition; or (b) stay the infringement proceedings pending a decision on

---

677. Article 33(3) UPCA.

the revocation procedure or a decision of the EPO and shall stay the infringement proceedings if it is of the view that there is a high likelihood that the relevant claims of the patent will be held to be invalid on any ground by the final decision of the EPO, which may be expected to be given rapidly.

In many Contracting Member States it is generally accepted that the validity question first needs to be answered before deciding on the infringement question. Therefore, it is to be expected that if the local or regional division of those countries refers the revocation action to the central division, the division shall in most cases not proceed with the infringement action but shall stay proceedings. However, it seems clear that much discussion before the Court of First Instance shall take place on the referral or not of the revocation action. The UPCA clearly states that the divisions can only decide *"after having heard the parties"*.

Rule 25.1 Rules of Procedure provides that the counterclaim for revocation of a defendant shall contain *"a statement of his position, if any, on the options provided for in Article 33(3) of the Agreement and Rule 37.4."*. Furthermore, according to Rule 29.1 Rules of Procedure, the defence to the counterclaim for revocation shall contain *"the claimant and the proprietor's response to the defendant's choice of option, if any, provided for in in Article 33(3) of the Agreement and Rule 37.4"*.

Rule 37 sets out the procedure for applying Article 33(3) UPCA. As soon as practicable after the closure of the written procedure, the Panel shall decide by way of order how to proceed with respect to the application of Article 33(3) UPCA. The parties shall be given an opportunity to be heard. Rule 264 Rules of Procedure provides that each time the Rules of Procedure provide that a party shall (or may) be given the opportunity to be heard, the Court shall (or may) request the parties to provide written submissions within a specified period and/or shall invite the parties to an oral hearing on a date fixed by the Court. The Court may also order that a hearing takes place by telephone or video conference. The panel shall set out in its order brief reasons for its decision.

The Panel may by order take an earlier decision if appropriate, having considered the parties' pleadings and having given the parties an opportunity to be heard.[678]

On the other hand, a lot shall depend on the quality of the local or regional divisions. If the local or regional division does not enjoy the confidence of the parties, parties can agree to refer the whole case to the central division. If local or regional divisions – despite the use of the Pool of Judges – would have unreliable case law, chances are that major patent cases brought before such divisions shall shift to the central division after agreement among the parties. However, it should be taken into account that despite the agreement of the parties, the discretion remains with the local or regional division. The parties cannot *"force"* the local or regional division to refer the whole case to the central division.

6. Independent revocation action

Revocation actions[679] are brought before the central division. The central division shall of course only be competent for such actions if no infringement actions are

---

678. Rule 37.2 Rules of Procedure.
679. Article 33(1)(d) UPCA.

already initiated by the patent proprietor, because if an infringement action is pending before a local or regional division such revocation action is in fact a counterclaim for revocation.

If an action for infringement between the same parties relating to the same patent has been brought before a local or a regional division, the revocation actions may only be brought before the same local or regional division.[680] The central division only has exclusive competence for *"independent"* or *"initial"* revocation actions.

On the other hand, if a revocation action is already initiated before the central division, the patent proprietor remains free to initiate an infringement action before the central division or before the division competent for (independent) infringement actions. So, if an action for revocation is pending before the central division, an action for infringement between the same parties relating to the same patent may be brought before any competent local or regional division or before the central division.[681] If the infringement action is brought before a local or regional division, the division concerned shall have the same possibilities to proceed as if a counterclaim for revocation were to be initiated in an infringement proceeding before a local or regional division (*supra*, Part Two, Chapter V C.5).

7. Non-infringement actions

The central division is competent for actions for declaration of non-infringement of patents and supplementary protection certificates.[682] Here again, the central division is only competent for such actions if no infringement actions are already initiated by the patent proprietor. If an action for infringement between the same parties relating to the same patent has been brought before a local or a regional division, the actions for declaration of non-infringement may only be brought before the same local or regional division.[683]

An action for declaration of non-infringement pending before the central division shall be stayed once an infringement action between the same parties or between the holder of an exclusive licence and the party requesting a declaration of non-infringement relating to the same patent is brought before a local or regional division within three months of the date on which the action was initiated before the central division.[684]

Consequently, no *"bifurcation"* possibility is provided for declarations of non-infringement and infringement actions. On the other hand, if a non-infringement action is initiated by the alleged infringing party before the central division, the patent proprietor is given a three-month period to initiate an infringement action before a local or regional division in order to let the infringement question be dealt with by the local or regional division of the place of infringement or the place of residence or (principal) place of business.

---

680. Article 33(4) UPCA.
681. Article 33(5) UPCA.
682. Article 33(4) UPCA.
683. Article 33(4) UPCA.
684. Article 33(6) UPCA.

Part Two – The Unified Patent Court

8. Actions against Unitary Patent tasks of the EPO

In Article 9 of the Unitary Patent Regulation, the EPO is granted several new tasks with respect to Unitary Patents. Actions which concern decisions of the EPO in carrying out these tasks can only be brought before the central division.[685]

9. General exception: choice of the parties

Except for actions concerning the decisions of the EPO in carrying out the tasks granted in Article 9 Unitary Patent Regulation, the parties can agree to bring all other actions before the division of their choice, including the central division. Consequently, parties can agree to deviate from the rules of competence set out in Article 33 UPCA.[686]

Such agreement between the parties can be concluded at the time of initiating proceedings or before, for example through a jurisdiction clause in an agreement with a licensee.

10. Relation between EPO oppositions and revocation actions

Revocation actions and counterclaims for revocation can be brought before the Court without the applicant having to file notice of opposition with the EPO.[687]

Conversely, a party must inform the Court of any pending revocation, limitation or opposition proceedings before the EPO, and of any request for accelerated processing before the EPO. The Court may (but is not obliged to) stay its proceedings when a rapid decision may be expected from the EPO.[688]

Rule 295(a) Rules of Procedure provides that the Court may stay proceedings where it is seized of an action relating to a patent which is also the subject of opposition proceedings or limitation proceedings (including subsequent appeal proceedings) before the EPO or a national authority where a decision in such proceedings may be expected to be given rapidly. Rule 298 provides that the Court may of its own motion or at the request of a party request that opposition proceedings or limitation proceedings (including any subsequent appeal proceedings) before the EPO be accelerated in accordance with the proceedings of the EPO. The Court may stay its proceedings pending the outcome of such request and any subsequent accelerated proceedings.

D. TERRITORIAL SCOPE OF THE DECISIONS OF THE COURT

One of the main goals of the Court is to ensure that parties no longer have to start proceedings in different or all Contracting Member States in order to enforce their patent rights in different or all Contracting Member States.

---

685. Article 33(9) UPCA.
686. Article 33(7) UPCA.
687. Article 33(8) UPCA.
688. Article 33(10) UPCA.

Article 34 UPCA provides that decisions of the Court shall cover in case of classic European Patents the territory of those Contracting Member States for which the European Patent has effect. This means that if a European Patent has been validated in five EU countries of which one country is not a Contracting Member State (e.g. Spain) and the Court subsequently revokes the patent, this revocation shall have effect in four EU Member States excluding Spain.

The unitary effect for decisions regarding Unitary Patents is laid down in Article 3(2) and (5) of the Unitary Patent Regulation (cf. *supra*).

Chapter VI
Sources of Law and Substantive Law

A. SOURCES OF LAW

When hearing a case brought before it, the Court shall base its decisions on:
- Union law, including the Unitary Patent Regulation and the Translation Regulation;
- the UPCA;
- the EPC;
- other international agreements applicable to patents and binding on all the Contracting Member States; and
- national law.[689]

Article 24 UPCA stresses that when applying the sources of law, the primacy of Union law has to be respected. In patent matters, we note the Biotech Directive[690] and the Enforcement Directive,[691] for example, as relevant instruments of Union law. To assess the validity of supplementary protection certificates, the Court shall rely on the EU Regulations regarding supplementary protection certificates for medicinal products and for plant varieties.[692]

In practice, the EPC shall be the predominant instrument for the Court to determine the validity of a patent. The basic requirements for patentability (novelty, inventive step and industrial application), as well as the patentable inventions and the exceptions to patentability, are laid down in the EPC. Furthermore, for infringement actions, Article 69 of the EPC and the Protocol on the Interpretation of Article 69 EPC shall be important for the extent of protection (interpretation of the claims) and more specifically the doctrine of equivalents.

In order to determine whether or not a patent is infringed, the UPCA shall be the go-to document. The UPCA contains six articles of substantive patent law,[693] regarding direct infringement, indirect infringement, limitations of the effect of a

---

689. Article 24(1) UPCA.
690. Directive 98/44/EC of the European Parliament and of the Council of 6 July 1998 on the legal protection of biotechnological inventions on the legal protection of biotechnological inventions.
691. Directive 2004/48/EC of the European Parliament and of the Council of 29 April 2004 on the enforcement of intellectual property rights.
692. EU Regulation No. 469/2009 of 6 May 2009 concerning the supplementary protection certificate for medicinal products; EU Regulation No. 1610/96 of 23 July 1996 concerning the creation of a supplementary protection certificate for plant protection products.
693. Articles 25–30 UPCA.

European or Unitary Patent, prior use, exhaustion of the rights of a European or Unitary Patent and the effects of supplementary protection certificates.

For Unitary Patents, Article 5(1) of the Unitary Patent Regulation provides that the Unitary Patent shall confer on its proprietor the right to prevent any third party from committing acts against which that patent provides protection throughout the territories of the Participating Member States in which it has unitary effect, subject to applicable limitations. Article 5(2) specifies that the scope of that right and its limitations shall be uniform in all Participating Member States in which the patent has unitary effect. Paragraph 3 of the same Article then states which national law shall determine these uniform rights and limitations. The acts against which the patent provides protection and the applicable limitations shall be those defined by the law applied to Unitary Patents in the Participating Member State whose national law is applicable to the European patent with unitary effect as an object of property in accordance with Article 7. At first sight, one could believe that this means that the infringement of the Unitary Patent shall be assessed according to provisions of a national law of one the Participating Member States. This is not the case. Since the UPCA shall apply to all the Participating Member States, this will mean that this Article is in fact a disguised reference to the provisions of substantive patent law mentioned in the UPCA.

Because many clauses of substantive patent law have been deleted from the Unitary Patent Regulation, the importance of national law shall nevertheless remain. National law shall be applicable to determine damages, to determine inventorship actions and in actions regarding the patents as an object of property.

For Unitary Patents, the applicable rules are to be found in different legislation:

- the principle of uniform protection, exhaustion or licences of rights are to be found in the Unitary Patent Regulation;
- the rules regarding direct infringement, indirect infringement, limitations and rights of prior use are to be found in the UPCA;
- the patentability provisions, the scope of protection[694] and the grounds on which a patent may be revoked[695] are to be found in the EPC;
- the rules regarding compulsory licences and the Unitary Patent as an object of property are to be found in the applicable national law.

To the extent that the Court shall base its decisions on national law, including where relevant the law of non-Contracting Member States (e.g. in case of European Patents valid in Member States of the European Patent Organisation which are non-EU Member States), the applicable law shall be determined:

(a) by directly applicable provisions of Union law containing private international law rules; or
(b) in the absence of directly applicable provisions of Union law or where they do not apply, by international instruments containing private international law rules; or

---

694. Article 69 EPC and the Protocol on the Interpretation of Article 69 EPC.
695. Article 138 EPC.

(c) in the absence of provisions referred to in points (a) and (b), by national provisions on private international law as determined by the Court.[696]

The law of non-Contracting Member States shall apply when designated by application of the abovementioned rules. This can in particular be the case in relation to direct infringement, indirect infringement, limitations of the effect, rights based on prior use, burden of proof and reversal of burden of proof, corrective measures in infringement proceedings, award of damages and period of limitation.

B.   SUBSTANTIVE PATENT LAW

The provisions of substantive patent law are included in the UPCA. As explained, for Unitary Patents these provisions were first included in the Unitary Patent Regulation, but were then transferred to the UPCA to avoid divergent jurisprudence for Unitary Patents and European Patents.

Only six articles of substantive patent law are available in the UPCA, as mentioned above. This is a major step forward in European harmonisation because Article 64 EPC currently provides that a European Patent confers on its proprietor from the date on which the mention of its grant is published in the European Patent Bulletin, in each Contracting Member State in respect of which it is granted, the same rights as would be conferred by a national patent granted in that State. The UPCA harmonises the national laws of the participating Contracting Member States on these aspects of substantive patent law.

1.   Direct use of the invention

A patent shall confer on its proprietor the right to prevent any third party not having the proprietor's consent from:

(a) making, offering, placing on the market or using a product which is the subject matter of the patent, or importing or storing the product for those purposes;

(b) using a process which is the subject matter of the patent or, where the third party knows, or should have known, that the use of the process is prohibited without the consent of the patent proprietor, offering the process for use within the territory of the Contracting Member States in which that patent has effect;

(c) offering, placing on the market, using, or importing or storing for those purposes a product obtained directly by a process which is the subject matter of the patent.[697]

---

696. Article 24(2) UPCA.
697. Article 25 UPCA.

2. Indirect use of the invention

A European Patent or a Unitary Patent shall confer on its proprietor the right to prevent any third party not having the proprietor's consent from supplying or offering to supply, within the territory of the Contracting Member States in which that patent has effect, any person other than a party entitled to exploit the patented invention, with means, relating to an essential element of that invention, for putting it into effect therein, when the third party knows, or should have known, that those means are suitable and intended for putting that invention into effect.[698]

This shall not apply when the means are staple commercial products, except where the third party induces the person supplied (i.e. the person to which the staple commercial products were supplied) to perform any acts of direct infringement.[699]

There shall remain an indirect infringement even when a third party not having the proprietor's consent supplies or offers to supply to certain persons bound by a limitation with means, relating to an essential element of that invention, for putting it into effect therein, when the third party knows, or should have known, that those means are suitable and intended for putting that invention into effect. In this respect, Article 26(3) UPCA stipulates that persons performing the acts referred to in Article 27(a) to (e) UPCA shall not be considered to be parties entitled to exploit the invention. This shall mean that if, for example, a third party, without the patent proprietor's consent, provides means, which are suitable or intended to put the invention into effect, to a person who uses the invention privately and for non-commercial purposes, this still can be considered as an indirect infringement.

For European Patents it can happen that during the transitional period the choice for a national court or for the Court will affect the existence of an indirect infringement. If brought before a national court, the means relating to an essential element of the invention shall have to be supplied within the territory of that Contracting Member State. If different steps or elements are necessary to have the means relating to an essential element of the invention, all these steps or elements have to be located in the same Contracting Member State. However, if brought before the Court, Article 26 UPCA provides that the means have to be supplied *within the territory of the Contracting Member States in which that patent has effect*. Here, it is sufficient that the different steps or elements are supplied in the territory where the European Patent has effect.

3. Limitations

The rights conferred by a European or Unitary Patent shall not extend to any of the following:
- acts done privately and for non-commercial purposes;
- acts done for experimental purposes relating to the subject matter of the patented invention;

---

698. Article 26(1) UPCA.
699. Article 26(2) UPCA.

- the use of biological material for the purpose of breeding, or discovering and developing other plant varieties;
- the use of biological material in accordance with Directive 98/44/EC,[700] for the purpose of breeding, or discovering and developing new plant varieties;

If this exception had been inserted in the Unitary Patent Regulation, an explicit reference to Union law would not have been necessary. However, after moving this exception to the UPCA, a reference to Union law was necessary to ensure that the UPCA fully respects the Union law. The Biotechnology Directive (Directive 98/44) may not be affected by an intergovernmental agreement.

- the acts allowed pursuant to Article 13(6) of Directive 2001/82/EC[701] or Article 10(6) of Directive 2001/83/EC[702] in respect of any patent covering the product within the meaning of either of those Directives (the *"Bolar exemption"*);
- the extemporaneous preparation by a pharmacy, for individual cases, of a medicine in accordance with a medical prescription or acts concerning the medicine so prepared;
- the use of the patented invention on board vessels of countries of the International Union for the Protection of Industrial Property (Paris Union) or members of the World Trade Organisation, other than those Contracting Member States in which that patent has effect, in the body of such vessel, in the machinery, tackle, gear and other accessories, when such vessels temporarily or accidentally enter the waters of a Contracting Member State in which that patent has effect, provided that the invention is used there exclusively for the needs of the vessel;
- the use of the patented invention in the construction or operation of aircraft or land vehicles or other means of transport of countries of the International Union for the Protection of Industrial Property (Paris Union) or members of the World Trade Organisation, other than those Contracting Member States in which that patent has effect, or of accessories to such aircraft or land vehicles, when these temporarily or accidentally enter the territory of a Contracting Member State in which that patent has effect;
- the acts specified in Article 27 of the Convention on International Civil Aviation of 7 December 1944, where these acts concern the aircraft of a country party to that Convention other than a Contracting Member State in which that patent has effect;
- the use by a farmer of the product of his harvest for propagation or multiplication by him on his own holding, provided that the plant propagating material was sold or otherwise commercialised to the farmer by or with

---

700. Directive 98/44/EC of 6 July 1998 on the legal protection of biotechnological inventions, *OJ* L 213, 30 July 1998, p. 13, including any subsequent amendments.
701. Directive 2001/82/EC of 6 November 2001 on the Community code relating to veterinary medicinal products, *OJ* L 311, 28 November 2001, p. 1, including any subsequent amendments.
702. Directive 2001/83/EC of 6 November 2001 on the Community code relating to medicinal products for human use, *OJ* L 311, 28 November 2001, p. 67, including any subsequent amendments.

the consent of the patent proprietor for agricultural use. The extent and the conditions for this use correspond to those under Article 14 of Regulation (EC) No. 2100/94;[703]
- the use by a farmer of protected livestock for an agricultural purpose, provided that the breeding stock or other animal reproductive material were sold or otherwise commercialised to the farmer by or with the consent of the patent proprietor. Such use includes making the animal or other animal reproductive material available for the purposes of pursuing the farmer's agricultural activity, but not the sale thereof within the framework of, or for the purpose of, a commercial reproductive activity;
- the acts and the use of the obtained information as allowed under Articles 5 and 6 of Council Directive 2009/24/EC,[704] in particular, by its provisions on decompilation and interoperability; and
- the acts allowed pursuant to Article 10 of Directive 98/44/EC.[705]

Although these limitations are similar to those applied in the national laws of the Contracting Member States, limitations in national laws can differ from those laid down in the UPCA. For example, the limitation for experimental use in Belgium concerns acts done for scientific purposes *with or on* the subject matter of the patented invention. For European Patents this can lead to the strange situation that during the transitional period of the Court, different limitations can apply depending on whether the claimant starts his infringement proceedings before a national court or before the Court. The national court shall apply the limitation from its national law, while the Court shall apply the limitation from the UPCA. Belgium and the Netherlands have, for example, aligned their national laws with the UPCA.

4. Prior use

Any person, who, if a national patent had been granted in respect of an invention, would have had, in a Contracting Member State, a right based on prior use of that invention or a right of personal possession of that invention, shall enjoy, in that Contracting Member State, the same rights in respect of a European or Unitary Patent for the same invention.[706]

For the rights based on prior use of the invention, Article 28 UPCA indirectly refers to national law. Only if a right based on prior use or a right of personal possession would be granted if the user had a national patent instead, shall the user have the same rights for prior use or personal possession of an invention laid down in a Unitary Patent.

---

703. Council Regulation No. 2100/94 of 27 July 1994 on Community plant variety rights, *OJ* L 227, 1 September 1994, p. 1, including any subsequent amendments.
704. Directive 2009/24/EC of 23 April 2009 on the legal protection of computer programs, *OJ* L 111, 5 May 2009, p. 16, including any subsequent amendments.
705. Directive 98/44/EC of 6 July 1998 on the legal protection of biotechnological inventions, *OJ* L 213, 30 July 1998, p. 13, including any subsequent amendments.
706. Article 28 UPCA.

5. Exhaustion of the rights conferred by a European Patent

The principle of exhaustion for Unitary Patents is laid down in Article 6 of the Unitary Patent Regulation. For European Patents, Article 29 UPCA provides that the rights conferred by a European Patent shall not extend to acts concerning a product covered by that patent after that product has been placed on the market in the Union by, or with the consent of, the patent proprietor, unless there are legitimate grounds for the patent proprietor to oppose further commercialisation of the product.

6. Effects of supplementary protection certificates

The provisions of the UPCA concerning patents shall apply *mutatis mutandis* to supplementary protection certificates to the extent that Union law does not provide otherwise. In the UPCA, supplementary protection certificates are to be understood as all supplementary protection certificates granted under Regulation No. 469/2009[707] or under Regulation No. 1610/96.[708]

Article 30 UPCA is intended to ensure that the provisions concerning European and Unitary Patents contained in the UPCA also apply to supplementary protection certificates.

---

[707]. Regulation (EC) No. 469/2009 of the European Parliament and of the Council of 6 May 2009 concerning the supplementary protection certificate for medicinal products, *OJ* L 152, 16 June 2009, p.1.

[708]. Regulation (EC) No. 1610/96 of the European Parliament and of the Council of 23 July 1996 concerning the creation of a supplementary certificate for plant protection products, *OJ* L 198, 8 August 1996, p.30.

Chapter VII
Organisation of Proceedings

A. STATUTE AND RULES OF PROCEDURE

The Statute and the Rules of Procedure are two important documents for understanding the organisation, functioning and procedures of the Court. According to the UPCA, the Statute lays down the details of the organisation and functioning of the Court,[709] while the Rules of Procedure lay down the details of the proceedings before the Court.[710]

The Statute is annexed to the UPCA and may be amended by decision of the Administrative Committee, on the basis of a proposal of the Court or a proposal of a Contracting Member State after consultation with the Court. However, such amendments cannot contradict or alter the UPCA.[711] As a matter of principle, the UPCA states that the Statute shall guarantee that the functioning of the Court is organised in the most efficient and cost-effective manner and shall ensure equitable access to justice.[712]

To properly understand the functioning of the Court, one needs to take into account three levels of rules. The general rules and principles are to be found in the UPCA. More detailed rules are included in the Statute and the most detailed and practical rules are provided for in the Rules of Procedure. In the relation between the three documents, the UPCA always prevails. In case of contradiction between the Rules of Procedure and the Statute, the Statute shall prevail.

One of the major problems the Court may encounter in its formation is that it cannot fall back on general rules of proceedings of the Contracting Member States. In normal circumstances, specialised courts have their own specific rules of proceedings for the subject matter concerned, but for the rest they rely upon the general rules of procedure of the Member States in or for which they operate. As a court common to all Contracting Member States, the Court cannot rely on procedural rules of a specific Member State (nor of the European Union) and has to fully establish its own rules of procedure. The advantage of this is that the Court shall not be confronted with conflicts between national procedural rules and its own rules of procedure. The disadvantage will be that the Court cannot rely on national rules to complete its own rules or provide interpretation of the Rules of Procedure.

---

709. Article 40(1) UPCA.
710. Article 41(1) UPCA.
711. Article 40(2) UPCA.
712. Article 40(3) UPCA.

The Rules of Procedure shall comply with the UPCA and the Statute[713] and need to be adopted by the Administrative Committee *"on the basis of broad consultations with stakeholders"*. The prior opinion of the European Commission on the compatibility of the Rules of Procedure with Union law needed to be requested.[714]

The Rules of Procedure may be amended by a decision of the Administrative Committee, on the basis of a proposal from the Court and after consultation with the European Commission. However, such amendments may not contradict or alter the UPCA or the Statute.[715]

For the Rules of Procedure, the UPCA sets out the following principles:

- the Rules of Procedure shall guarantee that the decisions of the Court are of the highest quality and that proceedings are organised in the most efficient and cost-effective manner;
- the Rules of Procedure shall ensure a fair balance between the legitimate interests of all parties;
- the Rules of Procedure shall provide for the required level of discretion of judges without impairing the predictability of proceedings for the parties.[716]

B. PROCEDURAL PRINCIPLES

The UPCA provides a number of procedural principles that should be respected by the Court.

First of all, the general principles of proportionality and fairness are reaffirmed. The Court shall deal with litigation in ways which are proportionate to the importance and complexity thereof. The Court shall ensure that the rules, procedures and remedies provided for in the UPCA and in the Statute are used in a fair and equitable manner and do not distort competition.[717]

Furthermore, the role of the Court in case management is determined. The Court shall actively manage the cases before it in accordance with the Rules of Procedure without impairing the freedom of the parties to determine the subject matter of, and the supporting evidence for, their case.[718]

A very special element regarding the proceedings is the clear choice of the UPCA for as many of electronic procedures as possible. The Court shall make best use of electronic procedures, such as the electronic filing of submissions of the parties and stating of evidence in electronic form, as well as video conferencing, in accordance with the Rules of Procedure.[719] The flexibility of the Court regarding electronic procedures can only be encouraged in further elaborating the functioning of the Court.

Finally, the proceedings shall be open to the public unless the Court decides to make them confidential, to the extent necessary, in the interest of one of the parties

---

713. Article 41(1) UPCA.
714. Article 41(2) UPCA.
715. Article 41(2), §2 UPCA.
716. Article 41(3) UPCA.
717. Article 42 UPCA.
718. Article 43 UPCA.
719. Article 44 UPCA.

or other affected persons, or in the general interest of justice or public order (see Part Three, Chapter VIII A.3).[720]

C. PARTIES AND REPRESENTATION

1. Parties

Any natural or legal person, or any body equivalent to a legal person entitled to initiate proceedings in accordance with its national law, shall have the capacity to be a party to the proceedings before the Court.[721] But having the capacity to be a party to the proceedings does not necessarily mean that they can start an action before the Court.

In any event, the patent proprietor is entitled to bring actions before the Court.[722] Unless the licensing agreement provides otherwise, an exclusive licensee shall also be entitled to bring actions before the Court under the same circumstances as the patent proprietor, provided that the patent proprietor is given prior notice.[723] The holder of a non-exclusive licence shall not be entitled to bring actions before the Court, unless the patent proprietor is given prior notice and insofar as expressly permitted by the licence agreement.[724] In actions brought by a licensee, the patent proprietor shall be entitled to join the action before the Court.[725] To make sure that as many persons as possible can bring actions before the Court, Article 47(6) UPCA provides that any other natural or legal person, or anybody entitled to bring actions in accordance with its national law, who is concerned by a patent, may bring actions in accordance with the Rules of Procedure. This *"catch-all"* section mainly refers to alleged infringers who can initiate revocation proceedings or declarations for non-infringement.

The validity of a patent cannot be contested in an action for infringement brought by the holder of a licence where the patent proprietor does not take part in the proceedings. The party in an action for infringement wanting to contest the validity of a patent shall have to bring actions against the patent proprietor.[726] Consequently, counterclaims for revocation can only be initiated if the patent proprietor is present in the infringement procedure.

The specific actions against decisions of the EPO in carrying out its new tasks referred to in Article 9 Unitary Patent Regulation, can be brought by any natural or legal person, or anybody entitled to bring actions in accordance with their national law and who is affected by the decision.[727]

---

720. Article 45 UPCA.
721. Article 46 UPCA.
722. Article 47(1) UPCA.
723. Article 47(2) UPCA.
724. Article 47(3) UPCA.
725. Article 47(4) UPCA.
726. Article 47(5) UPCA.
727. Article 47(7) UPCA.

2. Representation

a. General

Parties shall in principle be represented by lawyers before the Court. All lawyers authorised to practice before a court of a Contracting Member State can act before the Court.[728]

Besides lawyers, patent attorneys may under certain conditions also represent parties.

To be able to represent a party before the Court, the patent attorney should first of all be entitled to act as a professional representative before the EPO in accordance with Article 134 EPC. Article 134 EPC requires that the patent attorney appears on a list maintained for this purpose by the EPO. Any natural person who is a national of a Contracting Member State of the EPC, has his place of business or employment in a Contracting Member State and has passed the European qualifying examination may be entered on the list of professional representatives. The President of the EPO may grant exemption from the nationality requirement in special circumstances.[729]

Secondly, the European patent attorney should have appropriate qualifications.[730] The requirements for appropriate qualifications were established by the Administrative Committee in the "Rules on the European Patent Litigation Certificate and other appropriate qualifications"[731] of 22 February 2022 (hereafter "*EPLC Rules*"), which entered into force on 15 June 2022[732] (cf. *infra*). As an example of proof of appropriate qualifications, the UPCA refers to the European Patent Litigation Certificate.[733] The list of European patent attorneys entitled to represent parties before the Court shall be kept by the Registrar[734] and can be consulted and searched on the website of the Court.[735]

The representation before the Court has been subject to heated discussion between the different stakeholders.[736]

The Council of Bars and Law Societies of Europe (CCBE) was of the opinion that disputes involving patents are to be carried out by a suitably qualified and properly trained professional lawyer. According to the CCBE, disputes involving patents also involve many other areas of law in which a patent attorney will have no training or experience. The vague concept of a European Patent Litigation Certificate would not be a guarantee for the required level of training and the appropriate standards. Moreover, representatives have to be subject to clear, consistent rules of behaviour

---

728. Article 48(1) UPCA.
729. Article 134(7) EPC.
730. Article 48(2) UPCA.
731. Administrative Committee – Decision EPLC 22 February 2022, AC/06/22022022_rev_E; available on www.unified-patent-court.org
732. Article 48(3) UPCA.
733. Article 48(2) UPCA.
734. Article 48(3) UPCA.
735. www.unified-patent-court.org/en/registry/representation
736. For an overview of the different positions we refer to Volker "Falk" Metzler, "Representation before the future European and EU patents Court (EEUPC)", 8 October 2010, www.visaepatentes.com.

backed by an effective disciplinary procedure. Because in many EU Member States patent attorneys do not have a legal background, the CCBE was of the opinion that patent attorneys would not bring the same additional guarantees of professional behaviour as provided by bar members.[737]

Following the position paper of the CCBE, the Institute of Professional Representatives before the EPO (epi) responded with a position paper of 23 June 2010.[738] According to epi, European patent attorneys have technical qualifications, are highly experienced in patent matters, are regulated by a code of professional conduct, and will have training in the new procedures. epi found that the adoption of European patent attorneys as representatives will have significant cost benefits for the parties and provide effective litigation. For rules on professional conduct, epi refers to Article 11 of its Regulation on the establishment of an Institute of professional representatives before the EPO and the Regulation on discipline for professional representatives,[739] which prescribe certain rules of professional conduct for European patent attorneys. The Additional Rules of Procedure of the Disciplinary Committee govern the disciplinary committee of epi and the procedures of the Committee.

It appears that the Contracting Member States wanted to combine the traditions of the different Contracting Member States in the articles regarding representation. In a number of Contracting Member States (e.g. Germany, Austria, Poland and the Netherlands), patent attorneys have traditionally and by law been able to independently represent parties in validity and non-infringement patent cases before national courts. However, in most civil law countries, only attorneys-at-law can represent parties in court proceedings.

Before the Court, representation shall be open to European patent attorneys with appropriate qualifications. But if a patent attorney is not authorised to represent parties before the Court (e.g. because of lacking the appropriate qualifications), he shall in any event have the right to assist the representative (lawyer or other patent attorney with appropriate qualifications) before the Court. Representatives of the parties may be assisted by patent attorneys. The patent attorneys shall be allowed to speak at hearings of the Court in accordance with Rule 292 Rules of Procedure.[740] The term *"patent attorneys assisting a representative"* shall mean persons meeting the requirements of Rule 287.6(b) or 287.7 (i.e. a person who is recognised as eligible to give advice under the law of the state where he practises in relation to the protection of any invention or to the prosecution or litigation of any patent or patent application and is professionally consulted to give such advice, or a professional representative before the EPO pursuant to Article 134(1) EPC), and practising in a Contracting Member State.

---

737. Position paper of the Conseil des barreaux européens – Council of Bars and Law Societies of Europe, "Proposal for a European and Community Patents Court – CCBE Position regarding article 28", 19 February 2009, www.ccbe.eu.
738. http://216.92.57.242/downloads/Reports/10_33_23062010_representation-before-the-EEUPC.pdf.
739. http://www.patentepi.com/patentepi/en/Rules-and-Regulations/rules-and-regulations.php.
740. Article 48(5) UPCA.

Article 48(4) UPCA covers the attorney-client privilege for communications between a representative and the party or any other person. Representatives of the parties shall enjoy the rights and immunities necessary for the independent exercise of their duties, including the privilege from disclosure in proceedings before the Court in respect of communications between a representative and the party or any other person, under the conditions laid down in Rules 287–290 Rules of Procedure, unless such privilege is expressly waived by the party concerned. Patent attorneys who meet the requirements to be a representative before the Court shall now enjoy this privilege. Furthermore, the privilege shall also extend to *"any other person"*, which implies that communication between a lawyer and a patent attorney who assists the lawyer in a procedure before the Court (without being an official representative of the party concerned) shall also fall within the attorney-client privilege.

Representatives of the parties shall be obliged not to misrepresent cases or facts before the Court either knowingly or with good reason to know.[741] No explicit sanctions for representatives are provided in the UPCA for misrepresentation of cases or facts.

Article 48(7) UPCA states that representation by a lawyer or a patent attorney shall not be required in proceedings against decisions of the EPO in carrying out the tasks referred to in Article 9 Unitary Patent Regulation.[742]

b. Rules on the European Patent Litigation Certificate and appropriate qualifications

At its meeting of 3 September 2015, the Preparatory Committee agreed on the Rules on the European Patent Litigation Certificate and other appropriate qualifications (hereinafter *"Rules EPL Certificate"*). The Preparatory Committee prepared the draft Rules and they were adopted by the Administrative Committee of 22 February 2022 and entered into force on 15 June 2022.[743]

i. The European Patent Litigation Certificate

The European Patent Litigation Certificate (hereinafter the *"Certificate"*) may be issued by universities and other non-profit educational bodies of higher or professional education established in a Member State of the European Union as well as by the Unified Patent Court's Training Centre in Budapest to European patent attorneys entitled to act as professional representatives before the EPO pursuant to Article 134 of the European Patent Convention who have successfully completed a course on European patent litigation accredited pursuant to the Rules EPL Certificate (hereinafter referred to as the *"Course"*).[744]

The curriculum of the Course shall cover:

- a general introduction into law, including main aspects of European law;

---

741. Article 48(6) UPCA.
742. Article 32(1)(i) UPCA.
743. Article 48(3) UPCA.
744. Rule 2 of the Rules EPL Certificate.

Chapter VII – Organisation of Proceedings

- basic knowledge of private law, including contract law, company law and tort law, in both common and continental law, and private international law;
- the role, organisation and patent-related case law of the Court of Justice of the European Union, including case law on supplementary protection certificates;
- enforcement of patents, providing knowledge of Directive 2004/48 on the enforcement of intellectual property rights and relevant case law of the Court of Justice of the European Union;
- Unitary Patent protection, providing advanced knowledge of the Unitary Patent Regulation and the Translation Regulation, as well as the Rules relating to Unitary Patent Protection;
- a comparative overview on patent infringement proceedings and revocation of patents in Contracting Member States;
- the operation of the Court, providing advanced knowledge of the UPCA and the Unified Patent Court's Statute;
- litigation before the Court, providing advanced knowledge of procedures, litigation and advocacy skills, practice and case management before the Court, with special regard to the Rules of Procedure of the Unified Patent Court.[745]

Rule 3(2) of the Rules EPL Certificate provides that the Course shall focus in particular on the last four points mentioned above and shall include practical exercises on litigation and negotiation.

The minimum duration of the Course shall be 120 hours of lectures and practical training.[746] The Course shall be concluded by both a written and oral examination.[747] The Course may be provided in any official language of a Member State of the European Union.[748] Rule 5(2) of the Rules EPL Certificate provides that e-learning facilities are encouraged as an integral part of the Course, but that practical training always requires personal participation.

Universities and other non-profit educational bodies of higher or professional education established in an EU Member State may offer the Course subject to accreditation by the Administrative Committee.[749] Rules 7 and 8 of the Rules EPL Certificate describe the procedure that universities and non-profit educational bodies need to follow to receive accreditation. The request for accreditation shall be decided upon by the Administrative Committee on the basis of an opinion of the Advisory Committee. Accreditation is granted for five academic years following the date of the notification of the decision on accreditation.[750] A request for the prolongation of the accreditation for another five years may be filed one year before the expiry of the five-year period at the earliest. Participating educational bodies are required to report every year to the (Administrative Committee of the) Unified Patent Court on

---

745. Rule 3 of the Rules EPL Certificate.
746. Rule 4(1) of the Rules EPL Certificate.
747. Rule 4(2) of the Rules EPL Certificate.
748. Rule 5(1) of the Rules EPL Certificate.
749. Rule 6 of the Rules EPL Certificate.
750. Rule 8(4) of the Rules EPL Certificate.

the curriculum, results and statistics of the accredited Course.[751] The Training Centre, by offering the necessary infrastructural and organisational assets, shall assist the educational bodies that wish to provide a Course at the seat of the Training Centre as well, and may also facilitate e-learning options.[752] The Training Centre may also offer the Course itself.[753]

ii. Other appropriate qualifications

European patent attorneys holding a bachelor or master's degree in law according to relevant educational standards in an EU Member State or who have passed an equivalent state examination in law of a Member State of the European Union shall be deemed to have appropriate qualifications pursuant to Article 48(2) UPCA and may apply for registration on the list of entitled representatives.[754]

Rule 12 of the Rules EPL Certificate provides that during a transitional period of one year from the entry into force of the UPCA, two other qualifications shall also be deemed as appropriate qualifications for a European patent attorney. This Rule is also known as the *"grandfather provision"*.

The first appropriate qualification during a transitional period concerns the successful completion of one of the existing courses or certificates on patent law in different Member States, listed in Rule 12(a).

The second possible appropriate qualification during a transitional period is having represented a party alone without the assistance of a lawyer admitted to the relevant court or having acted as a judge in at least three patent infringement actions, initiated before a national court of a Contracting Member State within the five years preceding the application for registration.[755]

iii. Registration on the list of representatives

In case the European patent attorney wishing to represent parties before the Court has a Certificate, he shall lodge the Certificate with the Registrar and shall be registered on the list of representatives.[756]

If a European patent attorney wishing to represent parties before the Court wishes to be registered based on *"appropriate qualifications"*, he shall file his requests for recognition of other appropriate qualifications with the Registrar in one of the official languages of the EPO.[757]

If a request is based on a law degree or one of the courses on patent law mentioned in Rule 12(a), the request for recognition of other appropriate qualifications shall contain a copy of the respective diploma, certificate or other respective proof.[758]

---

751. Rule 9 of the Rules EPL Certificate.
752. Rule 10(1) of the Rules EPL Certificate.
753. Rule 10(2) of the Rules EPL Certificate.
754. Rule 11 of the Rules EPL Certificate.
755. Rule 12(b) of the Rules EPL Certificate.
756. Rule 13 of the Rules EPL Certificate.
757. Rule 14(1) of the Rules EPL Certificate.
758. Rule 14(2) of the Rules EPL Certificate.

If a request is based on experience as a representative or judge in three patent cases during the last five years, the request shall include all details necessary to identify the infringement actions the European patent attorney intends to rely on such as:

- name of the parties;
- court seized with the action;
- date of commencement of the proceedings.

Reasonably available evidence to support the request, such as a copy of the power of attorney, also needs to be submitted.[759] Rule 15 of the Rules EPL Certificate describes the examination procedure by the Registrar and the decision of the Registrar on the request for recognition of other appropriate qualifications.

Registrations of European patent attorneys on the list of representatives shall in principle be permanent, including registrations under the transitional grandfather provisions (Rule 12 of the Rules EPL Certificate).[760] Registration on the list shall cease to have effect in the event that the registered representative ceases to be a registered European patent attorney on the list of European patent attorneys maintained by the EPO. The Registrar will strike the name off the list, upon request or *ex officio*. In case the European patent attorney is re-entered on the list maintained by the EPO, he shall, upon his request, be re-entered by the Registrar on the list of representatives before the Court.[761] The Registrar shall also strike the name of an entitled representative from the list upon a final decision of a competent court or authority establishing that the registration on the list has been obtained by fraud – a conviction is not necessary.[762] The Registrar will of course strike the name of an entitled representative from the list upon his own request to this effect.

Decisions of the Registrar to enter a representative in the list of representatives before the Court may be challenged by any third party. Rules 17–20 of the Rules EPL Certificate provide a procedure for review of the decision of the Registrar to enter a representative in the list of representatives before the Court.

c. *Draft Code of Conduct for representatives*

Rule 290.2 Rules of Procedure provides that representatives who appear before the Court shall strictly comply with any code of conduct adopted for such representatives by the Administrative Committee.

The Preparatory Committee has made a draft Code of Conduct for representatives (hereafter the *"Code of Conduct"*). EPLAW, EPLIT and epi have assisted the Preparatory Committee in drafting the Code of Conduct. The draft Code of Conduct was approved by the Administrative Committee of the Court on 8 February 2023.

The Code contains only four articles. This should be no surprise since all representatives are already bound by national rules of conduct and/or rules of organisations.

---

759. Rule 14(3) of the Rules EPL Certificate.
760. Rule 16(1) of the Rules EPL Certificate.
761. Rule 16(2) of the Rules EPL Certificate.
762. Rule 16(3) of the Rules EPL Certificate.

In late 2013, EPLAW first formed a working group to assist the Court in developing a Code of Conduct. This working group undertook a comparative study of existing professional laws to identify needs as well as limitations for regulations within the Code of Conduct. The study focused on (a) conflicts and protection of confidential information; (b) duties to the Court; (c) experts and witnesses; and (d) miscellaneous (including contingency fees and record keeping). While it was strongly felt that harmonisation would be desirable for all topics, in particular (a) and (d) were found to be subject to numerous national rules, such that they could not be addressed in the Code of Conduct without the risk of creating conflicting laws. In contrast, (b) and (c) were considered to be able to be covered by the Code of Conduct without such risks.

In late 2014, EPLAW and EPLIT joined forces to develop a joint proposal for the Code of Conduct. In 2015, epi joined the preparations.

The starting point for this draft was the existing codes of conduct developed by the Council of Bars and Law Societies of Europe (CCBE) and epi. These were supplemented wherever differing national laws or traditions appeared to make clear rules desirable.

A point to note in the preamble of the Code of Conduct was Rule 291.1 Rules of Procedure regarding the exclusion of representatives from the proceedings. As presently drafted, this Rule would seem to compromise the position of both the client and his representative in ongoing litigation. The Code of Conduct points out that until any possible future joint disciplinary body is founded, a mechanism for referring such a matter to a relevant body for the respective national lawyers or the epi would seem more appropriate.

The articles of the Code of Conduct concern the field of application (Article 1), general conduct (Article 2), dealings with witnesses and party experts (Article 3) and a change of representation (Article 4).

The Code of Conduct shall apply to representatives as defined in Article 48(1) and (2) UPCA and to all activities of such representatives related to proceedings before the Court. Article 1 of the Code of Conduct makes it clear that representatives may at the same time be subject to other professional and commercial codes and laws. A note accompanying this article makes it clear that the reference to national professional laws is intended to remind practitioners that they may be subject to national, regional (e.g. epi or CCBE) or other codes of conduct in addition to this Code of Conduct. Also, for legal reasons, the scope of the Code of Conduct has to be limited to the scope required by the Rules of Procedure, i.e. in particular the relationship between the Court and representatives, and cannot contradict binding national law.

To avoid any doubt, in case of conflict between the Code of Conduct and the Rules of Procedure, the latter prevail.[763]

Article 2(1) of the Code of Conduct provides that in all dealings with the Court and its employees, a representative shall act respectfully and courteously and – based on sufficient education on the law and Rules governing the Court and proceedings before the Court – competently, and shall do everything possible to uphold the good reputation of his respective professional association. An accompanying note makes it clear that while the term *"competently"* is not and cannot be intended to impose

---

763. Article 1 Code of Conduct.

any formal requirement for continuing professional education, it seems important for enabling the Court to reach the objective of ensuring decisions of the highest quality that representatives inform themselves sufficiently about the new system and applicable law to prepare their cases correspondingly.

Article 2(2) of the Code of Conduct provides as a general rule that a representative must always have due regard for the fair conduct of proceedings. He shall exercise his rights in good faith and shall not abuse the Court process. He shall be reasonably accommodating and flexible regarding scheduling and routine matters.

Article 2(3) of the Code of Conduct provides that save to the extent necessary for ex parte procedures, no representative shall contact a judge about a specific case without the participation or prior consent of the representative of every other party to those proceedings. This rule is in line with most national codes of conduct for attorneys-at-law.

A representative shall act as an independent counsellor by serving the interests of his clients in an unbiased manner without regard to his personal feelings or interests.[764] A representative is responsible for taking appropriate steps to ensure the appropriate demeanour in Court of anyone accompanying him. For the purpose of this Article *"accompanying"* means attending in person or otherwise, such as by telephone or video link. *"In Court"* includes interim conferences, telephone conferences, video conferences or anything where there is an official communication between the representative and Court. *"Anyone"* includes inter alia clients and patent attorneys assisting the lawyers.

A representative shall be obliged not to misrepresent cases or facts before the Court either knowingly or with good reason to know or where the inaccuracy could reasonably have been discovered. If a representative becomes aware that he has inadvertently misled the Court, or that a witness has given evidence which is not true, the representative shall seek the client's consent to inform the Court as appropriate and in the absence of consent shall cease to represent the client. This addresses the situation where non-witness evidence is provided to the Court by the representative in good faith which turns out to be misleading later on, or where witness evidence turns out to be incorrect. An accompanying note makes it clear that the intention is not to introduce a US-style inequitable conduct doctrine.

A representative shall not disclose any document that is subject to privilege without the consent of the client. Privileged *"without prejudice"* inter partes correspondence shall not be submitted in the absence of a waiver of the privilege on both sides.[765] This is to emphasise that only a client can waive privilege and that privileged *"without prejudice"* inter partes correspondence shall not be submitted in absence of a waiver of the privilege on both sides.

Article 3 of the Code of Conduct provides rules regarding dealings with witnesses and party experts. A representative shall ensure that witnesses are at all times fully informed about their obligation to tell the truth and of their liability under applicable national law in the event of any breach of this obligation. Equally, a representative shall ensure that party experts are fully informed about their

---

764. Article 2(4) Code of Conduct.
765. Article 2(6) Code of Conduct.

obligation to assist the court impartially, being independent and objective and not advocating for any party.[766]

A representative may contact witnesses and party experts out of court in the context of a specific pending case in which they are involved, to verify the eligibility for their respective roles, to explain their roles, and to assist with the preparation of their evidence. A representative must do everything to ensure that the substance of the evidence of a witness or party expert solely reflects the witness's or expert's respective recollection or opinion.[767]

If required, the representative may arrange for reasonable compensation for the work of witnesses and party experts. The representative must upon request of the Court or upon reasonable request of a party inform the Court about the extent of that compensation.[768] While the Court has discretion to give or withhold grounds for such a request, any party should give reasons for their request to avoid unnecessary disclosure or related obligations. Whether such request is reasonable is up to the Court. Party experts are included alongside fact witnesses as their role under the Rules of Procedure is to provide for independent evidence. As part of a *"reasonable compensation"*, appropriate accommodation, travel costs, etc. for preparatory purposes should be allowable.

In the event of a change of representation (see Rule 293 Rules of Procedure), the former representative shall, unless the circumstances dictate otherwise, be responsible for effecting notification of the change to the Registry without undue delay.[769]

D. LANGUAGE OF THE PROCEEDINGS

1. Court of First Instance

a. *Local divisions*

The language of proceedings before any local division shall be an official European Union language which is the official language or one of the official languages of the Contracting Member State hosting the relevant division.[770] Additionally, Contracting Member States may designate one or more of the official languages of the EPO as the language of proceedings of their local division.[771] This means that a Contracting Member State hosting a local division may choose one or more of its official languages as languages of the proceedings of the local division. Besides that, the Contracting Member State may add to its chosen languages French, German and/or English (if this is not already an official language of the Contracting Member State).[772]

The language possibilities become clear with the example of Belgium. Belgium has three official languages, i.e. French, Dutch and German. Belgium has appointed

---

766. Article 3(1) Code of Conduct.
767. Article 3(2) Code of Conduct.
768. Article 3(3) Code of Conduct.
769. Article 4 Code of Conduct.
770. Article 49(1) UPCA.
771. Article 49(2) UPCA.
772. Article 14(1) EPC.

all these languages as official languages of its local division of the Court in Brussels. Theoretically, Belgium could have chosen only one or two of its official languages for the local division. Two of the official languages of Belgium are EPO languages (French and German). Belgium had the possibility to add English (the third official language of the EPO) as a language of proceedings for its local division, which it has done. Ultimately, Belgium will have four possible official languages (French, Dutch, German and English) for the proceedings at its local division.

The Registrar shall maintain a list of languages communicated by Contracting Member States pursuant to Article 49(1) and (2) UPCA as well as designations by Contracting Member States made pursuant to Rule 14.2(b) (designations that proceedings should be conducted in the official language of the region in which the defendant has his domicile or principal place of business) and Rule 14.2(c) (the indication that judges may use the official language of the Member State for oral proceedings and/or to deliver orders or decisions) (see further Part Three, Chapter VIII G). This list is available online on the website of the Court.

At the date of publication, the following languages were mentioned for the different local divisions:

Local divisions	*Languages*
Vienna (Austria)	German, English
Brussels (Belgium)	Dutch, French, German, English*
Copenhagen (Denmark)	Danish, English
Helsinki (Finland)	Finnish, Swedish, English
Paris (France)	French, English*
Düsseldorf (Germany)	German, English*
Hamburg (Germany)	German, English*
Mannheim (Germany)	German, English*
Munich (Germany)	German, English*
Milan (Italy)	Italian, English*
The Hague (the Netherlands)	Dutch, English
Lisbon (Portugal)	Portuguese, English
Ljubljana (Slovenia)	Slovenian, English

* with indication as to Rule 14.2(c) Rules of Procedure regarding the use of the official language(s) as to Rule 14.1(a) Rules of Procedure and/or the delivery of any order and any decision in the official language(s) as to Rule 14.1(a) RoP.

The Registrar shall return any pleading lodged in a language other than the language of proceedings.[773]

---

773. Rule 14.4 Rules of Procedure.

b. Regional divisions

The language of proceedings before any regional division shall be an official European Union language which is the official language or one of the official languages of the Contracting Member State hosting the division or the official language(s) designated by the Contracting Member States sharing a regional division.[774] Additionally, Contracting Member States may designate one or more of the official languages of the EPO as the language of proceedings of their regional division.[775]

Contracting Member States which join forces in a regional division can either choose to have the official language(s) of the Member State in which the regional division has its seat, or designate one or more official language(s) of the EPO. This means that in case four Contracting Member States having four different languages wish to establish a regional division with its seat in one of the four Contracting Member States, theoretically they could choose to have only one official language of one of the Contracting Member States sharing a division as an official language. They could also choose to appoint all national languages of the four Contracting Member States. Another option is to add one or more official languages of the EPO, such as German and English, to their national languages. Article 49 UPCA makes it possible for a regional division to designate an official EU language which is not one of the official languages of the Contracting Member States sharing a regional division. This is the choice the Nordic Baltic regional division has made. The Contracting Member States sharing that regional division (i.e. Estonia, Latvia, Lithuania and Sweden) have chosen to only appoint English as the official language of proceedings before the Nordic Baltic regional division, excluding all the official national languages of the Contracting Member States.

c. Central division

The language of proceedings at the central division shall be the language in which the patent concerned was granted.[776] Since the EPO only has three official languages which can be used to grant a European or Unitary Patent, proceedings before the central division shall always be in English, French or German.

The central division shall until 26 June 2024 have two locations (Paris and London) and as of 26 June 2024 three locations (with Milan as third location). But the place of the seat or section of the central division shall not affect the language regime of the proceedings, meaning that if the language of proceedings of a pharmaceutical patent was German, the Milan section of the central division shall have to perform the proceedings in German.

---

774. Article 49(1) UPCA.
775. Article 49(2) UPCA.
776. Article 49(6) UPCA.

d. General exception: use of the language in which the patent was granted

For proceedings before the local and regional divisions, there are three possible situations in which the language of proceedings can be switched to the language in which the patent was granted.

First, the parties may always agree on the use of the language in which the patent was granted as the language of proceedings, subject to approval by the competent panel.[777] If the panel does not approve their choice, the parties may request that the case be referred to the central division.[778] In case of agreement between the parties to use the language of the patent, any party may at any time during the written procedure lodge an *"Application by both parties"* to use the language in which the patent was granted as language of the proceedings. The procedure for an application by both parties to use the language in which the patent was granted is described in Rule 321 Rules of Procedure (see Part Three, Chapter VIII G.1).

Secondly, the competent panel itself may, on grounds of convenience and fairness, also decide on the use of the language in which the patent was granted as the language of proceedings, as long as all parties agree.[779] At any time during the written procedure and the interim procedure, the Judge-Rapporteur may, of his own motion or on a request by a party, after consulting the panel, propose to the parties that the language of the proceedings be changed to the language in which the patent was granted. If the parties and panel agree, the language of the proceedings shall be changed.[780]

Thirdly, Article 49(5) UPCA deals with the hypothesis that one of the parties requests to use the language in which the patent was granted as the language of the proceedings, but the other party does not agree. If a party wishes to use the language in which the patent was granted as the language of the proceedings the party shall include such Application in the Statement of claim, in the case of a claimant, or in the Statement of defence, in the case of a defendant. The Judge-Rapporteur shall forward the Application to the President of the Court of First Instance, who has to finally decide.[781] The President of the Court of First Instance shall invite the other party to indicate, within ten days, its position on the use of the language in which the patent was granted as language of the proceedings.[782] The President, having consulted the panel of the division, may order that the language in which the patent was granted shall be the language of the proceedings and may make the order conditional on specific translation or interpretation arrangements.[783] See further regarding the change of the language in the comments regarding Rules 321–324 (see Part Three, Chapter VIII G.1).

---

777. Article 49(3) UPCA.
778. Article 49(3) UPCA.
779. Article 49(4) UPCA.
780. Rule 322 Rules of Procedure.
781. Rule 323.1 Rules of Procedure.
782. Rule 323.2 Rules of Procedure.
783. Rule 323.3 Rules of Procedure.

2. Court of Appeal

In principle, the language of proceedings before the Court of Appeal shall be the language of proceedings as used before the Court of First Instance.[784]

However, the parties may also agree on the use of the language in which the patent was granted as the language of proceedings.[785] Even if in the first instance proceedings parties did not use the language in which the patent was granted, parties can still agree to do this at appeal level. Therefore, Rule 227 Rules of Procedure provides that the Statement of appeal and the Statement of grounds of appeal need to be drawn up:

(a) in the language of the proceedings before the Court of First Instance; or
(b) where the parties have agreed to use the language in which the patent was granted, in the language in which the patent was granted.

Where the parties have agreed to use the language in which the patent was granted, evidence of the respondent's agreement needs to be lodged by the appellant together with the Statement of appeal.

In exceptional cases and to the extent deemed appropriate, the Court of Appeal may decide on another official language of a Contracting Member State as the language of proceedings for the whole or part of the proceedings, subject to agreement by the parties.[786] Here again, we notice the flexibility of the UPCA with respect to the language of the proceedings.

If the language of the proceedings before the Court of Appeal is not the language of the proceedings before the Court of First Instance, the Judge-Rapporteur may order the appellant to lodge, within a time period to be specified, translations into the language of the proceedings before the Court of Appeal of:[787]

(a) written pleadings and other documents lodged by the parties before the Court of First Instance, as specified by the Judge-Rapporteur; and
(b) decisions or orders of the Court of First Instance.

The Judge-Rapporteur shall at the same time inform the appellant that if the appellant fails to lodge the translations within the time period specified, a decision by default may be given in accordance with Rule 357 Rules of Procedure. Should the appellant fail to lodge the translations within the period specified, the Judge-Rapporteur shall reject the appeal by a decision by default in accordance with Rule 357. He may give the appellant an opportunity to be heard beforehand.[788]

The appellant may request that documented costs of translations be taken into account when the Court fixes the amount of costs.[789]

---

784. Article 50(1) UPCA.
785. Article 50(2) UPCA.
786. Article 50(3) UPCA.
787. Rule 232.1 Rules of Procedure.
788. Rule 232.2 Rules of Procedure.
789. Rule 232.3 Rules of Procedure.

3. Translation and interpretation arrangements

Regarding translations, it should be remembered that Article 4(1) Translation Regulation provides that in the case of a dispute relating to a Unitary Patent, the patent proprietor shall provide at the request and the choice of an alleged infringer, a full translation of the Unitary Patent into an official language of the Participating Member State in which either the alleged infringement took place or in which the alleged infringer is domiciled.

Article 4(2) Translation Regulation provides that in the course of legal proceedings, a "*court competent in the territories of the participating Member States for disputes concerning European patents with unitary effect*" (= the Unified Patent Court) can request a full translation of the patent into the language of the proceedings of that court. Therefore, the Court can at all times oblige the patent proprietor to translate its Unitary Patent in the language of the proceedings.

On the other hand, any panel of the Court of First Instance and the Court of Appeal may, to the extent deemed appropriate, dispense with translation requirements.[790] If, for example, documents regarding the infringement are drafted in English, while the official language of the proceedings is French, the Court can decide to relieve the parties from translating.

At the request of one of the parties, and to the extent deemed appropriate, any division of the Court of First Instance and the Court of Appeal shall provide interpretation facilities to assist the parties concerned at oral proceedings.[791]

Since the proceedings before the central division can only be held in French, German or English, the UPCA provides special protection mechanisms for infringement actions dealt with by the central division. In cases where an action for infringement is brought before the central division, a defendant having its residence, principal place of business or place of business in an EU Member State shall have the right to obtain, upon request, translations of relevant documents in the language of the Member State of residence, principal place of business or, in the absence of residence or principal place of business, place of business, if the following three conditions are met:[792]

- jurisdiction is entrusted to the central division in accordance with Article 33(1) third or fourth subparagraph UPCA (i.e. actions against defendants located outside the territory of the Contracting Member States or actions relating to Contracting Member States that do not have a local or regional division); and
- the language of proceedings at the central division is a language which is not an official language of the EU Member State where the defendant has its residence, principal place of business or, in the absence of residence or principal place of business, place of business; and
- the defendant does not have proper knowledge of the language of the proceedings.

---

790. Article 51(1) UPCA.
791. Article 51(2) UPCA.
792. Article 51(3) UPCA.

E. PROCEEDINGS BEFORE THE COURT

1. Written, interim and oral procedure

The proceedings before the Court shall consist of a written, an interim and an oral procedure, in accordance with the Rules of Procedure. For further details on these stages of the procedure, please refer to Part Three, Chapter IV B, C and D.

Article 52(1) UPCA provides that all procedures shall be organised in a flexible and balanced manner.

The interim procedure is intended to explore settlement possibilities for the dispute. The interim procedure takes place after the written procedure. If appropriate, the Judge-Rapporteur, subject to a mandate of the full panel, shall be responsible for convening an interim hearing. That judge shall in particular explore with the parties the possibility for a settlement, including through mediation and/or arbitration by using the facilities of the Patent Mediation and Arbitration Centre.[793]

The oral procedure shall give parties the opportunity to explain their arguments properly. But the Court may, with the agreement of the parties, dispense with the oral hearing.[794] Given the broad tradition in several Contracting Member States to make use of the oral pleadings, it can be expected that this possibility to dispense with the oral hearing shall not lead to a systematic written procedure.

2. Means of evidence and burden of proof

Article 53 UPCA lists the means of giving or obtaining evidence that can be used in proceedings before the Court:

- hearing the parties;
- requests for information;
- production of documents;
- hearing witnesses;
- opinions by experts;
- inspection;
- comparative tests or experiments;
- sworn statements in writing (affidavits).

Rule 170 Rules of Procedure covers the means of evidence in more detail and adds the possible orders of the Court to obtain evidence. Rule 170 Rules of Procedure provides that in proceedings before the Court, the means of evidence shall in particular include the following:

(a) written evidence, whether printed, hand-written or drawn, in particular documents, written witness statements, plans, drawings, photographs;
(b) expert reports and reports on experiments carried out for the purpose of the proceedings;

---

793. Article 52(1) UPCA.
794. Article 52(3) UPCA.

(c) physical objects, in particular devices, products, embodiments, exhibits, models;
(d) electronic files and audio/video recordings.

Means of obtaining evidence shall include in particular the following:

(a) hearing of the parties;
(b) requests for information;
(c) production of documents;
(d) summoning, hearing and questioning of witnesses;
(e) appointing, receiving opinions from, summoning and hearing and questioning of experts;
(f) ordering inspection of a place or a physical object;
(g) conducting comparative tests and experiments;
(h) sworn statements in writing (written witness statements).

Rule 170.3 Rules of Procedure provides that means of obtaining evidence shall further include:

(a) ordering a party or a third party to produce evidence;
(b) ordering measures to preserve evidence.

Rules 170–201 Rules of Procedure govern the procedures and rules regarding evidence (see Part Three, Chapter V).

Questioning of witnesses and experts shall be under the control of the Court and be limited to what is necessary.[795] It was clearly the intention of the Contracting Member States to limit the use of oral questioning.

The burden of the proof of facts shall be on the party relying on those facts.[796]

Article 55 UPCA instals an important reversal of the burden of proof regarding the relationship between process patents and products. If the subject matter of a patent is a process for obtaining a new product, the identical product when produced without the consent of the patent proprietor shall, in the absence of proof to the contrary, be deemed to have been obtained by the patented process.

The reversal of the burden of proof shall also apply where there is a substantial likelihood that the identical product was made by the patented process and the patent proprietor has been unable, despite reasonable efforts, to determine the process actually used for such identical product.[797]

The presumption can be refuted by the alleged infringing party. But in the adduction of proof to the contrary, the legitimate interests of the defendant in protecting its manufacturing and trade secrets shall be taken into account.[798]

---

795. Article 52(2) UPCA.
796. Article 54 UPCA.
797. Article 55(2) UPCA.
798. Article 55 UPCA.

F. POWERS OF THE COURT

1. General powers

As a general principle, Article 56 UPCA provides that the Court may impose such measures, procedures and remedies as are laid down in the UPCA and may make its orders subject to conditions, in accordance with the Rules of Procedure.

The Court shall take due account of the interest of the parties and shall, before making an order, give any party the opportunity to be heard, unless this is incompatible with the effective enforcement of such order.[799] Measures for preserving evidence, as mentioned in Article 7 of Directive 2004/48 of 29 April 2004 on the enforcement of intellectual property rights (hereinafter the *"Enforcement Directive"*) and referred to in Article 60 UPCA, are an example of an order to which hearing the parties in most cases is incompatible with the enforcement of the order.

All other Articles of Chapter IV of the UPCA concern possible orders of the Court. Hereinafter, we have tried to list the orders in a way we feel meets the chronology of a patent case. Titles 2-8 concern orders which could help the Court in gathering evidence and deciding on the merits. The orders treated under titles 9-14 concern the consequences of a decision on the merits by the Court.

In order to help judges, the website of the Court has published a number of template documents and guidance which can be used for specific actions or orders. It concerns, among other things, template documents and guidance for a decision in an action for infringement with counterclaim for revocation, a decision in an action for a declaration of non-infringement, a decision allowing a Preliminary Objection, an order rejecting a Preliminary Objection, order on application of Article 33(3) UPCA, an order convening the interim conference, summons of the parties and party experts to the oral hearing, summons of a court expert, summons of witnesses to the oral hearing, an order for provisional measures, an order to inspect premises and to preserve evidence, an order to communicate information, and an order to freeze assets.

2. Order to preserve evidence and to inspect premises

Article 60 UPCA is very similar to Article 7 of the Enforcement Directive. Paragraphs 1, 2, 5, 6, 7, 8 and 9 of Article 60 are a quasi-identical rewrite of paragraphs 1-4 of Article 7 of the Enforcement Directive.

Measures to preserve evidence and inspection of premises can be ordered before the commencement of proceedings on the merits.[800]

At the request of an applicant who has presented reasonably available evidence to support the claim that the patent has been infringed or is about to be infringed, the Court may order prompt and effective provisional measures to preserve relevant evidence in respect of the alleged infringement, subject to the protection of confidential information.[801]

---

799. Article 56(2) UPCA.
800. Article 56(1) and (3) UPCA.
801. Article 60(1) UPCA.

Chapter VII – Organisation of Proceedings

Such measures may include a detailed description, with or without the taking of samples, or the physical seizure of the infringing products, and, in appropriate cases, the materials and implements used in the production and/or distribution of those products and the documents relating thereto.[802]

Furthermore, the Court may at the request of the applicant who has presented evidence to support the claim that the patent has been infringed or is about to be infringed, order the inspection of premises. Such inspection of premises shall be conducted by a person appointed by the Court in accordance with Rule 196.4 and 196.5 Rules of Procedure.[803] At the inspection of the premises the applicant himself shall not be present but may be represented by an independent professional practitioner whose name has to be specified in the Court's order.[804]

Although inspection of the premises is not included in the Enforcement Directive, it belongs in most Member States to the core of orders preserving evidence.

Measures shall be ordered, if necessary without the other party having been heard, in particular where any delay is likely to cause irreparable harm to the proprietor of the patent, or where there is a demonstrable risk of evidence being destroyed.[805]

The procedure to obtain an order to preserve evidence is set out in Rules 192-198 Rules of Procedure (see Part Three, Chapter V D). It is important to note that Rule 196.4 Rules of Procedure provides that the order to preserve evidence shall specify a person who shall carry out the measures and present a written Report on the measures to preserve evidence, all in accordance with the national law of the place where the measures are executed, to the Court within a time period to be specified. Therefore, the national law of the place where the measures are executed shall remain very important for orders to preserve evidence. In case of conflict regarding the execution of the order to preserve evidence, the Court shall apply the national law of the place where the order was executed.

Where measures to preserve evidence or inspect premises are ordered without the other party in the case having been heard, the parties affected shall be given notice, without delay and at the latest immediately after the execution of the measures. A review, including a right to be heard, shall take place upon request of the parties affected with a view to deciding, within a reasonable period after the notification of the measures, whether the measures are to be modified, revoked or confirmed.[806] The procedure for a review of the order to preserve evidence is laid down in Rule 197 Rules of Procedure.

The measures to preserve evidence may be subject to the lodging by the applicant of adequate security or an equivalent assurance intended to ensure compensation for any prejudice suffered by the defendant.[807]

The Court shall ensure that the measures to preserve evidence are revoked or otherwise cease to have effect, at the defendant's request, without prejudice to the damages which may be claimed, if the applicant does not bring, within a period

---

802. Article 60(2) UPCA.
803. Article 60(3) UPCA.
804. Article 60(4) UPCA; Rule 196.3 Rules of Procedure.
805. Article 60(5) UPCA.
806. Article 60(6) UPCA.
807. Article 60(7) UPCA.

not exceeding 31 calendar days or 20 working days, whichever is the longer, action leading to a decision on the merits of the case before the Court.[808]

Where the measures to preserve evidence are revoked, or where they lapse due to any act or omission by the applicant, or where it is subsequently found that there has been no infringement or threat of infringement of the patent, the Court may order the applicant, at the defendant's request, to provide the defendant with appropriate compensation for any damage suffered as a result of those measures.[809]

3. Freezing orders

At the request of an applicant who has presented reasonably available evidence to support the claim that the patent has been infringed or is about to be infringed, the Court may, even before the commencement of proceedings on the merits of the case, order a party not to remove from its jurisdiction any assets located therein, or not to deal in any assets, whether located within its jurisdiction or not.[810]

Article 60(5)-(9) UPCA regarding the measures preserving evidence by analogy and Rules 192–198 Rules of Procedure *mutatis mutandis*, shall apply to freezing orders. This means amongst other things that, also for freezing orders, the applicant needs to bring an action leading to a decision on the merits, within 31 calendar days or 20 working days, whichever is the longer, to uphold the freezing order, and if the freezing order is revoked, the applicant shall provide appropriate compensation for any damage suffered from the freezing order. The defendant has a right to review.

To protect the trade secrets, personal data or other confidential information of a party to the proceedings or of a third party, or to prevent an abuse of evidence, the Court may order that the collection and use of evidence in proceedings before it be restricted or prohibited or that access to such evidence be restricted to specific persons.[811] This shall be particularly important with respect to measures for preserving evidence and inspection of premises.

Rule 190.1 Rules of Procedure regarding an order to produce evidence and Rule 196.1 Rules of Procedure regarding an order to preserve evidence both provide that for the protection of confidential information the Court may order that the evidence be disclosed to certain named persons only and be subject to appropriate terms of non-disclosure.

4. Provisional and protective measures

To stop alleged infringers and prevent the increase of damages for the patent proprietor, the Court can order provisional and protective measures. Article 62 UPCA regarding such measures is similar to Article 9 of the Enforcement Directive.

The Court may, by way of order, grant injunctions against an alleged infringer or against an intermediary whose services are used by the alleged infringer, intended to prevent any imminent infringement, to prohibit, on a provisional basis and subject,

---

808. Article 60(8) UPCA and Rule 198.1 Rules of Procedure.
809. Article 60(9) UPCA and Rule 198.2 Rules of Procedure.
810. Article 61(1) UPCA and Rule 200.1 Rules of Procedure.
811. Article 58 UPCA.

where appropriate, to a recurring penalty payment, the continuation of the alleged infringement or to make such continuation subject to the lodging of guarantees intended to ensure the compensation of the rightholder.[812] This section of Article 62 is quasi-identical to Article 9(1) of the Enforcement Directive.

Before ordering such provisional and protective measures, the Court shall weigh up the interests of all parties. The Court shall have the discretion to weigh up the interests of the parties and in particular to take into account the potential harm to either of the parties resulting from the granting or the refusal of the injunction.[813] The weighing up of interest was not mentioned in the Enforcement Directive, but is a condition for provisional or protective measures applied in a number of Contracting Member States.[814] Article 62(2) UPCA only mentions the weighing up of the interests of the *"parties"*. In life sciences disputes, certain Contracting Member States also take into account the general interest (e.g. public health). Neither the UPCA nor the Rules of Procedure provide that the Court has to take into account the general interest.

The Court may also order the seizure or delivery up of products suspected of infringing a patent so as to prevent their entry into, or movement within the channels of commerce. If the applicant demonstrates circumstances likely to endanger the recovery of damages, the Court may order the precautionary seizure of the movable and immovable property of the alleged infringer, including blocking of the bank accounts and of other assets of the alleged infringer.[815]

For injunctions to prevent the continuation of the infringement and seizures, the Court may require the applicant to provide any reasonable evidence in order to satisfy itself with a sufficient degree of certainty that the applicant is the right-holder and that the applicant's right is being infringed, or that such infringement is imminent.[816]

Rule 211 Rules of Procedure summarises the different possibilities for the Court to order the provisional measures as following:

- injunctions against a defendant;
- the seizure or delivery up of the goods suspected of infringing a patent right so as to prevent their entry into or movement within the channels of commerce;
- if an applicant demonstrates circumstances likely to endanger the recovery of damages, a precautionary seizure of the movable and immovable property of the defendant, including the blocking of his bank accounts and other assets;
- an interim award of costs.

Just as for orders to preserve evidence and freezing orders, Article 60(5)-(9) UPCA regarding the measures preserving evidence shall apply by analogy to provisional and protective measures.[817] Rule 197.3 and 4 Rules of Procedure shall apply *mutatis mutandis*.

---

812. Article 62(1) UPCA.
813. Article 62(2) UPCA.
814. E.g. in Belgium Article 1369bis/1, §5 of the Procedural Code provides a weighing up of interests, including the general interest.
815. Article 62(3) UPCA.
816. Article 62(4) UPCA.
817. Article 62(5) UPCA.

5. Order to produce evidence

At the request of a party which has presented reasonably available evidence sufficient to support its claims and has, in substantiating those claims, specified evidence which lies in the control of the opposing party or a third party, the Court may order the opposing party or a third party to present such evidence, subject to the protection of confidential information. Such order shall not result in an obligation of self-incrimination.[818]

At the request of a party the Court may order, under the same conditions, the communication of banking, financial or commercial documents under the control of the opposing party, subject to the protection of confidential information.[819]

The order to produce evidence is intended to deal with the situation where one party sufficiently demonstrates that the counterparty possesses evidence which is not submitted. The Court has the power to order the production of such evidence.

The procedure for an order to produce evidence is described in Rule 190 Rules of Procedure (see Part Three, Chapter V C.1).

6. Court experts

The Court may at any time appoint court experts in order to provide expertise for specific aspects of the case.[820] This of course does not affect the right of the parties to produce its own expert evidence. It is common in patent cases that parties make use of expert opinions, such as opinions of patent attorneys, professors or researchers. When parties provide expert opinions that come to different conclusions, courts generally appoint a court expert.

The Court shall provide the court expert with all information necessary for the provision of the expert advice. An indicative list of experts shall be drawn up by the Court.[821] The indicative list shall be kept by the Registrar.[822] The UPCA does not provide any obligation for the Court to appoint an expert from the list of experts. Furthermore, neither the UPCA nor the Statute contain requirements for court experts. This means that the Court has a very broad discretion to appoint experts. The only limit seems to be any possible conflict of interest. Rule 185 Rules of Procedure governs the procedure for an appointment of a court expert (see Part Three, Chapter V.B). Rule 185.3 Rules of Procedure provides that the court expert shall possess the expertise, independence and impartiality required for being appointed as court expert. The parties shall be entitled to be heard on the expertise, independence and impartiality of the court expert.

The court experts shall guarantee independence and impartiality. The rules governing conflicts of interest applicable to judges set out in Article 7 of the Statute

---

818. Article 59(1) UPCA.
819. Article 59(2) UPCA.
820. Article 57(1) UPCA.
821. Rule 185.9 Rules of Procedure.
822. Article 57(2) UPCA.

shall by analogy apply to court experts.⁸²³ Therefore, court experts may not take part in the proceedings of a case in which they:

- have taken part as adviser;
- have been a party or have acted for one of the parties;
- have been called upon to pronounce as a member of a court, tribunal, board of appeal, arbitration or mediation panel, a commission of inquiry or in any other capacity;
- have a personal or financial interest in the case or in relation to one of the parties; or
- are related to one of the parties or the representatives of the parties by family ties.

Any party to an action may object to a court expert taking part in the proceedings on any of the listed grounds or where the court expert is suspected, with good reason, of partiality.[824]

It is not clear whether Article 7(3) of the Statute can be applied by analogy to court experts. Article 7(3) provides that when a judge considers that he should not take part in the judgment or examination of a particular case, he informs the President of the Court of First Instance (or in appeal cases the President of the Court of Appeal). In our opinion, the intervention of the President of the Court of First Instance is not necessary for court experts who consider themselves affected by a conflict of interest. Furthermore, a possible intervention of the President of the Court of First Instance (situated in Paris) risks affecting the efficiency of the proceedings.

Expert advice given to the Court by court experts shall be made available to the parties which shall have the possibility to comment on it.[825]

The UPCA does not contain any limitations regarding the mission of the court experts. Generally under national laws court experts are only authorised to comment on technical issues, and are not authorised to comment on points of law. The UPCA lacks any provisions regarding this aspect. Rule 186.3 Rules of Procedure provides that the court expert shall give expert advice only on questions which have been put to him. Rule 186.7 Rules of Procedure adds that the court expert has an overriding duty to assist the Court impartially on matters relevant to his area of expertise. He is to be independent and objective, and shall not act as an advocate for any party to the proceedings.

7. Power to order the communication of information

The Court may, in response to a justified and proportionate request of the applicant and in accordance with Rule 191 Rules of Procedure, order an infringer to inform the applicant of:

- the origin and distribution channels of the infringing products or processes;

---

823. Article 57(3) UPCA.
824. Article 5(4) Statute.
825. Article 57(4) UPCA.

- the quantities produced, manufactured, delivered, received or ordered, as well as the price obtained for the infringing products; and
- the identity of any third person involved in the production or distribution of the infringing products or in the use of the infringing process.[826]

The Court may also order any third party who:

(a) was found in the possession of the infringing products on a commercial scale or to be using an infringing process on a commercial scale;
(b) was found to be providing on a commercial scale services used in infringing activities; or
(c) was indicated by the person referred to in (a) or (b) as being involved in the production, manufacture or distribution of the infringing products or processes or in the provision of the services,

to provide the applicant with the aforementioned information.[827]

A previous version of Article 67[828] provided that the communication of information could be ordered against an *"alleged infringer"*. This opened up the possibility of ordering the communication of such information before the infringement was established. The current Article is clear that this order can only be granted once the infringement question has been answered by the Court.

The communication of this information gives the patent proprietor the opportunity to pursue not only the known infringer, but also the manufacturer, distributor, seller, service provider or any other third party involved in the infringement and/or infringing the patent.

8. Permanent injunctions in case of infringement

Where a decision is taken finding an infringement of a patent, the Court may grant an injunction against the infringer aimed at prohibiting the continuation of the infringement. The Court may also grant such an injunction against an intermediary whose services are being used by a third party to infringe a patent.[829] Article 63 UPCA is aligned with Article 11 of the Enforcement Directive.

Article 11 of the Enforcement Directive provides that non-compliance with an injunction shall, where appropriate, be subject to a recurring penalty payment, with a view to ensuring compliance. Normally penalty payments are to be paid by the infringing party to the plaintiff. However, Article 63 UPCA stipulates that, where appropriate, non-compliance with the injunction shall be subject to a periodic penalty payment that is payable to the Court.

Article 82(4) UPCA repeats that if a party does not comply with the terms of an order of the Court, that party may be sanctioned with a periodic penalty payment

---

826. Article 67(1) UPCA.
827. Article 67(2) UPCA.
828. Council working document 14268/12 of 27 September 2012, Draft UPCA on a Unified Patent Court and draft Statute – consolidated text", Article 39.
829. Article 63(1) UPCA.

which is payable to the Court, but stipulates that the penalty payment is *"without prejudice to the party's right to claim damages or security"*.[830]

Rule 354.3 Rules of Procedure provides that the Court's decisions and orders may provide for periodic penalty payments payable to the Court in the event that a party fails to comply with the terms of the order or an earlier order. The value of such payments shall be set by the Court having regard to the importance of the order in question.

If it is alleged that a party has failed to comply with the terms of the order of the Court, the first instance panel of the division in question may decide on penalty payments provided for in the order upon the request of the other party or of its own motion.[831] The procedure foreseen in Rule 264 shall apply. After having heard both parties (in accordance with Rule 264 Rules of Procedure), the Court may make an appropriate order which may be subject to an appeal.

9. Corrective measures in infringement proceedings

Without prejudice to any damages due to the injured party by reason of the infringement, and without compensation of any sort, the Court may order, at the request of the applicant, that appropriate measures be taken with regard to products found to be infringing a patent and, in appropriate cases, with regard to materials and implements principally used in the creation or manufacture of those products.[832] Article 64(1) UPCA is quasi-identical to Article 10(1) of the Enforcement Directive. But the measures enumerated by Article 64(2) are broader than the measures listed in Article 10(2) of the Enforcement Directive. Article 10(2) of the Enforcement Directive merely provides recall from the channels of commerce, definitive removal from the channels of commerce or destruction.

Corrective measures that can be ordered by the Court are the following:

- a declaration of infringement;
- recalling the products from the channels of commerce;
- depriving the product of its infringing property;
- definitively removing the products from the channels of commerce; or
- the destruction of the products and/or of the materials and implements concerned.[833]

Identical to Article 10(2) of the Enforcement Directive, Article 64(2) UPCA stipulates that the Court shall order that those measures be carried out at the expense of the infringer, unless particular reasons are invoked for not doing so.

In considering a request for corrective measures, the Court shall take into account the need for proportionality between the seriousness of the infringement and the remedies to be ordered, the willingness of the infringer to convert the materials into a non-infringing state, as well as the interests of third parties.[834] The willingness

---

830. Article 82(4) UPCA.
831. Rule 354.4 Rules of Procedure.
832. Article 64(1) UPCA.
833. Article 64(2) UPCA.
834. Article 64(4) UPCA.

of the infringer to convert the materials into a non-infringing state is not mentioned in Article 10(3) of the Enforcement Directive and was specifically included in the UPCA. Apparently, the Contracting Member States were of the opinion that corrective measures such as destruction and recall can be avoided if the infringing party corrects the infringement itself.

Unlike orders for protective and provisional measures, the interests of third parties are explicitly mentioned in Article 64(4) UPCA as an element that can be taken into account for ordering corrective measures.

10. Decision on the validity of a patent

The Court shall decide on the validity of a patent on the basis of an action for revocation or a counterclaim for revocation.[835]

The Court may revoke a classic European Patent or a Unitary Patent, either entirely or partly, only on the grounds referred to in Articles 138(1) and 139(2) EPC. These grounds are:

- the subject matter of the patent is not patentable under Articles 52 to 57 EPC: these Articles concern patentable inventions, exceptions to patentability, novelty, non-prejudicial disclosures, inventive step and industrial application;
- the patent does not disclose the invention in a manner sufficiently clear and complete for it to be carried out by a person skilled in the art;
- the subject matter of the patent extends beyond the content of the application as filed or, if the patent was granted on a divisional application or on a new application filed under Article 61 EPC[836] (European Patent applications filed by non-entitled persons), beyond the content of the earlier application as filed;
- the protection conferred by the patent has been extended;
- the proprietor of the European Patent is not entitled under Article 60, paragraph 1 EPC;[837]
- a national patent application and a national patent in a Contracting Member State has a prior right effect over a European Patent designating that Contracting Member State.[838]

---

835. Article 65(1) UPCA.
836. Article 61 EPC states: *"If by a final decision it is adjudged that a person other than the applicant is entitled to the grant of the European patent, that person may, in accordance with the Implementing Regulations:*
    (a) prosecute the European patent application as his own application in place of the applicant;
    (b) file a new European patent application in respect of the same invention; or
    (c) request that the European patent application be refused."
837. Article 60, §1 EPC states: *"The right to a European patent shall belong to the inventor or his successor in title. If the inventor is an employee, the right to a European patent shall be determined in accordance with the law of the State in which the employee is mainly employed; if the State in which the employee is mainly employed cannot be determined, the law to be applied shall be that of the State in which the employer has the place of business to which the employee is attached."*
838. Article 139(2) EPC.

Certain Contracting Member States have proceedings for transferring the ownership of a patent (application) in case of filings by non-entitled persons. Belgium, for example, has a specific procedure to transfer the ownership of a patent if the invention concerned was unlawfully relieved from the inventor or its successor in title or if a patent application was filed by setting aside a legal or contractual obligation.[839] An action to transfer the ownership of a patent is not included in the actions that can be brought before the Court.[840] Under the UPCA, the only possible reaction to filings by non-entitled persons is a claim for revocation of the patent.

In accordance with Article 138, §3 EPC the proprietor of a patent shall have the right to limit the patent by amending the claims in proceedings before the Court. The patent as thus limited shall form the basis for the proceedings.

If the grounds for revocation affect the patent only in part, the patent shall be limited by a corresponding amendment of the claims and revoked in part.[841]

To the extent that a patent has been revoked, it shall be deemed not to have had, from the outset, the effects specified in Articles 64 and 67 EPC.[842] Article 64 EPC stipulates that a patent confers on its proprietor from the date on which the mention of its grant is published in the European Patent Bulletin, in each Contracting Member State in respect of which it is granted, the same rights as would be conferred by a national patent granted in that State. Article 67 EPC deals with the rights conferred by a European Patent application after publication.

Where the Court, in a final decision, revokes a patent, either entirely or partly, it shall send a copy of the decision to the EPO and, with respect to a European Patent, to the national patent office of any Contracting Member State concerned.[843]

11.   Powers of the Court concerning decisions of the EPO

In actions concerning decisions of the EPO in carrying out the tasks referred to in Article 9 Unitary Patent Regulation, the Court may exercise any power entrusted to the EPO by Article 9 Unitary Patent Regulation, including the rectification of the Register for Unitary Patent Protection.[844]

The tasks of Article 9 of the Unitary Patent Regulation concern:

- the administration of requests for unitary effect by proprietors of European Patents;
- the inclusion and administration of a Register for Unitary Patent Protection within the European Patent Register;
- receiving and registering statements on licensing;
- withdrawal and licensing commitments undertaken in international standardisation bodies;
- the publication of the translations during the transitional period;

---

839. Article XI.10 of the Belgian Code of Economic Law.
840. Article 32(1) UPCA.
841. Article 65(3) UPCA.
842. Article 65(4) UPCA.
843. Article 65(5) UPCA.
844. Article 65(1) UPCA.

- the collection and administration of renewal fees for Unitary Patents;
- the collection and administration of additional fees paid in cases of late payment of renewal fees;
- the administration of a compensation scheme of translation costs for applicants filing European Patent applications in one of the official languages of the Union that is not an official language of the EPO.

Rules 85-98 Rules of Procedure govern the procedure for actions against decisions of the EPO in carrying out the aforementioned tasks (see Part Three, Chapter IV B.6). An action against a decision of the EPO shall have suspensive effect.[845]

If the EPO fails to carry out one of these specific tasks correctly, the Court can put itself in the place of the EPO and carry out the task itself or order the EPO to fulfil its task correctly. The EPO can also anticipate the outcome of an action against one of its decisions. If the EPO considers that the Application to annul or alter a decision of the Office is well founded, it shall within two months of the date of receipt of the Application:

- rectify the contested decision in accordance with the order or remedy sought by the claimant; and
- inform the Court that the decision has been rectified.

Where the Court is informed by the EPO that the contested decision has been rectified, it shall inform the claimant that the action is closed.[846]

The most common action against a decision of the EPO will be the Application to annul a decision of the EPO to reject a request for unitary effect. This action is governed by Rule 97 Rules of Procedure.

For actions against decisions of the EPO regarding Unitary Patents, the parties shall bear their own costs.[847] This is an exception to the general arrangement regarding costs, set out in Article 69 UPCA.

12. Award of damages

a. Determination of the damages

The Article on the award of damages in the UPCA is again based on the Enforcement Directive.

Article 68 UPCA is to a large extent identical to Article 13 of the Enforcement Directive. The only difference is that Article 68(2) UPCA gives clear guidance as to the aim and limits of damages. The injured party shall, to the extent possible, be placed in the position as it would have been in if no infringement had taken place. The infringer shall not benefit from the infringement and damages may not be punitive.[848] This section confirms the civil law tradition of damage determination. Both parties should be placed as far as possible in the same position as would have occurred

---

845. Rule 86 Rules of Procedure.
846. Rule 91 Rules of Procedure.
847. Article 66(2) UPCA.
848. Article 68(2) UPCA.

in the absence of an infringement. To reach that goal, the Court can take away all elements by which the infringer benefited from the infringement, but in doing so the Court cannot go any further than the theoretical position in which both parties would have been if no infringement had taken place. The common law concept of punitive damages is clearly rejected by the Contracting Member States.

Furthermore, the UPCA and the Enforcement Directive clearly distinguish between an infringer who knowingly, or with reasonable grounds to know, has infringed the patent and an infringer who did not know, or did not have reasonable grounds to know he was infringing a patent.

The Court shall, at the request of the injured party, order the infringer who knowingly, or with reasonable grounds to know, engaged in a patent infringing activity, to pay the injured party damages appropriate to the harm actually suffered by that party as a result of the infringement.[849]

When the Court sets the damages:

(a) it shall take into account all appropriate aspects, such as the negative economic consequences, including lost profits, which the injured party has suffered, any unfair profits made by the infringer and, in appropriate cases, elements other than economic factors, such as the moral prejudice caused to the injured party by the infringement; or
(b) as an alternative to (a), it may, in appropriate cases, set the damages as a lump sum on the basis of elements such as at least the amount of the royalties or fees which would have been due if the infringer had requested authorisation to use the patent in question.[850]

Where the infringer did not knowingly, or with reasonable grounds to know, engage in the infringing activity, the Court may order the recovery of profits or the payment of compensation.[851]

In order to assess whether the infringer knowingly infringed a Unitary Patent, special attention should be given to Article 4(4) Translation Regulation. This Article provides that in the case of a dispute concerning a claim for damages, the court hearing the dispute shall take into consideration that the alleged infringer (in particular where the alleged infringer is an SME, a natural person or a non-profit organisation, a university or a public research organisation) may have acted without knowing or having reasonable grounds to know that he was infringing the patent before having been provided by the patent proprietor with a full translation of the Unitary Patent into an official language of the Participating Member State in which either the alleged infringement took place or in which the alleged infringer is domiciled.

The procedure for the determination of damages and compensation is laid down in Rules 125–144 Rules of Procedure (see Part Three, Chapter IV E.1). The determination of the amount of damages ordered for the successful party may be the subject of separate proceedings.[852] Where the successful party wishes to have the amount of damages determined, it shall, no later than one year from service of

---

849. Article 68(1) UPCA.
850. Article 68(3) UPCA.
851. Article 68(4) UPCA.
852. Rule 125 Rules of Procedure.

the final decision on the merits (including any final decision on appeal) on both infringement and validity, lodge an Application for the determination of damages, which may include a request for an order to lay open books.[853] The Request to lay open books is governed by Rules 141-144 Rules of Procedure (see Part Three, Chapter IV E.2)

b.   Period of limitation

For all forms of financial compensation, the UPCA contains a period of limitation. Actions relating to all forms of financial compensation may not be brought more than five years after the date on which the applicant became aware, or had reasonable grounds to become aware, of the latest fact justifying the action.[854] The reference to *"all forms of financial compensation"* makes it clear that the period of limitation also applies to claims regarding legal costs and expenses for corrective measures.

The injured party can only go back five years for damages. The limitation to five years is meant to prevent patent proprietors from first tolerating an infringement until the lapse of the 20-year term of a patent (or longer in case of a supplementary protection certificate) and then at the end claiming damages for the full twenty years. The period of limitation encourages patent proprietors to bring action against infringement within a reasonable period of time.

13.   Recoverable legal costs

Article 69(1) UPCA provides that reasonable and proportionate legal costs and other expenses incurred by the successful party shall, as a general rule, be borne by the unsuccessful party, unless equity requires otherwise, up to a ceiling set in accordance with the Rules of Procedure.

Where a party succeeds only in part or in exceptional circumstances, the Court may order that costs be apportioned equitably or that the parties bear their own costs.[855] A party should bear any unnecessary costs it has caused the Court or another party.[856]

Although this Article is identical to Article 14 of the Enforcement Directive, the principle that the successful party pays is not implemented in all Contracting Member States in the same way. Belgium for example has a system of lump sum compensation for attorney fees and costs. The lump sum compensation principle is laid down in the Procedural Code[857] and a Royal Decree determines the actual sums that can be granted by the judge.[858] In a patent case between a Belgian telecom provider and a non-practising entity, the Court of Appeal, by order of 26 January

---

853. Rule 126 Rules of Procedure.
854. Article 72(1) UPCA.
855. Article 69(2) UPCA.
856. Article 69(3) UPCA.
857. Article 1022 of the Belgian Procedural Code.
858. Royal Decree of 26 October 2007 regarding the determination of the tariff of the procedural compensation meant in Article 1022 of the Procedural Code and the determination of the date of entry into force of the Articles 1 to 13 of the Law of 21 April 2007 regarding the

2015, referred the following question to the CJEU for a preliminary ruling: *"Do the terms 'reasonable and proportionate legal costs and other expenses' in Article 14 of the Enforcement Directive preclude the Belgian legislation which offers courts the possibility of taking into account certain well-defined features specific to the case and which provides for a system of varying flat rates in respect of costs for the assistance of a lawyer?".* On 28 July 2016 the CJEU ruled that Article 14 of Directive 2004/48 must be interpreted as not precluding national legislation which provides that the unsuccessful party is to be ordered to pay the legal costs incurred by the successful party, offers the courts responsible for making that order the possibility of taking into account features specific to the case before it, and provides for a flat-rate scheme for the reimbursement of costs for the assistance of a lawyer, subject to the condition that those rates ensure that the costs to be borne by the unsuccessful party are reasonable, which it is for the referring court to determine. However, Article 14 of that Directive precludes national legislation from providing flat-rates which, owing to the maximum amounts that it contains being too low, do not ensure that, at the very least, a significant and appropriate part of the reasonable costs incurred by the successful party are borne by the unsuccessful party.

Rules 150–157 Rules of Procedure govern the procedure for cost decisions. A cost decision may be the subject of separate proceedings following a decision on the merits and, if applicable, a decision for the determination of damages.[859] The Court may also order an interim award of costs to the successful party in the decision on the merits or in a decision for the determination of damages, subject to any conditions that the Court may decide.[860]

On 26 February 2016, the Preparatory Committee published a draft decision (for approval by the Administrative Committee) on the scale of recoverable cost ceilings (hereinafter "Decision on cost ceilings") and draft Guidelines for the determination of Court fees and the ceiling of recoverable costs of the successful party. Due to the lack of time that had passed between the draft and the final entry into force of the UPCA, the contracting parties could have decided to amend the amounts. However, in order to remain attractive, the Member States decided not to make any changes to the amounts. The Administrative Committee of the Court adopted the Decision on cost ceilings on 24 April 2023.

The Preamble to the Decision on cost ceilings stresses that the ceiling on the recoverable representation costs is only one of the safeguards against undue cost recovery, and the last one to apply when the Court makes its decision on costs. First, only reasonable and proportionate legal costs and other expenses incurred by the successful party may be recovered from the unsuccessful party. Moreover, equity may also serve as a self-standing ground for rendering the general rule inapplicable. Furthermore, in case of partial success or in exceptional circumstances, the Court may order the parties to bear their own costs, or apply a different apportionment of cost, based on equity. Unnecessary costs caused to the Court or the other party shall be borne by the party incurring them, which means that even the successful

---

recovery of fees and costs connected to legal advice by a lawyer, *Belgian Official Gazette*, 9 November 2007.
859. Rule 150.1 Rules of Procedure.
860. Rule 150.2 Rules of Procedure.

party has to reimburse costs caused that are deemed unnecessary by the Court. Only the recoverable costs established in compliance with these principles is measured against the ceilings set forth in this Decision. There is a large margin of discretion for the Court when applying the safeguarding principles before making a cost decision, and thus, the ceilings are only to be regarded as a safety net, i.e. an absolute cap on recoverable representation costs applicable in every case. The Preamble reflects the concern that the ceilings should not be viewed as the default level of recoverable costs for all cases of that value.

The scale of ceilings for recoverable costs are the following:

Value of the proceeding	*Ceiling for recoverable costs*
Up to and including EUR 250,000	Up to EUR 38,000
Up to and including EUR 500,000	Up to EUR 56,000
Up to and including EUR 1,000,000	Up to EUR 112,000
Up to and including EUR 2,000,000	Up to EUR 200,000
Up to and including EUR 4,000,000	Up to EUR 400,000
Up to and including EUR 8,000,000	Up to EUR 600,000
Up to and including EUR 16,000,000	Up to EUR 800,000
Up to and including EUR 30,000,000	Up to EUR 1,200,000
Up to and including EUR 50,000,000	Up to EUR 1,500,000
More than EUR 50,000,000	Up to EUR 2,000,000

Article 1(2) of the Decision on cost ceilings provides that the ceilings of recoverable costs shall apply to representation costs. Article 69(2) UPCA clearly provides that *"reasonable and proportionate legal costs and other expenses"* incurred by the successful party are borne by the unsuccessful party up to a ceiling, and therefore does not limit the recoverability to *"representation costs"*. Consequently, all other legal costs and expenses, even if they go beyond the amounts of the ceilings, can be recovered. Rule 152 Rules of Procedure confirms this reading, only this Rule provides that the Administrative Committee shall adopt a scale of recoverable costs which shall set ceilings for such costs by reference to the value of the dispute. Rules 153–155 Rules of Procedure dealing with compensation for costs of experts of the parties, costs of witnesses and costs of interpreters and translators do not mention any ceiling.

The ceiling shall be applied to each instance of the Court proceedings regardless of the number of parties, claims or patents concerned.[861] In case of partial success, the ceiling applicable in the case shall correspond to the proportion of success of the party seeking cost recovery.[862] It remains to be seen how the Court will determine and quantify the *"proportion of success"*. For example, if a revocation action fails but a declaration of non-infringement is granted, how will that reflect the cost ceilings?

---

861. Article 1(3) of the Decision on cost ceilings.
862. Article 1(4) of the Decision on cost ceilings.

Fifty-fifty, or a bigger portion for the non-infringing party since the final result is that the patent proprietor does not obtain anything from that party?

In limited situations, the Court may upon request by one party, having regard to the financial capability of all the parties in the light of the principle of fair access to justice, raise the ceilings:

- by up to 50% of the applicable level in the scale corresponding to a value of the proceeding up to and including EUR 1 million;
- by up to 25% of the applicable level in the scale corresponding to a value of the proceeding of more than EUR 1 million and up to and including EUR 50 million;
- up to EUR 5 million in cases with a value of the proceeding of more than EUR 50 million.[863]

As examples of such *"limited situations"* the Decision on cost ceilings names the particular complexity of the case or multiple languages used in the proceeding. However, it is clear that these examples are not exhaustive.

Upon request of one of the parties, the Court may also lower the ceiling applicable with regard to that party if, in the event that the requesting party is unsuccessful, the amount of recoverable costs of representation to be awarded to the successful party would threaten the economic existence of the requesting party, especially if the latter is a micro-enterprise, SME, non-profit organisation, university, public research organisation or natural person.[864] When deciding upon a request to lower the ceiling, the Court shall take into consideration all available information on the parties and circumstances, including, where possible, the procedural behaviour of the parties, the applicable level of the ceiling for recoverable costs in comparison with the annual turnover of both parties, the type of economic activity of both parties, as well as the impact the lowering of the ceiling would have on the other party.[865]

A request to raise or lower the ceiling shall be made as soon as possible and practicable in the proceeding. This may be with the Statement of claim by the plaintiff, or with the Statement of defence by the defendant but shall be lodged in sufficient time to enable the Court to make a decision before closure of the interim procedure. The request shall include all reasonably available evidence.[866] The request shall be dealt with by the Court without delay after having heard the parties and at the latest before closure of the interim procedure.[867]

The Administrative Committee shall review this Decision on cost ceilings within two years after the entry into force of the UPCA, and thereafter every three years.[868]

At the request of the defendant, the Court may order the applicant to provide adequate security for the legal costs and other expenses incurred by the defendant which the applicant may be liable to bear, in particular in the case of orders to produce

---

863. Article 2(1) of the Decision on cost ceilings.
864. Article 2(2) of the Decision on cost ceilings.
865. Article 2(3) of the Decision on cost ceilings.
866. Article 2(4) of the Decision on cost ceilings.
867. Article 2(5) of the Decision on cost ceilings.
868. Article 3 of the Decision on cost ceilings.

evidence,[869] orders to preserve evidence and to inspect premises,[870] freezing orders[871] and provisional and protective measures.[872]

Since the cost ceilings are determined as a function of the value of the action, it is important to know how the Court will determine the value of the action. The Preparatory Committee agreed in February 2016 on draft Guidelines for establishing the value of actions (hereinafter *"Guidelines for Valuation"*). The Guidelines for Valuation were adopted by the Administrative Committee of 24 April 2023. They are available on the website of the Court. These Guidelines for Valuation are also important to determine the Court fees (see Part Three, Chapter IX).

The Preamble to the Guidelines for Valuation provides that the purpose of the Guidelines is to provide Court judges for both the Court of First Instance and the Court Appeal with a method for establishing the value of actions for the determination of Court fees and the ceilings for the recoverable costs for the representatives of the successful party. However, the Guidelines for Valuation do not interfere with the liberty of judges to apply in a given case other methods which may be required by the circumstances of the case. The Guidelines for Valuation clearly indicate that the most practicable method, in most cases, will be a valuation based on an appropriate licence fee. The valuation should relate to the summed up values of the main remedies claimed (injunction for the future, damages for the past), not excluding, where appropriate, the value of other remedies claimed. Where the parties agree on a valuation the Court should in principle base its valuation on their estimate.

For the valuation of an infringement action, a declaration of non-infringement, an action for compensation for licence of right, the Guidelines for Valuation set out a method for a royalty calculation. This method is described in Part Three, Chapter IX A.1.g regarding Rule 370 Rules of Procedure. For the determination of the value of a revocation action or a counterclaim for revocation, Title II.2(b) of the Guidelines for Valuation provides that this value should be determined having regard to the value of the patent to be revoked. The Guidelines for Valuation further provide that in the absence of relevant information, (i) the value of a revocation action may be assumed to be equal to the value of an appropriate licence fee calculated on the basis of the turnover of the parties for the remaining lifetime of the patent; and (ii) the value of the revocation counterclaim may be assumed as being equal to the value of the infringement action (calculated according to a royalty calculation set out in the Guidelines for Valuation) plus up to 50%. If the revocation action concerns more than one patent, the value of each patent should be calculated separately and the values determined should be added together to become the value of the action. The value of the infringement action and the value of the revocation counterclaim pending before the same division should be added together for determining the level of recoverable costs.

Title II.5(b) of the Guidelines for Valuation provides that in case of application for interim relief pursuant to Article 62 UPCA (*"provisional and protective measures"*) which is not followed by an infringement action on the merits, the value of an

---

869. Article 59 UPCA.
870. Article 60 UPCA.
871. Article 61 UPCA.
872. Article 62 UPCA.

Chapter VII – Organisation of Proceedings

application for interim relief for determining the level of the recoverable costs should be calculated at 66% of the value calculated for revocation actions.

G. COURT FEES AND LEGAL AID

1. Court fees

Parties to proceedings before the Court shall pay Court fees.[873]

The Table of Court fees was prepared by the Preparatory Committee and finally approved at its 14th meeting on 24/25 February 2016. The Administrative Committee adopted the Table of Court Fees on 8 July 2022. The Court fees are set by the Administrative Committee. They shall consist of a fixed fee, combined with a value-based fee above a pre-defined ceiling. Article 36(3) e UPCA stipulates that the Court fees shall be fixed at such a level as to ensure a right balance between (i) the principle of fair access to justice, in particular for small and medium-sized enterprises, micro-entities, natural persons, non-profit organisations, universities and public research organisations; (ii) an adequate contribution of the parties for the costs incurred by the Court, recognising the economic benefits to the parties involved; and (iii) the objective of a self-financing Court with balanced finances. The level of the Court fees shall be reviewed periodically by the Administrative Committee. Targeted support measures for small and medium-sized enterprises and micro entities may be considered.[874]

The following section regarding Court fees was included in the draft declaration of the Contracting Member States concerning the preparations for the coming into operation of the UPCA:

> *"The Signatory States consider that the fee system of the Unified Patent Court should be straightforward and predictable for the users. Accordingly, the Unified Patent Court should apply a mixed system of fixed and value-based fees. The Court should be accessible for parties with limited resources. Thus the Court fees should be set at an appropriate level. Whilst all users of the Unified Patent Court should contribute to its financing, users having more significant economic interests should provide a reasonable and proportionate contribution to the functioning of the Court, on the basis of an additional value-based fee, proportionate to the economic value of the case at stake in the specific procedure, applicable above a predefined ceiling. The fee system should provide adequate and specific tools to ensure proper access for small and medium-sized enterprises, micro entities, natural persons, non-profit organizations, universities and public research organizations to the Unified Patent Court, especially in relation to cases of high economic value."*[875]

---

873. Article 70(1) UPCA.
874. Article 36(3) UPCA.
875. Updated draft declaration of the contracting Member States concerning the preparations for the coming into operation of the Unified Patent Court agreement, 14 November 2012, Council Document 16221/12, section 8.

Court fees shall be paid in advance, unless the Rules of Procedure provide otherwise. Any party which has not paid a prescribed Court fee may be excluded from further participation in the proceedings.[876]

The amounts of the Court fees and the methods for determining the fees are set out in Rule 370 Rules of Procedure. We refer to Part Three, Chapter IX A regarding Rules 370 and 371 for a detailed description of the rules on Court fees.

2. Legal aid

For natural persons, the UPCA provides the possibility for legal aid. Legal persons are excluded from obtaining legal aid. A party who is a natural person and who is unable to meet the costs of the proceedings, either wholly or in part, may at any time apply for legal aid.[877] The conditions and rules for granting of legal aid are laid down in Rules 375–382 (see Part Three, Chapter IX B).

H. APPEAL PROCEEDINGS

1. Appeal

The decisions on the merits of the Court of First Instance, as well as all orders the Court of First Instance may decide upon during the course of proceedings, can be appealed.

An appeal against a decision of the Court of First Instance may be brought before the Court of Appeal by any party which has been unsuccessful, in whole or in part, in its submissions, within two months of the date of the notification of the decision.[878]

While the appeal term for decisions of the Court is quite long, the appeal term for specific orders is only fifteen calendar days. An appeal against an order of the Court of First Instance may be brought before the Court of Appeal by any party which has been unsuccessful, in whole or in part, in its submissions:

(a) for the orders that decide to use, with the agreement of the parties, the language in which the patent was granted as the language of proceedings,[879] orders to produce evidence,[880] orders to preserve evidence and to inspect premises,[881] freezing orders,[882] orders for provisional and protective measures[883] and orders to communicate information,[884] within fifteen calendar days of the notification of the order to the applicant;

---

876. Article 70(2) UPCA.
877. Article 70(1) UPCA.
878. Article 73(1) UPCA.
879. Article 49(5) UPCA.
880. Article 59 UPCA.
881. Article 60 UPCA.
882. Article 61 UPCA.
883. Article 62 UPCA.
884. Article 67 UPCA.

Chapter VII – Organisation of Proceedings

For these orders, the term starts at the date of notification since certain measures can be ordered without the other party being heard.
(b) for orders other than referred to in point (a):
   (i) together with the decision, or
   (ii) where the Court grants leave to appeal,
within fifteen days of the notification of the Court's decision to that effect.[885]

Rule 220 Rules of Procedure repeats that an appeal by a party adversely affected may be brought against:

- final decisions of the Court of First Instance;
- decisions terminating proceedings as regards one of the parties;
- the orders mentioned under point (a) above.

Orders other than those referred to in point (a) above, may be either the subject of an appeal together with the appeal against the decision or may be appealed with the leave of the Court of First Instance within fifteen days of service of the Court's decision to that effect.[886]

"*Leave to appeal*" is a common law concept which has been introduced in the Unified Patent Court system. It can be seen as a permission to appeal. If for example an order for the appointment of a Court expert or the protection of confidential information is rendered by the Court before the whole case is decided, to appeal such order the permission of the Court itself is needed. Such permission is called "*leave to appeal*". In the event of a refusal of the Court of First Instance to grant leave within fifteen days of the order of one of its panels, a request for a discretionary review to the Court of Appeal may be made within fifteen calendar days from the end of that period.[887] The Registrar shall assign the request for a discretionary review to the standing judge. The standing judge may deny the request without giving reasons. If the standing judge allows the request after having heard the other party, he shall order what further steps, if any, the parties shall take and within what time limits, and the President of the Court of Appeal shall assign the review to a panel of the Court of Appeal for a decision. The Court of Appeal may consult the presiding judge or the Judge-Rapporteur on the panel of the Court of First Instance which has refused the leave order.[888]

The appeal against a decision or an order of the Court of First Instance may be based on points of law and matters of fact.[889] The Court of Appeal may hear appeals against separate decisions on the merits in infringement proceedings and in validity proceedings together.[890]

For new facts and new evidence that is only presented for the first time in appeal, the UPCA provides a threshold. New facts and new evidence may only be introduced where the submission thereof by the party concerned could not reasonably

---

885. Article 73(2) UPCA.
886. Rule 220.2 Rules of Procedure.
887. Rule 220.3 Rules of Procedure.
888. Rule 220.4 Rules of Procedure.
889. Article 73(3) UPCA.
890. Rule 220.5 Rules of Procedure.

have been expected during proceedings before the Court of First Instance.[891] Rule 222.2 Rules of Procedure repeats that requests, facts and evidence which have not been submitted by a party during proceedings before the Court of First Instance may be disregarded by the Court of Appeal, but clarifies that when exercising discretion, the Court shall in particular take into account:

- whether a party seeking to lodge new submissions is able to justify that the new submissions could not reasonably have been made during proceedings before the Court of First Instance;
- the relevance of the new submissions for the decision on the appeal;
- the position of the other party regarding the lodging of the new submissions.

2. Effects of an appeal

Only decisions on actions or counterclaims for revocation and on actions regarding decisions of the EPO in carrying out the tasks referred to in Article 9 of the Unitary Patent Regulation, shall always have suspensive effect.[892]

For all other actions, an appeal shall not have suspensive effect unless the Court of Appeal decides otherwise at the motivated request of one of the parties. Rule 223 provides that a party may lodge an Application for suspensive effect which shall set out the reasons why the lodging of the appeal shall have suspensive effect and the facts, evidence and arguments relied on. The Court of Appeal shall decide on the Application *"without delay"*.[893] In cases of extreme urgency the applicant may apply at any time without formality for an order for suspensive effect to the standing judge. The standing judge shall have all the powers of the Court of Appeal and shall decide the procedure to be followed on the application, which may include a subsequent written application.[894] There shall be no suspensive effect for an appeal of an order pursuant to Rule 220.2 (orders appealed together with the decision or appealed with leave of the Court of First Instance), Rule 220.3 (discretionary review by the Court of Appeal against a refusal of the Court of First Instance to grant leave) and Rule 221.3 (appeal against cost decisions).[895]

The non-suspensive effect of decisions in infringement cases are new for a number of Contracting Member States.

If a defendant brings a counterclaim for revocation in an infringement case and the Court eventually decides that the patent is valid and infringed, the plaintiff shall be entitled to demand from the defendant to cease the patent infringement, even if the defendant has appealed the decision regarding the validity of the patent.

An appeal against an order that decides to use, at the request of one of the parties, the language in which the patent was granted as the language of proceedings,[896]

---

891. Article 73(4) UPCA.
892. Article 74(2) UPCA.
893. Article 74(1) UPCA; Rule 223.3 Rules of Procedure.
894. Rule 223.4 Rules of Procedure.
895. Rule 223.5 Rules of Procedure (as amended by Amendment 22 (to Rule 223) as adopted by the Administrative Committee on 8 July 2022).
896. Article 49(5) UPCA.

an order to produce evidence,[897] an order to preserve evidence and to inspect premises,[898] a freezing order,[899] an order for provisional and protective measures[900] or an order to communicate information,[901] shall not prevent the continuation of the main proceedings. However, the Court of First Instance shall not give a decision in the main proceedings before the decision of the Court of Appeal concerning an appealed order has been given.[902]

3. Decision on appeal and referral back

If an appeal is well-founded, the Court of Appeal shall revoke the decision of the Court of First Instance and give a final decision. The Court of Appeal may in exceptional cases refer the case back to the Court of First Instance for decision.[903]

Rule 242 Rules of Procedure provides that the Court of Appeal shall either reject the appeal or set the decision or order aside totally or in part substituting its own decision or order, including an order for costs both in respect of the proceedings at first instance and on appeal. The Court of Appeal may:

- exercise any power within the competence of the Court of First Instance;
- in exceptional circumstances refer the action back to the Court of First Instance for decision or for retrial.

It is unclear in which cases a referral back to the Court of First Instance shall be necessary. However, Rule 242.2(b) Rules of Procedure provides one situation which shall in normal circumstances not be considered as an *"exceptional circumstance"* justifying a referral back, i.e. the situation in which the Court of First Instance failed to decide an issue which it is necessary for the Court of Appeal to decide on appeal.

Where a case is referred back to the Court of First Instance, the Court of First Instance shall be bound by the decision of the Court of Appeal on points of law.[904] Rule 243.2 Rules of Procedure further provides that the Court of First Instance shall be bound by the decision of the Court of Appeal and its *"ratio decidendi"*. The decision referring an action back to the Court of First Instance shall specify whether the same panel whose earlier decision or order is revoked shall deal further with the action or whether another panel shall be appointed by the presiding judge of the division concerned.[905]

---

897. Article 59 UPCA.
898. Article 60 UPCA.
899. Article 61 UPCA.
900. Article 62 UPCA.
901. Article 67 UPCA.
902. Article 74(3) UPCA.
903. Article 75(1) UPCA.
904. Article 75(2) UPCA.
905. Rule 243.1 Rules of Procedure.

I. DECISIONS

1. Basis for decisions

The Court shall decide in accordance with the requests submitted by the parties and shall not award more than is requested.[906] This general procedural principle has as a consequence that the Court is bound for its decision by the matters presented by the parties. The judges of the Court cannot refuse to decide upon the submitted requests, but on the other hand may go no further than such submitted requests.

Decisions on the merits may only be based on grounds, facts and evidence which were submitted by the parties or introduced into the procedure by an order of the Court and on which the parties have had an opportunity to present their comments.[907]

The Court shall evaluate evidence freely and independently.[908]

2. Formal requirements of decisions

Decisions and orders of the Court shall be reasoned and shall be given in writing in accordance with Rules 350-351 Rules of Procedure.[909] Decisions and orders of the Court shall be delivered in the language of proceedings.[910] Rule 14.2(c) Rules of Procedure introduced an important exception to this principle. The Judge-Rapporteur may order in the interests of the panel that judges may use the official language of their Member State to make any order and deliver any decision together with a certified translation in the language of proceedings.

Decisions of the Court shall contain the names of the judges deciding the case.[911]

Decisions shall be signed by the judges deciding the case and by the Registrar for decisions of the Court of Appeal. For decisions of the Court of First Instance, the Deputy-Registrar and the deciding judges shall sign. The decisions shall be read in open court.[912]

3. Decisions and dissenting opinions

a. Decision making process

Decisions and orders of the Court shall be taken by a majority of the panel.[913] Normally, a panel shall be composed of three judges (*supra*, Part Two, Chapter III A.1), but if a technically qualified judge is added in case of a counterclaim for revocation, there shall be an even number of judges. When a panel sits in a composition of an even

---

906. Article 76(1) UPCA.
907. Article 76(2) UPCA.
908. Article 76(3) UPCA.
909. Article 77(1) UPCA.
910. Article 77(2) UPCA.
911. Article 35(4) Statute.
912. Article 35(5) Statute.
913. Article 78 UPCA.

Chapter VII - Organisation of Proceedings

number of judges, decisions of the Court shall be taken by a majority of the panel.[914] In case of equal vote, the vote of the presiding judge shall prevail.[915]

The deliberations of the Court shall be and shall remain secret.[916] The Court shall deliberate in closed session. The presiding judge shall preside over the deliberations. Only those judges who were present at the oral hearing may take part in the deliberations on the decision. The deliberation of the Court shall take place as soon as possible after the closure of the oral hearing.[917]

In the event of one of the judges on a panel being prevented from attending, a judge from another panel may be called upon to sit in accordance with the Rules of Procedure.[918]

In cases where the Court of Appeal shall take a decision sitting as a full court (*supra*, Part Two, Chapter III B), such decision shall be valid only if it is taken by at least three-quarters of the judges comprising the full court.[919]

b.   *Dissenting opinions*

Following the common law tradition, any judge on the panel may, in exceptional circumstances, express a dissenting opinion separately from the decision of the Court.[920] A dissenting opinion expressed separately by a judge on a panel shall be reasoned, given in writing and shall be signed by the judge expressing this opinion.[921] Any dissenting opinion shall be attached to the Court's decision.[922]

c.   *Decisions by default*

The Statute also provides the possibility for decisions by default, under certain circumstances. At the request of a party to an action, a decision by default may be given in accordance with Rules 355–357 Rules of Procedure, where the other party, after having been served with a document instituting proceedings or with an equivalent document, fails to file written submissions in defence or fails to appear at the oral hearing.[923]

An objection against a decision by default may be lodged within one month of it being notified to the party against which the default decision has been given. The objection shall not have the effect of staying enforcement of the decision by default unless the Court decides otherwise.[924] The Application to set aside a decision by default is governed by Rule 356 Rules of Procedure.

---

914. Article 35(1) Statute.
915. Article 78(1) UPCA and Article 35(1) Statute.
916. Article 34 Statute.
917. Rule 344 Rules of Procedure.
918. Article 35(2) Statute.
919. Article 35(3) Statute.
920. Article 78(2) UPCA.
921. Article 36 Statute.
922. Rule 350.3 Rules of Procedure.
923. Article 37(1) Statute.
924. Article 37(2) Statute.

4. Settlement decisions

The parties may, at any time in the course of proceedings, conclude their case by way of settlement, which shall be confirmed by a decision of the Court in accordance with Rule 365 Rules of Procedure.[925] Article 79 UPCA provides that a patent may not be revoked or limited by way of settlement.

This does not mean that parties cannot agree on the limitation of a patent, but in such case the patent proprietor who agrees to limit its patent should do so by a unilateral limitation notified to the respective national offices of the Member States in which a European Patent is validated (or to the EPO in case of a Unitary Patent), not by a settlement confirmed by a decision of the Court.[926]

5. Publication of decisions

Article 80 UPCA provides that the Court may order, at the request of the applicant and at the expense of the infringer, appropriate measures for the dissemination of information concerning the Court's decision, including displaying the decision and publishing it in full or in part in public media.

Although this Article is included in Chapter VI of the UPCA, which deals with decisions of the Court, it gives the Court the power to order publication measures. Publication measures are in fact a remedy for the plaintiff in patent cases, and would therefore have been better included in Chapter IV of the UPCA (*"Powers of the Court"*). The wording of Article 54 is identical to Article 15 of the Enforcement Directive.

6. Rehearing

The Unified Patent Court system does not include a *"Cassation"* or *"Supreme Court"* instance controlling the correct application of the law. But the UPCA does provide the possibility for a rehearing, which could be considered as an exceptional (third) instance after the normal appeal term has lapsed or after an appeal decision. A request for rehearing after a final decision of the Court may exceptionally be granted by the Court of Appeal in the following circumstances:

- on discovery of a fact by the party requesting the rehearing which is of such a nature as to be a decisive factor and which, when the decision was given, was unknown to the party requesting the rehearing; such request may only be granted on the basis of an act which was held, by a final decision of a national court, to constitute a criminal offence; or
- in the event of a fundamental procedural defect, in particular when a defendant who did not appear before the Court was not served with the document initiating the proceedings or an equivalent document in sufficient time and in such a way as to enable him to arrange for the defence.[927]

---

925. Article 79 UPCA.
926. Article 9(1)(b) Unitary Patent Regulation.
927. Article 81(1) UPCA.

The term for a request for rehearing is ten years from the date of the decision but not later than two months from the date of the discovery of the new fact or of the procedural defect. Such request shall not have suspensive effect unless the Court of Appeal decides otherwise.[928]

Rule 245 Rules of Procedure executes Article 81 UPCA as follows: an Application for rehearing may be lodged by any party adversely affected by a final decision either of the Court of First Instance for which the time for lodging an appeal has expired or of the Court of Appeal. The Application for rehearing shall be lodged at the Court of Appeal within the following periods:

- where the Application for rehearing is based on the ground of a fundamental procedural defect, within two months of the discovery of the fundamental defect or of service of the final decision, whichever is the later;
- where the Application for rehearing is based on an act which has been held, by a final court decision, to constitute a criminal offence, within two months of the date on which the criminal offence has been so held or service of the final decision, whichever is the later;
- but in any event no later than ten years from service of the final decision.

If the request for a rehearing is well-founded, the Court of Appeal shall set aside, in whole or in part, the decision under review and re-open the proceedings for a new trial and decision, in accordance with Rule 255 Rules of Procedure.[929] Persons using patents which are the subject matter of a decision under review and who act in good faith should be allowed to continue using such patents.[930] The question shall be how the further use of a patent shall be taken into account for the calculation of damages, if the re-hearing results in a final decision of infringement. Can an alleged infringer who was successful in an infringement procedure that was reheard afterwards be held liable for acts committed after the first final (non-infringement) decision of the Court and before the final (infringement) decision resulting from the rehearing?

7. Enforcement of decisions and orders

Decisions and orders of the Court shall be enforceable in any Contracting Member State. An order for the enforcement of a decision shall be appended to the decision by the Court.[931] Decisions and orders of the Court shall be directly enforceable from their date of service in each Contracting Member State.[932]

Where appropriate, the enforcement of a decision may be subject to the provision of security or an equivalent assurance to ensure compensation for any damage suffered, in particular in the case of injunctions.[933]

Enforcement shall take place in accordance with the enforcement procedures and conditions governed by the law of the particular Contracting Member State

---

928. Article 81(2) UPCA.
929. Article 81(3) UPCA.
930. Article 81(4) UPCA.
931. Article 82(1) UPCA.
932. Rule 354.1 Rules of Procedure.
933. Article 82(2) UPCA.

where enforcement takes place.[934] Any decision of the Court shall be enforced under the same conditions as a decision given in the Contracting Member State where the enforcement takes place.[935]

---

934. Rule 354.1 Rules of Procedure.
935. Article 82(3) UPCA.

Chapter VIII
Finance of the Court

A. BUDGET OF THE COURT

The budget of the Court shall be financed by the Court's own financial revenues and at least in the transitional period of seven years after the date of entry into force (*infra*), as necessary, by contributions from the Contracting Member States. The budget shall be balanced.[936]

The Court's own financial revenues shall comprise Court fees and other revenues.[937] Other revenues could be the penalty payments payable to the Court in case of non-respect of orders or injunctions[938] (*supra*, Part Two, Chapter VI F.9).

If the Court is unable to balance its budget out of its own resources, the Contracting Member States shall remit to it special financial contributions.[939]

The training framework for judges[940] and the operating costs of the Patent Arbitration and Mediation Centre[941] shall be financed by the budget of the Court.

B. FINANCING OF THE COURT

The operating costs of the Court shall be covered by the budget of the Court, in accordance with the Statute.

On the date of entry into force of the UPCA, the Contracting Member States need to provide the initial financial contributions necessary for the setting up of the Court.[942]

The basis for the calculations of the financial contributions of the Contracting Member States was subject to extensive political discussions in the European Competitiveness Council. Finally, the Competitiveness Council of 5 December 2011 agreed that during the initial transitional period (the first seven years) the financial contributions should be based on the number of European Patents in force and the number of European Patents litigated in the Member State concerned.[943]

---

936. Article 36(1) UPCA.
937. Article 36(2) UPCA.
938. Article 63(2) UPCA.
939. Article 36(4) UPCA.
940. Article 38 UPCA.
941. Article 39 UPCA
942. Article 37(2) UPCA.
943. Council of the European Union, *Draft UPCA on the creation of a Unified Patent Court, Presidency compromise text*, Council working document 18239/11 of 6 December 2011, p. 2.

Therefore, Article 37(3) UPCA provides that during the initial transitional period of seven years, starting from the date of the entry into force of this UPCA, the contribution by each Contracting Member State having ratified or acceded to the UPCA *before the entry into force* thereof shall be calculated on the basis of the number of European Patents having effect in the territory of that State on the date of entry into force of this UPCA and the number of European Patents with respect to which actions for infringement or for revocation have been brought before the national courts of that State in the year preceding entry into force of this UPCA.

During the same initial transitional period of seven years, for Member States which ratify, or accede to, this UPCA *after the entry into force* thereof, the contributions shall be calculated on the basis of the number of European Patents having effect in the territory of the ratifying or acceding Member State on the date of the ratification or accession and the number of European Patents with respect to which actions for infringement or for revocation have been brought before the national courts of the ratifying or acceding Member State in the year preceding the ratification or accession.

After the transitional period, it is expected that the Court shall be self-financing. If it is not the case and exceptional contributions by the Contracting Member States become necessary, they shall be determined in accordance with the scale for the distribution of annual renewal fees for Unitary Patents applicable at the time the contribution becomes necessary.[944]

Besides the purely financial contributions of Contracting Member States, the Court also needs facilities and administrative support. Contracting Member States setting up a local division shall provide the facilities necessary for that purpose. Contracting Member States sharing a regional division shall provide jointly the facilities necessary for that purpose. And the Contracting Member States hosting the central division, its sections or the Court of Appeal (France, the UK, Germany and Luxembourg), shall provide the facilities necessary for that purpose.[945]

During the initial transitional period of seven years, the Contracting Member States concerned shall provide administrative support staff, without prejudice to the Statute of that staff. The addition *"without prejudice to the Statute of that staff"* refers to the fact that the Administrative Committee (and not the Contracting Member States) shall establish the Staff Regulations of officials and other servants of the Court.[946]

C. OPERATING THE BUDGET

The budget shall be adopted by the Budget Committee on a proposal from the Presidium.[947] The Presidium shall submit the draft budget of the Court to the Budget Committee no later than the date prescribed in the Financial Regulations.[948]

The budget shall be drawn up in accordance with the generally accepted accounting principles laid down in the Financial Regulations. These Financial Regulations have been adopted by the Administrative Committee on 22 February 2022 and

---

944. Article 37(4) UPCA.
945. Article 37(1) UPCA.
946. Article 16(2) UPCA.
947. Article 26 Statute.
948. Article 30 Statute.

Chapter VIII – Finance of the Court

amended by decision of 24 April 2023. They are available on the website of the Court. They include arrangements relating to the establishment and implementation of the budget and for the rendering and auditing of accounts, the method and procedure whereby the payments and contributions, including the initial financial contributions of the Contracting Member States, are to be made available to the Court, the rules concerning the responsibilities of authorising and accounting officers[949] and the arrangements for their supervision, and the generally accepted accounting principles on which the budget and the annual financial statements are to be based.[950] The Financial Regulations shall be amended by the Administrative Committee on proposal of the Court.

The Registrar shall be responsible for the implementation of the budget in accordance with the Financial Regulations.[951] The Registrar shall annually make a statement on the accounts of the preceding financial year relating to the implementation of the budget which shall be approved by the Presidium.[952]

The accounting period shall commence on 1 January and end on 31 December.[953] If, at the beginning of the accounting period, the budget has not been adopted by the Budget Committee, the Court can make use of a provisional budget divided into provisional twelfths. Then expenditure may be effected on a monthly basis per heading or other division of the budget, in accordance with the Financial Regulations, up to one-twelfth of the budget appropriations for the preceding accounting period, provided that the appropriations thus made available to the Presidium do not exceed one-twelfth of those provided for in the draft budget.[954] The Budget Committee may authorise expenditure in excess of one-twelfth of the budget appropriations for the preceding accounting period.[955]

In a normal budget, the expenditure entered in the budget shall be authorised for the duration of one accounting period unless the Financial Regulations provide otherwise.[956] In accordance with the Financial Regulations, any appropriations, other than those relating to staff costs, which are unexpended at the end of the accounting period may be carried forward, but not beyond the end of the following accounting period.[957] Appropriations shall be set out under different headings according to type and purpose of the expenditure, and subdivided, to the extent necessary, in accordance with the Financial Regulations.[958]

Within the budget, the Presidium may, in accordance with the Financial Regulations, transfer funds between the various headings or subheadings.[959]

---

949. In the draft version of the Statute it was not clear if this would be the officers of the Court or of each division of the Court.
950. Article 33 Statute.
951. Article 26(3) Statute.
952. Article 26(4) Statute.
953. Article 29 Statute.
954. Article 31(1) Statute.
955. Article 31(2) Statute.
956. Article 27(1) Statute.
957. Article 27(2) Statute.
958. Article 27(3) Statute.
959. Article 26(2) Statute.

The budget of the Court may include appropriations for unforeseeable expenditure. The employment of these appropriations by the Court shall be subject to the prior approval of the Budget Committee.[960]

The annual financial statements of the Court shall be examined by independent auditors. The auditors shall be appointed and if necessary dismissed by the Budget Committee.[961] The audit, which shall be based on professional auditing standards and shall take place, if necessary, in situ, shall ascertain that the budget has been implemented in a lawful and proper manner and that the financial administration of the Court has been conducted in accordance with the principles of economy and sound financial management. The auditors shall draw up a report after the end of each accounting period containing a signed audit opinion.[962] The Presidium shall submit to the Budget Committee the annual financial statements of the Court and the annual budget implementation statement for the preceding accounting period, together with the auditors' report.[963]

The Budget Committee shall approve the annual accounts together with the auditors' report and shall discharge the Presidium in respect of the implementation of the budget.[964]

---

960. Article 28 Statute.
961. Article 32(1) Statute.
962. Article 32(2) Statute.
963. Article 32(3) Statute.
964. Article 32(4) Statute.

Chapter IX
Implementation and Operation of the UPCA

A. TRANSITIONAL REGIME AND OPT-OUT

1. Immediate and exclusive jurisdiction for Unitary Patents

The Court system shall immediately have exclusive jurisdiction for Unitary Patents. There will be no possibility for a proprietor of a Unitary Patent to "*escape*" from the jurisdiction of the Court. This is logical since the main intention of the Unitary Patent Regulation is to provide a title with equal effect in all participating EU Member States. To be of consequence, the proprietor of a Unitary Patent should be able to enforce its patent in the same territory at the same time.

2. European Patents: national courts or Unified Patent Court

The situation is different for the classic European Patents. At the time most proprietors of European Patents obtained their title or applied for it, the Court was not yet in place. It is possible that had proprietors of European Patents known that the Court system would be applied to their patent, they would have decided not to apply for a European Patent, but instead have chosen national protection for their invention. Therefore, the UPCA contains a transitional period in which European Patent proprietors can still bring action before national courts. In other words, the claimant may choose between the Court (the new system) and the national courts (the old EPC system).

The Competitiveness Council of 5 December 2011 decided that the transitional period in which actions for European Patents can still be brought before the national court should be fixed at seven years, with the possibility of prolongation for a maximum of up to a further seven years. During the transitional period of seven years after the date of entry into force of the UPCA, an action for infringement or for revocation of a European Patent or an action for infringement or for declaration of invalidity of a supplementary protection certificate issued for a product protected by a European Patent may still be brought before national courts or other competent national authorities.[965] Consequently, during the transitional period parties shall have the choice to either start infringement or revocation proceedings at a national court or at the Court.

An action pending before a national court at the end of the transitional period shall not be affected by the expiry of the transitional period.[966]

---

965. Article 83(1) UPCA.
966. Article 83(2) UPCA.

3. Opt-out for European Patents

For European Patents the UPCA provides the possibility to avoid Unified Patent Court jurisdiction for the lifetime of the patent (and supplementary protection certificate). The only condition for opting out is that no action has been brought before the Court. Also Unified Patent Court proceedings that have already been concluded preclude an opt-out.

Unless an action has already been brought before the Court, proprietors of or applicants for a European Patent granted or applied for prior to the end of the transitional period, as well as a holder of a supplementary protection certificate issued for a product protected by a European Patent, shall have the possibility to opt-out from the exclusive jurisdiction of the Court. To this end they shall notify the Registry by the latest one month before expiry of the transitional period. After the transitional period, patent proprietors can no longer opt-out their European Patents. The opt-out shall take effect upon its entry into the Register for Unitary Patent Protection.[967]

The opt-out possibility was a result of political compromise, undermining to some extent the whole purpose of a transitional period. Normally a transitional period is meant to provide a smooth transition to a new system. Here, for European Patents it shall be possible to completely avoid the jurisdiction of the Court during the full life cycle of a patent. This has of course everything to do with the reluctance certain (major) patent proprietors felt vis-à-vis the Court.

An opt-out can always be withdrawn if no action has already been brought before a national court. In this respect, Article 83(4) UPCA stipulates that unless an action has already been brought before a national court, proprietors of or applicants for European Patents or holders of supplementary protection certificates issued for a product protected by a European Patent, who made use of the opt-out shall be entitled to withdraw their opt-out at any moment. In this event they shall notify the Registry accordingly. The Withdrawal of the opt-out shall take effect upon its entry into the Registry.[968] It remains to be seen how the Court will interpret *"action"*. Should this be considered as all actions as mentioned in Article 32 of the Agreement?

Rule 5 Rules of Procedure governs the Application to opt-out and withdraw an opt-out. Under Part Three, Chapter III J we describe the different conditions and rules regarding opting out.

Five years after the entry into force of the UPCA, the Administrative Committee shall carry out a broad consultation with the users of the patent system and a survey on the number of European Patents and supplementary protection certificates issued for products protected by European Patents with respect to which actions for infringement or for revocation or declaration of invalidity are still brought before the national courts, the reasons for this and the implications thereof. On the basis of this consultation and an opinion of the Court, the Administrative Committee may decide to prolong the transitional period by up to seven years.[969]

If the transitional period is prolonged, patent proprietors shall still be able to go to national courts for the enforcement of a European Patent and defendants shall be

---

967. Article 83(3) UPCA.
968. Article 83(4) UPCA.
969. Article 83(5) UPCA.

able to revoke European Patents before national courts during a period of fourteen years. As a transitional period, this is very long and equals almost three-quarters of the total duration of a patent. Taking into account that the grant of a European Patent takes several years, some European Patents granted at the same time as the date of signing of the UPCA shall have lapsed before the end of the prolonged transitional period.

At the end of June 2023 (one month after the start date of the Court (1 June 2023)) 535,152 patents and patent applications were reported to have been opted-out of the jurisdiction of the Unified Patent Court. At the same time, 54 withdrawals and 220 removals of opt-outs have been requested, of which 52 were automatic withdrawals due to requests for unitary effect of opted-out patents.[970] During the last weeks of the sunrise period, the opt-outs reached a peak of just over 36,336 patents and applications opted-out on 30 May 2023, the day before the UPC's Case Management System was taken offline for upgrades.

Since the opening of the Court, the number of opt-outs has stabilised to around 2,700 applications and 7,600 patents per week. This compares to around 3,700 applications filed per week at the EPO and approximately 1,500 patents granted per week by the EPO.[971] This could indicate that during the first month many patent owners were still reviewing and considering their patent portfolios for opt-out.

The most patents and applications opted-out by absolute number were published in the name of Huawei Technologies (5,384), Honeywell International (4,724), The Boeing Company (4,441), Microsoft Technology Licensing (4,328) and Samsung Electronics (3,939). This shows that major technology and telecom companies are keeping their patents away for the time being from the jurisdiction of the Court. Whilst the companies in this top five list are all outside the EU, the thirty-nine member states of the European Patent Organisation still account for over 45.4% of all opt-outs when looking at the country of the first-named applicant or proprietor.[972]

4. National proceedings: in or out?

The drafting of Article 83 UPCA was not the best job the Contracting Member States did during the preparation of the Unitary Patent package. Although from the outset one might expect Article 83 to provide an *"in or out"* regime towards the jurisdiction of the Court for a particular patent, this was not exactly the result.

Article 83(1) UPCA provides that during a transitional period of seven years after the date of entry into force of this Agreement, an action for infringement or for revocation of a European Patent or an action for infringement or for declaration of

---

970. Laurence Lai, "UPC opt-outs: statistics and trends one month in", Kluwer Patent Blog, 2 July 2023, https://patentblog.kluweriplaw.com/2023/07/02/upc-opt-outs-statistics-and-trends-one-month-in/
971. Laurence Lai, "UPC opt-outs: statistics and trends one month in", Kluwer Patent Blog, 2 July 2023, https://patentblog.kluweriplaw.com/2023/07/02/upc-opt-outs-statistics-and-trends-one-month-in/
972. Laurence Lai, "UPC opt-outs: statistics and trends one month in", Kluwer Patent Blog, 2 July 2023, https://patentblog.kluweriplaw.com/2023/07/02/upc-opt-outs-statistics-and-trends-one-month-in/

invalidity of a supplementary protection certificate issued for a product protected by a European Patent "*may still be brought before national courts or other competent national authorities*". This Article does not state that national proceedings preclude another action before the Court. In practice, this shall mean that if, for example, a party starts a revocation action before the central division of the Court, the patent proprietor can still start a national infringement procedure. Conversely, if a patent proprietor starts a national infringement action, the defendant can still choose to attack the validity of the patent before the Court. In such case the *lis pendens* rules of the Brussels I (recast) Regulation shall apply. However, under Part Two, Chapter V A we explained that these *lis pendens* rules also leave a great deal of uncertainty. In our opinion such situations could be very negative for the initial purpose of the Court. The Court has been created to avoid as much as possible parallel litigation and conflicting case law and lower the costs of patent enforcement in Europe. If in practice, the Court or national courts are used strategically to start new battlefields during a patent dispute, the purpose of reducing complexity and costs shall move further away. There are objective reasons to defend a transitional regime and an opt-out: proprietors of European Patents did not know at the time they filed for patent protection that the Court would come into existence during the lifetime of their patent. However, we do not see a clear reason to knowingly leave open the possibility for disputing parties to battle each other both before the Court and before national courts regarding the same patent. It would have been advisable to clearly foresee in the UPCA that if one of the parties makes a choice for a national or a Unified Patent Court proceeding, this has the immediate consequence that all counterclaims are dealt with by the same level of jurisdiction. Only the future will tell if such parallel litigation will become a real problem for the success of the Court.

What is clear from the UPCA and the Rules of Proceedings is that if a European Patent has opted out from the jurisdiction of the Court and national proceedings regarding that patent are started, the opt-out can no longer be withdrawn.[973] The same goes if the patent has not been opted out and proceedings are started before the Court regarding that patent, in such case the patent can no longer be opted out, even if the proceedings before the Court have been concluded.[974]

5. National proceedings: application of the UPCA?

Another ambiguity that appeared from Article 83(3) was the question of whether national courts had to apply the provisions of the UPCA in proceedings regarding European Patents. This question gave rise to an interpretative note of the Preparatory Committee in January 2014. The interpretative note is published on the website of the Court.

The interpretative note points out that Article 83(3) UPCA provides applicants or holders of such patents during a transitional period the possibility to opt-out from "*the exclusive jurisdiction*" of the Court. Some had taken the view that the consequence of opting out (or from bringing a case to a national court during the transitional period) is that while the Court is no longer competent in that specific

---

973. Rule 5.9 Rules of Procedure.
974. Rule 5.7 Rules of Procedure.

case, the Agreement itself remains applicable. The competent national court would therefore be obliged to apply the provisions of the Agreement, in particular the provisions with regard to substantive patent law (Chapter V). In other words, national law would be superseded by the Agreement, even if a patent is opted out or the case is brought before a national court.

Another view was that, if a patent is opted out (or if during the transitional period the case is brought before the national court), the UPCA no longer applies to the patent concerned and the competent national court has to apply the applicable national law only.

In its analysis, the Preparatory Committee tries to find the *ratio legis* of Article 83 UPCA. From the Recitals and Article 1 of the Agreement, it deduces that it was the wish of the Contracting Member States to improve the enforcement of patents and the defence against unfounded claims and patents which should be revoked, and to enhance legal certainty by setting up a Court. The Court should be devised to ensure expeditious and high quality decisions, striking a fair balance between the interests of right holders and other parties and taking into account the need for proportionality and flexibility. It was the choice of the Contracting Member States that these goals could best be achieved by setting up a court common to those Contracting Member States that would have exclusive competence in respect of European Patents and European patents with unitary effect. This is reflected in the title of the instrument that was used: Agreement on a Unified Patent Court.

According to the Preparatory Committee, the underlying idea is that by attributing competence with regard to patent cases to one court exclusively, uniform interpretation of the applicable law is best guaranteed. Although composed of different divisions, the Court is a single court with a single appeal body that safeguards the uniform interpretation of the applicable rules (most notably the agreement itself, its Rules of Procedure, the applicable European Union law and the European Patent Convention). This is in contrast with the current situation where different national courts are interpreting substantial patent law. As far as EU law is concerned, EU legislation has been provided for in the area of supplementary protection certificates for medicinal and plant products and the directive on legal protection of biotechnological inventions, for which a uniform interpretation can today be achieved by referring interpretative questions to the European Court of Justice. However, large areas of law remain for which the uniform interpretation is not guaranteed by a single court.

The Preparatory Committee deduces from the texts that the legislator has clearly not chosen to achieve a uniform application of substantive patent law through obligatory harmonisation of national patent law. There is no provision in the UPCA that obliges the Contracting Member States to do so. In this regard, the Agreement differs from the EU trade mark system, where the regulation establishing the EU trade mark is accompanied by an EU Directive harmonising national trade mark systems and preliminary questions can be posed to the European Court of Justice. There is no possibility for national judges to refer interpretative questions to the Court. As a consequence, application of the substantive patent law that is contained in the UPCA by national courts would seriously bear the risk of diverging interpretations, which would be contradictory to the goals of the UPCA.

The note deduces that it was the purpose of the Contracting Member States to create a new jurisdiction in order for substantive patent law to be interpreted by a court common to the Contracting Member States exclusively (i.e. the Unified Patent Court). It was not intended to be obligatory to harmonise national patent law, nor was it intended that national courts would have jurisdiction with regard to the agreement itself. As far as the transitional regime is concerned, it should be concluded that this aims at allowing parties for a limited period of time to continue the current practice whereby national courts have jurisdiction with regard to applications for European Patents and to European Patents, thereby applying national law. *Mutatis mutandis*, the above would apply to supplementary protection certificates that have been issued.

From the above, the Preparatory Committee concludes in its interpretative note that if an application for a European Patent, a European Patent or a supplementary protection certificate that has been issued for a product protected by a European Patent is opted out (or during the transitional period the case is brought before a national court), the UPCA no longer applies to the application for a European Patent, the European Patent or the supplementary protection certificate concerned. As a consequence the competent national court shall have to apply only the applicable national law and not the UPCA.

B. RATIFICATION AND ENTRY INTO FORCE

1. Signature, ratification and accession

The UPCA was in fact a treaty between initially twenty-five Member States of the European Union. The number of EU Member States dropped to twenty-four after Brexit.

The UPCA is subject to ratification in accordance with the respective constitutional requirements of the EU Member States. Instruments of ratification were deposited with the General Secretariat of the Council of the European Union (the Depositary).[975]

Each Member State having signed the UPCA has an obligation to notify the European Commission of its ratification of the UPCA at the time of the deposit of its ratification instrument,[976] as prescribed by Article 18(3) of the Unitary Patent Regulation. The Commission shall publish in the Official Journal of the European Union the date of entry into force of the UPCA and a list of the Member States that have ratified the UPCA at the date of entry into force. The Commission shall thereafter regularly update the list of the Participating Member States which have ratified the UPCA and shall publish such updated list in the Official Journal of the European Union.[977] In practice, the list of ratifications and dates of deposit are published on the website of the Court.

The UPCA shall be open to accession by any EU Member State. Instruments of accession shall be deposited with the Depositary.[978]

---

975. Article 84(2) UPCA.
976. Article 84(3) UPCA.
977. Article 18(3) Unitary Patent Regulation.
978. Article 84(4) UPCA.

The Depositary draws up certified true copies of the UPCA and transmits them to the governments of all signatory or acceding Member States.[979] The Depositary notifies the governments of the signatory or acceding Member States of:

- any signature;
- the deposit of any instrument of ratification or accession;
- the date of entry into force of this UPCA.[980]

The Depositary shall also register the UPCA with the Secretariat of the United Nations.[981]

All information on the status of the ratifications of the Contracting Member States can be found on the Court website. At the date of publication of this book, eighteen Member States have ratified the UPCA. These Member States are:

- Austria (6 August 2013)
- France (14 March 2014)
- Sweden (5 June 2014)
- Belgium (6 June 2014)
- Denmark (20 June 2014)
- Portugal (28 August 2014)
- Malta (9 December 2014)
- Luxembourg (22 May 2015)
- Finland (19 January 2016)
- Bulgaria (3 June 2016)
- the Netherlands (14 September 2016)
- Italy (10 February 2017)
- Estonia (1 August 2017)
- Lithuania (24 August 2017)
- Latvia (11 January 2018)
- Slovenia (15 October 2021)
- Germany (17 February 2023)

2. Revision

The UPCA shall be of unlimited duration,[982] but a possibility for revision is included in Article 87.

Either seven years after the entry into force of this UPCA or once 2,000 infringement cases have been decided by the Court, whichever is the later point in time, and if necessary at regular intervals thereafter, a broad consultation with the users of the patent system shall be carried out by the Administrative Committee on the functioning, efficiency and cost-effectiveness of the Court and on the trust and confidence of users of the patent system in the quality of the Court's decisions. On the basis of this consultation and an opinion of the Court, the Administrative Committee may

---

979. Article 85(1) UPCA.
980. Article 85(2) UPCA.
981. Article 85(3) UPCA.
982. Article 86 UPCA.

decide to revise the UPCA with a view to improving the functioning of the Court.[983] The Administrative Committee may also amend this UPCA to bring it into line with an international treaty relating to patents or Union law.[984]

Some Contracting Member States have argued in the European Council that a review of the UPCA should require unanimity on the Administrative Committee. Other Contracting Member States feared that unanimity may render a necessary review too difficult. The Competitiveness Council of 5 December 2011 decided as a compromise to maintain the three-quarters majority on the Administrative Committee for review of the UPCA, but to give Member States the possibility to reject a review on the basis of their relevant internal decision making procedures.[985] For this reason, a decision of the Administrative Committee for revision shall not take effect if a Contracting Member State declares within twelve months of the date of the decision, on the basis of its relevant internal decision making procedures, that it does not wish to be bound by the decision. In this case, a Review Conference of the Contracting Member States shall be convened.[986]

3. Authentic languages of the UPCA

The UPCA shall be drawn up in a single original in the English, French and German languages, each text being equally authentic.[987] After signature of the originals, the UPCA shall be translated in all other official languages of the Contracting Member States. The translations of the UPCA are available on the website of the Court (www.unified-patent-court.org).

The texts of the UPCA that are drawn up in official languages of Contracting Member States other than English, French and German shall, if they have been approved by the Administrative Committee, be considered as official texts. In the event of divergences between the various texts, the texts of the authentic English, French and German originals shall prevail.[988]

Nothing is provided to solve any divergences between the English, French and German texts.

4. Entry into force

There was a general agreement between the Contracting Member States that the UPCA should enter into force once a minimum number of Member States have ratified the UPCA. In previous versions, nine Member States were proposed.[989] But

---

983. Article 87(1) UPCA.
984. Article 87(2) UPCA.
985. Council of the European Union, *Draft UPCA on the creation of a Unified Patent Court, Presidency compromise text*, Council working document 18239/11 of 6 December 2011, p. 4.
986. Article 87(3) UPCA.
987. Article 88(1) UPCA.
988. Article 88(2) UPCA.
989. Council of the European Union, *Draft UPCA on the creation of a Unified Patent Court, revised presidency text*, Council working document 16741/11 of 11 November 2011.

the Competitiveness Council of 5 December 2011 finally decided to set the number of Member States to ratify the UPCA before entering into force at thirteen Member States.[990]

Article 89 of the UPCA provides that the UPCA shall enter into force on 1 January 2014 or on the first day of the fourth month after the deposit of the thirteenth instrument of ratification or accession, including the three EU Member States in which the highest number of European Patents had effect in the year preceding the year in which the signature of the UPCA takes place, or on the first day of the fourth month after the date of entry into force of the amendments to Regulation (EC) 44/200113 of 22 December 2000 on jurisdiction and the recognition and enforcement of judgments in civil and commercial matters, concerning its relationship with this UPCA, whichever is the latest.

The three EU Member States in which the highest number of European Patents had effect during 2012 were Germany, France and the United Kingdom. Therefore, the UPCA would initially have entered into force after ratification by thirteen Contracting Member States, including Germany, France and the United Kingdom. After Brexit, the ratification of Germany, France and Italy was needed since Italy was the fourth EU Member State where the highest number of European Patents had effect during 2012.

Any ratification or accession after the entry into force of this UPCA shall take effect on the first day of the fourth month after the deposit of the instrument of ratification or accession.[991]

Finally, the UPCA entered into force on 1 June 2023, which was the first day of the fourth month after the deposit by Germany (on 17 February 2023) of the instrument of ratification.

5. Brexit

In 2016 it was expected that Germany would be the last of the three mandatory Member States to ratify. Germany would hold the key for giving the green light to the Court. The plan was that the UK would ratify first and then Germany.

During 2016 the UK government was preparing its ratification process. At that time observers considered the Court would become operational by the end of 2016. But that was without taking into account the Brexit referendum of 23 June 2016. Like a bolt from the blue, the UK voted in June 2016 in favour of exiting the EU. From that moment on, it was clear that the UK would not be able to ratify in the months following the Brexit referendum. Moreover, a great deal of uncertainty arose within the patent community as to whether or not the UK would still be able to ratify the UPCA at all. Certain people even considered that this could be the end of the Unitary Patent package. This uncertainty lasted until 28 November 2016.

At the EU Competitiveness Council of 28 November 2016 Baroness Neville-Rolfe announced that notwithstanding the upcoming Brexit, the UK would soon ratify the UPCA. At the same time, the UK government launched a press release with

---

990. Council of the European Union, *Draft UPCA on the creation of a Unified Patent Court, Presidency compromise text*, Council working document 18239/11 of 6 December 2011, p. 4.
991. Article 89(2) UPCA.

the unambiguous title and subtitle: *"UK signals green light to Unified Patent Court Agreement. The UK government has confirmed it is proceeding with preparations to ratify the Unified Patent Court Agreement."* The press release explained:

> *"This is part of the process needed to realise the Unitary Patent and Unified Patent Court (UPCA). Under the new regime, businesses will be able to protect and enforce their patent rights across Europe in a more streamlined way – with a single patent and through a single patent court. The court will make it easier for British businesses to protect their ideas and inventions from being illegally copied by companies in other countries."*

The press release also included the following statement of UK Minister of State for Intellectual Property, Baroness Neville-Rolfe, which she also used during the EU Competitive Council:

> *"The new system will provide an option for businesses that need to protect their inventions across Europe. The UK has been working with partners in Europe to develop this option.*
>
> *As the Prime Minister has said, for as long as we are members of the EU, the UK will continue to play a full and active role. We will seek the best deal possible as we negotiate a new agreement with the European Union. We want that deal to reflect the kind of mature, cooperative relationship that close friends and allies enjoy. We want it to involve free trade, in goods and services. We want it to give British companies the maximum freedom to trade with and operate in the Single Market – and let European businesses do the same in the UK.*
>
> *But the decision to proceed with ratification should not be seen as pre-empting the UK's objectives or position in the forthcoming negotiations with the EU."*[992]

For the record, the press release ended with a note for editors that *"the UPC itself is not an EU institution, it is an international patent court. The judiciary appointed include UK judges."*

It was expected that UK would ratify the UPCA by March 2017. The UK officially started the procedure of Article 50 of the Treaty on European Union (TEU), i.e. the official exit procedure for EU Member States, on 30 March 2017. In April, the UK had still not ratified the UPCA. It was then said that the UK would ratify after the parliamentary approval of the Protocol on Privileges and Immunities of Judges, which was planned for after the Easter holidays (end of April 2017). Instead of announcing ratification of the UPCA, Prime Minister Theresa May announced on 18 April 2017 to hold elections in the UK on 8 June 2017. Once again, a setback for the start of the Court.

After the UK elections, the UK resumed its legislative process by publishing on 26 June 2017 the draft of the remaining piece of secondary legislation required to enable the UK to ratify the UPC Agreement, i.e. the Unified Patent Court (Immunities and Privileges) Order 2017.[993] The UK finally ratified the UPCA on 26 April 2018.

---

992. https://www.gov.uk/government/news/uk-signals-green-light-to-unified-patent-court-agreement.
993. http://www.legislation.gov.uk/ukdsi/2017/9780111158555/contents.

Chapter IX – Implementation and Operation of the UPCA

However, with the change of government in the UK, the new administration decided in early 2020 not to proceed with the Unified Patent Court. Consequently, the UK has withdrawn its ratification on, and effective as from, 20 July 2020. That marked the end of the UK's participation in the UPCA.

6. Provisional application

Although the UPCA provides a period of three to four months between the last necessary ratification and the entry into force of the UPCA depending on the date of the month on which the ratification occurs, the Contracting Member States considered that in order to provide a smooth transition into the operational phase and to ensure the proper functioning of the Court before the entry into force of the UPCA, a provisional application of the UPCA was needed.

In the margins of the Competitiveness Council meeting of 1 October 2015, the Contracting Member States signed a Protocol to the UPCA on provisional application (hereinafter *"Protocol Provisional Application"*), allowing some parts of the UPCA to be applied early. The Contracting Member States considered that the provisional application should concern only the institutional, organisational and financial provisions of the UPCA and should be limited to what is strictly necessary to ensure the smooth transition into the operational phase.

Article 1 of the Protocol Provisional Application sums up the Articles of the UPCA and the Statute that shall enter into provisional application upon the entry into force of this Protocol. Articles 1–2 (Nature of the Court and definitions), Articles 4–5 (Legal status and liability), Article 6(1) (Structure of the Court), Article 7 (the Court of First Instance), Articles 10–19 (the Registry, the committees, the judges of the Court), Article 35(1), (3) and (4) (Patent Mediation and Arbitration Centre), Articles 36–41 (Financial provisions, Statute, Rules of Procedure) and Article 71(3) (Level of and rules relating to legal aid) of the UPCA, and Articles 1–7(1) (Judges), Article 7(5) (Presidium's role in impartiality discussions), Articles 9–18 (End of duties, removal, training and remuneration of judges, President of the Court of Appeal, President of the Court of First Instance, Presidium, staff, judicial vacations, setting up local or regional division), Article 20(1) (List with judges for Pool of Judges), Articles 22–28 (the Registry and Budget), Article 30 (Preparation of the Budget), Article 32 (Auditing of accounts) and Article 33 (Financial regulations) of the Statute of the Unified Patent Court shall enter into provisional application among the Parties.

The period of provisional application was meant to be used to take the final decisions on the practical set up of the Court, for example the recruitment of judges and testing of IT systems, and of course as a sunrise period for early registrations of opt-outs.

Chapter X
Unified Patent Court Website and Case Management System

From the start of its activities, the Preparatory Committee decided to set up a specific website with the domain name www.unified-patent-court.org. The initial communication plan of the Preparatory Committee provided that the website would be used to publish:

- general information such as the composition, the organisation and the target dates of the Committee;
- questions and answers relevant to the Court;
- basic texts such as the Agreement on a Unified Patent Court, the Regulations on the Unitary Patent system and its translation regime, the Organisational Rules of the Committee, the Communication Plan and the Roadmap;
- proposals and other documents which have reached an appropriate stage; and
- the launch of written consultations with stakeholders.

During the preparatory phase, this website was indeed used for the abovementioned purposes. Amongst other things, the Preparatory Committee posted in the *"News"* section short reports of its meetings and decisions and in the *"Documents"* section a number of draft documents (Rules of Procedure, Rules regarding Court fees, etc.).

Furthermore, at a very early stage the Preparatory Committee published a test version of the Case Management System (CMS) of the Unified Patent Court on its website. Given the international character of the Court, it will be very important for parties, representatives, judges and the registry to have a swift access to all relevant case documents.

During the sunrise period and the first weeks of the Court, the CMS appeared to be a weak spot of the Court. In the final days of the sunrise period, the CMS had to be taken down in order to manage the large number of opt-outs. Also during the first weeks of the UPC, judges and users experienced issues with the CMS. It is to be expected that these initial hiccups can be set aside quickly and that the advantages of a completely electronic case management system can be used.

PART THREE:

THE RULES OF PROCEDURE OF THE UNIFIED PATENT COURT

Chapter I
Introduction

A. FRAMEWORK

As described in the first part of this book, the UPCA introduces, in its Part III, the principles of the Unified Patent Court's (hereafter referred to as the *"Court"*) procedural law. Article 41 UPCA states that the Rules of Procedure (hereafter referred to as the *"Rules"*) will lay down the details of the proceedings before the Court. The Rules need to comply with the UPCA and the Statute. This principle is explicitly reiterated in the Rules, where Rule 1.1 states that in the event of a conflict between the provisions of the UPCA or Statute and those of the Rules, the provisions of the UPCA or Statute will prevail.

The Rules should guarantee that Court decisions are of the highest quality and proceedings should be organised in the most efficient and cost-effective manner. A fair balance should be ensured between the legitimate interests of all parties. The Rules need to provide for the required level of discretion for the judges without impairing predictability of proceedings for the parties.[994]

B. LEGAL HISTORY OF THE RULES

Upon the signature of the UPCA, the Contracting Member States commenced the necessary preparations for its ratification. In line with these efforts the Contracting Member States set up a *"Preparatory Committee"* in charge of preparing the practical arrangements for the early establishment and coming into operation of the Court.

The Preparatory Committee focused on five main work streams: legal framework, financial aspects, IT, facilities, and human resources and training. The legal framework stream was divided in several sub-streams, one of which was the Rules of Procedure (Group). Although it was initially the aim that these sub-streams would be staffed by experts and the Preparatory Committee would take more (political) national stances, in reality the national interests were already prominently present during discussions in the substreams.

To avoid further delay a small Drafting Committee[995] of expert judges and lawyers was appointed to take the work forward. The purpose of the Drafting

---

994. Article 41(3).
995. Members of the Drafting Committee: Mr K. Mooney (UK), Mr C. Floyd (UK), Mr K. Grabinski (GE), Mr W. Tilmann (GE), Mme A. Pezard (FR), Mr P. Véron (FR) and Mr W. Hoyng (NL).

Committee was to assist the Preparatory Committee to complete the draft Rules.[996] The Rules of Procedure Group held several meetings in Berlin under the presidency of Johannes Karcher, also the president of the legal working group. Mr Karcher was in direct contact with the Drafting Committee. The Drafting Committee participated in the last two meetings of the Rules of Procedure Group in Berlin (organised in 2015). Throughout 2016 and early 2017 the Drafting Committee held meetings which resulted in adjustments to the Rules.

The history of the Rules is quite different to that of national procedural laws. Where the fundamental principles may be an amalgam of national procedural (patent) law, the actual expression of these principles in the Rules was based on a pragmatic approach where practitioners (judges and lawyers) were in the driver's seat.

An issue to which the drafters were confronted, or better found a consensus on, was the mixture of common and civil law. It was indeed the principle aim of the Drafting Committee to articulate in one body of rules national procedural rules which were held to be beneficial by the patent community as being advantageous in decision taking with regard to patent procedures. This meant that national rules from common law and civil law traditions needed to be merged into one set of procedural rules.[997]

Also the opinion of the stakeholders played an important role in the drafting process of the Rules. This is explicitly foreseen in Article 41(2) UPCA were it is stated that the Administrative Committee should adopt the Rules *"on the basis of broad consultations with stakeholders"*. The purpose was to construct viable proceedings. Such a pragmatic approach overshadows interpretative problems of the Articles of the UPCA and the Rules themselves. In other words: the Rules can sometimes be understood from a pragmatic point of view but the question arises as to whether the Court, confronted with interpretative problems, has the same power to set aside a legalistic view for a pragmatic solution.

It is in this respect that the principle laid down in Rule 1.1 might become important not only when applying the Rules but also when the Court needs to decide

---

996. In reality the mentioned Drafting Committee had already a history of drafting the rules for the Court. A historical overview of the Court and its Rules has been provided inter alia in K. Mooney, "The Unified Patent Court and its Rules of Procedure", Hoyng-bundel – *Liber Amicorum Willem Hoyng Litigator* (Amsterdam, 2013) 432–457; K. Grabinski, "An Overview of the Draft Rules of Procedure for the Unified Patent Court", LES Nouvelles (September 2013), 154–169 and A. Plomer, "A Unitary Patent for a (Dis)United Europe: the Long Shadow of History", ICC 46:5 (August 2015), 508–533, E. De Gryse and V. Vanovermeire, "Toekomstperspectieven voor de rechtshandhaving in het octrooirecht: De EU-verordening betreffende het octrooi met eenheidswerking en de creatie van het 'gemeenschappelijk octrooigerecht'", *T.B.H.* (2013/4), 215–230 and G. Gathem, "Protéger ses inventions dans l'Union européenne: le brevet européen à effet unitaire et la juridiction unifiiée du brevet", *Journal de droit européen (2014)*, 274–282.
997. After Brexit this led to a strange situation that besides Ireland no other common law country is a Contracting Member State, while an important influence of (or rather balance with) common law can be detected in the Rules of Procedure. Therefore, it could be of importance for the interpretation of the Rules of Procedure and the UPC as a whole that Ireland, after the Irish government announced on 28 June 2022 to hold a referendum (in 2023 or 2024) on the approval to ratify the UPCA, becomes active part of the system.

on the legality of a certain rule in view of the UPCA and/or Statute.[998] Some of the Rules (subject of discussion and in its final version agreed upon based on a political consensus) came into existence based on an *ex post* interpretation of the UPCA aimed at fitting the proposed Rule to a pragmatic solution. Whether such reasoning will stand in court will not always be certain. The same applies with the interpretation of some of the FAQ provided by the Preparatory Committee on its website (www.unified-patent-court.org).[999]

Two drafts (the 15th draft dated 31 May 2013[1000] and the 17th draft dated 31 October 2014) were subject to public consultations.[1001] Based on the received comments the 18th draft emerged on 1 July 2015. This was the first draft to be presented to the Preparatory Committee on 10 July 2015. It was dealt with and agreed upon by the Preparatory Committee on 10 October 2015. The agreement resulted in the publication of the 18th Version of the Rules on 19 October 2015 followed by a public hearing held in Trier on 26 November 2016 to which over 70 organisations and also judges had been invited. Based on this consultation and after a meeting of the Drafting Committee on 15 March 2017, the "final" 18th Version was published on the website of the Preparatory Committee on 10 April 2017.

The 18th Version of the Rules was presented to the Administrative Committee at its inaugural meeting of 22 February 2022. After this presentation some further amendments were discussed. As it falls within the powers of the Administrative Committee[1002] to adopt the final Rules[1003] (with a majority of three-quarters of the Contracting Member States), the Rules were adopted by decision of 8 July 2022 with the amendments of Annex I to the text approved by the Preparatory Committee on 15 March 2017 contained in Annex II. The decision by the Administrative Committee entered into force on 1 September 2022.

C. TEMPLATES AND GUIDANCES

In order to ensure a unified, European and consistent appearance and content of orders and decisions of the Court, a set of templates and guidances hereto have been drafted. They can be accessed through the CMS.

The templates and guidances are non-binding. Therefore, they should be considered as practical tools (*"Informal check-list"*) for the judges of the Court but also as a tool for Its users to double check (e.g.) formal requirements. It Is important

---

998. Rules which may be the subject of such interpretative discussion include Rule 5, Rule 11.2, and Rule 14 (see *infra*).
999. Cf. transitional regime Rule 5 *juncto* Article 83(1).
1000. This draft was opened for public consultation at the end of June 2013 until the end of September 2013 and some 600 comments were received.
1001. The main areas of concern during the first consultation can be listed as follows: Languages (Rule 14), Transitional regime (Rule 5), Procedural appeals (Rule 220), Bifurcation (application of Article 33), Injunctions (criteria) (inter alia Rules 205–213), Forum shopping, patent trolls, amicus briefs (former Rule 318) and quality of appointed judges.
1002. The Administrative Committee is composed of one representative of each Contracting Member State (Article 12(1)).
1003. Article 12(4).

to note that neither the templates neither the guidances were drafted to limit the judges' independence.

At the time of publication the following downloadable templates with guidance were available:

- Order to communicate information
- Decision in an action for a declaration of non-infringement
- Decision in an action for Infringement with counterclaim for revocation
- Decision allowing a preliminary objection
- Order convening interim conference
- Order rejecting a preliminary objection
- Summons of a court expert
- Order on Application of Article 33(3) UPCA
- Order to inspect premises and to preserve evidence
- Order for provisional measures
- Order to freeze assets
- Summons of parties and party expert to the oral hearing
- Summons of witnesses to the oral hearing
- General template for decisions and orders (UPC Court of First Instance)
- General template for decisions and orders (UPC Court of Appeal)

Chapter II
Preamble

The Preamble to the Rules refers to the Articles of the UPCA dealing with *proportionality*,[1004] *flexibility*, *fairness* and *equity* regarding its application and interpretation (cf. Article 41(3), Article 42(1) and (2) and Article 52(1)).[1005] These terms are further elaborated in the Preamble.

Proportionality should be ensured by giving due consideration to the nature and complexity of each action and its importance.[1006] An important principle set forward in the Preamble[1007] is that the Rules should be applied in a *flexible* and *balanced* manner allowing the judges the required level of discretion to organise proceedings in the most efficient and cost-effective manner. Discretion is introduced several times in the Rules in order to allow a pragmatic and flexible approach to solve legal issues. As mentioned above, the Rules were constructed by practitioners looking for practical and pragmatic solutions. Finally, *fairness* and *equity* should be ensured by having regard to the legitimate interests of all parties.[1008]

In accordance with the aforementioned principles, the Court should apply and interpret the Rules in a way that ensures decisions of the highest quality.[1009]

Proceedings should be organised in such a way as to allow the final oral hearing on the issues of infringement and validity at first instance to take place within one year. Decisions on the costs and/or damages may take place at the same time or *as soon as practicable* thereafter.[1010] The possible consecutive structure of the proceedings (at least regarding costs and damages) is explicitly articulated in this paragraph. This consecutive organisation of the proceedings could have a beneficial impact on ADR in general and on the success of the Patent Mediation and Arbitration Centre[1011] (to which actions regarding issues such as damages may be referred with the consent of the parties) in particular. This seems in line with national jurisdictional patent practice where, after a decision has been made regarding invalidity and/or infringement, the damages and costs are often settled (with or without the aid of formal ADR proceedings).

1004. See also regarding the importance of *"proportionality"*: S. Granata, "Rules of procedure of the UPC, a judge's perspective", in D. Matthews and P. Torremans (eds.), *Research Handbook on European Patent Law: The European Patent Convention, the European Patent with Unitary Effect and Unified Patent Court* (De Gruyter, 2023).
1005. Preamble 2.
1006. Preamble 3.
1007. Preamble 4.
1008. Preamble 5.
1009. Preamble 6.
1010. Preamble 7.
1011. Article 35.

Case management should be organised in such a way that the aimed for objectives are met. One of the objectives of the UPC is public access to written pleadings and evidence (limited access) and to the decisions and orders of the Court (full access). The CMS plays an important role in this respect.[1012]

A burden is placed on the parties to set out their full case as early as possible in the proceedings. The procedure can be characterised as *"front-loaded"* and, taking into account the envisaged term of one year for proceedings to lead to a decision (at least on infringement and invalidity) in combination with the means of evidence, one could even characterise the proceedings as *"pre-loaded"*.

The Court should endeavour to ensure consistent application and interpretation of the Rules. Due consideration should be given to this objective in any decision concerning leave to appeal against procedural orders.[1013]

1012. Cf. Amendment 24 (to Rule 262) as adopted by the Administrative Committee on 8 July 2022.
1013. Preamble 8.

Chapter III
Application and Interpretation of the Rules of Procedure

A. INTRODUCTION

Under this general title some diverse yet fundamental issues are clarified in the Rules.

An important Rule 5 is introduced regarding proceedings to opt-out (and the withdrawal of an opt-out). It is probably this Rule, together with Rule 14 (language regime), which was redrafted manifold times during the drafting process. Each of the modifications resulted from remarks made during the public consultations. The written consultation organised between May and December 2013 gave rise to more than 1,000 pages of comments. At the same time, a large number of interested attendees had to be refused participation in the oral public consultation.[1014] Rule 5 was also one of the Rules which was finally amended in 2022 during the last amendment round of the Rules by the Administrative Committee before the entry into force on 1 September 2022.[1015]

B. APPLICATION OF THE RULES AND GENERAL PRINCIPLES OF INTERPRETATION

After reiterating the general principle regarding a possible conflict between the provisions of the UPCA and/or the Statute on the one hand and the Rules on the other hand,[1016] the first Rule[1017] stipulates that where the Rules provide for the Court to perform any act other than an act exclusively reserved for a panel of the Court, the President of the Court of First Instance or the President of the Court of Appeal, that act may be performed by:

(a) the presiding judge or the Judge-Rapporteur on the panel to which the action has been assigned,
(b) a single legally qualified judge where the action has been assigned to a single judge,
(c) the standing judge designated pursuant to Rule 345(5).

1014. Held in Trier on 26 November 2014.
1015. E.g. in Rule 5.1(b) it was clarified that the Application to opt-out shall be made in respect of *"all of the states for which the European patent has been granted"*, instead of *"all of the Contracting Member States for which the European patent has been granted"*.
1016. Rule 1.1.
1017. Rule 1.2.

C. SUPPLEMENTARY PROTECTION CERTIFICATES

Rule 2 clarifies the situation wherein an SPC is the object of proceedings regulated by these Rules. The expressions *"patent"* and *"proprietor"* shall then include, whenever appropriate, respectively, an SPC as defined in Article 2(h) and granted in respect of the *patent* and the *proprietor* of such certificate.[1018] References in the Rules to *"the language in which the patent was granted"*, means *that* language and not the language in which a supplementary certificate in respect of the patent was granted.[1019]

D. POWER OF THE STAFF OF THE REGISTRY AND SUB-REGISTRY TO PERFORM FUNCTIONS OF THE REGISTRY

Where the Rules refer to the Registry or Registrar and provide to perform any act, that reference includes the Deputy-Registrar and the relevant sub-registry. Such act may be performed by the Registrar, the Deputy-Registrar or by a member of staff of the Registry or relevant sub-registry.[1020] Such reference including the Deputy-Registrar and sub-registry only applies in connection with the Court of First Instance.[1021]

E. LODGING OF DOCUMENTS

Written pleadings and documents need to be lodged at the Registry and signed in electronic form, making use of the official online forms.[1022] For this purpose, the Preparatory Committee has set up a Case Management System (CMS). The receipt of the documents will be confirmed by automatic issue of an electronic receipt, which should indicate the date and local time of the receipt. The format of the official forms available online has not been decided yet (at the time of writing this 3th Edition of this book the definite forms were not available). When going through the Rules, more than 250 forms or templates seem necessary. One of the initial tasks of the Court will undoubtedly be the drafting of these forms/templates. In order to facilitate the formal examination by the Registry[1023] and/or the examination of time schedules, it is necessary that the user is obliged to complete the information to be examined in a preformatted document.

Reference can be made to the (non-binding) Templates and Guidelines for the judges (but also users) of the UPC accessible through the CMS.

1018. Rule 2.1.
1019. Rule 2.2.
1020. Rule 3.
1021. On the level of the Court of Appeal, reference to Registry and Registrar cannot refer to the Deputy-Registrar and the sub-registry as they have no competence on this level (cf. Article 25(3) Statute).
1022. Rule 4.1. For all separate procedural documents online guidance will be provided in the form of standardised documents. Such online guidance should be available for any written action to be taken by a party. The CMS requires that written pleadings are signed electronically. By Amendment 1 (to Rule 4.1) adopted by the Administrative Committee on 8 July 2022, the requirement of signature was introduced in the Rules.
1023. Cf. Examination as to formal requirements (Rule 16).

Chapter III – Application and Interpretation of the Rules of Procedure

As electronic communication (and forms) are clearly promoted, the only exception to lodge a document in hard-copy is *"where it would not be possible (...) for the reason that the (CMS) has ceased to function"*.[1024] The electronic copy of the document should be lodged as soon as practicable thereafter.[1025] It should be noted that no time extension is foreseen for such lodging in hard-copy when the CMS has ceased to function. Therefore, it would seem advisable for lodgers to keep in mind the necessary time to lodge a document in hard-copy should the CMS cease to function.

F. SERVICE AND SUPPLY OF ORDERS, DECISIONS AND WRITTEN PLEADINGS AND OTHER DOCUMENTS BY THE REGISTRY

Rule 6 sets out the principles regarding the service and supply of orders, decisions, written pleadings and other documents by the Registry. As a general principle, the Registry needs to serve orders and decisions of the Court on the parties and written pleadings of a party to the other party *as soon as practicable*. If applicable the Registry should inform the parties of the opportunity to reply or to take any other appropriate step in the proceedings and of any time period for doing so.[1026] Further, the Registry needs to supply *as soon as practicable* to the parties' copies of documents referred to it and lodged pleadings and written evidence.[1027]

Should a party lodge pleadings in a language other than the language of proceedings, the Registry should return any such pleadings.[1028]

Where the postal or electronic address for service provided by a party pursuant to the Rules has changed, that party should give notice in writing to the Registry and to every other party as soon as such change has taken place.[1029]

When setting the term within which an action should be taken by the Registry/Court the term *"as soon as practicable"* is frequently used. It seems that no specified time limits have been set in order to avoid liability of the Registry/Court.

G. INTRODUCTION TO LANGUAGE REGIME

All procedural written documents (including the written pleadings and evidence) should be lodged in the language of proceedings unless the Court or the Rules provide otherwise.[1030] Article 49 deals with the language of proceedings at first instance level and Article 50 at the appeal level (cf. *supra*).

1024. This sole exception to the general rule of electronically lodging of documents was introduced by Amendment 1 (to Rule 4.2) adopted by the Administrative Committee on 8 July 2022. Before this amendment *"any reason"* was accepted to lodge the documents in hard-copy instead of electronically. This amendment seems to make clear that if the impossibility would be caused at the lodgers' end, it will not be accepted to lodge documents in hard-copy and/or electronically after the foreseen time period (see Rules 300–301).
1025. Rule 4.2.
1026. Rule 6.1.
1027. Rule 6.2.
1028. Rule 14.4.
1029. Rule 6.3.
1030. Rule 7.1.

Hereafter, an introductory overview is provided of the language regime. For a more detailed procedural exploration of the Rules (specifically regarding changing the language of proceedings at the subsequent levels) we refer to the respective parts hereafter (and their accompanying flowcharts).

At *first instance level* and before a *local or regional division* the following principles should be taken into consideration:

- The language of proceedings may be an official EU language which is the official language or one of the official languages of the Contracting Member State hosting the relevant division, or the official language(s) designated by the Contracting Member States sharing a regional division.[1031]
- The language of proceedings may be one or more of the official languages of the EPO so designated by the Contracting Member States as the language of proceedings of their local or regional division.[1032]
- If the competent panel so approves, parties may agree on the use of the language in which the patent was granted as language of the proceedings. If the panel does not approve, the parties may request that the action be heard by the central division.[1033]
- With the agreement of the parties, the competent panel may decide (on grounds of convenience and fairness) on the use of the language in which the patent was granted.[1034]
- At the request of one of the parties and after having heard the other parties and the competent panel, the President of the Court of First Instance may (on grounds of fairness and taking into account all relevant circumstances, including the position of the parties, in particular the position of the defendant) decide on the use of the language in which the patent was granted as language of proceedings. In such action the President of the Court of First Instance will assess the need for specific translation and interpretation arrangements.[1035]

Rule 7 and Article 49 UPCA are to be read together with Rule 14. Rule 14, dealing with the use of languages under Article 49(1) and 49(2) UPCA, is a rule that has been discussed *in extenso* in the expert group and during public consultations. The Rule reflects a political consensus taking into regard the particular language regimes within some Contracting Member States (especially Belgium) and the level of knowledge of a foreign language (read English) by the judges of a Contracting Member State.

Three different interests can be identified as leading the way to the actual Rule 14.

First interest: the claimant should have the freedom of choice regarding the languages he prefers. This is a principle that has been set to limit any explicit interference by a Contracting Member State or by the language regimes of a Contracting

---

1031. Article 49(1) UPCA.
1032. Article 49(2) UPCA.
1033. Article 49(3) UPCA.
1034. Article 49(4) UPCA.
1035. Article 49(5) UPCA.

Member State. This principle is translated explicitly in Rule 14.1 where it provides that the proceedings shall be conducted:

(a) in the official language or one of the official languages designated as language(s) of proceedings pursuant to Article 49(1); or
(b) in a language designated as additional language of proceedings by a Contracting Member State pursuant to Article 49(2).

The second interest relates to the specific linguistic situation in a Contracting Member State hosting a local division or participating in a regional division for which several languages have been designated.[1036] If an action is introduced before a division having designated several languages the claimant may choose as the language of proceedings any designated language.[1037] On the other hand, in proceedings before a local or regional division in a Contracting Member State against a defendant who has his domicile or principal place of business in that Contracting Member State where the action could not be brought before any other local or regional division,[1038] proceedings should be conducted in the official language of the Contracting Member State (paragraph 1(a)). Where a designation by a Contracting Member State having several official regional languages so indicates, proceedings shall be conducted in the official language of the region in which the defendant has his domicile or principal place of business. Where there are two or more such defendants whose domiciles or principal places of business have different regional languages, the claimant may choose the language from the regional languages in question. Where a designation by a Contracting Member State having several official languages so indicates, proceedings shall be conducted in the official language of the defendant. Where there are two or more such defendants with different official languages, the claimant may choose one of the official languages.[1039]

This means, for example, that if a claimant brings an action before the local division in Belgium, the claimant can choose in principle French, Dutch, German (i.e. the official national languages of Belgium) or English (the EPO language designated by Belgium as an additional language of its local division) as the language of proceedings. The choice of the claimant is limited if the claimant cannot bring the same action before any other local or regional division (due to the fact that there are no infringements outside Belgium). In that case, the claimant is obliged to conduct the proceedings in the official language of the region in which the defendant has his domicile or principal place of business. For Belgium, this means that the claimant shall have to conduct the proceedings in Dutch if the defendant has his domicile or principal place of business in the Dutch language area (Flanders), in French if the defendant has his domicile or principal place of business in the French language area (Walloon area) or in German if the defendant has his domicile or principal place of business in the German language area (nine municipalities surrounding Eupen). For the bilingual Brussels capital region, the claimant can choose between French and Dutch.

1036. Article 49(1) and 49(2) UPCA.
1037. Rule 14.2(a).
1038. Pursuant to Article 33(1)(a) UPCA.
1039. Rule 14.2(b).

The third interest (introduced only from the end of 2014, articulated the first time in the 16th draft) concerns the expected limited knowledge of foreign languages of a panel of judges. In the 18th draft it is provided that where a designation of an additional language under Article 49(2) for a regional division or for one or more local division(s) hosted in a Member State so indicates, the Judge-Rapporteur may order in the interest of the panel that in the oral proceedings judges may use the language according to Rule 14.1(a) and/or that the Court may make any order and deliver any decision in the language according to Rule 14.1(a) together with a certified translation for the purpose of Rule 118.8 into the language according to Rule 14.1(b).[1040]

This means that if, for example, English is opted for by the claimant as being the language of proceedings, panels of local divisions that have a different language as a national language (e.g. German) may always use their national language during the oral proceedings and for writing their orders and judgments. If the panel makes use of this possibility, a certified translation needs to be provided by the panel for orders and judgments.

In order to facilitate the different language regimes before the local and regional division, the Registry will maintain online a publicly available list of languages communicated by the Contracting Member States pursuant the Article 49(1) and 49(2) as well as designations by the Contracting Member States pursuant to Rule 14.2(b) and 14.2(c)[1041]

Whether this language regime, specifically Rule 14.2(c), was foreseen by the Contracting Member States, in other words whether the Rules are in line with the prevailing Agreement, may ultimately have to be decided by the Court of Appeal.

However, it is doubtful that should the Court of Appeal decide that the language regime, as expressed in the Rules, contradicts the (will of the Contracting Member States as laid down in the) UPCA, this would result in the nullity of the proceedings at first instance.

At *first instance level* and before the *central division* the language of proceedings is the language in which the patent concerned was granted.[1042]

At *the appeal level*, the language of proceedings should be the language of proceedings before the Court of First Instance. The possibility is foreseen to change the language at this level either if parties agree to change the language into the language in which the patent was granted[1043] or if the Court of Appeal decides on another official language of a Contracting Member State and this subject to the agreement of the parties.[1044] It should be noted that the Rules themselves remain silent regarding this last possibility.

Should documents be translated it is not necessary to provide a formal certification by a translator as to the accuracy thereof unless (i) the accuracy is challenged, (ii) the Court orders a certificate, or (iii) the Rules require such a certificate.[1045]

1040. Rule 14.2(c).
1041. Rule 14.3.
1042. Article 49(9) UPCA.
1043. Article 50(2) UPCA.
1044. Article 50(3) UPCA.
1045. Rule 7.2.

Chapter III – Application and Interpretation of the Rules of Procedure

H. REPRESENTATION, COMMUNICATION WITH THE COURT AND PROPRIETORSHIP OF A PATENT

A party should be represented in accordance with Article 48 UPCA unless otherwise provided by the Rules.[1046] For the purpose of all proceedings, where the Rules provide that should a party perform an act (or that should any act be performed upon a party), that act shall be considered to be performed by or upon the representative of the party.[1047]

A party is obliged to communicate any communication with the Court to the other party. This obligation is limited to sending a copy of the communication and does not apply when the Court is obliged to send a copy to the other party.[1048] No sanctions have been provided when this obligation has not been complied with. The question may arise as to whether communication to the Court without sending a copy to the other party should be disregarded as having an influence on the rights of defence and/or whether such a deficiency can be corrected and if so, within which time frame.[1049]

Under Rule 8.4 and 8.5, a difference is introduced between the proprietorship of a Unitary Patent and of a European Patent.

- Regarding a *Unitary Patent*, the person shown in the Register for Unitary Patent Protection referred to in Regulation (EU) No. 1257/2012[1050] as the proprietor shall be treated as such. If during proceedings before the Court a new proprietor is recorded in the Register for Unitary Patent Protection, the former registered proprietor may apply to the Court pursuant to Rule 305.1(c) for the substitution of the new proprietor.[1051]
- Regarding a *European Patent*, and taking into consideration the lack of a central register, the following solution has been worked out:[1052]
    (a) in relation to the *proprietor* of a European Patent, the person entitled to be registered as proprietor under the law of each Contracting Member State in which such European Patent has been validated shall be treated as the proprietor whether or not such person is in fact recorded in the national patent register; and
    (b) in relation to the *applicant* for a European Patent, the person entitled to be registered as applicant whether or not such person is in fact recorded as such in the European Patent Register kept by the EPO, shall be considered as the applicant.

For the purposes of Rule 8.5, there shall be a rebuttable presumption that the person shown in each national patent register and the European Patent Register kept by the EPO is the person entitled to be registered as proprietor or applicant, as the case may be.

1046. Rule 8.1 with reference to Rules 5, 88 and 378.5.
1047. Rule 8.2.
1048. Rule 8.3.
1049. In such case Article 2(2) of the Code of Conduct may apply.
1050. More specifically Article 9(1)(g) and (h) of the mentioned Regulation.
1051. Rule 8.4.
1052. Rule 8.5.

A presumption of ownership is introduced[1053] regarding actions to be directed against the patent proprietor[1054] and actions for the Declaration of non-infringement[1055] in relation to European Patents. For the purpose of these proceedings the person shown in the national patent register as the proprietor shall be treated as such for each Contracting Member State or, should no such person be registered in a national patent register, the last person shown recorded as proprietor in the European Patent Register kept by the EPO shall be considered as the proprietor.

The rules regarding proprietorship shall become particularly important for the opt-out of European Patents (cf. *infra*). Since the Rules provide that all (co-)proprietors need to opt-out, the proprietors shall be responsible for making sure that all proprietors entitled to be registered as proprietor are mentioned in the opt-out. Neither the EPO nor Registry need to check whether the opt-out has been properly performed. In case the Application to opt-out is demanded by patent attorneys, they shall have to perform due diligence in order to certify whether they are authorised to perform this act by all patent proprietors. It is therefore their responsibility to check whether opt-outs are performed correctly. The patent attorney shall not be able to rely on the European Patent Register to decide who the proprietor of a European Patent is. In most cases in which patents are transferred or co-owned (including the split per Member State of the ownership), patent proprietors do not bother to register the transfer or co-ownership. Rule 5.1(b) clearly provides that all proprietors of a European Patent need to lodge the Application to opt-out. If the person lodging the Application to opt-out is not recorded as the proprietor or applicant in the European Patent Register, that person needs to lodge a Declaration of proprietorship.

The opt-out procedure is meant to be "*mechanical*". Therefore, if afterwards it appears that the opt-out was not requested properly and the patent was subject to a Court procedure (e.g. revocation action), the liability of the patent attorney could be triggered. It is important for patent attorneys to carefully address questions concerning the opt-out, certainly if it concerns large patent portfolios.

I.   POWERS OF THE COURT

Rule 9 lists the powers of the Court. The Court may, at any stage of the proceedings, of its own motion or on reasoned request by a party, order a party to take any step, answer any question or provide any clarification or evidence, within time periods to be specified.[1056] Should a time limit not be respected as provided in the Rules and/or by the Court, the Court may disregard such step, fact, evidence or argument.[1057] For disregarding such step, fact, evidence or argument it seems that no reasoned request is necessary. The Court may take such decision of its own motion. The Rules remain silent as to which elements will be taken into consideration when

---

1053. Rule 8.6.
1054. Rule 42.
1055. Rule 60.
1056. Rule 9.1.
1057. Rule 9.2.

disregarding such steps, facts, evidence or arguments.[1058] It would seem reasonable that the touchstone would be the interest of the other party. If the other party is not disadvantaged in proceedings, it would seem reasonable not to disregard such step, fact, evidence or argument not timely introduced. On the other hand, the Court may always extend (even retrospectively) or, except for the time periods stipulated regarding the Revocation of an order to preserve evidence,[1059] the Revocation for provisional measures[1060] and the Lodging of a Statement of appeal,[1061] shorten a time period.[1062] Such decision can only be made on a reasoned request by the other party and not of the Court's own motion.

The importance of this Rule 9 cannot be highlighted enough. Rule 9 allows the court to manage the case (of its "own motion") in the most suitable manner, should the rules not foresee a specific solution to a procedural issue. Further, Rule 9 allows the court to solve CMS-problems which cannot be solved in a timely manner taking into consideration the strict time limits set out in the Rules. But also for the parties Rule 9 might be of mayor importance as it allows them to file a reasoned request to solve a specific procedural problem or make a procedural request for which the rules do not provide a tailor-made solution.

J. APPLICATION TO OPT-OUT AND WITHDRAWAL OF OPT-OUT

Rule 5 sets out the procedure for lodging an Application to opt-out and Withdrawal of an opt-out[1063] regarding any patent or application.

Where Rule 8 stipulates the requirements for representation before the UPC, Rule 5.4 explicitly states that this Rule 8 does not apply to Applications to opt-out and to withdraw. As such, right holders themselves (or anyone they may appoint) can proceed with the declaration without representation.

Graphically this Rule can be presented as in the following flowcharts.

As mentioned, the opt-out system for European Patents (including expired European Patents) has been the subject of numerous comments from the patent community. As the interventions regarding this rule are so numerous, it would go beyond the scope of this publication to make a reference to each and any consecutive change and alternative view on the subject.[1064] However, it became clear that the

---

1058. Amendment 31a (to Rule 355) adopted by the Administrative Committee on 8 July 2022 provides some guidelines (but limited to decisions by default) that, even when the time limits have been exceeded, consideration should be given to the fact that the service of the claim or counterclaim was effected in sufficient time to enable the defendant to enter a defence. This consideration was introduced after consultation with the European Commission and was based on the far reaching consequences of default judgments on the right of defence of the defaulting party. Such consideration seems only explicitly foreseen regarding such default judgments.
1059. Rule 198.1.
1060. Rule 213.1.
1061. Rule 224.1.
1062. Rule 9.3 and Rule 9.4.
1063. In conformity with Article 83(3).
1064. W. Tilmann, "The European Patent Package: Opt-out or use the UPC", Hoyng-bundel (2013) – *Liber Amicorum Willem Hoyng Litigator*, Amsterdam, 458–465.

Part Three – The Rules of Procedure of the Unified Patent Court

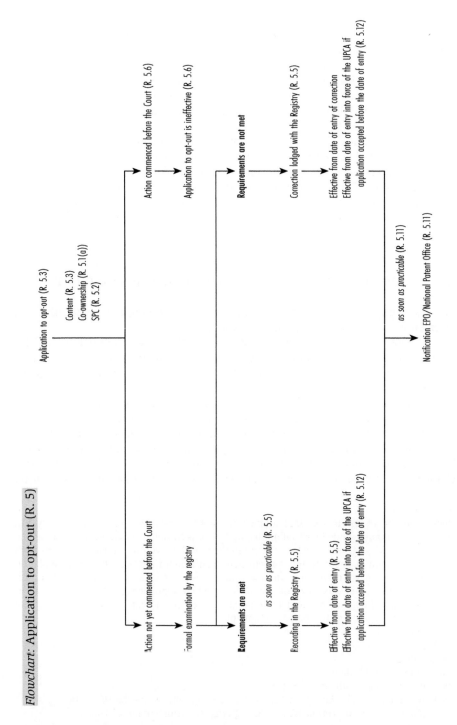

Chapter III – Application and Interpretation of the Rules of Procedure

Flowchart: Application to withdraw (R. 5)

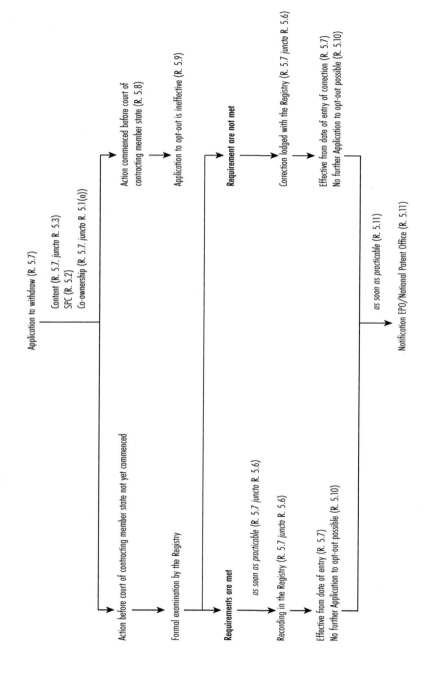

industry, which was historically the driving force for obtaining a central judicial system in Europe,[1065] was at the same time in favour of a broad transitional phase.[1066]

Rule 5 has an important influence on business strategies during the transitional regime and is without doubt the most discussed Rule at the managerial level. In the Rules, a balance has been sought between on the one hand constructing a safe harbour for those users in doubt of the effectiveness of the Court and on the other hand putting into place some gentle pressure to participate in the new system.

When examining Article 83 in conjunction with Rule 5 there seems to be two routes to opt-out. Either by declaration (i.e. the Application to opt-out),[1067] or by introducing an action (Article 83(3)[1068]). When an action has been introduced before a national court (related to a non-opted out patent), *no concurrent jurisdiction* by the Court seems possible.[1069] During the transitional phase the national court and the Court are considered as alternative courts.[1070]

This is expressed by the construction of Rules 5.7 and 5.9 introduced in the 16th draft (in the 18th Draft Rules Rule 5.6 and 5.8.). These Rules stipulate that:

- once an action regarding a patent/patent application subject of an Application to opt-out has been initiated before the Court on a date prior to the date of entry of the Application or date of correction *irrespective of whether the action is pending or has been concluded*, such an Application shall remain ineffective (Rule 5.6); and

---

1065. E. Van Zimmeren, "Recente ontwikkelingen in het Octrooirecht: het Europees Octrooi met Eenheidswerking in de 'Spotlight'", in *Recht in beweging 22e VRG Alumnidag 2015* (Antwerpen, Maklu, 2015), 358–360.

1066. This transitional phase reflects the difficult equilibrium between the reason of a uniform judicial system and the economical impact hereof on local economies (cf. A. Plomer, "A Unitary Patent for a (Dis)United Europe: the Long Shadow of History", ICC, August 2015, Volume 46, Issue 5, pp. 508–533) or multinationals' interests (based on risk spreading).

1067. As the opt-out can be notified until the very last day of the transitional period, the Application to opt-out gives the patent holder the possibility to remove his European Patent from the jurisdiction of the Court for the whole life of that patent.

1068. In Article 83(3) the possibility to opt-out from the exclusive competence of the Court is detailed but conditional on the fact that no action has been brought before the Court.

1069. Regarding the concurrent jurisdiction, it is important to note that the UPCA and the Rules remain silent as to whether the principle of no concurrent jurisdiction should be understood as such that any action commenced before the Court or the court of a Contracting Member State would bar the introduction of any action (be it the same or a different one) before the alternative court or that no concurrent jurisdiction is possible regarding that specific introduced action.

1070. That the national court and the Court are to be considered as alternatives, is in line with the objectives of the Unified Patent Court system (inter alia legal certainty for the patentees). Nevertheless, some critical issues remain as the patentee loses his control on the procedural path as an action introduced by a possible infringer before a national court will block his access to the Court. This may result in a *"race to the court"*. A further issue is whether such national proceedings can block proceedings before the Court when the case, introduced before a national court, is clearly inadmissible (e.g. validity action before a Belgian national court regarding the validity of a German part of a European Patent).

Chapter III – Application and Interpretation of the Rules of Procedure

– once an action has been commenced before a court of a Contracting Member State (in a matter over which the court also has jurisdiction pursuant to Article 32) in respect of a patent/patent application contained in an Application to withdraw on a date prior to the date of entry of the Application to withdraw or date of correction *irrespective of whether the action is pending or has been concluded*, such an Application shall remain ineffective (Rule 5.8).[1071] In cases 545571/2023 and 551054/2023 the court of first instance of the UPC (local division UPC Helsinki (Finland)), taking into considerations the specific facts of the case and applying Article 83(4) UPCA and Rule 5.8), that also an action commenced before June 1st, 2023, before a national court (in a matter over which the UPC also has jurisdiction pursuant to Article 32) made the withdrawal of an earlier opt-out ineffective. The panel decided that the UPC had no jurisdiction regarding based on the effective earlier opt-out. In this case the national action was still pending.[1072]

Rule 5.7 describes the possibility and requirements to *withdraw an opt-out*. Rule 5.10 provides that once a patent/patent application has been subject to an Application to withdraw, a subsequent Application to opt-out will not be registered. This means that there can only be one Application to opt-out (and withdrawal) per patent.

A *sunrise period* has been introduced in the Rules stating that Applications to opt-out or to withdraw the opt-out accepted by the Registry before the entry into force of the UPCA shall be treated as entered in the Register on the date of entry into force of the UPCA.[1073] This rule aims at avoiding a multitude of Applications from being introduced on the date of entry into force of the UPCA. Three days after the start of the sunrise period on 1 March 2023, 199 opt-outs were registered in the CMS. Forty-five of those 199 (25%) concerned opt-outs for patent *applications*.[1074]

Rule 5.1(a) deals with *the situation of co-ownership*. This Rule provides that *all* proprietors or applicants need to lodge the Application to opt-out. Should the person lodging an Application to opt-out not be recorded as the proprietor or applicant in the registers referred to in Rule 8.5(a) and (b) respectively, these person(s) should lodge a Declaration of proprietorship pursuant to Rule 8.5. Rule 5.3(e) provides that the Declaration of proprietorship must be contained in the Application to opt-out. The proprietorship of a European Patent/application, more specifically, the correctness of this information has been an element of discussion in the expert group

---

1071. In this respect, it should be noted that the Preparatory Committee on its website states that it will be possible for a party to initiate a revocation action before the Court even if the proprietor of the European Patent has initiated an infringement action before a national patent. The only possibility for the proprietor to avoid a centralised revocation action would be to make use of the Application to opt-out from the jurisdiction of the Court. (FAQ as found on www.unified-patent-court.org dd. 17 December 2015.)
1072. In application of Rule 210.4(as one of the cases concerned an application for provisional measures) and exceptionally, the decision was given orally on September 21th, 2023 at the end of the oral hearing. The written decision (with further motivation) was not available at the time of drafting this chapter. It is likely that this case may give rise to an appeal.
1073. Rule 5.12.
1074. Laurence Lai, "3 days of UPC sunrise in numbers", 4 March 2023, Kluwer Patent Blog.

as an up-to-date centralised register does not exist at the EPO level. The Rules of Procedure clarify that a *"proprietor"* of a European Patent is the person *"entitled to be registered as proprietor(s) under the law of each Contracting Member State in which the European Patent has been validated"*, whether or not such person is in fact recorded in the register maintained in the Contracting Member State. For persons registered in each national patent register and the European Patent Register there is a rebuttable presumption that such person is entitled to be registered as proprietor.[1075] But since this presumption is rebuttable, it will be the task of the parties (and their representatives) to verify the ownership rights.[1076] Neither the EPO nor the Court will do so. The opt-out procedure is meant to be *"mechanical"*. Therefore, it could appear afterwards that, despite an Application to opt-out, the opt-out was not executed by all the patent proprietors and the Court is competent after all.

The Rules state clearly that the Application to opt-out,[1077] and the Application to withdraw,[1078] should be made in respect of all of the states for which the European Patent has been granted or which have been designated in the application.[1079] This means that not only the UPC Member States should be indicated in the Application, but all states of the European Patent Organisation for which the patent was granted or (for applications) that were designated in the application.

An important part of Rule 5 has been reserved for *SPCs*. Rule 5.2 clarifies that any Application to opt-out or Application to withdraw extends to any SPC based on the European Patent. Where any such SPC has been granted on the date of lodging the Application to opt-out or the Application to withdraw, the holder(s) of the SPC shall, if different from the proprietor of the patent, lodge the Application to opt-out or the Application to withdraw *together* with the proprietor. Should the SPC be granted subsequent to the lodging of the Application to opt-out, the opt-out shall take effect automatically on grant of the SPC. Rule 5.2(c) further makes it clear that the specific situation of Rules 5.6 and 5.8 (relationship between proceedings introduced before the Court or before a court of a Member State and effectiveness of the Application to opt-out / withdraw) applies for SPCs providing that:

1075. Rule 8.5(c).
1076. The examination hereof is left to the Registry when a procedure is commenced. If the defendant would develop an argument regarding entitlement, it seems that such argumentation would not be possible as a preliminary remark, but should be dealt with on its merits. Where Rule 5A.3 articulates a specific procedure regarding an Application to remove an unauthorised Application to opt-out or unauthorised withdrawal of an opt-out (decision by Registrar and if necessary a review by the President of the Court of Appeal) such procedure seems not available in light of the formal examination by the Registry regarding entitlement.
1077. Rule 5.1(b).
1078. Rule 5.7.
1079. Before Amendment 2 (to Rule 5.1(b) and Rule 5.7) adopted by the Administrative Committee on 8 July 2022 the Application to opt out and to withdraw should have been made in respect to *"[a]ll of the Contracting Member States"*. This wording was found to be inconsistent with the indivisibility of the Application to opt-out and to withdraw. In its explanatory notes the Administrative Committee states that such wording would imply that the UPC solely would have jurisdiction over Contracting Member States, which is held not to be the case.

Chapter III – Application and Interpretation of the Rules of Procedure

(i) actions in respect of a European Patent shall apply to all SPCs based on that European Patent;
(ii) actions in respect of an SPC shall apply to the European Patent on which such SPC is based; and
(iii) actions in respect of an SPC shall apply to all other SPCs based on the same European Patent.

Rule 5.2(d) clarifies that it is not possible for SPCs based on a *Unitary Patent* to opt-out.

Rule 5.9[1080] has been reserved for the situation where *an application for a European Patent subject to an opt-out becomes (after grant) a Unitary Patent*. In such case the Application to opt-out shall be deemed to be withdrawn. This withdrawal should be entered as soon as practicable in the Register.

On 26 February 2016 the Preparatory Committee of the Unified Patent Court published the Rules on Court fees and recoverable costs for the Court. The explanatory note that accompanied these Rules explained that – although Rule 5.5 (16th Draft and omitted in the 18th Draft) contains the possibility to charge a fee for an Application for and Withdrawal of an opt-out – there was a clear consensus in consultation responses that the opt-out fee had to be removed or lowered. Finally, the Preparatory Committee decided that no opt-out fee or a fee for a Withdrawal of an opt-out shall be charged. The Preparatory Committee explained this decision by referring to the commitment made by the Preparatory Committee that the fees for both the Application to opt-out and its withdrawal are set to reclaim administrative costs only and that the Court would not profit from either of these. The Preparatory Committee wrote in the explanatory note that they gathered more information as to how the proposed opt-out process will work and that the administration burden rests almost entirely with the applicant. Furthermore, any cost to the Court associated with the opt-out is related to processing the fee. There is no additional cost for the Case Management System to process Applications to opt-out if there is no fee. Requiring applicants to make payment generates costs for the Court which would not be needed if there were no fee. So, removing the fee would remove the cost. Further, it also eliminates the problem of how to process payments particularly during provisional applications and honours the commitment already made only to reclaim administrative costs of the Application to opt-out.

By Amendment 3 (introduction Rule 5A) adopted by the Administrative Committee on 8 July 2022 a new Rule was introduced regarding the Application to

---

1080. This Rule is necessary as the territorial scope of the first European patents with unitary effect will in all likelihood not cover all twenty-five Member States participating in enhanced cooperation (see Article 18(2), 2nd sub-paragraph, Regulation 1257/2012/EU). For the Member States that have not ratified the UPCA, a European Patent may still be obtained and this in addition to a European patent with unitary effect. Rule 5.10 further identifies the effect of the opt-out of a European Patent application if a European patent with unitary effect not covering all participating Member States is obtained. In this situation the opt-out shall be deemed to be withdrawn only in respect of the Contracting Member States covered by the European patent with unitary effect. In Contracting Member States that have not ratified the UPCA, a European Patent may be validated and, if so, the opt-out shall be effective for that European Patent.

remove an unauthorised Application to opt-out or unauthorised withdrawal of an opt-out. Rule 5A.1 states that the proprietor of a European Patent or the applicant for a published application for a European Patent or holder of a supplementary protection certificate in relation to which an Application to opt-out or withdraw the opt-out is entered in the register may lodge an Application to remove the entry of an unauthorised Application to opt-out or withdrawal of the opt-out from the Registry setting out the reasons.[1081] The decision on such an Application for removal is to be made by the Registrar and may be subject to an Application for review to the President of the Court of Appeal of the UPC.

1081. Rule 5A.2 further states that the Registrar should indicate whether an Application to opt-out or Application to witdraw is subject to an Application for removal.

Chapter III – Application and Interpretation of the Rules of Procedure

Flowchart: Application for removal (Rule 5A)

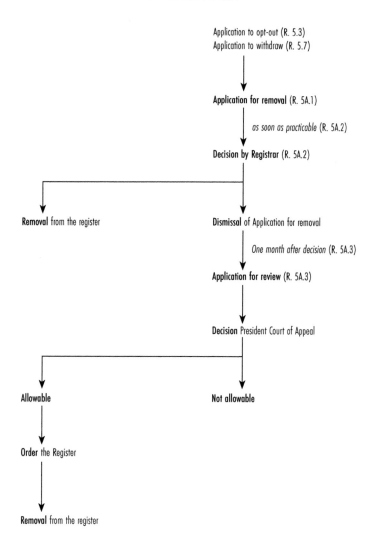

Chapter IV

(Part 1) Procedures before the Court of First Instance (Rules 10–159): Stages of the Proceeding (inter partes proceedings)

A.   BIRDS' EYE VIEW

The Rules make a clear distinction between the following actions:[1082]

- Infringement Action
- Revocation Action
- Action for Declaration of non-infringement
- Actions within Article 33(5) and 33(6) UPCA
- Action for Compensation for licences on the basis of Article 8 of Regulation (EU) No. 1257/2012.
- Action against decisions of the EPO in carrying out the tasks referred to in Article 9 of Regulation (EU) No. 1257/2012

The following distinctive stages of proceedings are identifiable in the Rules:[1083]

- a written procedure, which generally comprises:
  - a Statement of claim
  - a Statement of defence
  - a Reply to statement of defence
  - a Rejoinder to the reply to the statement of defence
- an interim procedure, which may include an interim conference with the parties;
- an oral procedure, which includes an oral hearing of the parties, unless the Court dispenses with the oral hearing with the agreement of the parties;

and where necessary:

- a procedure for the award of damages; and/or
- a procedure for cost orders.

1082. Article 32(1)(a-j).
1083. Rule 10.

The exceptional action is the *"Action for Compensation for licenses on the basis or Article 8 of the Regulation (EU) No. 1257/2012 implementing enhanced cooperation in the area of the creation of Unitary Patent Protection"*.[1084]

In any of the above stages, the Court, more specifically the Judge-Rapporteur, may propose the parties make use of the facilities of the Patent Mediation and Arbitration Centre (hereafter referred to as the "Centre") in order to settle or to explore a settlement of the dispute.[1085] Such exploration of the possibilities of a settlement is one of the aims of the interim conference described hereafter.[1086] Should parties attempt to settle, such attempt should not have a negative effect on their rights under the Rules.[1087]

The terms of a settlement or arbitral award by consent may be confirmed on the request of a party by a decision of the Court.[1088] An important change was introduced by adding the wording *"irrespective of whether it was reached using the facilities of the Centre or otherwise"* after the words *"settlement or arbitral award by consent"*. By adding this wording the exclusivity regarding mediation or arbitration, which might have been claimed by the Centre based on Article 35 UPCA, has been restricted.[1089] Rule 11.2 also clarifies the type of arbitral award that can be enforced as a settlement under Article 82 UPCA by specifying that the parties must have consented to the arbitral award. The parties may agree on costs to be awarded or may request the Court to decide on costs to be awarded through a procedure which is *mutatis mutandis* the same as the procedure for a cost decision in Court proceedings.[1090]

Save for the purpose of enforcing the terms of any such settlement agreement, no documents, expressed opinions, proposals, concession, suggestions, and so on may be relied upon as evidence by the Court or the parties in proceedings before the Court or any other court, unless it was agreed by parties that such matter was made on an *"open basis"* and freely disclosable to the Court or any other court[1091].[1092]

1. Examination as to formal requirements

Before examining the distinct stages of the proceedings, it should be noted that the examination as to the formal requirements, usually performed by the Registry, is standardised in different actions.

1084. Rule 80.
1085. Rule 11.1.
1086. Rule 104(d)
1087. Article 8 of Directive 2008/52/EC on certain aspects of mediation in civil and commercial matters which provides that Member States (MS) shall *"ensure that parties who choose mediation in an attempt to settle a dispute are not subsequently prevented from initiating judicial proceedings or arbitration in relation to that dispute by the expiry of limitation or prescription periods during the mediation process"*.
1088. Rule 11.2.
1089. See Part Two, Chapter II F, *supra*.
1090. Rules 150–156.
1091. Rule 11.3.
1092. As the courts of the Contracting Member States are not bound by the Rules and the Court is considered a national court, Article 7 Directive 2008/52/EC on certain aspects of mediation in civil and commercial matters will apply.

Chapter IV – (Part 1) Procedures before the Court of First Instance (Rules 10–159)

Flowchart: Bird's eye view

1. Principle (R. 10)

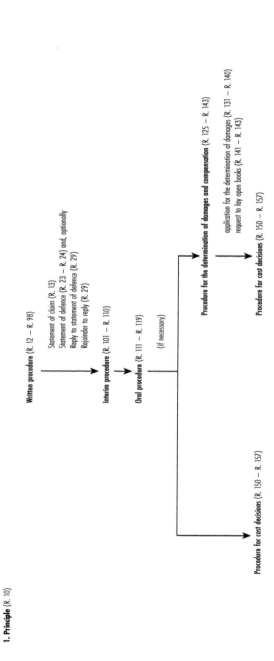

2. Exception (R. 80): "Action for Compensation for licences on the basis of Art. 8 of the Regulation (EU) No. 1257/2012 implementing enhanced cooperation in the area of the creation of unitary patent protection"

3. Settlement (R. 11) (R. 365)

Written procedure
Interim procedure (if requested)
Oral procedure
Procedure for the determination of damages
Procedure for cost orders

Part Three – The Rules of Procedure of the Unified Patent Court

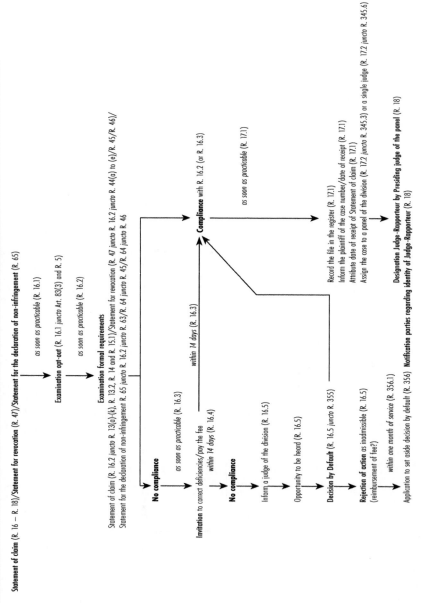

Flowchart: Examination as to formal requirements (R. 16/R. 17) and designation of Judge-Rapporteur (R. 18)

Throughout the Rules reference is made to Rules 16 and 17 (for the introductory Statement of claim) and Rule 27 (for the Statement of defence) each time a formal examination is to be considered (if appropriate using the indication *mutatis mutandis*).

A similar structure in the Rules applies regarding the *Designation of the Judge-Rapporteur*[1093] following the formal examination by the Registry of the introductory statements and the *further schedule*[1094] upon the formal examination of the subsequent defence statements.

In the following actions a reference is made to (i) Rules 16 and 17 (regarding Statement of claim) and Rule 27 (regarding Statement of defence), (ii) Rule 18 (designation of the Judge-Rapporteur) and Rule 28 (further schedule):

Infringement action
- Statement of claim (Rules 16/17/18)
- Statement of defence (either including a counterclaim for revocation or not) (Rules 27/28)

Revocation action
- Statement for revocation (Rules 16/17/18)
- Defence to revocation (Rules 27/28)

Action for declaration of non-infringement
- Statement for the declaration of non-infringement (Rules 16/17/18)
- Defence to statement for the declaration of non-infringement (Rules 27/28)

Actions within Article 33(5) and 33(6)
- Rule 70.2 *juncto* Rules 16/17
- Rule 71.2 *juncto* Rules 16/17

By Amendment 8 (to Rule 27) adopted by the Administrative Committee on 8 July 2022 the examination by the Registry of the requirements of Rule 25.1(g) – (h) was introduced for the Counterclaim for revocation as it is considered a complaint in a separate action.[1095]

Where reference is made to the formal examination of the Statement of claim (Rule 16) it is not always clear which specific Rule(s) should apply. For example in Rule 16.2, reference is made to the requirements of Rule 13.1(a) to (k). When Rule 47 refers to Rules 16 to 18 being applied *mutatis mutandis*, it is not clear which specific requirements of Rule 44.1(a) to (j) should be examined. By reference it seems that only Rule 44.1(a) to (e) are part of the formal examination. The same remark should be formulated when reading Rule 65. The Rules remain silent as to which parts of Rule 62(a) to (j) should be formally examined. Because of the reference, it seems that only Rule 62(a) to (f) should be examined.

1093. Rule 18.
1094. Rule 28.
1095. The explanatory notes make clear that *only* Rule 25.1(g) and (h) should be subject to formal examination as the other formal requirements were already the subject of the examination of the Statement of claim and the Statement of defence.

Flowchart: Examination as to formal requirements. Statement of defence (R. 27)

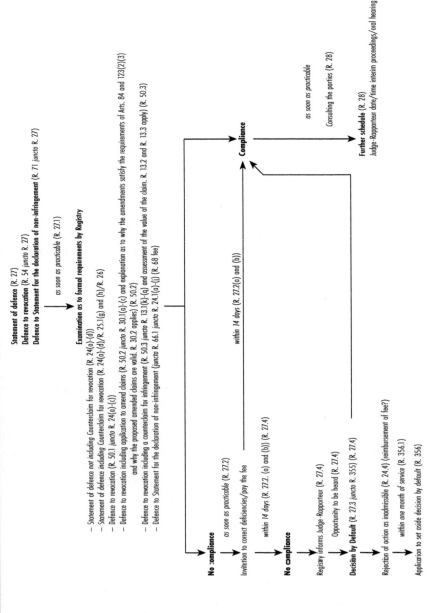

Chapter IV – (Part 1) Procedures before the Court of First Instance (Rules 10–159)

Rule 50.3 regarding the Defence to revocation indicates that the Defence should provide an explanation as to why the amendments satisfy the requirements of Articles 84 and 123(2) and (3) and why the proposed amendments are valid. The question may arise as to whether the examination hereof should be considered a formal examination to be performed by the Registry.

Where a procedure is foreseen for the applicant to be heard if the Registry would decide that the (formal) requirements are not met,[1096] it is not explicitly foreseen at which stage of the proceedings a defendant can argue that a decision of compliance of the formal requirements was flawed. As most of the formal requirements are not explicitly mentioned in Rule 19.1(a)[1097] argumentation regarding non-compliance of the formal requirements seem to have to be decided after the Preliminary Objections.

2. Preliminary Objection

A further procedural element similar to different actions is the *Preliminary Objection* as stipulated in Rules 19 to 21. In the following actions, reference is made to such objection:

- Infringement Action (Rules 19 to 21)
- Revocation Action (Rule 48)[1098]
- Action for declaration of non-infringement (Rule 66)[1099]

The Preliminary Objection may concern:[1100]

- The jurisdiction and competence of the Court, including any objection that an Application to opt-out pursuant to Rule 5 applies to the patent that is the subject of the proceedings.[1101]
- The competence of the division indicated by the claimant.[1102]
- The language of the Statement concerned.[1103]

The language in which the Preliminary Objection should be drawn up is governed by Rule 14.[1104] As no specific exceptions have been furnished in Rule 14 regarding a Preliminary Objection, the general language regime should be applied.[1105]

1096. Rule 16.5.
1097. With a clear exception for the examination of the jurisdiction and competence of the court, including any objection than an opt-out pursuant to Rule 5 applies to the patent that is the subject of the proceedings. It will depend on how broad *"jurisdiction and competence"* will be interpreted to include other formal requirements.
1098. With reference to Rules 19.1 to 3, 19.5 to 7, 20 and 21.
1099. With reference to Rules 19.1 to 3, 19.5 to 7, 20 and 21.
1100. Rule 19.1.
1101. Whether the patent/patent application is the subject of an opt-out is therefore not only examined during at the formal stage (when the Statement of claim is introduced (cf. Rule 16.1), but may also be the subject of a Preliminary Objection (Rule 19.1(a)).
1102. With reference to Rule 13.1.i.
1103. With reference to Rule 14.
1104. Rule 19.3.
1105. In earlier versions of the Draft Rules (up to the 17th draft) the possibility to use alternative languages was foreseen. In the 14th Draft as an alternative such Preliminary Objection

Part Three – The Rules of Procedure of the Unified Patent Court

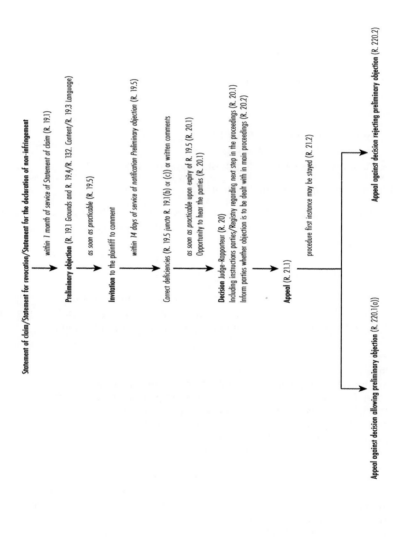

Chapter IV – (Part 1) Procedures before the Court of First Instance (Rules 10–159)

If no Preliminary Objection is lodged within the provided time period,[1106] such failure shall be treated as a submission to the jurisdiction and competence of the Court and the competence of the division opted for by the claimant.[1107]

The defendant may request, by Preliminary Objection, transferral to the central division pursuant to Article 33(2) should the action been commenced before a regional division.[1108]

The actual procedure is detailed in the flowchart.

3. Value-based fee for the infringement action

The value-based fee is governed by Part 6 Rules (and specifically Rules 370.6 and 371.4).

Rule 370.6 refers to guidelines laid down in a decision by the Administrative Committee (and further discussed under Part Three, Chapter 9 A.1.g).

Rule 371.4 stipulates that at first instance the value will be determined based on the claimant's assessment of the value at the time of lodging the relevant pleading or application. Should a higher value be determined by the Judge-Rapporteur the claimant will need to pay the remaining fee (within ten days of service of the order determining the value of the action). Should the value be lower, the Court shall reimburse the claimant.

Rule 371.4 refers to the following Rules in view of the order to be made by the Judge-Rapporteur:

- Rule 22: regarding an infringement action. The Rule refers to Rule 370.6 and indicates that the order should be taken during the interim procedure.
- Rule 60: regarding a counterclaim for infringement. The Rule refers to Rule 370.6 and indicates that the order should be taken during the interim procedure.
- Rule 74: regarding an action for a declaration of non-infringement. The Rule refers to Rule 370.6 and indicates that the order should be taken during the interim procedure.
- Rule 133: regarding an application for the determination of damages. Here no explicit reference is made to Rule 370.6 but merely to Part 6 of the Rules in general.

---

could be drafted in the language of the Contracting Member State where the defendant had his residence or principal place of business. In the 17th Draft the alternative language was limited to one of the official languages of the EPO.

1106. Rule 19.1 states within one month of service of the Statement of claim.
1107. Rule 19.6. Whether the claimant has the opportunity to object regarding the competence of the Division should the Registry have allocated a case to the seat or a single section of the central division based on the application of Rule 17, is not explicitly foreseen.
1108. Rule 19.4. The Preliminary objection shall in such a case contain all facts and evidence supporting the existence of the same infringement in the territories of three or more regional divisions. The Rule explains the application of Rule 19.1(b) in the case of applying Article 33(2) §2.

Part Three – The Rules of Procedure of the Unified Patent Court

Flowchart: Distribution of actions between the seats of the Central Division and its sections (R. 17 and R. 345.3)

1. Action involving **single patent** with **single classification** (R. 17.3(a))

    Allocation by Registry based on the classification of the patent according to Annex II UPCA
    Assignment to a specific panel based on action-distribution-scheme (R. 345.3)

Panel of the seat or the section of the central division

2. Action involved **more than one patent** and majority of patents with **single classification** (R. 17.3(b))

    Allocation by Registry based on the classification of the patent according to Annex II UPCA
    Assignment to a specific panel based on action-distribution-scheme (R. 345.3)

Panel of the seat or the section of the central division

3. Action involves **single patent** with **more than one classification** (R. 17.3(c)(i))

    Allocation by Registry appropriate to the first classification of the patent according to Annex II UPCA
    Assignment to a specific panel based on action-distribution-scheme (R. 345.3)

Presiding judge of the panel of the Seat or the section of the central division

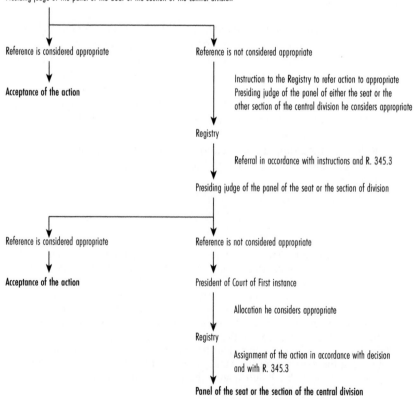

Reference is considered appropriate

Acceptance of the action

Reference is not considered appropriate

    Instruction to the Registry to refer action to appropriate Presiding judge of the panel of either the seat or the other section of the central division he considers appropriate

Registry

    Referral in accordance with instructions and R. 345.3

Presiding judge of the panel of the seat or the section of division

Reference is considered appropriate

Acceptance of the action

Reference is not considered appropriate

President of Court of First instance

    Allocation he considers appropriate

Registry

    Assignment of the action in accordance with decision and with R. 345.3

Panel of the seat or the section of the central division

Chapter IV – (Part 1) Procedures before the Court of First Instance (Rules 10–159)

Flowchart: Distribution of actions between the seats of the Central Division and its sections (R. 17 and R. 345.3) *(cont.)*

4. Actions involves **more than one patent** and **no majoriry with a single classification** corresponding to the seat or the one of the section of the central division (R. 17.3(c)(ii))

        ↓   Allocation by Registry appropriate to the first classification of the patent according to Annex II UPCA
            Assignment to a specific panel based on action-distribution-scheme (R. 345.3)

Presiding judge of the panel of the Seat or the section of the central division

↓   ↓

Reference is considered appropriate   Reference is not considered appropriate

↓   ↓

Acceptance of the action   Instruction to the Registry to refer action to appropriate Presiding judge of the panel of either the seat or the other section of the central division he considers appropriate

                       ↓

                       Registry

                       ↓   Referral in accordance with instructions and R. 345.3

Presiding judge of the panel of the seat or the section of division

↓   ↓

Reference is considered appropriate   Reference is not considered appropriate

↓   ↓

Acceptance of the action   President of Court of First instance

                       ↓   Allocation he considers appropriate

                       Registry

                       ↓   Assignment of the action in accordance with decision and with R. 345.3

Panel of the seat or the section of the central division

As will be mentioned hereafter, the value of the case not only plays a role with regard to the fees to be paid to the Court but is also important for the procedure for cost decisions (see *infra* Part Three, Chapter IV F) and specifically for Rule 152.2 regarding the recovery of the representation costs and the ceiling for recoverable costs that makes reference to the value of the proceedings.

4. Distribution of actions

The distribution of actions between the seat of the central division is straightforward when the action involves *a single patent having a single classification*[1109] or *involves more than one patent and a majority of the patents have a single classification* appropriate to the seat or a single section of the central division according to Annex II of the UPCA:[1110]

(a) Where an action involves a single patent having a single classification, the Registry shall allocate the action to the seat or the section of the central division appropriate to the classification of the patent.[1111] Subsequently, the Registry[1112] shall assign the action to a panel[1113] in accordance with the action-distribution scheme as set out in Rule 345(3).

(b) Where an action involves more than one patent and a majority of the patents have a single classification appropriate to the seat or a single section of the central division (cf. Annex II UPCA), the Registry shall allocate the action to the seat or that section of the central division. Subsequently, the Registry shall assign the action to a panel in accordance with the action-distribution scheme as set out in Rule 345(3).

When the action involves *a single patent having more than one classification or where the action involves more than one patent and no majority of the patents have a single classification corresponding to the seat or to one of the sections of the central division*, the allocation becomes more complicated:[1114]

(c) Where neither of the above apply, namely where (i) the action involves a single patent having more than one classification or (ii) where the action involves more than one patent and no majority of the patents have a single classification corresponding to the seat or to one of the sections of the central division, the Registry shall assign the action in accordance with the action-distribution scheme as set out in Rule 345.3 to the panel of the seat or the section[1115] appropriate to the first classification of either the single patent or, where the action involves more than one patent, the patent first listed

---

1109. Rule 17.3(a).
1110. Rule 17.3(a) and (b).
1111. Cf. Annex II UPCA.
1112. In the earlier version of the Rules reference was made to the *"presiding judge of the seat of that section"*. As this position does not exist, the necessary adjustments were made in Rule 17.3(a) to (c) and Rule 345.
1113. See Rule 345(1) regarding the appointment of this judge by the Presidium.
1114. Rule 17.3(c).
1115. See Rule 345(1) regarding the appointment of this judge by the Presidium.

Chapter IV – (Part 1) Procedures before the Court of First Instance (Rules 10-159)

in the Statement of claim.[1116] If the presiding judge of the respective panel considers that the reference of the action is appropriate, he shall accept it. If he considers otherwise, he shall instruct the Registry to refer the action in accordance with the action-distribution scheme as set out in Rule 345.3 to the presiding judge of the panel of either the seat or the other section of the central division he considers appropriate. The referred to presiding judge of that panel once again has to consider whether the re-allocation of the action is appropriate. If he considers otherwise, it is up to the President of the Court of First Instance to allocate the action to the seat or the other section of the central division he considers appropriate. Subsequently, the Registry shall assign the action to a panel in accordance with the action-distribution scheme as set out in Rule 345.3.

B. (CHAPTER 1) WRITTEN PROCEDURE (RULES 12-96)

1. Infringement action (Rules 12-41)

When examining the infringement action flowchart, it is important to take the following in consideration:

- Where the claimant is *not the proprietor* of the patent, all references to the claimant regarding an application to amend the patent should be read as including the proprietor.[1117] The Rules do not provide an indication as to which deadlines apply when a conflict of interests exists between the claimant non-proprietor and the proprietor becoming a party in the proceedings following Rule 25.2. The Rules set one term for the Defence to the counterclaim for revocation and the Reply to the statement of defence (Rule 29(d)) regardless of whether this has been drafted by the claimant non-proprietor (and the proprietor at the same time became a party in the proceedings (based on Rule 25.2)). It will be up to the Judge-Rapporteur to *case manage* such a situation.
- The Defence to the counterclaim (by the proprietor of the patent) may include an *Application to amend the patent*.[1118] Such Application should contain the proposed amendments of the claims of the patent concerned and/or specification, including where appropriate one or more alternative sets of claims (auxiliary requests)[1119] and this in the language in which the patent was granted. Where the language of the proceedings is not the language in which the patent was granted, the proprietor should lodge a translation of the proposed amendments in the language of the proceedings, and where the patent is a Unitary Patent, in the language of the defendant's domicile in a Member State of the EU or of the place of the alleged infringement or

---

1116. Cf. Annex II UPCA.
1117. Rule 29(f).
1118. Rule 30.
1119. Rule 30.1(a).

Part Three – The Rules of Procedure of the Unified Patent Court

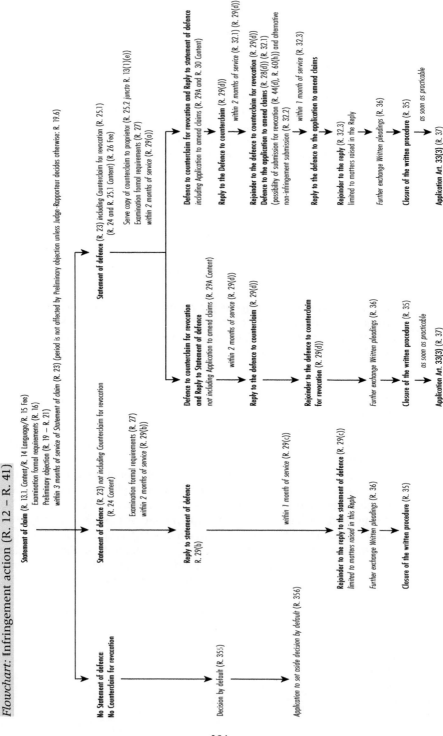

Chapter IV – (Part 1) Procedures before the Court of First Instance (Rules 10-159)

threatened infringement in a Contracting Member State if so requested by the defendant.
- A party to the proceedings may lodge an *Application for allocating a technically qualified judge to the panel*. Such an Application needs to contain an indication of the relevant field of technology[1120] and should be lodged as early as possible in the written procedure. An Application lodged after the closure of the written procedure may only be granted if justified in view of changed circumstances. Changed circumstances could comprise new submissions presented by the other party and allowed by the Court. If the requirements have been complied with and the Judge-Rapporteur has been consulted, the President of the Court of First Instance will allocate a technically qualified judge to the panel. Rule 33.2 is not too clear as to whether the request can be denied by the President of the Court of First Instance. *On the one hand* the rule provides that the President of the Court of First Instance *"shall"* allocate a technically qualified judge if the mentioned requirements are met, while *on the other hand* the obligation to consult the Judge-Rapporteur would imply that the Judge-Rapporteur could advise, taking in consideration the specific circumstances of the case (e.g. procedural strategy to delay the written procedure), that the allocation of a technically qualified judge is not necessary.[1121]

The Judge-Rapporteur himself may at any time during the written procedure, after consulting the presiding judge and the parties, request the President of the Court of First Instance to *allocate a technically qualified judge to the panel*.[1122]

In the event a technically qualified judge is allocated to the panel, it might be beneficial for the proceedings that the technically qualified judge masters the language of proceedings. The Rules remain silent on this matter.
- Any *request to amend the patent* after the term allowed to include an Application to amend the patent into the Defence to the counterclaim for revocation following Rule 30 will only be admitted into the proceedings with the permission of the Court.[1123]
- The terms as set out in the Rules should be strictly observed. However, the Judge-Rapporteur may, on a reasoned request by a party (lodged before the date on which he intends to close the written procedure (cf. Rule 35(a))), allow the *exchange of further written pleadings*.[1124] The Rules remain silent as to whether the Judge-Rapporteur is obliged to allow a request made by all parties regarding the further exchange of further written pleadings. Based on case management principles, it would be reasonable that the

---

1120. Rule 33.1-3.
1121. This could be of importance when such an application based on Rule 33 is introduced during the written phase upon an application for provisional measures (see Rules 205-213) (in the case where the defendant is summoned). However, one may hold that, as no reference can be found in the mentioned Rules, such an application is not possible in summary proceedings.
1122. Rule 34.
1123. Rule 30.2.
1124. Rule 36.

Part Three – The Rules of Procedure of the Unified Patent Court

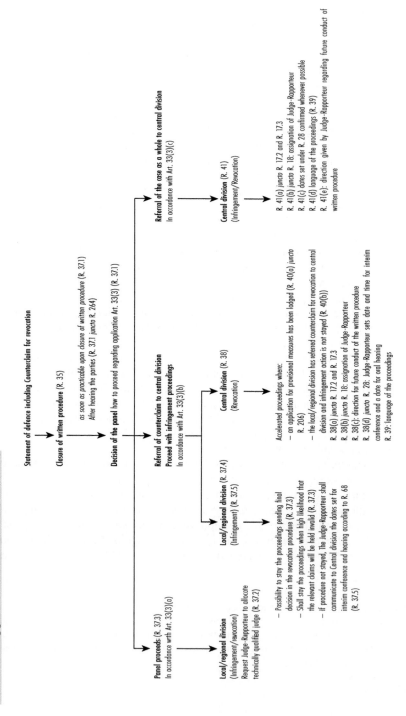

Judge-Rapporteur may ignore such a mutual request if he believes that additional argumentation is not necessary to adjudicate the case.

The application of Article 33(3) UPCA *juncto* Rule 37 is represented graphically below. For convenience, Article 33(3) UPCA is cited hereunder:

> *"A counterclaim for revocation as referred to in Article 32(1)(e) may be brought in the case of an action for infringement as referred to in Article 32(1)(a). The local or regional division concerned shall, after having heard the parties, have the discretion either to:*
> *(a) proceed with both the infringement action and with the counterclaim for revocation and request the President of the Court of First Instance to allocate from the Pool of Judges in accordance with Article 18(3) a technically qualified judge with qualifications and experience in the field of technology concerned;*
> *(b) refer the counterclaim for decision to the central division and suspend or proceed with the infringement proceedings; or*
> *(c) with agreement of the parties, refer the case for decision to the central division."*

In our view, the following considerations may come into play when the Court has to decide on the referral of the action as a whole or in part to the central division:

- amendments of the patent;
- complexity of the technical nature of the patent;
- new points of law;
- mismatch between the timing of hearings in case of referral;
- the language in which the case would be dealt with before the different divisions (and the need for translations);
- duplication of considerations of evidence or issues;
- costs of a referral;
- squeeze between infringement and validity issues.

Regarding the language of the proceedings upon application of Article 33(3) UPCA, the following rules apply:

- *Language of the proceedings in case of a Counterclaim for revocation is referred to the central division under Article 33(3)(b) UPCA.* If the case is referred to the central division under Article 33(3)(b) UPCA, the language regime depends on whether the language of proceedings before the local or regional division is the language in which the patent was granted:
  • Where the language of the proceedings before the regional division or the local division which referred the Counterclaim for revocation to the central division is *not the language in which the patent was granted*, the Judge-Rapporteur may order that the parties lodge, within a period of one month, a translation into the language in which the patent was granted of any written pleadings and such other documents lodged during the written procedure as the Judge-Rapporteur may direct.[1125]

1125. Rule 39.1.

Part Three – The Rules of Procedure of the Unified Patent Court

Flowchart: Revocation action (R. 42 – R. 60)

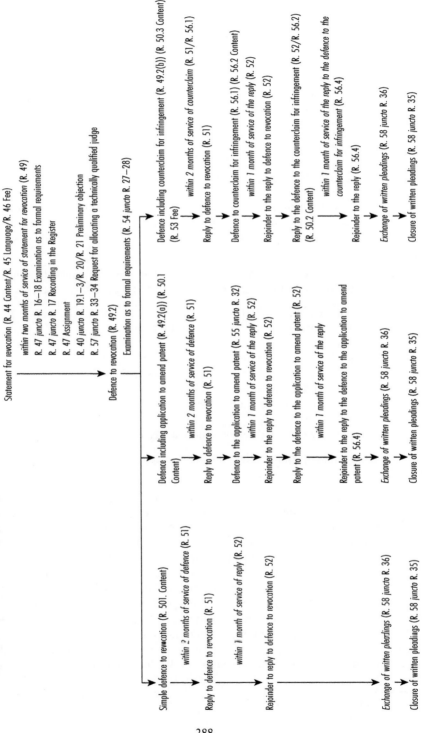

Where appropriate, the Judge-Rapporteur may specify in his order that only excerpts of parties' written pleadings and other documents need to be translated.[1126]
- Where the language of the proceedings before the regional or the local division is *the language in which the patent was granted*, the pleadings (served in accordance with Rules 24, 25, 29, 29A., 30 and 32) shall stand.[1127]
– *Language of the proceedings when the central division deals with the action under Article 33(3)(c) UPCA*. Rule 39 applies *mutatis mutandis*:[1128] the Judge-Rapporteur may order that the parties lodge a translation in the language in which the patent was granted of any written pleadings lodged during the written procedure. Where appropriate, the Judge-Rapporteur may specify in his order that only excerpts of parties' written pleadings and other documents need to be translated. Otherwise the pleadings lodged during the written procedure will stand.[1129]

2. Revocation action (Rules 42–60)

Any action for revocation of a patent should be directed against the proprietor of the patent.[1130] In case the action has been commenced against a registered proprietor of a European Patent under Rule 8.6,[1131] but he is not the actual proprietor (in the sense of Rule 8.5), the registered proprietor will have to apply for the substitution as soon as practicable after being served the Statement for revocation.[1132]

The Statement for revocation should be drawn up in the language in which the patent was granted.[1133] Where the parties have agreed to bring the action before a local or a regional division in accordance with Article 33(7) UPCA, the Statement for revocation should be drawn up in one of the languages referred to in Rule 14.1(a) and Rule 14.1(b).

3. Action for declaration of non-infringement (Rules 61–74)

The Court can declare that the performance of a specific act does not, or a proposed act would not, constitute an infringement of a patent.[1134] Such declaration can be

---

1126. Rule 39.2.
1127. Rule 39.3.
1128. Rule 41(d).
1129. Rule 41(d).
1130. Rule 42.1.
1131. Rule 8.6 provides that for the purpose of proceedings pursuant to Rules 42 and 61, the person shown in the register of patents maintained in each Contracting Member State in which the European Patent has been validated as the proprietor, shall be treated as the proprietor for each Contracting Member State. If no such person is registered in the national patent register, the last person shown recorded as proprietor in the European Patent Register kept by the EPO shall be treated as the proprietor.
1132. Rule 42.2.
1133. Rule 45.1.
1134. Rule 61.1.

Part Three – The Rules of Procedure of the Unified Patent Court

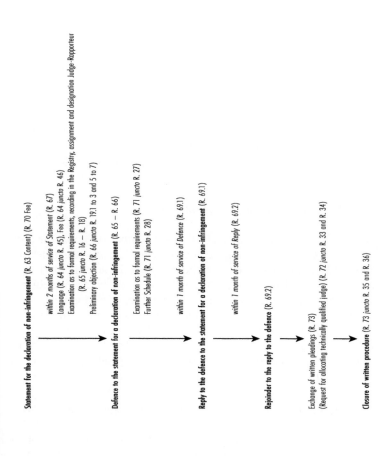

Flowchart: Action for Declaration of non-infringement (R. 61 – R. 74)

Chapter IV – (Part 1) Procedures before the Court of First Instance (Rules 10-159)

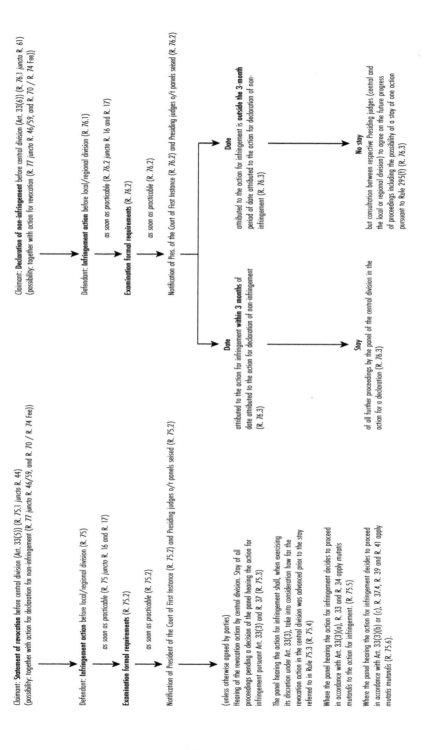

made in proceedings between the person doing or proposing to do the act and the patent proprietor or licensee entitled to commence infringement proceedings:[1135]

- if the patent proprietor or such licensee has asserted that the act is an infringement, or
- if no such assertion has been made by the patent proprietor or licensee, if:
  (a) that person has applied in writing to the proprietor or licensee for a written acknowledgment to the effect of the declaration claimed, and has provided him with full particulars in writing of the act in question and
  (b) the proprietor or licensee has refused or failed to give any such acknowledgment within one month.

The Action for declaration of non-infringement should be directed against the proprietor of the patent or the licensee who has asserted an infringement or refused or failed to give an acknowledgement pursuant to Rule 61.1(b).[1136]

In case the action has been commenced against a registered proprietor of a European Patent under Rule 8.6, but the registered proprietor is not the actual proprietor (within the meaning of Rule 8.5), each such registered proprietor shall have to apply for the substitution as soon as practicable after being served the Statement for a declaration of non-infringement.[1137]

In earlier drafts, Rule 66.2 described in detail rules regarding a Defence to the statement for a declaration of non-infringement including a counterclaim for infringement. The final version of Rule 66.2 only makes a reference to Rule 12.5 which provides that the Judge-Rapporteur may allow the exchange of further written pleadings, within time periods to be specified.

4. Actions within Article 33(5) and (6) UPCA (Rules 75-77)

The flowchart should be examined together with Article 33(5) and (6) UPCA, which for convenience is cited hereunder:

"Article 33: Competence of the divisions of the Court of First Instance

(1) ...

...

(5) If an action for revocation as referred to in Article 32(1)(d)) is pending before the central division, an action for infringement as referred to in Article 32(1)(a) between the same parties relating to the same patent may be brought before any division in accordance with paragraph 1 of this Article or before the central division. The local or regional division concerned shall have the discretion to proceed in accordance with paragraph 2 of this Article.

(6) An action for declaration of non-infringement as referred to in Article 32(1)(b) pending before the central division shall be stayed once an infringement

---

1135. Pursuant to Article 47.
1136. Rule 61.2.
1137. Rule 61.3.

action as referred to in Article 32(1)(a) between the same parties or between the holder of an exclusive licence and the party requesting a declaration of non-infringement relating to the same patent is brought before a local or regional division within three months of the date on which the action was initiated before the central division."

5. Actions for compensation for licences on the basis of Article 8 of the Unitary Patent Regulation (Rule 80)

Article 8 of Regulation (EU) 1257/2012 enables the proprietor of a Unitary Patent to file a statement with the EPO that he is prepared to allow any person to use the invention as a licensee in return for appropriate compensation (contractual licence).

The Court has exclusive jurisdiction in respect of Actions for compensation for licences on the basis of Article 8 of the Unitary Patent Regulation.[1138]

The Application for appropriate compensation[1139] shall contain:

(a) particulars in accordance with Rule 13(a) to (d);
(b) information on the filing of the statement as referred to in Article 8(1) of the Unitary Patent Regulation;
(c) the licence agreement referred to in Article 8(2) of the Unitary Patent Regulation.

Rules 132, 133, 135 and 137 to 140 (regarding proceedings related to the applications for the determination of damages) apply *mutatis mutandis*[1140] to the procedure for appropriate compensation.

Flowchart: Actions against a decision by the EPO with regard to Art. 9 Regulation (EU) No. 1257/2012 implementing enhanced cooperation in the area of the creation of unitary patent protection (R. 85 – R. 88)

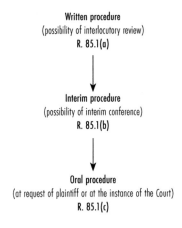

1138. Article 32(1)(h).
1139. Rule 80(1) and (3) regarding the fee.
1140. Rule 80.2.

Part Three – The Rules of Procedure of the Unified Patent Court

Flowchart: Formal requirements: Actions against a decision by the EPO with regard to Art. 9 Regulation (EU) No. 1257/2012 implementing enhanced cooperation in the area of the creation of unitary patent protection (I) (R. 85 – R. 98)

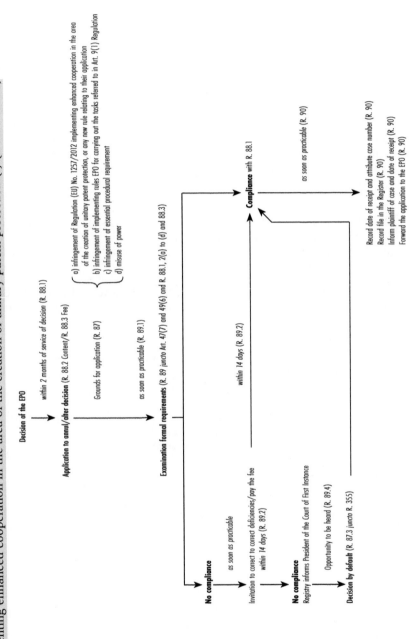

Chapter IV – (Part 1) Procedures before the Court of First Instance (Rules 10–159)

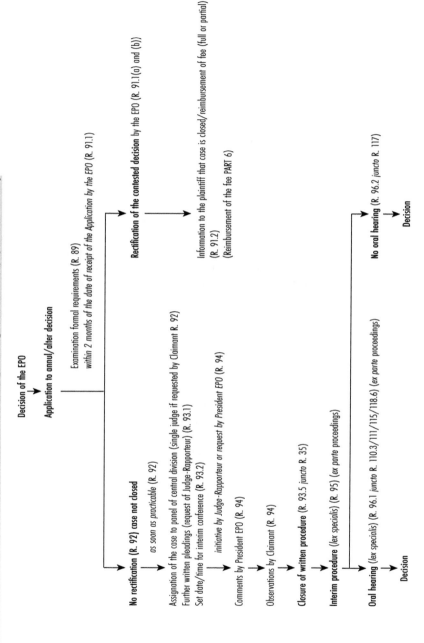

Flowchart: Actions against a decision by the EPO with regard to Art. 9 Regulation (EU) No. 1257/2012 implementing enhanced cooperation in the area of the creation of unitary patent protection (II) (R. 85 – R. 98)

6. Actions against a decision of the EPO in carrying out the tasks referred to in Article 9 Unitary Patent Regulation (Rules 85–98)

Article 9 of the Unitary Patent Regulation lays down the tasks, within the meaning of Article 143 EPC, which the Participating Member States entrust to the EPO. The EPO shall carry out these tasks in conformity with its internal rules. The EPO shall administer requests for unitary effect, include and administer in the European Patent Register entries relating to Unitary Patents, receive and register statements on licensing, ensure the publication of the translations required during the transitional period, collect and administer the renewal fees (as well as additional fees), administer the distribution of a part of the collected renewal fees to the Participating Member States and administer a compensation scheme of translation costs for applicants filing European Patent applications in one of the official languages of the Union that is not an official language of the EPO.

The Participating Member States should ensure that requests by the patent proprietor for unitary effect are submitted in the language of the proceedings as defined in Article 14(3) of the EPC no later than one month after the mention of the grant is published in the European Patent Bulletin. The Participating Member States should also ensure that the unitary effect is indicated in the Register, if the relevant conditions are fulfilled. The EPO should be informed of limitations and revocations of European Patents with unitary effect.

The Court has exclusive jurisdiction in respect of actions concerning decisions of the EPO in carrying out the tasks referred to in Article 9 of the Unitary Patent Regulation (Article 32 UPCA).

The application should be lodged in the language in which the patent was granted.[1141]

During the interim procedure, the Judge-Rapporteur invites the claimant to indicate whether he wishes that an oral hearing be convened. The Judge-Rapporteur may convene an oral hearing at his own instance.[1142]

It should be noted that Rule 94 (as added in one of the last redrafts of this Rule) clarifies that the President of the EPO can be invited to provide comments not only in first instance but also in appeal.

Should an oral hearing be convened the rules on closure of the interim procedure,[1143] role of the presiding judge,[1144] its public nature[1145] and time-frame for delivering the decision[1146] apply.

Should an oral hearing not be convened, the panel should decide in accordance with Rule 117 regarding the absence of both parties from the oral hearing.[1147]

Rule 97 provides a specific procedure to annul a decision of the EPO to reject a request for unitary effect.

1141. Rule 88.1.
1142. Rule 95.
1143. Rule 110.3.
1144. Rule 111.
1145. Rule 115.
1146. Rule 118.6.
1147. Rule 96.

Chapter IV – (Part 1) Procedures before the Court of First Instance (Rules 10–159)

Flowchart: Application to annul a decision of the office to reject a request for unitary effect (R. 97)

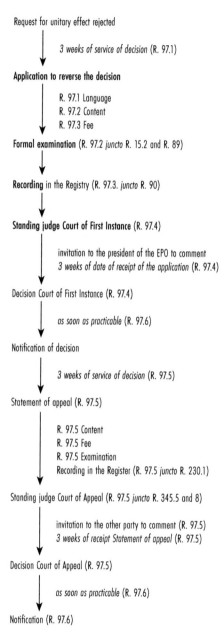

C. (CHAPTER 2) INTERIM PROCEDURE (RULES 101–110)

While the Judge-Rapporteur plays an important role during the written procedure, his role as a case manager is prominent during the interim procedure. Please note that the interim procedure should be completed within three months of the closure of the written procedure (unless that would infringe the principle of proportionality).[1148]

The interim procedure is structured in such a way as to make sure that when the case is pleaded during the oral phase, issues that may arise during the oral phase, will have already been dealt with upfront allowing the panel to focus on deciding upon the actual arguments of the parties.

Therefore, during the interim procedure, the Judge-Rapporteur should make all necessary preparations for the oral hearing.[1149] This managerial task of the Judge-Rapporteur is important to allow to the panel to take its decision within the intended time-frame.

As some of the issues to be prepared or decided by the Judge-Rapporteur may be essential for the final decision-taking process, the Judge-Rapporteur may decide to hold an interim conference during the interim procedure[1150] (if necessary on more than one occasion). The issues that should be addressed or decided upon during the interim procedure are listed in a general way in Rule 104 (with the title *"Aim of the interim conference"*), but could actually be interpreted as a *checks-and-balances* rule for the Judge-Rapporteur of the issues to be addressed during the interim procedure (in view of the preparation of the oral hearing). The extent of the managerial powers of the Judge-Rapporteur can therefore be derived from Rule 104 which lists the actions and decisions he can take. Some of these orders are related to the further progress of the proceedings (Rule 104(c) and (e)), the actual oral hearing to be held in the next phase (Rule 104(a), (b)), the physical or non-physical nature (video-conference) of the oral hearing or a separate hearing of witnesses and experts[1151] (Rule 104 (h)), or the exploration of the possibility of a settlement. However, he should also take decisions related to the value of the action (Rule 104 (i) *juncto* Rule 370.6) and the value of the proceedings (Rule 104 (j) *juncto* Rule 152.3) as those will no longer be dealt with during the oral procedure.

As mentioned, in order to realise the aims as set out in Rule 104, the Judge-Rapporteur may decide to hold an interim conference. But an interim conference is not considered to be necessary as such if the aims can be fulfilled without an interim conference.[1152] Whether or not he decides to hold an interim conference, the

---

1148. Rule 101.3.
1149. Amendment 14 (to Rule 104 (h)) adopted by the Administrative Committee on 8 July 2022 introduced the possibility for the Judge-Rapporteur to order (after consultation with the presiding judge and the parties) that the oral hearing or a separate hearing of witnesses and experts be wholly or partly conducted by video-conference in accordance with Rule 112.3 (which itself is the subject of Amendment 15 adopted by the Administrative Committee on 8 July 2022).
1150. Rule 101.1.
1151. In consultation with presiding judge of the panel and the parties.
1152. Where Rule 105.5 states that the Judge-Rapporteur should issue an order setting out the decisions taken *"following the interim conference"*, Rule 103.1 implies that he can also issues such orders without organising an interim conference.

Chapter IV – (Part 1) Procedures before the Court of First Instance (Rules 10–159)

Flowchart: Interim procedure (R. 101 – R. 110)

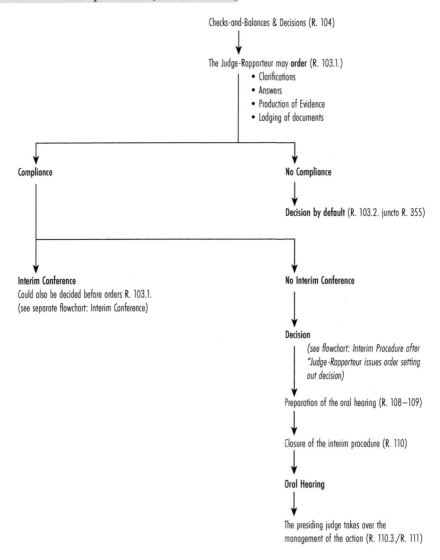

Judge-Rapporteur may order the parties to provide clarifications on specific points, to answer specific questions, to produce evidence or to lodge specific documents.[1153] In such order the Judge-Rapporteur should inform the party concerned that failing to comply with the time period specified may lead to a decision by default.[1154]

1153. Rule 103.1.
1154. Rule 103.2.

Part Three – The Rules of Procedure of the Unified Patent Court

Flowchart: Interim conference (R. 104 – R. 110)

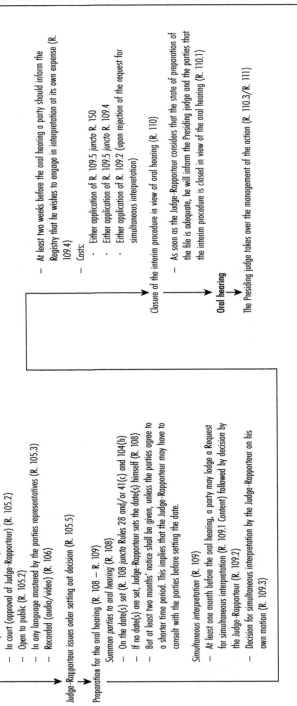

Chapter IV – (Part 1) Procedures before the Court of First Instance (Rules 10-159)

The interim conference itself may be held in any language agreed by parties' representatives[1155] and is graphically represented in the flowchart.

The Judge-Rapporteur has the obligation to ensure a fair, orderly and efficient interim procedure.[1156]

An important rule is that the Judge-Rapporteur may refer any matter to the panel for decision and the panel may, of its own motion, review any decision or order made by the Judge-Rapporteur or the conduct of the interim procedure.[1157] Any party may request that a decision or order of the Judge-Rapporteur be referred to the panel for a review.[1158] Pending such review, the decision or order made by the Judge-Rapporteur is effective.

Because there is no case law to rely on and to augment harmonisation on a procedural level, it would seem reasonable for the Judge-Rapporteur during the first months and even the first years of the establishment of the Court to refer (on his own motion) most of the procedural matters to the panel for collegial decisions. Should the Judge-Rapporteur not refer to the panel of its own motion, it would seem beneficial for the parties to request such referral. The Rules remain silent on whether the Judge-Rapporteur can ignore such a (mutual) request. However, ignoring the request could be based on sound case management if the request would be solely used to delay proceedings.

D. (CHAPTER 3) ORAL PROCEDURE (RULES 111-119)

1. The actual oral procedure (Rules 111-119)

For the purposes of case management, the presiding judge – who takes over the management of the action as of the oral hearing[1159] – shall:[1160]

(a) have all authority to ensure fair, orderly and efficient oral procedure; and
(b) ensure that the action is ready for decision on the merits at the end of the oral hearing.

The oral hearing will be held before the panel and this under the control of the presiding judge.[1161] The hearing will consist of:

(a) the hearing of the parties' oral submissions;
(b) the hearing of witnesses and experts under the control of the presiding judge).[1162] [1163]

1155. Rule 105.3.
1156. Rule 101.2.
1157. Rule 102.1.
1158. Rule 102.2 *juncto* Rule 333.
1159. Rule 110.3.
1160. Rule 111.
1161. Rule 112.1.
1162. Rule 112.2(b). as amended by Amendment 15 (to Rule 112) as adopted by the Administrative Committee of 8 July 2022.
1163. The actual hearing of the witnesses and experts by the panel is part of the oral hearing (managed by the Presiding Judge). However, during the interim procedure the

Part Three – The Rules of Procedure of the Unified Patent Court

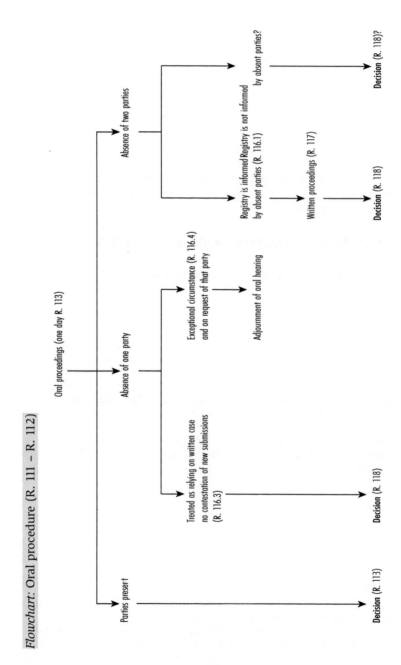

Amendment 15 (introduction of Rule 112.3) adopted by the Administrative Committee on 8 July 2022 introduced a general rule[1164] for the main hearing to be held by video-conference based on the importance such procedures gained after the COVID-19 pandemic. Rule 112.3(a) allows the parties, representatives or accompanying person to attend the oral hearing by video-conference, while Rule 112.3(b) enables the Court to hear parties, witnesses or experts through electronic means, such as video-conferences.[1165] Rule 112.3(c) enables the Court to hold the whole oral hearing by video-conference. Even if a party or all parties would not agree to such oral hearings by video-conference the Court can still make such decision if it considers it *"appropriate (...) due to exceptional circumstances"*.[1166] It may be expected that if none of the parties agree to a video-conference a physical oral hearing will be organised. The principle of publicity was respected by introducing Rule 112.3 (second paragraph) by providing that the oral hearings should be transmitted simultaneously in picture and sound to the courtroom.[1167]

The presiding judge and the judges on the panel may provide a preliminary introduction to the action and put questions to the parties, to the parties' representatives and to any witness or expert.[1168] Parties may put questions to the witness (under the control of the managing presiding judge).[1169]

The witness may give his evidence in a language other than the language of proceedings.[1170]

Translations of oral witness statements could be considered as costs of the proceedings (cf. Rule 150.1). For party experts, it seems reasonable that the language used by the party expert should be the language of proceedings since it is up to the parties to choose their own (language skilled) expert. Therefore, should a translator

---

Judge-Rapporteur may hold preparatory *discussions* with the witnesses and experts with a view to properly prepare the oral hearing (Rule 104(f) and related herewith Rule 104(g)-(h)). Where before amendment Rule 112.2(b) indicated that witnesses and experts could only be heard *"if ordered during the interim procedure"* (by the Judge-Rapporteur), the *amended* Rule 112.2(b) seems to indicate that hearing of witnesses and experts is the standard for the oral hearing. The explanatory notes to the amendment do not indicate whether the hearing of witnesses and experts is dependent on an order by the Judge-Rapporteur. One might argue that is still the case because, should the hearing be the norm, no order to hear expert and witnesses would be necessary and this Rule (Rule 104) was not amended on 8 July 2022.

1164. Before this amendment video-conferences were only foreseen in specific circumstances applicable to the interim hearing (Rule 105.1), examination of witnesses (Rule 178.6) and fair hearing (Rule 264).
1165. It is not clear why Rule 112.3(a) and (c) mentions *"video-conference"* and Rule 112.3(b) mentions *"electronic means, such as video-conference"*.
1166. In the explanatory notes to this amendment the *"exceptional circumstances"* mentioned as examples are travel restrictions or disproportionality (long journey for short and simple oral hearings).
1167. Whether the judges should be present in the courtroom or have the possibility to also conduct and join oral hearings by video-conference outside the courtroom is not mentioned.
1168. Rule 112.4.
1169. Rule 112.5.
1170. Rule 112.6.

be necessary it would seem reasonable to argue that these costs should be borne by the relevant party.

The presiding judge needs to endeavour to complete the oral hearing within one day. The presiding judge may set time limits for parties' oral submissions in advance of the oral hearing.[1171] The oral testimony is limited to issues identified by the Judge-Rapporteur or the presiding judge as having to be decided on the basis of oral evidence[1172] and may be limited if the panel is sufficiently informed.[1173]

In exceptional cases, the Court may, after hearing the parties' oral submissions, decide to adjourn proceedings and call for further evidence.[1174]

The oral hearing and any separate hearing of witnesses is open to the public unless the Court decides to make a hearing confidential in the interests of one or both parties or third parties or in the general interests of justice or public order. An audio recording shall be made of the hearing.[1175]

The wording *"in good time"* in Rule 116.1 for providing a time frame within which a party should inform the Registry of its desire not to be represented at the oral hearing might be considered flexible but may give rise to some practical (organisation of the oral hearing) and legal problems (regarding the consequences when this information does not reach the Registry *"in good time"*).

Regarding the reliance on the written case, the flowchart reflects a consensus between on the one hand the need to protect a party absent from an oral hearing against new submissions made by the other party during the oral hearing and, on the other hand, the need of the panel to bring proceedings to an end and reach a decision on the merits despite the absence of the party.

The Rules[1176] ensure that an absent party is treated as relying only on its written case. As the Rules do not seem to hold that the absent party automatically contests new submissions made by the other (present) party during the oral hearing, it will lie at the discretion of the Court whether to admit new submissions in the proceedings and – if admitted – whether they are of such relevance to the decision that the oral hearing should be adjourned so that the party absent from the oral hearing shall be given an opportunity to be heard. In light of such a decision the Court should also consider whether such new submissions (including possibly new arguments) should not be disregarded based on Rule 9.2.[1177] Reference could be made to Rule 222.2 where the discretion of the Court of Appeal is dealt with regarding new requests, facts and evidence which had not been introduced during proceedings before the Court of First Instance. It would seem reasonable that the Court of First Instance applies an equivalent discretion.

1171. Rule 113.1.
1172. Rule 113.2.
1173. Rule 113.3.
1174. Rule 114.
1175. Rule 115.
1176. Rule 116.3.
1177. This Rule stipulates that the Court may disregard any step, fact, evidence or argument submitted by a party not in accordance with a time limit set by the Court or the Rules.

2. The decision on the merits (Rules 118-119)

In addition to the orders and measures and without prejudice to the discretion of the Court referred to in Articles 63 (permanent injunction), 64 (corrective measures in infringement proceedings), 67 (order to communicate information) and 80 (publication of decision), the Court can (if requested) order the payment of damages and compensation.[1178] The amount of the damages and the compensation may be stated in the order or determined in separate proceedings.[1179]

It is generally felt that tension exists between the power of the Court to order payments instead of an injunction and the right under Article 25 recognising the right to prevent the use of the invention without the consent of the patent proprietor as the core right of the patent proprietor. It seems that only under exceptional circumstances should the Court use its discretion and not render such an order to prevent the use of the invention.

Rule 118 went through considerable changes during the drafting process. Rule 118.2 in the 16th draft (now deleted) stated the following:

> 2. Without prejudice to the general discretion provided for in Articles 63 and 64 of the UPCA, in appropriate cases and at the request of the party liable to the orders and measures provided for in paragraph 1 the Court may order damages and/or compensation to be paid to the injured party instead of applying the orders and measures if that person acted unintentionally and without negligence, if execution of the orders and measures in question would cause such party disproportionate harm and if damages and/or compensation to the injured party appear to the Court to be reasonably satisfactory.

In an earlier version of Rule 118.2 a number of cumulative requirements were explicitly mentioned. The Drafting Committee (backed by the Expert Committee) felt that a scenario in which an infringer acted not only unintentionally but also without any negligence would be difficult to imagine and that therefore the provision could in practice hardly apply. Furthermore, the deletion of the wording that stems from Article 12 of Enforcement Directive 2004/48/EC is in line with EU law since the Directive does not impose this provision on Member States (*"Member States may provide"*).

Should a revocation action be pending before the central division while there are pending infringement proceedings before a local or regional division, the local or regional division:[1180]

(a) may render its decision on the merits of the infringement claim, including its orders, under the condition subsequent pursuant to Article 56(1) UPCA that the patent is not held to be wholly or partially invalid by the final decision in the revocation proceedings or a final decision of the EPO or under any other term or condition; or

(b) may stay the infringement proceedings pending a decision in the revocation proceedings or a decision of the EPO and shall stay the infringement proceedings if it is of the view that there is a high likelihood that the relevant claims

---

1178. Cf. Articles 68 and 32(1)(f).
1179. Rule 118.1 *juncto* Rules 125-144.
1180. Rule 118.2.

of the patent will be held to be invalid on any ground by the final decision in the revocation proceedings or of the EPO (where it is expected that the such decision will be given rapidly).

Rule 118.2 was heavily debated during the drafting process and the final version is intended to mitigate the risks for negative effects of the so-called bifurcation possibility. The bifurcation (as it is known in Germany) could lead to the situation that the Court decides upon infringement before first analysing the validity of a patent. Rule 118.2 is intended to provide more guarantees to defendants so that there will not normally be an enforceable decision regarding infringement before the Court has decided upon the validity of a patent.

Where, in the decision on the merits of a direct action or a counterclaim for revocation, the patent is found to be entirely or partially invalid, the Court may revoke the patent entirely or partially according to Article 65 (decision on the validity of a patent).[1181]

Where the Court has made orders, in accordance with Rule 118.2(a) (i.e. a decision on the merits regarding the infringement claim under the condition subsequent that the patent is valid), any party may apply to the local or regional division within two months following a final decision of the central division or the Court of Appeal on the validity of the patent for orders consequential on such final decision.[1182]

The Court shall decide in principle on the obligation to bear the legal costs in accordance with Article 69. In view of such a decision the Court may order (in advance of the decision) that parties submit a preliminary estimate of the legal costs they will seek to recover.[1183]

The Court will decide on the merits *as soon as possible* after the closure of the oral hearing. The Court endeavours to issue the reasoned decision on the merits in writing within six weeks of the oral hearing and should provide the reasons for its decision.[1184] The Court may render its decision immediately after the closure of the oral hearing and provide its reasons on a subsequent date.[1185] The Rules remain silent as to when the Court may render a decision immediately and when the decision is communicated together with its reasons. It may be expected that immediate decisions are exceptional.

The orders of the Court referred to above are enforceable on the defendant only after:

- the claimant has notified the Court which part of the orders he intends to enforce and the said notice has been served on the defendant by the Registry;
- a certified translation of the orders[1186] in the official language of a Contracting Member State in which the enforcement has taken place; and

---

1181. Rule 118.3.
1182. Rule 354.4 *juncto* Rule 118.4.
1183. Rule 118.5.
1184. Rule 118.6.
1185. Rule 118.7.
1186. In accordance with Rule 7.2.

– said notice (and certified translation) has been served on the defendant by the Registry.[1187]

The Court may subject any order or measure to a security to be given by the successful party to the unsuccessful party.[1188]

The Court may order an interim award of damages to the successful party in its decisions on the merits. The Court may subject such an award to any conditions. Rule 119 provides that the award should at least cover the expected costs of the procedure for the award of damages and compensation on the part of the successful party.

E. (CHAPTER 4) PROCEDURE FOR THE DETERMINATION OF DAMAGES AND COMPENSATION (RULES 125–144)

1. Application for the determination of damages (Rules 131–140)

It is most likely when the damage assessment is straightforward that the Court will decide on the damages together with its decision on the infringement.

However, should the damage assessment demand a more elaborate deliberation due to either the complexity of the case or the lack of information to decide on the issue, two options emerge:

- the Court decides in its decision on the merits regarding the infringement on the principles of the damage assessment (leaving aside the precise calculation of the amount of damages); or
- the Court deals with all aspects of the damage assessment in separate proceedings. In such cases Rules 125 to 144 apply.

The determination shall include the determination of the amount of compensation, if any, to be awarded as a result of the provisional protection conferred by a published European Patent application[1189] and compensation to be paid pursuant to Rule 118.1, 198.2, 213.2 and 354.2. Rule 125 *in fine* makes it clear that the expression *"damages"* includes such compensation and interest at the rate and for the period that the Court shall decide.

The consecutive nature of these damages proceedings and the managerial function of the Judge-Rapporteur as settlement seeker,[1190] could result in a high number of settlements between the parties regarding damages. Indirectly this could form a stimulus to use the Patent Mediation and Arbitration Centre.

When it is up to the Court to decide on the damages, the procedure may include a separate request from the claimant to lay open books.

Regarding the actual damages proceedings, reference can be made to the following flowcharts. Regarding the substantive law on the determination of damages, Article 68 UPCA applies.

1187. Rule 118.8. This is an exception on the general rule that translations should not to be certified.
1188. Rule 118.8 *in fine* with reference to Rule 352.
1189. Cf. Article 32(1)(f) and Article 67 EPC.
1190. Rule 11 and Rule 104(d).

Part Three – The Rules of Procedure of the Unified Patent Court

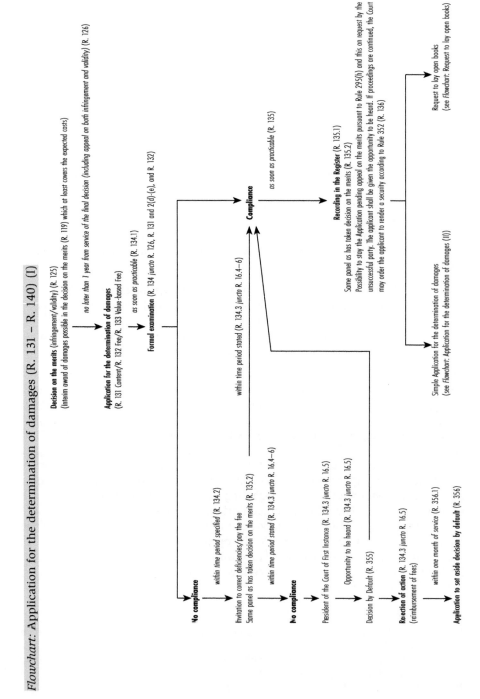

Flowchart: Application for the determination of damages (R. 131 – R. 140) (I)

Chapter IV – (Part 1) Procedures before the Court of First Instance (Rules 10-159)

Flowchart: Application for the determination of damages (R. 131 – R. 140) (II)

Application for the determination of damages

Examination of formal requirements (R. 134)
Possible stay of the Application pending appeals on the merits (R. 136)
within 2 months of service (R. 137)

Acceptance of the claim (R. 137.1)

Order for the award of damages (by Judge-Rapporteur) (R. 137.1)

Defence to the application for the determination of damages R. 137.2/R. 138 Content

within 1 month of service (R. 139)

Reply to the defence for the determination of damages (R. 139)

within 1 month of service (R. 139)

Rejoinder to the Reply (R. 138)

Further Exchange of written pleadings ordered by Judge-Rapporteur (R. 140.1)

Interim Proceedings (R. 140.2 *juncto* Chpt. 2) (reduced timetable possible)

Oral Proceedings (R. 140.2 *juncto* Chpt. 3) (reduced timetable possible)

309

Part Three – The Rules of Procedure of the Unified Patent Court

2. Request to lay open books (Rules 141–144)

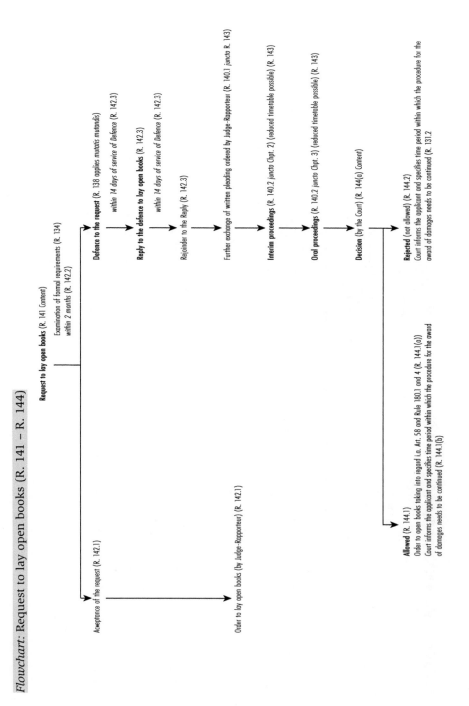

Chapter IV – (Part 1) Procedures before the Court of First Instance (Rules 10–159)

F. (CHAPTER 5) PROCEDURE FOR COST ORDERS (RULES 150–157)

A cost order may be the subject of separate proceedings following a decision on the merits and, if applicable, a decision for the determination of damages.[1191]

Flowchart: Procedure for cost orders (R. 150 – R. 157)

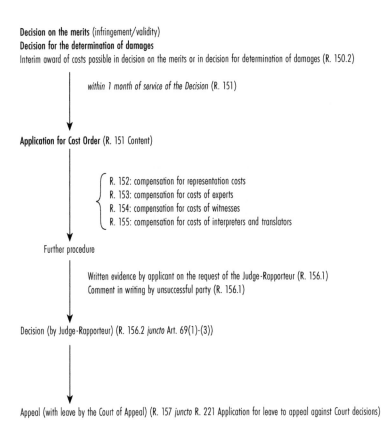

The cost decision shall cover costs incurred in the proceedings by the Court such as costs for simultaneous interpretation and costs incurred pursuant to Rules 173, 180.1, 185.7, 188 and 201, and, subject to Rules 152 to 156, the costs of the successful party including Court fees paid by that party.[1192] Costs for interpretation and translation necessary for the judges of the Court in order to conduct the action in the language of

---

1191. Rule 150.1.
1192. Cf. Rule 151(d).

proceedings are borne solely by the Court.[1193] The Court may order an interim award of costs to the successful party in the decision on the merits or in a decision for the determination of damages, subject to any conditions that the Court may decide.[1194]

Specific importance should be given to the compensation for representation costs. Rule 152.2 refers to the scale of ceilings for recoverable costs by reference to the value of the proceedings. Where the value of the proceedings was not already the subject of an order by the Judge-Rapporteur (i.e. where only a fixed fee is due), the party requesting the representation costs to be recovered should assess the value for the purpose of calculating the applicable ceiling. The other party will be heard. Reference is further made to Rule 370.6.

G. (CHAPTER 6) SECURITY FOR COSTS (RULES 158–159)

The Court may at any time (but following a reasoned request by a party) order the other party to provide (within a specified time period) adequate security for the legal costs and other expenses incurred and/or to be incurred by the requesting party, which the other party may be liable to bear. Should the Court decide to order such security, it should decide whether it is appropriate to order the security by deposit or bank guarantee.[1195] An order for security can only be made after the parties have been given the opportunity to be heard.[1196]

The order for security may be either the subject of an appeal together with the appeal against the decision or may be appealed with the leave of the Court of First Instance within fifteen days of service of the Court's decision to that effect.[1197]

Should the party concerned fail to provide adequate security within the given time frame, a decision by default may follow in accordance with Rule 355.[1198]

Except where deposits are rendered pursuant to Rule 180.2,[1199] the Court may order that either or both parties provide adequate security (by deposit or bank guarantee) to cover costs incurred and/or to be incurred in the proceedings by the Court, pending a cost decision pursuant to Rule 150.1.[1200] The same rules as mentioned above regarding the hearing of parties and appeal apply.

1193. The question arises as to which level of language skills a judge should have to be part of the panel. It would be beneficial for the users of the Court and its credibility for judges to have adequate language skills to hear and judge the case without the need for interpretation or translation.
1194. Rule 150.2.
1195. Rule 158.1.
1196. Rule 158.2.
1197. Rule 158.3 *juncto* Rule 220.2.
1198. Rule 158.4 (obligation to inform the party concerned) and 5 (decision by default).
1199. Conditional summoning of the witness upon the deposit of a sum sufficient to recover the expenses as mentioned in Rule 180.1.
1200. Rule 159.

Chapter V
(Part 2) Evidence (Rules 170–201)

Means of evidence and means of obtaining evidence. The evidence to be relied on should be considered at an early stage in proceedings. The claimant should include the evidence relied on,[1201] where available, as early as the Statement of claim and an indication of any further evidence which will be offered in support. The means of the evidence are set out in a non-exhaustive list in Rule 170.1. The means of obtaining evidence are listed under Rule 170.2 and 170.3.

Flowchart: Means of evidence and means of obtaining evidence (R. 170)

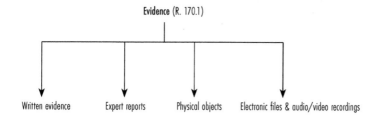

Means of obtaining evidence (R. 170.2)

- hearing of parties (R. 170.2(a))
- summoning, hearing and questioning of witnesses (R. 170.2(b))
- appointing and hearing experts (R. 170.2(c))
- order to produce evidence (R. 170.2(d))
- order to inspect place of physical object (R. 170.2(e))
- order to preserve evidence (R. 170.2(f))
- conducting comparative test and experiments (R. 170.2(g))
- sworn statements in writing (written witness evidence) (R. 170.2(h))
- ordering a part or third party to produce evidence (R. 170.3(a))
- ordering measures to preserve evidence (R. 170.3(b))

Offering of evidence. A party making a statement of fact that is contested or likely to be contested by the other party, has to indicate the means of evidence to prove it. In case of failure to indicate the means of evidence regarding a contested fact, the

---

1201. Rule 13.1(m) with reference to Rule 170.1.

Court may take such failure into account when deciding the issue.[1202] Rule 171.2 is an important rule regarding the weight that should be given to a statement of fact. The Rule provides that a fact which is not specifically contested by any party is held to be true as between the parties. In practice this will probably lead to a formal statement that unless otherwise indicated all factual statements are contested.

Duty to produce evidence. Should evidence be available to a party regarding a statement of fact that is contested or likely to be contested by the other party, such evidence must be produced by the party making that statement of fact.[1203] The Court may order a party making a statement of fact to produce evidence that lies in the control of that party.[1204] Failure to produce the evidence will be taken into account by the Court when deciding on the issue.

Judicial cooperation in the taking of evidence. For the judicial cooperation in the taking of evidence, reference is made to the following instruments and means (if applicable):

1. Regulation (EU) No. 2020/1783[1205]
2. The Hague Convention of 18 March 1970 on the Taking of Evidence Abroad in Civil or Commercial Matters or any other applicable convention or agreement; or
3. to the extent that there is no such convention or agreement in force, national law on the procedures to be followed for the judicial cooperation in the taking of evidence.

A. (CHAPTER 1) WITNESSES AND EXPERTS OF THE PARTIES (RULES 175–181)

Hearing of the witnesses. Before hearing the witness, the presiding judge shall ask the witness to make the declaration provided in Rule 178.1.[1206] The hearing of a witness shall start with the confirmation of the evidence given therein. The witness may elaborate on the evidence contained in his written witness statement.[1207] Thereafter, the judges may put questions to the witness.[1208] Then, under the control

---

1202. Rule 171.1.
1203. Rule 172.1.
1204. Rule 172.2.
1205. The explanatory notes to Amendment 17 (to Rule 173) adopted by the Administrative Committee on 8 July 2022 note that this regulation does not apply in case of judicial cooperation with a national court of the same State where the UPC division is located as it only applies to cross border scenarios. The question could be raised as to whether this regulation would not apply for any UPC division if judicial cooperation is requested with a court of a Contracting Member State, as the UPC is considered a *common court* to the Contracting Member States. One could make reference to divisional issues where the Brussel I (recast) Regulation does not seem to apply.
1206. *"I solemnly, sincerely and truly declare and affirm that the evidence I shall give shall be the truth, the whole truth and nothing but the truth."*
1207. Rule 178.3.
1208. Rule 178.4.

Chapter V – (Part 2) Evidence (Rules 170–201)

Flowchart: Witnesses (R. 175 – R. 181)

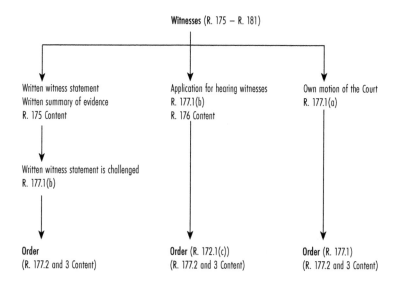

of the presiding judge, the representatives of the parties may put questions to the witness. The presiding judge may prohibit any question which is not designed to adduce admissible evidence.[1209] In other words, the presiding judge may decide that a certain question is not admissible and as such does not need to be answered.

The Court may allow a witness to give evidence through electronic means, such as video-conference.[1210]

Should the Court consent, the witness may give evidence in a language other than the language of proceedings.[1211]

Duties of the witnesses. The listed duties of the witnesses comprise:
- obeying the summons and attending the oral hearing;[1212]
- giving evidence;[1213] and
- making the declaration under Rule 178.1.[1214]

1209. Rule 178.5.
1210. Where this possibility was included as a separate Rule (old Rule 178.6) this is covered by the amended Rule 112.3(b) adopted by the Administrative Committee on 8 July 2022 (Amendment 18).
1211. Rule 178.6. The same Rule can be found under Rule 112.5. The written witness statement (Rule 175.2) as well as the application for hearing a witness in person (Rule 176) should set out the language in which the witness shall/should give evidence.
1212. Rule 179.1.
1213. Rule 179.2.
1214. Rule 179.2 *juncto* Rule 178.1.

Should the witness not respect his obligations, the Court may impose a pecuniary sanction[1215] and may order that all further summons be served at the witness's own expense.[1216] Finally, the Court may send a letter rogatory to the competent national court.[1217]

Nobody can be obliged to sign a written witness statement or to give evidence at an oral hearing if he is a spouse, partner equal to a spouse under applicable national law, descendant, sibling or parent of a party. A witness may also refuse to answer questions if answering them would violate a professional privilege or other duty of confidentiality imposed by the national law applicable to the witness or expose him or his spouse, partner equal to a spouse under applicable national law, descendant, sibling or parent to criminal prosecution under applicable national law.[1218] The rules remain silent as to whether this rule allows a witness to refuse to disclose documents based on a contractual (civil) obligation of confidentiality towards a third party.

Should a witness give false evidence, the Court may report this to the competent authorities of the Contracting Member State whose courts have criminal jurisdiction.[1219]

Reimbursement of expenses of the witnesses. A witness shall be entitled to reimbursement of expenses for travelling and stay, and loss of income caused by his hearing in person.[1220] After the witness has carried out his duties and upon his request, the Registry shall make a payment to the witness towards the expenses incurred.

Where a party has lodged an Application for the hearing of a witness in person, the Court shall make the summoning of the witness conditional upon the deposit of a sum sufficient to cover the expenses referred to above.[1221]

Experts of the parties. A party has the possibility to provide expert evidence that it considers necessary, subject to the orders of the Court referred to in Rule 104(e)[1222] and Rule 113.2(b)[1223] [1224] An order of the Court to call upon an expert shall additionally set out that:[1225]

- An expert has a duty to assist the Court impartially on matters relevant to his area of expertise which overrides any duty to the party retaining him.[1226]
- An expert is to be independent and objective, and shall not act as an advocate for any party to the proceedings.[1227]

1215. A maximum is set for the pecuniary sanction.
1216. Rule 179.2.
1217. Rule 179.2 *juncto* Rule 202.
1218. Rule 179.3.
1219. Rule 179.4.
1220. Rule 180.1.
1221. Rule 180.2.
1222. This Rule refers to the interim conference where the Judge-Rapporteur may order experts to be called upon.
1223. This Rule refers to the actual hearing of the expert under the control of the presiding judge.
1224. Rule 181.
1225. Additional to Rule 177 dealing with the order summoning a witness to the oral hearing.
1226. Rule 181.2(a).
1227. Rule 181.2(b).

Chapter V – (Part 2) Evidence (Rules 170–201)

B.   (CHAPTER 2) COURT EXPERTS (RULES 185–188)

Flowchart: Experts (R. 181 – R. 188)

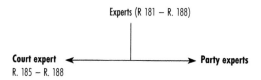

Appointed after hearing parties (R. 185.1)

cf. Procedure witnesses (R. 181 *juncto* R. 175 – R. 180)

The parties may make suggestions regarding the identity of the court expert, his technical background and the questions to be put to him (R. 185.2). The Registry maintains a list of experts (R. 185.9).

The court expert is responsible to the Court and needs to possess the expertise, independence and impartiality required for being appointed as court expert (185.3). He is appointed by order and required upon receipt of the order to confirm in writing that he will present the expert report within the time period specified by the Court (R. 185.6). If an appointed court expert does not present his report within the time period specified or, if extended at the expert's request, the extended period, the Court may appoint another expert in his place. The Court may hold the expert liable for all or part of the costs of appointing and reimbursing another expert (R. 185.8).

The duties of the court expert are stipulated under Rule 186.

The court expert shall be under supervision of the Court and shall inform the Court of his/her progress (R. 186.2). He/she shall only answer the questions which are put to him (R. 186.3). Any communication shall be presented to all parties (R. 186.4). He shall not communicate the contents of his report to third parties (R. 186.5) and he shall attend the oral hearings (if requested by the Court) answering the questions from the Court and the parties (R. 186.6). As a party expert, the court expert shall be independent and objective (R. 186.7).

Upon presentation of the final report to the Court, parties are invited to comment on it either in writing or during the oral hearing (R. 187).

Regarding the hearing of the expert, reference is made to the hearing of witnesses (R. 188 *juncto* R. 178 – R. 180).

C. (CHAPTER 3) ORDER TO PRODUCE EVIDENCE AND COMMUNICATE INFORMATION (RULES 190–191)

1. Order to produce evidence (Rule 190)

Where a party has presented reasonably available and plausible evidence in support of its claims and has specified evidence which lies in the control of the other party or a third party, the Court may (on a reasoned request introduced by the party specifying such evidence) order that party or third party to produce such evidence.

For the protection of confidential information, the Court may order that the evidence be disclosed to certain named persons only and be subject to appropriate terms of non-disclosure.[1228]

The order should specify:[1229]

(a) under which conditions, in what form and within what time period the evidence needs to be produced; and
(b) any sanction which may be imposed if the evidence is not produced according to the order.

The order will indicate that an appeal may be brought in accordance with Article 73 UPCA and Rule 220.1.[1230]

If a party fails to comply with an order to produce evidence, the Court shall take such failure into account when deciding on the issue in question.[1231]

If an order to produce evidence is requested during written and interim procedures, the Judge-Rapporteur may make such order in these procedures having given the other/third party an opportunity to be heard.[1232]

Should a third party be ordered to produce evidence, the interests of that third party shall be duly taken into account.[1233] The Rules do not provide the opportunity for the third party to be heard. A further issue is whether this third party can appeal such order. This might only be possible if the third party – by means of the order – is considered a party to the proceedings.

To intervene, the party who has been ordered to produce evidence may intervene on his own motion,[1234] may be invited by the Judge-Rapporteur[1235] or be forced to intervene[1236] (see also relevant flowcharts).

An order to produce evidence is subject to the provisions of Rule 179.3 (duties of the witnesses), Rule 287 (attorney-client privilege) and Rule 288 (litigation privilege).[1237]

1228. Rule 190.1.
1229. Rule 190.4.
1230. Rule 190.6.
1231. Rule 190.7.
1232. Rule 190.2 and 3.
1233. Rule 190.5.
1234. Rule 313.
1235. Rule 316.
1236. Rule 316A.
1237. Rule 190.6.

Chapter V – (Part 2) Evidence (Rules 170–201)

2. Order to communicate information (R. 191)

The Court may in response to a reasoned request of a party order the other party or any third party to communicate information in the control of that other party or third party where such information is reasonably necessary for the purpose of advancing that party's case. Rules 190.1, 190.5 and 190.6 regarding an order to preclude evidence shall apply *mutatis mutandis*.[1238]

D. (CHAPTER 4) ORDER TO PRESERVE EVIDENCE (*SAISIE*) AND ORDER FOR INSPECTION (RULES 192–199)

Flowchart: Order to preserve evidence (*saisie*) (R. 192 – R. 198) and order for inspection (R. 199) (same Rules apply)

Application for preserving evidence (R. 192.1) (R. 192.2 and 3 Content) (R. 192.3 Language) (R. 182.5 Fee)

An Application for preserving evidence may be lodged by a party (within the meaning of Article 47) at the division where the applicant has commenced infringement proceedings *on the merits*. If the application is lodged before proceedings *on the merits* have been started, it shall be lodged at the division where the applicant intends to start proceedings on the merits

Case not pending (R. 193.1)

Language (R. 192.4)
Application is dealt with in accordance to (R. 193.1):
– R. 16 (examination as to formal requirements)
– R. 17.1(a)-(c) and 2 (date of receipt, recording Registry, case number, assignment to panel)
– R. 18 (designation of Judge-Rapporteur by Presiding judge)

Case pending (R. 193.2)

Language (R. 192.4)
Application shall immediately be
– examined on formalities (cfr. R. 16)
– forwarded to the panel or to judge (cfr. R. 17.2. and R. 194.3–4)

1238. Rule 191.

Part Three – The Rules of Procedure of the Unified Patent Court

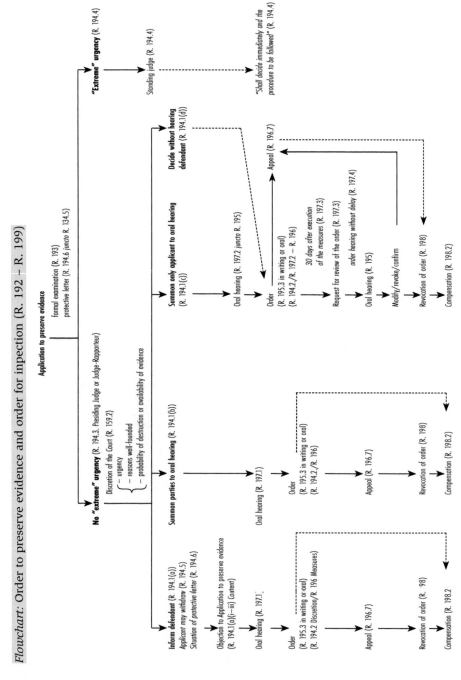

Flowchart: Order to preserve evidence and order for inpection (R. 192 – R. 199)

Combining the burden placed on the parties to set their full case as early as possible allowing the final hearing on the issues on infringement and validity at first instance to take place within one year (mentioned in the preamble) and the non-preferential list of the means of evidence, will actually lead to a *pre-loaded* procedure where all evidence should be in place when introducing the action. As such, the order to preserve evidence (*saisie*) and the order for inspection might take an important place in the means of obtaining evidence.

1. Order to preserve evidence (*saisie*) (Rules 192–198)

The components and consecutive stages of the proceedings to preserve evidence (and/or for inspection) are set out in the above flowcharts.

When analysing the provided flowcharts and applicable Rules, the following additional remarks should be made:

- Where this application is lodged after main proceedings on the merits of the action have been initiated before the Court, the Application needs to be drawn up in the *language of the proceedings*.[1239] Where the Application is lodged before main proceedings on the merits of the action have been initiated before the Court, Rule 14 applies *mutatis mutandis*.
- Rule 194.1(d) provides that the Court has discretion to decide on the Application without having heard the defendant. This is the situation of the *saisie-contrefaçon* as we know it for example in France and Belgium.
- The *protective letter* is dealt with in the Part 3 of the Rules dealing with provisional measures (Part 3 – Provisional Measures). The specific procedural steps that apply after a protective letter has been lodged are mentioned in Chapter 4 of Part 2 (Part 2 – Evidence) of the Rules dealing with the order to preserve evidence (and the order for inspection). However, within the specific procedure related to the order to preserve evidence/order for inspection, a (deliberate) difference seems to emerge. Rule 194.6 only refers to Rule 207 and not to any of the consecutive Rules related to protective letters (e.g. Rule 209.2(d) which states that in exercising its discretion under Rule 209.1 the existence of a protective letter should be taken into consideration which is not reiterated in Rule 194.2(c)). This seems to be a deliberate choice by the drafters. The reason would be that the protective letter is considered a pre-emptive defence against a possible request for provisional measures and not (or less) against a request for an ex-parte provisional measure.
- The Rules make a distinction between "*extreme urgency*" (Rule 194.4 leading to a specific procedural path where the standing judge can choose for a tailored procedure to be followed) and a situation "*where any delay is likely to cause irreparable harm to the applicant or where there is a demonstrable risk of evidence to be destroyed or otherwise ceasing to be available*" (Rule 197.1 justifying why measures may be ordered without having heard the defendant). The Rules remain silent on how such distinction should be made

---

1239. Rule 192.4.

and whether the situation described under Rule 197.1 can be automatically considered as qualifying as *"extreme urgency"* under Rule 194.4.
- Rule 196.3 states that the order is *immediately enforceable*. The term *"immediately"* could mean that the obligations for the claimant under Rule 118.8 (enforceability of decision on the merits) are not applicable. The order must in any event be served in accordance with Rule 354.1 to be enforceable. This means that enforcement shall always take place in accordance with the enforcement procedures and conditions governed by the law of the particular Contracting Member State where enforcement takes place.
- Rule 196.4 leaves some uncertainty regarding *the person who has to carry out the measures and present a written report on the measures to preserve evidence*. The Rule states that the specification of the person and the written report should be in accordance with national law of the place where the measures are executed. Therefore, it seems necessary for the Court to carefully examine whether its order (and more specifically the appointed person and his duties) is in conformity with national law. Where the measures are requested for one Contracting Member State this will not be too difficult. The difficulty may arise when the requested order is enforceable in several Contracting Member States (e.g. a plurality of production units) with different and possibly contradictory national rules on the issue.
- Finally, the Rules remain silent as to what should be done with gathered evidence (based on an order *"without hearing the defendant"* (Rule 197)) *during appeal proceedings* when the order was not maintained after review. After review, it might be opportune to request the Court to secure the evidence (by the appointed expert or by a bailiff) until the term to appeal has lapsed or the appeal has been decided on, whichever is the longest.

Order on the application for preserving evidence. In deciding an Application to preserve evidence, the Court can, in particular, order:[1240]

(a) preserving evidence by detailed description, with or without the taking of samples;
(b) physical seizure of allegedly infringing goods;
(c) physical seizure of the materials and implements used in the production and/or distribution of these goods and any related document.
(d) the preservation and disclosure of digital media and data and the disclosure of any passwords necessary to access them.

For the protection of confidential information, the Court may order that any of the above be disclosed only to certain named persons and subject to appropriate terms of non-disclosure.

An order to preserve evidence shall specify that, unless otherwise ordered by the Court, the outcome of the measures to preserve evidence may only be used in the proceedings on the merits of the case.[1241]

1240. Rule 196.1.
1241. Rule 196.2.

The Court may set conditions on the enforceability of the order, specifying in particular:

(a) who may represent the applicant when the measures to preserve evidence are being carried out and under what conditions; or
(b) any security which shall be provided by the applicant.

Otherwise, the order to preserve evidence shall be immediately enforceable.

If necessary, the Court may set penalties applicable to the applicant if these conditions are not observed. The Rules remain silent as to whom these penalties should be paid. Taking into consideration Rule 354.3, it seems reasonable to argue that these penalties are to be paid to the Court.

The order to preserve evidence shall specify a person who shall carry out the measures ordered and present a written report on the measures to preserve evidence (all in accordance with the national law where the measures are executed) to the Court within a time period to be specified.[1242] This person specified should be a professional person or expert, who guarantees expertise, independence and impartiality.[1243] Where appropriate and allowed under applicable national law, the person may be a bailiff or assisted by a bailiff.[1244]

Under no circumstance may an employee or director of the applicant be present at the execution of the measures. The prohibition of employees or directors of the applicant to be present may differ from the current situation in some Contracting Member States.

The Court may order the applicant to provide adequate security for the legal costs and other expenses and compensation for any injury incurred or likely to be incurred by the defendant which the applicant may be liable to bear.[1245] The Court shall do so where the order to preserve evidence was made without the defendant having been heard, unless there are special circumstances not to do so.[1246] The Court shall decide whether it is appropriate to order the security by deposit or bank guarantee.

Revocation of an order to preserve evidence. An order to preserve evidence is revoked or otherwise ceases to have effect upon request of the defendant (without prejudice to damages which may be claimed) if within a time period not exceeding 31 calendar

---

1242. Rule 196.4.
1243. Rule 196.5.
1244. The reference to national law (especially also regarding the execution of orders to preserve evidence) could make the similar existing national orders to preserve evidence remain equally popular, certainly when taking into account that the evidence gathered by means of such national order can be equally used during proceedings before the UPC. On the other hand, for orders to preserve evidence that need to be performed simultaneously in different UPC Contracting States, the UPC order to preserve evidence could become more popular.
1245. Rule 196.6.
1246. E.g. no damages can be incurred or only an inexpensive sample is seized in order to preserve evidence.

days or 20 working days (whichever is longer), the applicant does not commence proceedings on the merits of the case before the Court.[1247] [1248]

Where the measures to preserve evidence are revoked, or where they lapse due to any act or omission by the applicant, or where it is subsequently found that there has been no infringement or threat of infringement of the patent right, the Court may order the applicant, upon request of the defendant, to provide the defendant with appropriate compensation for any injury caused by those measures.[1249]

2. Order for Inspection (Rule 199)

The Court may, on a reasoned request by a party,[1250] order an inspection of products, devices, methods, premises or local situations *in situ*. For the sake of protection of confidential information, the Court may order that any of the above be disclosed only to certain named persons and subject to appropriate terms of non-disclosure in accordance with Article 58.[1251]

The Rules relating to the order to preserve evidence apply *mutatis mutandis*.[1252] This implies that the above flowcharts regarding the order to preserve evidence (*saisie*) are applicable.

E. (CHAPTER 5) OTHER EVIDENCE (RULES 200-204)

1. Order to freeze assets (Rule 200)

Where a party has presented reasonably available and plausible evidence in support of its claim that a patent has been or is about to be infringed, the Court may (whether before or after proceedings have been commenced) order a party not to remove from

---

1247. Rule 198.1. Reference can be made regarding this rule to Article 50(6) TRIPS Agreement and Article 7(3) Directive 2004/48/EC.
1248. Special attention should be given to the fact that this Rule 198.1 refers to proceedings on the merits before the Court (with capital). This could mean that should proceedings on the merits be initiated before a national court (based on evidence gathered during the execution of an Order to preserve evidence obtained from the UPC) the order could be revoked (or cease to have effect). This is different for similar actions before a Belgian court for example (order for descriptive measures) where proceedings on the merits can indeed be initiated before another national court or before the UPC, without having any effect on the evidence gathered. The Rules regarding this issue are in conformity with Article 68(8) UPCA which also refers to the Court (with a capital 'C'). As such and having regard to the principle that in case of contradiction the UPCA prevails on the Rules, the Rules could not be construed in such a way that Rule 198.1 could allow proceedings on the merits before any court within the given time frame to prevent the revocation of the order.
1249. Rule 198.2. Reference can be made to Rule 354.2.
1250. In earlier versions of the draft Rules (up to 15th draft), the Court could order such an inspection of its own motion (but after hearing the parties).
1251. Rule 199.1.
1252. Rule 199.2 *juncto* Rules 192 to 198.

its jurisdiction any assets or particular assets located therein nor to deal in any assets, whether located within its jurisdiction or not.[1253]

The rules relating to the order to preserve evidence apply *mutatis mutandis*.[1254] This implies that the above flowcharts regarding the order to preserve evidence (*saisie*) are applicable.

When seeking an order to freeze assets, the applicant should initiate proceedings on the merits of the case within the time period determined in accordance with Article 60(8) (i.e. a period of not exceeding 31 calendar days or 20 working days).[1255]

2. Experiments ordered by the Court (Rule 201)

Flowchart: Experiments ordered by the Court (R. 201)

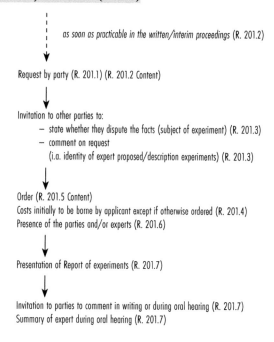

1253. Rule 200.1.
1254. Rule 200.2 *juncto* Rules 192 to 198.
1255. Article 61(2) *juncto* Article 60(8).

Chapter VI

(Part 3) Provisional Measures (*summary proceedings*) (Rules 205–213)

A. OVERVIEW OF THE PROCEEDINGS (RULES 205–213)

Summary proceedings before the Court of First Instance consist of a written procedure followed by an oral hearing.[1256]

The consecutive stages of the Application for provisional measures are detailed in the relevant flowcharts.

The flowchart should be examined in conjunction with the following additional remarks.

Subject to an Application for provisional measures, the Court may order the following *provisional measures*:[1257]

(a) injunctions against a defendant;
(b) the seizure or delivery up of the goods suspected of infringing a patent right so as to prevent their entry into or movement within the channels of commerce;
(c) a precautionary seizure of the movable and immovable property of the defendant, including the blocking of his bank accounts and other assets, if an applicant demonstrates circumstances likely to endanger the recovery of damages;
(d) an interim award of costs.

Regarding *the discretion of the Court* upon issuing an order, the following rules are to be taken into consideration:

> **Rule 209.2.** In exercising its discretion regarding (i) informing the defendant and inviting him to lodge an Objection to the Application, (ii) summoning the parties to the oral hearing, or (iii) summoning only the defendant to the oral hearing, the Court takes in particular into account:
> (a) whether the patent has been upheld in an opposition procedure before the EPO or has been the subject of proceedings in any other court;
> (b) the urgency of the action;
> (c) whether the applicant has requested provisional measures without hearing the defendant and whether the reasons for not hearing the defendant appear well-founded;

1256. No interim procedure is foreseen.
1257. Rule 211.

Part Three – The Rules of Procedure of the Unified Patent Court

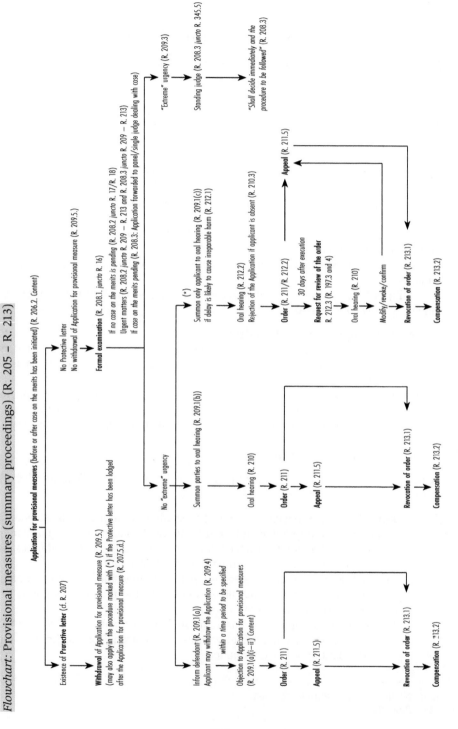

Flowchart: Provisional measures (summary proceedings) (R. 205 – R. 213)

(d) any Protective letter filed by the defendant; the Court needs to consider summoning parties to an oral hearing if a relevant Protective letter has been filed by the defendant.

Rule 211.2. In taking its decision the Court shall be satisfied with a sufficient degree of certainty that the applicant is entitled to commence proceedings pursuant to Article 47 UPCA, that the patent in question is valid and that his right is being infringed, or that such infringement is imminent.

Rule 211.3. In taking its decision on the Application for provisional measures, the Court shall have the discretion to weigh up the interests of the parties.

Rule 211.4. The Court should have regard to any unreasonable delay in seeking provisional measures.

Rule 211.5. The Court may order the applicant to provide adequate security for appropriate compensation for any injury likely to be caused to the defendant which the applicant may be liable to bear in the event that the Court revokes the order for provisional measures. The Court shall do so where interim measures are ordered without the defendant having been heard unless there are special circumstances not to do so.[1258] The Court shall decide whether it is appropriate to order the security by deposit or bank guarantee. The order shall be effective only after the security has been given in accordance with the Court's decision.

In two instances the applicant is given the opportunity *to withdraw his Application for provisional measures* and request the Court that the mentioned Application remains confidential:

- Either when the applicant has applied for provisional measures without hearing the defendant and the Court decides not to grant provisional measures without hearing the defendant.[1259]
- Or when the patent subject of the Application for provisional matters is the subject of a Protective letter.[1260] The Rules remain silent as to when and how the applicant is informed of the existence of such Protective letter. It would seem reasonable to assume that he is informed thereof before the formal examination.

B. PROTECTIVE LETTER (RULE 207)

If a person, entitled to initiate proceedings under Article 47 UPCA, considers it likely that an Application for provisional measures against him as a defendant may be lodged before the Court in the near future, he may file a Protective letter.[1261] The Protective letter should be filed with the Registry in the language of the patent, *should* contain

---

1258. For example, when no damages can occur.
1259. Rule 209.4.
1260. Rule 209.5 (with reference to Rule 209.4).
1261. Rule 207.1.

the elements as listed under Rule 207.2 and *may* contain the elements as listed under Rule 207.3. Upon filing a Protective letter a fee of EUR 200 should be paid.[1262]

The consecutive stages related to lodging a Protective letter are detailed in the flowchart.

Flowchart: Protective letter (R. 207)

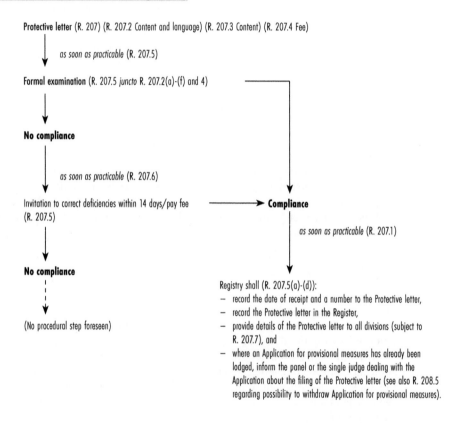

Where an Application for provisional measures is subsequently lodged, the Registrar forwards a copy of the Protective letter to the panel or judge appointed under Rule 208 together with the Application for provisional measures and forwards a copy to the applicant *as soon as practicable*.[1263]

The Protective letter will not be publicly available. Only when it has been forwarded to the applicant will the letter be publicly available in the Register.[1264]

1262. Rule 207.4.
1263. Rule 207.8.
1264. Rule 207.7.

Chapter VI – (Part 3) Provisional Measures (*summary proceedings*) (Rules 205-213)

If no Application for provisional measures has been lodged within six months from the date of receipt of the Protective letter, the Protective letter is removed from the Register unless the person who has lodged the Protective letter has, prior to the expiry of such period, applied for an extension of six months and paid a fee for the extension.[1265] Further extensions may be obtained on further payment of the fee.

No formal procedure has been foreseen should the defendant not have complied with the requirements of Rule 207.2. The Rules remain silent as to when and how the applicant is informed regarding a final decision (made by whom?) if he has not respected the requirements of Rule 207.2.

1265. Rule 207.9.

Chapter VII
(Part 4) Procedures before the Court of Appeal (Rules 220–254)

A. INTRODUCTORY AND BASIS RULES (RULES 220–223)

1. Appealable decisions (Rule 220)

Article 73(1) UPCA provides that an appeal against a decision of the Court of First Instance may be brought before the Court of Appeal by any party that has been unsuccessful, in whole or part, in its submissions and this within two months of the date of notification of the decision.

Under Article 73(2)(a) UPCA, certain orders of the Court of First Instance referred to in Articles 49(5), 59 to 62 and 67 (including orders to produce evidence and to inspect premises or orders for provisional measures which have a particular impact on the parties) may also be appealed. The different appealable decisions and orders of the Court are listed under Rule 220.1:[1266]

- (a) final decisions of the Court of First Instance,
- (b) decisions terminating proceedings as regards one of the parties,
- (c) orders referred to in Articles 49(5),[1267] 59,[1268] 60,[1269] 61,[1270] 62,[1271] or 67[1272] UPCA.

Under Article 73(2)(b) UPCA other procedural orders which are not mentioned under Article 73(2)(a) may in principle only be appealed together with the appeal against the final decision of the Court of First Instance or if the Court grants leave to appeal.

The duality seems to find its basis in the interest of the parties touched upon. Most of the procedural orders not mentioned under Article 73(2)(a) do not seem to touch upon basic interests of the parties. In the interest of efficiency, an appeal against such orders should be dealt with together with the appeal against the final decision. On the other hand, for orders touching upon the interests of parties, it was held desirable that they are appealable separately. This situation is addressed in Rule

---

1266. Rule 220.1.
1267. Decision by the President of Court of First Instance on the use of the language in which the patent was granted as language of proceedings.
1268. Order to present evidence which lies in the control of the opposing party or a third party.
1269. Order to preserve evidence and to inspect premises.
1270. Freezing orders.
1271. Provisional and protective measures.
1272. Power to order the communication of information.

Part Three – The Rules of Procedure of the Unified Patent Court

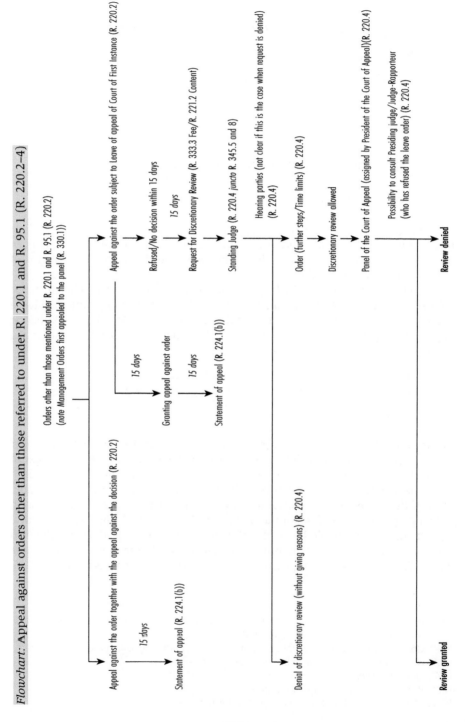

Chapter VII – (Part 4) Procedures before the Court of Appeal (Rules 220-254)

220.2 providing that orders *other than* those referred in Rule 220.1 may be either the subject of an appeal together with the appeal against the decision or may be appealed with the leave of the Court of First Instance within fifteen days of service of the Court's decision to that effect.[1273]

Rule 220.2 seems to be construed in such a way as to give the Court of Appeal means to control procedural orders of the Court of First Instance but at the same time allowing the Court of Appeal to limit its intervention to cases of particular importance. The aim seems to be to avoid systematic appeals which would risk stalling proceedings.

It is understood that, where the first instance procedural order is given by the Judge-Rapporteur, the party adversely affected must request first an early review by the panel of the Court of First Instance (Rules 102.2 and 333.1). Therefore, an application for a discretionary review by the Court of Appeal only applies to orders given or upheld by the first instance panel.

In the event of a refusal of the Court of First Instance to grant leave within fifteen days of the order of one of its panels or the Court not acting within this time period, a request for a discretionary review to the Court of Appeal[1274] may be made within fifteen calendar days from the end of that period.[1275] Such an appeal will not have suspensive effect.[1276]

The Registrar shall assign the request for a discretionary review to the standing judge.[1277] The standing judge may deny the request without giving reasons.[1278]

If the standing judge allows the request after having heard the other party, he shall order what further steps, if any, the parties shall take and within what time limits, and the President of the Court of Appeal shall assign the review to a panel of the Court of Appeal for a decision. The Court of Appeal may consult the presiding judge or the Judge-Rapporteur on the panel of the Court of First Instance which has refused the leave order.

Finally, this Rule clarifies that the Court of Appeal may hear appeals against separate decisions on the merits in infringement proceedings and in validity proceedings together.[1279]

1273. Rule 220.2.
1274. Setting out the matters referred to in Rule 221.2.
1275. Rule 220.3.
1276. Rule 223.5 (Amendment 22 (to Rule 223) adopted by the Administrative Committee on 8 July 2022).
1277. Rule 220.4 *juncto* Rule 345(5) and (8).
1278. Whether such denial (but also allowance) without giving reasons is in line with Article 77 (providing that all decisions and orders of the Court shall be reasoned) remains to be seen.
1279. Rule 221.5.

Flowchart: Overview leave of appeal against cost decisions (R. 221)

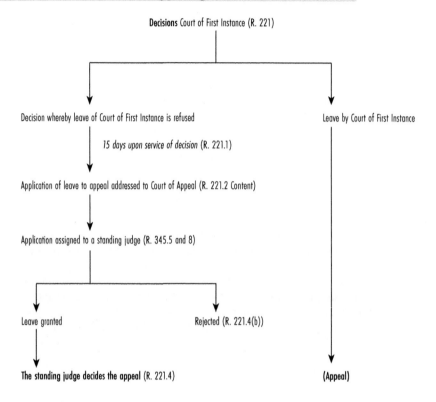

2. Application for leave of appeal against cost decisions (Rule 221)

A party adversely affected by a decision referred to in Rule 157[1280] may lodge an Application for leave of appeal within fifteen days of service of the decision of the Court.[1281] Such an appeal will not have suspensive effect.[1282]

1280. This Rule does not refer to a decision. Most probably Rule 156.2 is meant. Rule 157 states that an appeal is admittable against decisions by the Judge-Rapporteur as to costs in accordance with Rule 221.
1281. Rule 220.1.
1282. Rule 223.5 (Amendment 22 (to Rule 223) adopted by the Administrative Committee on 8 July 2022).

3. Subject matter before the Court of Appeal (Rule 222)

Requests, facts, evidence and arguments submitted by the parties under Rules 221,[1283] 225,[1284] 226,[1285] 236[1286] and 238[1287] constitute the subject matter of the proceedings before the Court of Appeal.[1288]

Requests, facts and evidence not submitted by a party during proceedings before the Court of First Instance may be disregarded by the Court of Appeal. When exercising its discretion, the Court takes into account:[1289]

(a) whether a party seeking to lodge new submissions is able to justify that the new submissions could not reasonably have been made during proceedings before the Court of First Instance;
(b) whether the new submissions are highly relevant for the decision on the appeal;
(c) the position of the other party regarding the lodging of the new submissions.

It would be problematic if an evaluation as described in Rule 222.2(b) might already imply a decision. Most probably such an evaluation can only be made when reading/ examining all submissions (also these introduced *after* the statement of grounds of appeal). Furthermore, the Rules remain silent as to at what point in time the Court of Appeal will need to take a decision regarding new requests, facts, evidence or arguments. More specifically whether this decision should be taken either after all written arguments have been introduced or at that moment in time when the new requests, facts and evidence have been introduced.

1283. Application for leave of appeal against cost decisions.
1284. Statement of appeal.
1285. Statement of grounds of appeal.
1286. Statement of response.
1287. Reply to a statement of cross-appeal.
1288. Rule 222.1.
1289. It would have been opportune that a parallel rule as the one under Rule 220.2 was introduced under Rule 116 / Rule 9.5 regarding new submissions introduced during the oral proceedings before the Court of First Instance.

Part Three – The Rules of Procedure of the Unified Patent Court

4. Application for suspensive effect (Rule 223)

Flowchart: Application for suspensive effect (R. 223)

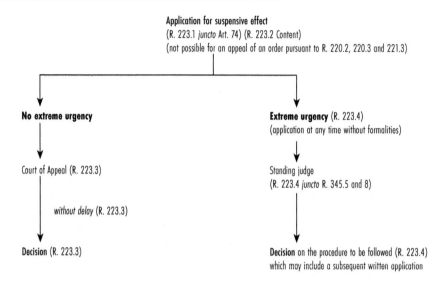

B. (CHAPTER 1) WRITTEN PROCEDURE (RULES 224–238A)

Rule 229.5 states that if the applicant has not lodged its Statement of appeal within two months of service (or within fifteen days of service for certain orders and decisions), the Registry shall inform the President of the Court of Appeal who shall reject the appeal as inadmissible.[1290] Although the Rule mentions that the appellant may be given the opportunity to be heard, it appears that the President has no discretion to accept Statements of appeal lodged after the term (*"shall reject"*). However, the appellant can still rely on Rule 234 regarding challenges to inadmissible appeals. The appellant may challenge a decision to reject the appeal as inadmissible under Rules 224.1 (late lodging) or 233.2 (failure to amend a Statement of grounds of appeal).

Translation of file. A comprehensive rule has been introduced regarding the translation of the file. If the language of the proceedings before the Court of Appeal is not the language of the proceedings before the Court of First Instance, the Judge-Rapporteur may order the appellant to lodge, within a time period to be specified, translations into the language of the proceedings before the Court of Appeal of:

(a) written pleadings and other documents lodged by the parties before the Court of First Instance, as specified by the Judge-Rapporteur; and
(b) decisions or orders of the Court of First Instance.[1291]

1290. Rule 224.1.
1291. Rule 232.1.

Chapter VII – (Part 4) Procedures before the Court of Appeal (Rules 220–254)

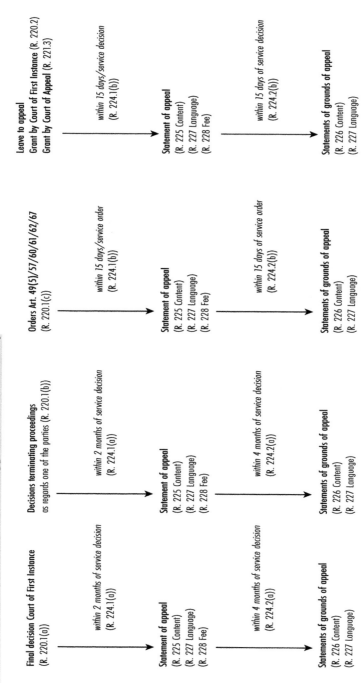

Part Three – The Rules of Procedure of the Unified Patent Court

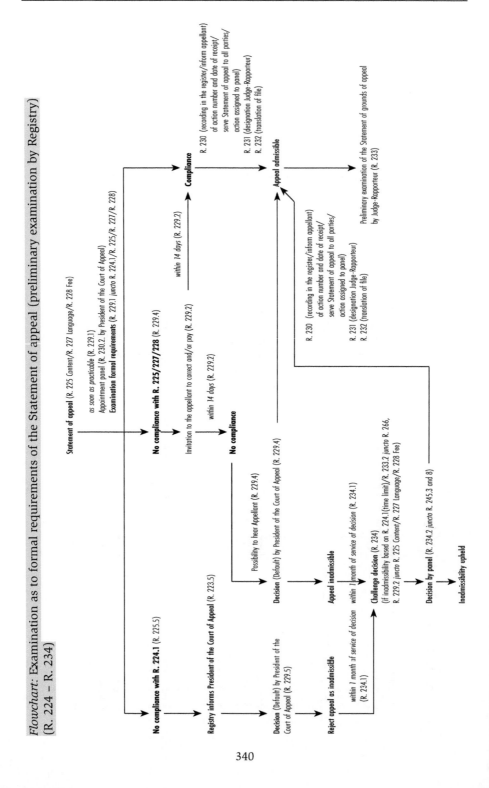

Flowchart: Examination as to formal requirements of the Statement of appeal (preliminary examination by Registry) (R. 224 – R. 234)

Chapter VII – (Part 4) Procedures before the Court of Appeal (Rules 220–254)

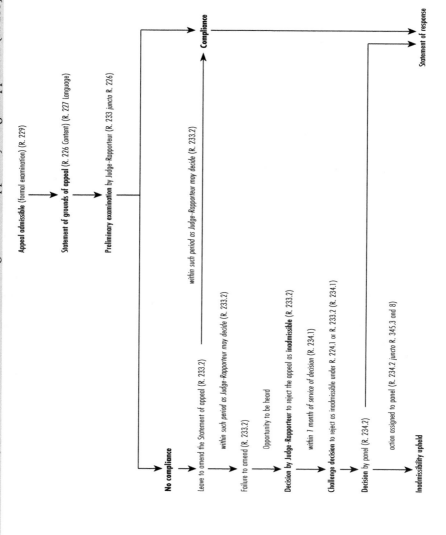

Flowchart: Preliminary examination of the Statement of grounds of appeal by Judge-Rapporteur (R. 233)

Should the appellant fail to lodge the translations within the time period specified, the Judge-Rapporteur shall reject the appeal by a default decision,[1292] with the possibility of hearing the appellant.[1293]

The appellant may request that costs of translations be taken into account when the Court fixes the amount of costs in accordance with Part 1, Chapter 5.[1294]

Change of language of proceedings at the appeal level. Based on Article 50(2) and (3) UPCA two situations seem to emerge when the language of the proceedings before the Court of Appeal is not the language of the proceedings before the Court of First Instance:

- either if parties agree to change the language into the language in which the patent was granted.[1295] This change is referred to under Rule 227.1(b);
- or if the Court of Appeal decides on another official language of a Contracting Member State and this subject to the agreement of the parties.[1296] Where a reference is made to this possibility under Rule 227.1(a), the Rules remain silent as to when the Court of Appeal would decide on such change of language. It is important to note that throughout the procedure this is the only possibility to change the language of proceedings to a language other than the language in which the patent is granted.

Bifurcation and language of proceedings at the appeal level. A situation which is not specifically foreseen is the language of proceedings before the Court of Appeal in the situation of a bifurcated case and in which different languages are used in the infringement and validity proceedings. The FAQ page of the Court[1297] states that in such an event, the language of the main action (i.e. infringement) heard by the local or regional division should prevail but this principle seems not to be articulated in the Rules.

An alternative approach might be that the language of the first decision appealed (which will most likely be the decision on validity in a language of the patent) will prevail and this upon application by the Court of Appeal of Rule 227.1(a) (*juncto* Article 50(2) UPCA). However, in the unlikely event that the parties do not agree to such a change (a condition explicitly stipulated under Article 50(2) UPCA), it seems that the Rules do not provide a solution other than to conduct the appeal proceedings (on validity and infringement) in a different language.

Rule 238A. – Referral to the full Court. The panel to which the action has been assigned may refer it to the full Court of Appeal if, on a proposal from the presiding judge, it considers the case to be of exceptional importance and, in particular, where the decision in the action may affect the consistency and unity of the case law of the

---

1292. Cf. Rule 354.
1293. Rule 233.2.
1294. Rule 233.3.
1295. Article 50(2).
1296. Article 50(3).
1297. Available on 13 April 2017.

Chapter VII – (Part 4) Procedures before the Court of Appeal (Rules 220-254)

Court.[1298] The decision needs to be taken by a three-quarters majority of the judges of the full Court.[1299]

The presiding judge on the panel shall request that the President of the Court of Appeal and the two judges of the Court of Appeal who are members of the Presidium appoint the judges of the Court of Appeal to the full Court. The appointees shall be the President of the Court of Appeal and not less than ten (legal and technical) judges of the Court of Appeal to represent the initial two panels of the Court of Appeal. In the event that the Court of Appeal shall have more than two panels, the appointees to the full Court shall increase by five judges (legal and technical) for each additional panel.[1300]

C. (CHAPTER 2) INTERIM PROCEDURE (RULE 239)

See flowchart under Part Three, Chapter VII D '(Chapter 3) Oral Procedure (Rules 240-241)' *infra*.

1298. Rule 238.A.1.
1299. Rule 238.A.3.
1300. Rule 238.A.2.

Part Three – The Rules of Procedure of the Unified Patent Court

D. (CHAPTER 3) ORAL PROCEDURE (RULES 240–241)

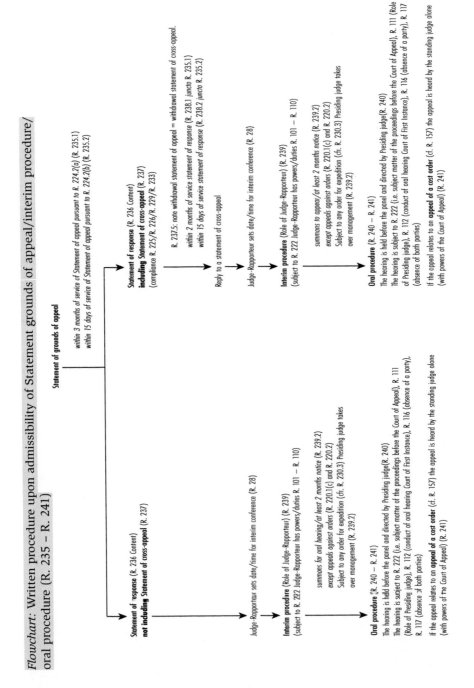

Flowchart: Written procedure upon admissibility of Statement grounds of appeal/interim procedure/oral procedure (R. 235 – R. 241)

Chapter VII – (Part 4) Procedures before the Court of Appeal (Rules 220–254)

E. (CHAPTER 4) DECISIONS AND EFFECTS OF DECISIONS (RULES 242–243)

Flowchart: Decisions and effects of decisions (R. 242 – R. 243)

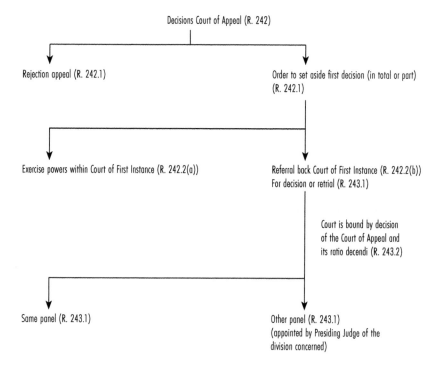

Part Three – The Rules of Procedure of the Unified Patent Court

F. (CHAPTER 5) PROCEDURE FOR APPLICATION FOR REHEARING (RULES 245–254)

Flowchart: Procedure for Application for rehearing (R. 245 – R. 255)

Final decision of the Court of First Instance (for which the time for lodging an appeal has expired) or the Court of Appeal

    Time limitations
    — Within two months of the discovery of the fundamental defect or of service of the final decision, whichever is the later (in case of a fundamental procedural defect listed under R. 247) (R. 245.2(a))
    — Within two months of the date on which the criminal offence has been so held or service of the final decision, whichever is the later (based on a criminal offence decided by a final court under R. 249) (R. 245.2(b))
    — In any event no later than ten years of service of the final decision (R. 245.2(c))

    If based on a fundamental procedural defect the following conditions should be met (R. 248):
    — Objection was raised during the proceedings before the Court of First Instance or the Court of Appeal and dismissed by the Court.
    — Objection could not be raised during the proceedings before the Court of First Instance or the Court of Appeal
    — An appeal could be brought in respect of the defect but failed to do so.

Application for rehearing lodged at the Court of Appeal (R. 245.2) (R. 246 Content) (R. 250 Fee) (R. 251 *juncto* R. 230.1 Recording in the Registry)

    R. 252: no suspense effect unless the Court of Appeal decides otherwise
    as soon as practicable (R. 253.1)

Formal examination by Registry (R. 253 *juncto* R. 245, 246, and 250)
    (it is not clear whether the Registry should also examine R. 248 and 249)

as soon as practicable (R. 253.1)

No compliance
    within 14 days (R. 253.2)
Invitation to correct deficiencies and/or pay fee (R. 253.2) → **Compliance**
    within 14 days (R. 253.2)

No compliance → **Application admissible**
    See also next flowchart "Application for rehearing by the Panel"

    hear petitioner

Decision Standing judge (R. 253.2 *juncto* R. 345.5 and 8)

Application inadmissible

Examination Application for rehearing (R. 255)

hearing of the parties (R. 255)

Rejected (R. 255(a))   Allowed (R. 255(b))

Reopen proceedings

Chapter VII – (Part 4) Procedures before the Court of Appeal (Rules 220–254)

Flowchart: Application for rehearing by the Panel (R. 254 and R. 255)

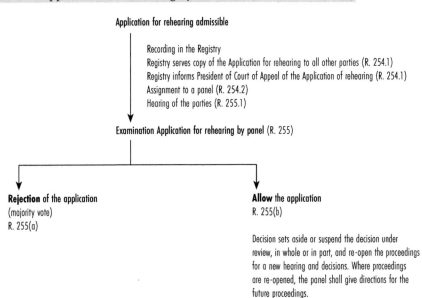

Part Three – The Rules of Procedure of the Unified Patent Court

G. (CHAPTER 6) PROCEDURE FOR APPLICATION FOR REHEARING (RULES 295–304)

Flowchart: Application for rehearing by the Panel (R. 254 and R. 255)

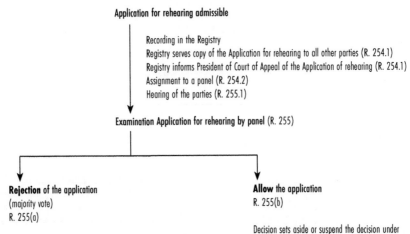

Chapter VIII
(Part 5) General Provisions

A. (CHAPTER 1) GENERAL PROCEDURAL PROVISIONS (RULES 260–266)

1. Examination by the Registry of its own motion (Rule 260)

The Registry examines, *as soon as practicable* in the proceedings, of its own motion, whether an Application to opt-out has effect for the patent or patents concerned.[1301] This Rule does not seem to add any alternative obligation to the one to be performed during the formal examination.[1302] The Registry was already furnished with the task of examining whether one or more of the patents concerned (regarding the Statement of claim but *mutatis mutandis* repeated throughout the Rules regarding other actions) are the object of an opt-out.

In the event the Registry identifies that two or more actions between the same parties and concerning the same patent are initiated before several divisions, it informs *as soon as practicable* the divisions concerned.[1303] The Rules remain silent as to how the divisions should proceed in case an action has been introduced between the same parties and concerning the same patent in several divisions. In our view, the Brussels I (recast) Regulation[1304] shall apply in such cases. Article 31 of the Brussels I (recast) Regulation provides that where actions come within the exclusive jurisdiction of several courts, any court other than the court first seized shall decline jurisdiction in favour of that court.

2. Date of pleadings (Rule 261)

All pleadings bear a time and date that is the time and date of receipt of pleadings at the Registry. The time shall be the local time of the Registry[1305] which might have implications in view of the time periods (to be dealt with under Rules 300 and 301).

1301. Rule 260.1.
1302. Rule 16.1.
1303. Rule 260.2.
1304. Regulation No. 1215/2012 of 12 December 2012 on jurisdiction and the recognition and enforcement of judgments in civil and commercial matters (recast), *OJ* L 351/1, 20 December 2012.
1305. Rule 261.

Part Three – The Rules of Procedure of the Unified Patent Court

3. **Public access to the Register (Rule 262)**[1306]

As a general rule and without prejudice to Articles 58 and 60(1) UPCA[1307] and subject to Rules 190.1,[1308] 194.5,[1309] 196.1,[1310] 197.4,[1311] 199.1,[1312] 207.7,[1313] 209.4,[1314] 315.2[1315] and 365.2:[1316]

- decisions and orders made by the Court shall be published;
- written pleadings and evidence[1317] lodged at the Court will be available to

---

1306. The authors point out that on the date of publication of this book some minor changes were discussed among the expert group regarding the access to the Register which may give rise to some changes to the mentioned Rules.
1307. These Articles deal with the protection of confidential information. In particular Article 58 UPCA states that the Court may limit access to evidence used in proceedings to specific persons.
1308. For the protection of confidential information the Court may order that the evidence be disclosed to certain named persons only and subject to appropriate terms of non-disclosure.
1309. If the Court decides to inform the defendant about the Application to preserve evidence, it will first allow the applicant the possibility to withdraw the Application. In the event of such withdrawal of his Application to preserve evidence, the applicant may request the Court to order that the Application and its contents shall remain confidential.
1310. In its order on the Application to preserve evidence, the Court may order that any of the evidence to be disclosed pursuant to its order may only be disclosed to certain named persons and subject to appropriate terms of non-disclosure.
1311. Should an order to preserve evidence be modified or revoked after a Request of a review has been introduced (Rule 197.3), the Court shall oblige the persons to whom confidential information has been disclosed to keep this information confidential.
1312. The same rules as mentioned regarding the Application to preserve evidence apply for the Application for inspection.
1313. The Protective letter shall not be publicly available in the Register until it has been forwarded to the applicant of the Application for provisional measures.
1314. On an Application for provisional measures without hearing the defendant and the Court would decide not to grant provisional measures without hearing the defendant, the applicant may withdraw the Application and may request that the Court orders the Application and the contents of the Application to remain confidential. Which elements the Court will take into consideration to allow or deny such a request will depend on the circumstances of the case.
1315. On a reasoned request by a party, the Court, for the protection of confidential information, may order that a pleading or part of a pleading of an intervener be disclosed only to certain named persons and subject to appropriate terms of non-disclosure.
1316. At the request of parties, the Court may order that details of a settlement are to be kept confidential in a Court decision confirming the settlement. Which elements the Court will take into consideration to allow or deny such a request will depend on the circumstances of the case.
1317. This includes *written* and *non-written* evidence as is made clear in the explanatory notes to Amendment 24 (to Rule 262) as adopted by the Administrative Committee on 8 July 2022.

Chapter VIII – (Part 5) General Provisions

the public upon reasoned request[1318] to the Registry.[1319] A decision will be taken by the Judge-Rapporteur after consulting the parties.

The amended Rule 262.1[1320] further refers to the need of confidentiality as expressed in the General Data Protection Regulation (EU) 2016/569 and the request to keep certain information confidential (as detailed under Rule 262.2).

Although explicitly referred to in Rule 262.1, it would seem advisable that an applicant requesting an order to preserve evidence or for inspection without hearing (or informing) the defendant and/or a provisional measure without hearing (or informing) the defendant, would make clear in his application that, should the application be rejected and the defendant is not heard or informed, such decision should not be published (stating the reasons).

Under Rule 262.2 it is foreseen that a party can request that certain information of written pleadings or evidence is kept confidential and this by providing specific reasons for such confidentiality.[1321] The Registry shall not make content of the Register available to the public until fourteen days after all the recipients took note. Further, the Registrar shall ensure that information subject to such a request shall not be made available pending an Application for an order to exclude information from public access[1322] or an appeal.[1323]

This approach may be different to some national proceedings where the written pleadings, written evidence, decisions and orders lodged by parties are only accessible to the parties.

The Application for an order to exclude information from public access should contain:[1324]

(a) details of the information alleged to be confidential or otherwise to be restricted;
(b) the grounds upon which the information should be restricted; and
(c) the purpose for which the information is needed.

1318. Some argue that the fact that the request is *"reasoned"* should be enough to allow access to the written pleadings and evidence. This seems to be contradicted by the fact that the Judge-Rapporteur needs to take a *decision* and as such evaluate the *"reasons"*. Whether academic reasons could be considered sufficient and/or whether (requesting) non-parties to the proceedings will be heard remains to be seen.
1319. The explanatory notes to Amendment 24 (to Rule 262) as adopted by the Administrative Committee on 8 July 2022 clarify that the Contracting Member State is configured in a way that the public can take note of the *existence* of documents and orders but not their contents.
1320. Amendment 24 (to Rule 262) as adopted by the Administrative Committee on 8 July 2022.
1321. Rule 261.1 (in fine) Where a party requests that parts of written pleadings or written evidence shall be kept confidential, it shall also provide copies of the said documents with the relevant parts redacted when making the request.
1322. Rule 262.1 *juncto* Rule 262.2.
1323. Rule 262.1 *juncto* Rule 220.2.
1324. Rule 262.3.

Upon receiving the mentioned Application, the Court may invite written comments from the parties prior to making any order.[1325] The Court should allow the Application unless legitimate reasons given by the party concerned for the confidentiality of the information outweigh the interest of the applicant to access such information.[1326] The Registrar should take all such steps necessary with regard to the access to the Register to give effect to the Court order.[1327]

4. Protection of Confidential Information (Rule 262A)

Flowchart: Protection of confidential information (R. 262A)

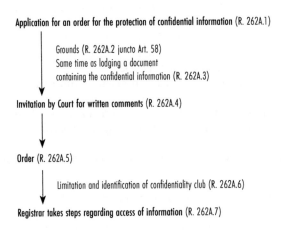

Amendment 25 (introduction of new Rule 262A) adopted by the Administrative Committee on 8 July 2022 deals with the question of ordering confidentiality of the information made available under Rule 262 or the collection and use of evidence towards the other party.[1328] Under Rule 262A.1, a party is given the opportunity to introduce an Application to the Court for an order that certain information contained in its pleadings or the collection and use of evidence in proceedings may be restricted or prohibited or that access to such information or evidence be restricted to specific persons.

The procedure is graphically explained by the flowchart.

1325. Rule 262.5.
1326. Rule 262.6.
1327. Rule 262.7
1328. Amendments adopted by the Administrative Committee on 8 July 2022 were made to several other rules where reference is made to Rule 262. More specifically Amendment 4 (to Rule 13), Amendment 6 (to Rule 24), Amendment 7 (to Rule 25), Amendment 9 (to Rule 29A), Amendment 10 (to Rule 44), Amendment 12 (to Rule 63), Amendment 13 (to Rule 88).

Rule 262A.5 provides some guidance to the proportionality weighting by the Court indicating that grounds relied upon by the applicant that the order "significantly" should outweigh the interest of the other party to have full access to the information and evidence in question to allow the application.

Rule 262A.6 states that the number of persons as indicated in the application shall be no greater than necessary in order to ensure compliance with the right of the parties to the legal proceedings to an effective remedy and to a fair trial, and shall include at least one natural person from each party and the respective lawyers or other representatives of those parties to the legal proceedings.[1329]

5. Leave to change claim or amend case (Rule 263)

At any stage of the proceedings, a party can apply to the Court for leave to change its claim or to amend its case, including adding a counterclaim.[1330] Such application should explain the reasons why such a change or amendment was not included in the original pleading. Leave will only be granted if, all circumstances considered, the party seeking the amendment can satisfy the Court that:[1331]

(a) the amendment in question could not have been made with reasonable diligence at an earlier stage; and
(b) the amendment will not unreasonably hinder the other party in the conduct of its action.

In contrast, leave to limit a claim in an action *unconditionally* should always be granted.[1332] Should leave be granted, the Court may reconsider fees already paid in the light of an amendment.[1333] The Court has discretionary power regarding the reconsideration of the fees.

6. An opportunity to be heard (Rule 264)

Where the Rules provide that a party or parties shall or may be given an opportunity to be heard (before the Court makes an order or takes action), the Court shall or may (as the case may be) request the parties to provide written submissions within a specified period and/or (may) invite the parties to an oral hearing on a date fixed by the Court. The Court could also order a hearing by telephone or video-conference.[1334]

1329. This rule is in line with Article 9 of the Directive (EU) 2016/943 of 8 June 2016 on the protection of undisclosed know-how and business information (trade secrets) against their unlawful acquisition, use and disclosure which is stated in the explanatory notes to Amendment 25 (and specifically Rule 262A.6).
1330. Rule 263.1.
1331. Rule 263.2.
1332. Rule 263.3.
1333. Rule 263.4.
1334. Rule 264.

7. Withdrawal (Rule 265)

As long as there is no final decision, a claimant can apply for withdrawal of his action. The Court will decide after hearing the other party (or parties). The Application to withdraw is not permitted if the other party has a legitimate interest in the action being decided by the Court.[1335] If withdrawal is allowed, the Court shall:[1336]

(a) give a decision declaring the proceedings closed;
(b) order the decision to be entered on the Register; and
(c) issue a cost decision.[1337]

Such withdrawal shall have no effect on any counterclaim in the action. The Court may refer a counterclaim for revocation to the central division.[1338]

8. Preliminary references to the CJEU (Rule 266)

At any stage of the proceedings, where a question is raised before the Court for which in its opinion it is necessary to request a preliminary judgment of the CJEU before the Court can give judgment, the Court of First Instance *may* and the Court of Appeal *shall* request the CJEU to give a ruling thereon.[1339] In requesting[1340] the ruling, the procedures set out in the Rules of the CJEU will be followed.[1341] If the Court requests the CJEU to apply its expedited procedure, the request shall in addition set out:[1342]

(a) matters of fact and law which establish its urgency; and
(b) reasons why an urgent ruling is appropriate.

Unless otherwise decided by the Court, the proceedings are stayed until the CJEU has given a preliminary ruling on the question.[1343] By adding this rule, compliance is ensured with EU law and Article 38(2) Unified Patent Court Statute. A stay of the entire proceedings is not compulsory[1344] but rather an option.[1345] However, Rule 266.5 clarifies that the Court cannot give its judgment before the CJEU has ruled on the request.

1335. Rule 265.1.
1336. Rule 265.2.
1337. In accordance with Part 1, Chapter 5.
1338. Rule 265.2 in fine.
1339. Rule 266.1.
1340. In which case the Registrar shall as soon as practicable forward the request and request to apply the expedited procedure to the Registrar of the CJEU.
1341. Rule 266.2.
1342. Rule 266.3.
1343. Rule 266.5.
1344. Cf. Article 267 Treaty on the Function of the European Union.
1345. Rule 266.5.

9. Actions pursuant to Article 22 UPCA[1346] (Rule 267)

Where an action for damages has been brought against a Contracting Member State pursuant to Article 22 UPCA, the President of the Court of Appeal shall, as soon as practicable following a request from the competent authority in the Contracting Member State, provide the competent authority with copies of all pleadings, evidence, decisions and orders available to the Court in its proceedings that are relevant to the action for damages. The President of the Court of Appeal shall have an opportunity to comment.[1347]

B. (CHAPTER 2) SERVICE (RULES 270-279)

1. Service within the Contracting Member States or by agreement (Rules 270-272)

a. Scope of this section (Rule 270)

For the service of the Statement of claim (to be understood as all pleadings in actions for which the Court has been awarded exclusive competence[1348]) within the Contracting Member States, the law of the European Union on the service of documents in civil and commercial matters[1349] and the Rules set out in this Section (with specific reference to Rule 271.2) apply.

The Rules establish a system of service of documents which *expedite or further simplify* the service mechanisms in the mentioned Service Regulation.

b. Service of the Statement of claim (Rule 271)

According to Article 44 UPCA, the Court shall make best use of electronic procedures.

Rule 271 used to define the requirements to be met for a secure system for service. With Amendment 26 (to Rules 270, 271, 272, 274, 275 and 278) adopted by the Administrative Committee on 8 July 2022, the Administrative Committee has decided that these requirements are no longer necessary to mention separately as they are included in the Service Regulation (Regulation (EU) 2020/1784).

Rule 271.1(a) allows electronic service directly on the defendant, as provided for in Article 19(1) of the Regulation (EU) 2020/1784. The following two options are available:

(i) using a qualified electronic registered delivery services if the defendant has consented to it (Article 19(1)(a)). Such secure systems need to meet the standards contained in Regulation (EU) No. 910/2014. The document served electronically must use a trust service provider established by the EU or an electronic identification scheme notified by a Member State (Article 2(1)

1346. Liability for damage caused by infringements of Union law.
1347. Rule 267.
1348. Cf. Article 32(1).
1349. Regulation (EU) 2020/1784

Regulation (EU) No. 910/2014). A list of systems is published by the Commission under Article 9(2) Regulation (EU) No. 910/2014. The requirements for electronic signatures are contained in Articles 25 et seq. of Regulation (EU) No. 910/2014.

(ii) Service by simple e-mail where the addressee has consented to it and he confirms receipt of the document with an acknowledgement of receipt, including the date of receipt as is provided in Article 19(1)(b) Regulation (EU) 2020/1748

Rule 272.1(b) and (c) provide for the possibility to serve the Statement of claim to a representative of the defendant.[1350]

Rule 272.2 highlights the importance of the Contracting Member State by indicating that where a representative accepts service on behalf of a party, service may be affected within this Contracting Member State. In the explanatory notes to the introduction of this new Rule the Administrative Committee stated that this provision should be regarded as a *"lex specialis"* to Regulation (EU) 2020/1784. As a legal basis, the Administrative Committee refers to Article 29(2) of Regulation (EU) 2020/1784 and to the European Court of Justice working in the same manner in its internal system.

For the purpose of serving a Statement for revocation[1351] or a Statement for declaration of non-infringement,[1352] the reference to *representatives* under Rule 271.2(b) or (c) shall additionally include professional representatives and legal practitioners as defined in Article 134 EPC who are recorded as the appointed representative for the patent, the subject of the proceedings, in the Register or in the national patent register.[1353]

Rule 274.4 sets forth the possible means of service for the situation where service by electronic means would not be possible. Service in such a case can be secured by:

(i) any other method foreseen in the Service Regulation (Regulation (EU) 2020/1784), in particular by registered letter with acknowledgement of receipt or equivalent; or[1354] [1355]

(ii) in the event service could not be effected by registered letter with acknowledgment, any other method could be used permitted by the law of the Member State of the EU where service is to be effected or authorized by the Court under Rule 275.

1350. Either upon information of the defendant providing the electronic address of the representative (in conformity with Rule 8.1) or upon notification of the representative that he accepts service of Statement of claim on behalf of the defendant at an electronic address.
1351. Rule 44.
1352. Rule 62.
1353. Rule 271.3.
1354. Cfr. Article 18 Regulation (EU) 2020/1784.
1355. Other possibilities mentioned in the explanatory means consist in the use of agencies, diplomatic service or direct service (cfr. Articles 8 et seq., 17, 20 Regulation (EU) 2020/1784.

Service under the above-mentioned rules should be effected at the following place:[1356]

(a) where the defendant is a company or other legal person: at its statutory seat, central administration or principal place of business within the Contracting Member State or at any place within the Contracting Member State where the company or other legal person has a permanent or temporary place of business;[1357] or
(b) where the defendant is an individual: at his usual or last known residence within the Contracting Member State; or
(c) for the purpose of serving a Statement for revocation[1358] or serving a Statement for a declaration of non-infringement,[1359] at the place of business of a professional representative or legal practitioner as defined in Article 134 EPC who is recorded as the appointed representative for the patent, the subject of the proceedings, in the Register or of the patent office of a Contracting Member State.

The actual *day* on which a Statement of claim is deemed to be served on the defendant depends on the means by which it is served:[1360]

(a) where service takes place by means of electronic communication: the *day* on which the relevant electronic message was sent (GMT + 1); or
(b) where service takes place by registered letter with acknowledgment of receipt or equivalent shall be deemed to be served on the addressee: the *tenth day* following posting unless it has failed to reach the addressee, has in fact reached him on a later date or acknowledgment of receipt or equivalent has not been returned. Such service shall, except where Rule 271.8 applies, be deemed effective even if acceptance of the letter has been refused.

Rule 270.7 states the obligation for the Registry to advise the defendant that he may refuse to accept a Statement of claim if it is not written or not accompanied by a translation into a language that he understands or that is an official language of the place where service is to be effected. The Registry should enclose with the document to be served form L in Annex I of Regulation (EU) 2020/1784.

In the event the defendant is entitled to refuse service and where he has notified such refusal to the Registry within two weeks of the attempted service together with an indication of the language(s) he understands, the Registry shall inform the claimant. The claimant shall provide to the Registry translations of at least the Statement of claim and the information required in Rule 13.1(a) to (p) in a language provided for by Rule 271.7.

1356. Rule 271.5.
1357. By mentioning *"temporary place of business"* it is clear that service can be effected at, for example, trade fairs.
1358. Rule 44.
1359. Rule 62.
1360. Rule 271.6.

c. Notice of the service and non-service of the Statement of claim (Rule 272)

The Registry informs the claimant of the date on which the Statement of claim is deemed served.[1361]

Should the Registry have served the Statement of claim by registered letter with acknowledgement of receipt or equivalent and the Statement of claim is returned to the Registry, the Registry informs the claimant thereof.[1362] This rule applies *mutatis mutandis* where the Registry has served the Statement of claim by means of electronic communication or by fax and the relevant electronic message or fax appears not to have been received.[1363]

2. Service outside the Contracting Member States (Rules 273-274)

A Statement of claim is to be served outside the Contracting Member States:[1364]

(a) by any method provided by:
   (i) the Service Regulation (Regulation (EU) 2020/1784) where it applies; or
   (ii) the Hague Service Convention or any other applicable convention or agreement where it applies; or
   (iii) (to the extent that there is no such convention in force) either by service through diplomatic or consular channels from the Contracting Member State in which the Registry is established;
(b) where service under (a) could not be effected, by any method permitted by the law of the state where service is to be effected or as authorised by the Court.[1365]

The chosen method is conditional on the fact that it is not contrary to the law of the state where service is effected.[1366]

The Registry informs the claimant of the date on which the Statement of claim is deemed served under Rule 274.1 and shall inform the claimant if for any reason service pursuant to the mentioned Rule cannot be effected.[1367]

3. Service by an alternative method (Rule 275)

Where service in accordance with Section 1 (Service within the Contracting Member States) or Section 2 (Service outside the Contracting Member States) could not be effected and on an application by the claimant that there is a good reason to authorise service by a method or at a place not otherwise permitted by the Rules, the Court

---

1361. Rule 272.1 *juncto* Rule 271.5.
1362. Rule 272.2.
1363. Rule 272.3.
1364. Rule 274.1.
1365. Cf. Rule 275 (Service of the Statement of claim by an alternative method or at an alternative place).
1366. Rule 274.2.
1367. Rule 274.3 and 4.

may by way of order permit service by an alternative method or at an alternative place.[1368] On a reasoned request, the Court may order that steps already taken to bring the Statement of claim to the attention of the defendant by an alternative method or at an alternative place is good service.[1369] Such order should specify:[1370]

(a) the method or place of service;
(b) the date on which the Statement of claim is deemed served; and
(c) the period for filing the Statement of defence.

No order for alternative service that permits service in a manner that is contrary to the law of the state where service is to be effected can be made.[1371]

4. Service of Orders, Decisions and Written Pleadings (Rules 276–279)

a. *Service of orders and decisions (Rule 276)*

Any order or decision of the Court needs to be served on each of the parties in accordance with the provisions of Section 1 (Service within a Contracting Member State of by agreement), Section 2 (Service outside the Contracting Member State) and Section 3 (Service by an alternative method), as the case may be.[1372]

Decisions by default,[1373] resulting from the failure of the defendant to lodge a Defence to revocation[1374] or to lodge a Defence to the statement for a declaration of non-infringement[1375] within the time limit set by the Rules of Procedure or by the Court, may be served on the defendant at the place of business of a professional representative or legal practitioner as defined in Article 134 EPC who is recorded as the appointed representative in the Register or in the national patent register[1376] for the subject Unitary Patent, being the subject of the proceedings.

b. *Decisions by default under Part 5, Chapter 11 (Rule 277)*

In the event that the Court renders a decision by default, it should satisfy itself that either:[1377]

(a) the Statement of claim was served by a method prescribed by the internal law of the state addressed for the service of documents in domestic actions upon persons who are within its territory; or
(b) the Statement of claim was actually served on the defendant according to Chapter 2.

1368. Rule 275.1.
1369. Rule 275.2.
1370. Rule 275.3.
1371. Rule 273.4.
1372. Rule 276.1.
1373. Pursuant to Rule 355.
1374. Cf. Rule 50.
1375. Cf. Rule 65
1376. Rule 276.2.
1377. Rule 277.

c. Service of written pleadings and other document (Rule 278)

As soon as practicable (after written pleadings have been received at the Registry), the Registry should serve the pleadings and any other document lodged with the pleadings on the other party by means of electronic communication except if the pleadings contain a request for an *ex parte* proceeding.[1378] Where service by means of electronic communication cannot be effected, the Registry serves the written pleadings on the party by:[1379]

(a) registered letter with acknowledgement of receipt or equivalent; or
(b) any method authorised by the Court under Rule 275.

Service under registered letter with advice of delivery needs to be effected at the following place:[1380]

(a) where the party is a company or other legal person: at its statutory seat, central administration, principal place of business or at any place within the Contracting Member State where the company or other legal person has a place of business; or
(b) where the party is an individual: at his usual or last known residence within the Contracting Member State.

Where a party is represented pursuant to Rule 8.1, the pleadings and other documents referred to above shall be served on that representative. Rule 278.2 shall apply *mutatis mutandis*.[1381]

d. Change of electronic address for service (Rule 279)

Where the electronic address for service of a party changes, that party must give notice in writing of the change as soon as it has taken place to the Registry and every other party.[1382]

C. (CHAPTER 3) RIGHTS AND OBLIGATIONS OF REPRESENTATIVES (RULES 284–293)

1. Duty of representatives not to misrepresent facts or cases (Rule 284)

A representative of a party shall not misrepresent cases or facts before the Court either knowingly or with good reasons to know. Although such a rule should be applauded, the Rules remain silent as to what the actual sanctions or implications for the action would be, especially if the misrepresentation occurs in *ex parte* proceedings and/or in actions where the claimant has requested not to hear the defendant.

1378. Rule 278.1.
1379. Rule 278.2.
1380. Rule 278.3.
1381. Rule 278.5.
1382. Rule 279 with reference to Rule 6.3.

2. Powers of Attorney (Rule 285)

Unless his representative powers are challenged and the Court orders production of a written authority, the claim of a representative to be representing a party is accepted as such.[1383] By Amendment 27 (to Rule 285) as adopted by the Administrative Committee on 8 July 2022, Rule 285.2 was introduced allowing the Court to exclude a representative from the proceedings following a successful challenge to his representative powers.

3. Certificate that a representative is authorised to practise before the Court (Rule 286)

A representative pursuant to Article 48(1) UPCA[1384] should lodge a certificate at the Registry stating that he is a lawyer authorised to practise before a court of a Member State of the European Union.[1385] A lawyer within the meaning of Article 48(1) is a person who is authorised to pursue professional activities under a title referred to in Article 1 of Directive 98/5/EC and (by way of exception) a person with equivalent legal professional qualifications who, owing to national rules, is permitted to practise in patent infringement and invalidity litigation but not under such title. In subsequent actions the representative may refer to the certificate previously lodged.[1386] Discussions regarding specific situations in Finland and Sweden have led to the broad definition of the term "lawyer". By adding the specific wording in Rule 286.1 wherein it is clear that the qualifications which are considered are of "legal" nature, the distinction between lawyers (cf. Article 48(1) and Rule 286.1) and European Patent attorneys (cf. Article 48(2) and Rule 286.2) remains untouched.

A representative pursuant to Article 48(2)[1387] should lodge a European Patent Litigation Certificate as defined by the Administrative Committee at the Registry or otherwise justify that he has appropriate qualifications to represent a party before the Court. In subsequent actions such representative may refer to the certificate or other evidence of appropriate qualification previously lodged.[1388]

4. Attorney-client privilege (Rule 287)

As an introduction to this Rule (but also to Rule 288 – Litigation privilege), it is important to clarify the terms "*lawyer*" and "*patent attorney*":

- The term "*lawyer*" means a person as defined above[1389] and any other person who is qualified to practise as a lawyer and to give legal advice under the

---

1383. Rule 285.1.
1384. This article concerns lawyers.
1385. By making reference to a Member State of the EU clarifies that lawyers authorised to practise before courts of the EU (which are not Contracting Member States) may also lodge the certificate.
1386. Rule 286.1.
1387. This article concerns patent attorneys.
1388. Rule 286.2.
1389. Rule 286.1 (a person who is authorised to pursue professional activities under a title

law of the state where he practises and who is professionally instructed to give such advice.[1390]
- The term *"patent attorney"* shall include a person who is recognised as eligible to give advice under the law of the state where he practises in relation to the protection of any invention or to the prosecution or litigation of any patent or patent application and is professionally consulted to give such advice[1391] and includes a professional representative before the EPO pursuant to Article 134(1) EPC.[1392]

Where a client seeks advice from a lawyer he has instructed in a professional capacity, whether in court or otherwise, any confidential communication (whether written or oral) between them relating to the seeking or the provision of that advice is privileged[1393] from disclosure, whilst it remains confidential, in any proceedings before the Court or in arbitration or mediation proceedings before the Centre.[1394] The privilege applies also to communications between a client and a lawyer or patent attorney employed by the client and instructed to act in a professional capacity, whether in connection with proceedings before the Court or otherwise.[1395] Furthermore, the privilege extends to the product of the work of the lawyer or patent attorney (including communications between lawyers and/or patent attorneys employed in the same firm or entity or between lawyers and/or patent attorneys employed by the same client) and to any record of a privileged communication.[1396]

The privilege prevents the lawyer or patent attorney or agent and his client from being questioned or examined regarding the contents or nature of their communications.[1397] The privilege may be expressly waived by the client.[1398]

5. Litigation privilege (Rule 288)

Where a client, or a lawyer or patent attorney as specified above[1399] instructed by a client in a professional capacity, communicates confidentially with a third party for the purposes of obtaining information or evidence of any nature for the purpose of or for use in any proceedings, including proceedings before the EPO, such communications shall be privileged from disclosure in the same way and to the same extent as provided for in Rule 287.

---

referred to in Article 1 of Directive 98/5/EC and by way of exception a person with equivalent legal professional qualifications who, owing to national rules, is permitted to practise in patent infringement and invalidity litigation but not under such title).
1390. Rule 287.6(a).
1391. Rule 287.6(b).
1392. Rule 287.7.
1393. A privilege that may be waived according to Rule 287.5.
1394. Rule 287.1.
1395. Rule 287.2.
1396. Rule 287.3.
1397. Rule 287.4.
1398. Rule 287.5.
1399. With reference to Rules 287.1, 2, 6 and 7.

Chapter VIII – (Part 5) General Provisions

6. Privileges, immunities and facilities (Rule 289)

Representatives appearing before the Court or before any judicial authority to which it has addressed letters rogatory,[1400] enjoy immunity in respect of words spoken or written by them concerning the action or the parties.[1401] Representatives enjoy the following further privileges and facilities:[1402]

- (a) papers and documents relating to the proceedings are exempted from both search and seizure;
- (b) any allegedly infringing product or device relating to the proceedings is exempted from both search and seizure when brought to the Court for the purposes of the proceedings.

In the event of a dispute, customs officials or police may seal those papers, documents or allegedly infringing products or devices. Such sealed papers, documents or allegedly infringing products or devices need to be immediately forwarded to the Court for inspection in the presence of the Registrar and of the person concerned.[1403]

Although not specified, it is up to the parties to send these papers, documents or allegedly infringing products or devices to the Court. The incurred costs related to this obligation need to be considered as costs of proceedings to which Rule 150.1 will apply.

The Court may waive the immunity where it considers that a representative is guilty of conduct which is contrary to the proper conduct of proceedings.[1404]

7. Powers of the Court as regards representatives (Rule 290)

The Court has the powers normally accorded to courts of law, under the conditions laid down in Rule 291 as regards representatives who appear before it.[1405] Representatives who appear before the Court shall strictly comply with any code of conduct adopted for such representatives by the Administrative Committee.[1406]

8. Exclusion from the proceedings (Rule 291)

If the Court considers that the conduct of a party's representative towards the Court, towards any judge of the Court or towards any member of the staff of the Registry is incompatible with the dignity of the Court or with the requirements of the proper administration of justice, or that such representative uses his rights for purposes other than those for which they were granted, it shall so inform the person concerned. On the same grounds, the Court may at any time, after having given the person concerned an opportunity to be heard, exclude that person from the proceedings by way of order.

1400. Cf. Rule 202.
1401. Rule 289.1.
1402. Rule 289.2.
1403. Rule 289.3.
1404. Rule 289.5.
1405. Rule 290.1.
1406. Rule 290.2.

Such order has immediate effect.[1407] Where a party's representative is excluded from the proceedings, the proceedings shall be stayed for a period fixed by the presiding judge in order to enable the party concerned to appoint another representative.[1408]

9. Patent attorneys' right of audience (Rule 292)

For the purposes of Article 48(4) UPCA, the term *"patent attorneys"* assisting a representative referred to in Article 48(1) and/or Article 48(2) UPCA shall mean persons meeting the requirements of Rule 287.6(b) or Rule 287.7 and practising in a Contracting Member State.[1409] Such patent attorneys are allowed to speak at hearings of the Court at the discretion of the Court and subject to the representative's responsibility to coordinate the presentation of a party's case.[1410] The privileges as mentioned under the above Rules 285[1411] and 287 to 291 shall apply *mutatis mutandis*.[1412]

10. Change of a representative (Rule 293)

Any change of representative takes effect from the receipt by the Registry of a notification that a new representative shall in future be representing the party concerned. Until the moment where such statement is received, the former representative remains responsible for the conduct of the proceedings and for communications between the Court and the party concerned.

11. Removal from the register of representatives (Rule 294)

By Amendment 28a (to Rule 294) as adopted by the Administrative Committee on 8 July 2022 a new Rule has been introduced dealing with an application to remove a representative from the register of representatives.[1413] Such application should be made either by the representative himself in the event he retires or for any other reason ceases to satisfy the requirements of Rule 286 or by a representative on behalf of a listed representative who has died.

1407. Rule 291.1.
1408. Rule 291.2.
1409. Rule 292.1.
1410. Rule 292.2.
1411. Rule 285 was added to this Rule by Amendment 28 (to Rule 292) adopted by the Administrative Committee on 8 July 2022 to allow the Court to order the assisting patent attorney to produce a mandate.
1412. Rule 292.3.
1413. The explanatory notes to this amendment further clarify that there is no need for a corresponding rule for patent attorneys (and this by referring to the Rules on the European Patent Litigation Certificate and Other Appropriate Qualifications Pursuant to Article 48(2) of the Agreement on a Unified Patent Court (EPLC) which include a provision dealing with this issue (Rule 16).

Chapter VIII – (Part 5) General Provisions

D. (CHAPTER 4) STAY OF PROCEEDINGS (RULES 295-298)

1. Stay of proceedings (Rule 295)

In the following situations, proceedings may be stayed by the Court:
- (a) where the Court is seized of an action relating to a patent which is also the subject of opposition proceedings or limitation proceedings (including subsequent appeal proceedings) before the EPO or a national authority where a decision in such proceedings may be expected to be given rapidly. It is unclear how the Court shall interpret the term *"rapidly"* for decisions of national authorities. If the touchstone is a term comparable to the time frame of a decision of the EPO in opposition proceedings, rapidly can be easily interpreted as a couple of years;
- (b) where it is seized of an action relating to a supplementary protection certificate which is also the subject of proceedings before a national court or authority;
- (c) where an appeal is brought before the Court of Appeal against a decision or order of the Court of First Instance:
  (i) disposing of the substantive issues in part only; or
  (ii) disposing of an admissibility issue or a Preliminary Objection;
- (d) at the joint request of the parties;
- (e) in case of infringement proceedings during the written procedure when the central division deals with a Counterclaim for revocation under Article 33(3);[1414]
- (f) in case of a revocation action and subsequent infringement action in a local or regional division and actions for declaration of non-infringement within Article 33(6);[1415]
- (g) in case of infringement proceedings pending a decision in the revocation procedure or a decision of the EPO;[1416]
- (h) regarding an application for a determination of damages pursuant to Rule 136;[1417]
- (i) preliminary references to the CJEU;[1418]
- (j) in case of death or demise of a party or insolvency of a party.[1419]
- (k) in case of a party objecting to a judge taking part in the proceedings in application of Article 7 Statute;[1420]
- (l) to give effect to Union law,[1421] in particular the provisions of Regulation (EU) No. 1215/2012 (recast Brussels I) and the Lugano Convention; or

---

1414. Rule 37.
1415. Rules 75 and 76.
1416. Rule 118.
1417. Rule 136.
1418. Rule 266.
1419. Rules 310 and 311.
1420. Rule 346.
1421. Adding the general wording *"Union law"* compared with earlier versions of the drafts seems to imply that the application of Union law is general and not limited to the Union

(m) in any other case where the proper administration of justice requires so. This last catch-all provision empowers the Court to stay the proceedings for any reason it holds appropriate.[1422]

2. Duration and effects of a stay of proceedings (Rule 296)

The stay of proceedings shall take effect on the date indicated in the order to stay or, in the absence of such an indication, on the date of that order. The Court should stipulate what effect the stay has on any existing orders.[1423] Where the order to stay does not fix the length of the stay, it ends on the date indicated in the order to resume proceedings or, in the absence of such indication, on the date of the order to resume.[1424] While proceedings are stayed, time shall cease to run for the purposes of procedural periods. Time begins to run afresh for the purposes of procedural periods from the date on which the stay of proceedings comes to an end.[1425]

3. Resumption of proceedings (Rule 297)

An order to resume[1426] (before the end of the stay) will be rendered by the Judge-Rapporteur after hearing the parties. The Judge-Rapporteur may refer the matter to the panel.

4. Accelerated proceedings before the EPO (Rule 298)

The Court may of its own motion or at the request of a party request that opposition proceedings or limitation proceedings (including any subsequent appeal proceedings) before the EPO be accelerated in accordance with the proceedings of the EPO. The Court may stay its proceedings[1427] pending the outcome of such request and any subsequent accelerated proceedings.

E. (CHAPTER 5) TIME PERIODS (RULES 300-301)

1. Calculation of periods (Rule 300)

Any period of time prescribed by the UPCA, the Statute or the Rules for the taking of any procedural step is laid down in terms of full days, weeks, months or years and is calculated taking the following in consideration:

---

law as mentioned in the Rules.
1422. E.g. If a request would be made for an order for a security for costs (R. 158-159) the Court could decide to stay the proceedings during the given time frame to allow the party to comply with the order.
1423. Rule 296.1.
1424. Rule 296.2.
1425. Rule 296.3.
1426. Cf. Rule 296.2.
1427. In accordance with Rule 295.

(a) computation shall start on the day following the day on which the relevant event occurred; in the case of service of a document, the relevant event shall be the receipt of that document in accordance with Part 5, Chapter 2;
(b) when a period is expressed as one year or a certain number of years, it shall expire in the relevant subsequent year in the month having the same name and on the day having the same number as the month and the day on which the said event occurred. If the relevant subsequent month has no day with the same number, the period shall expire on the last day of that month;
(c) when a period is expressed as one month or a certain number of months, it shall expire in the relevant subsequent month on the day which has the same number as the day on which the said event occurred. If the relevant subsequent month has no day with the same number, the period shall expire on the last day of that month;
(d) when a period is expressed as one week or a certain number of weeks, it shall expire in the relevant subsequent week on the day having the same name as the day on which the said event occurred;
(e) day shall mean a calendar day unless expressed as a working day;
(f) calendar days shall include official holidays of the Contracting Member State in which the division or the seat of the central division or its section concerned or the Court of Appeal is located, as well as Saturdays and Sundays;
(g) working days shall not include official holidays of the Contracting Member State in which the division or the seat of the central division or its section concerned or the Court of Appeal is located, Saturdays and Sundays;
(h) periods shall not be suspended during the judicial vacations.

2. Automatic extension of periods (Rule 301)

If a period expires on a Saturday, Sunday or official holiday of the Contracting Member State in which the division or section of the central division concerned or the Court of Appeal is located, this period shall be extended until the end of the first following working day.[1428] This Rule also applies if documents filed in electronic form cannot be received by the Court.[1429]

F. (CHAPTER 6) PARTIES TO PROCEEDINGS (RULES 302–320)

1. Plurality of parties (Rules 302–303)

a. *Plurality of claimants or patents (Rule 302)*

The Court is empowered to order that proceedings initiated by a plurality of claimants or in respect of a plurality of patents be heard in separate proceedings.[1430]

1428. Rule 301.1.
1429. Rule 301.2.
1430. Rule 302.1.

Should separate proceedings be ordered, the Court decides on the payment of a new fee (or fees).[1431]

Where it is in the interests of justice, the Court may order that parallel infringement or revocation proceedings relating to the same patent (or patents) and before the same local or regional division or the central division or the Court of Appeal, are heard together.[1432] Hearing the cases together does not seem to imply that they are joined. Joining of more than one action concerning the same patent is regulated by Rule 340.

Cases (more than one action concerning the same patent) pending before different panels in the Court of First Instance can be joined if the conditions of Rule 340 are met (i.e. interests of the proper administration of justice and of avoiding inconsistent decisions). In such case the panels may order by agreement at any time and after hearing the parties that two or more actions shall be heard together. Rule 340 provides that when applying this rule it is of no importance whether or not the cases are pending between the same parties.

A difference between Rule 302 and Rule 340 seems to be that under Rule 302 (hearing together of the cases) the Court[1433] *orders*, while under Rule 340 the decision to join is reserved for a mutual *panel decision*.[1434] A further important difference is that under Rule 302 the Court seems to be empowered by its own motion to hear the cases together, while the actual joining of the cases (under Rule 340) should be requested by the parties.

b. *Plurality of defendants (Rule 303)*

Proceedings may be initiated against a plurality of defendants[1435] in the event the Court has competence in respect of all of the defendants.

The Court may separate the proceedings into two or more separate proceedings against different defendants.[1436] If separate proceedings are ordered and the Court does not decide otherwise, the claimants in the new proceedings should pay a new Court fee,[1437] unless the Court would decide otherwise. The Rules remain silent as to when no new Court fees should be paid.

1431. Rule 302.2 *juncto* Part 6.
1432. Rule 302.3.
1433. Reference can be made to Rule 1.2 stating that if the Rules provide the Court to perform an act, that act may be performed by the mentioned single judge.
1434. Rule 340.1.
1435. Rule 303.1.
1436. Rule 303.2.
1437. Rule 302.3 *juncto* Part 6.

Chapter VIII – (Part 5) General Provisions

2. Change in Parties (Rules 305–306)

a. *Change in parties (Rule 305)*

On application by a party and upon hearing the parties, the Court may order a person to be added as, or to cease to be, or to be substituted for a party.[1438] When ordering a person to become a party or to cease to be a party, the Court may make appropriate orders as to payment of Court fees and costs as regards such party.[1439]

b. *Consequences for the proceedings (Rule 306)*

Should a party be added, removed or substituted, the Court shall give directions to regulate the consequences as to case management[1440] and determine the extent to which a new party is bound by the proceedings as then constituted.[1441]

3. Death, Demise or Insolvency of a Party (Rules 310–311)

a. *Death or demise of a party (Rule 310)*

In principle, proceedings are stayed until a party who has died or ceased to exist, is replaced by his successor.[1442] The Court may specify a period in this respect. If there are more than two parties to the proceedings, the Court may decide that proceedings between the remaining parties are continued separately and that the stay only concerns the proceedings regarding the party who no longer exists.[1443]

If the successor to the party who died or ceased to exist does not continue the proceedings of his own motion, within a period specified by the Court, any other party may apply to have the successor added to or substituted for a party.[1444]

Rule 310 refers to Rule 305 (Change in parties) to decide who shall be added or substituted as a party and provides that Rule 306 (Consequences for the proceedings) shall apply *mutatis mutandis*.[1445]

b. *Insolvency of a party (Rule 311)*

If a party is declared insolvent under the national law of his residence or principal place of business or (in the absence of residence or principal place of business) place of business proceedings, the Court may stay the proceedings for up to three months. Proceedings may be stayed until the competent national authority or person

---

1438. Rule 305.1 and 2
1439. Rule 305.3.
1440. Rule 306.1.
1441. Rule 306.2.
1442. Rule 310.1.
1443. Rule 310.2.
1444. Rule 310.3.
1445. Rule 310.4.

dealing with the insolvency has decided whether to continue the proceedings or not. The Rules remain silent as to whether the three months are a maximum term independent of the decision of the competent national authority or person dealing with the insolvency or whether after the term of three months the proceedings could be further stayed (for an additional period of three months) awaiting the decision of said authority or person.

Where said competent national authority or person decides not to continue the proceedings, the Court may decide, upon a reasoned request by the other party, that the proceedings should be continued in accordance with the applicable national insolvency law.[1446]

Proceedings may also be stayed at the request of a temporary administrator who has been appointed before a party is declared insolvent.[1447]

The claimant may withdraw the action against an insolvent defendant. Such withdrawal will not prejudice the action against other parties.[1448]

If the proceedings are continued, the effect of a decision of the Court as regards the insolvent party in the action is determined by the national law applicable to the insolvency proceedings.[1449]

4. Transfer of patent (Rule 312)

If a patent or patent application is transferred for one or more Contracting Member States, after proceedings have been initiated before the Court, the Court may authorise the new proprietor to be added as a party or substituted for a party pursuant Rule 305 (Change in parties) to the extent that the patent and the claims in the proceedings have been transferred to him.[1450] As is already the case today, this Rule again shows that when transferring a patent (or other intellectual property right) it is very important to include in the transfer agreement the right to take action against past infringements. If the new proprietor takes over the proceedings, no new Court fee needs to be paid, even if the new proprietor is represented by a new representative.[1451]

Should the new proprietor not wish to take over the proceedings, any decision in proceedings that has been recorded in the Register is binding upon him.[1452]

5. Intervention (Rules 313–317)

An Application to intervene may be lodged at any stage of the Proceedings before the Court of First Instance or the Court of Appeal by any person establishing a legal interest in the result of an action submitted to the Court (hereinafter the "*intervener*").[1453] However, the Application to intervene is only admissible if made

---

1446. Rule 311.1.
1447. Rule 311.2.
1448. Rule 311.3.
1449. Rule 311.4.
1450. Rule 312.1.
1451. Rule 312.2.
1452. Rule 312.3.
1453. Rule 313.1.

Chapter VIII – (Part 5) General Provisions

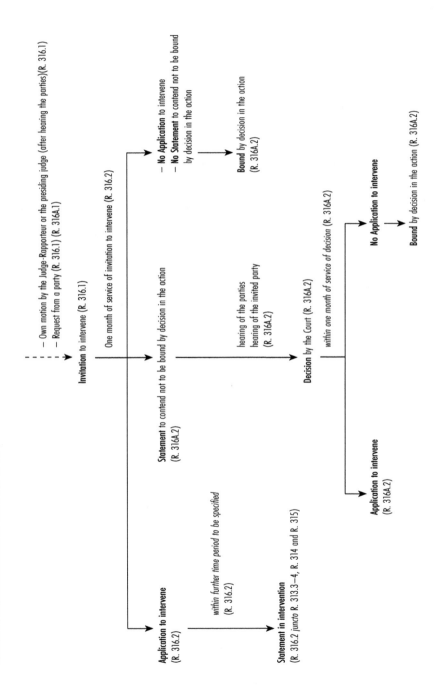

Flowchart: Invitation to intervene (R. 316 – R. 316A)

Part Three – The Rules of Procedure of the Unified Patent Court

Flowchart: Intervention overview (R. 313 – R. 317)

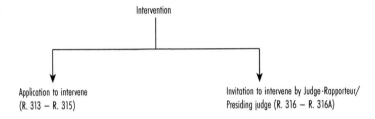

Flowchart: Application to intervene (R. 313 – R. 315)

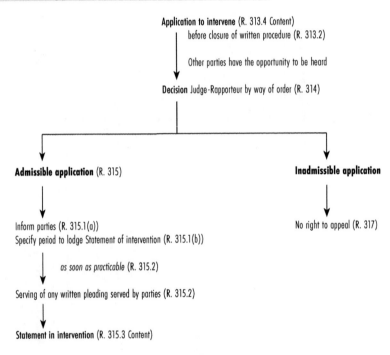

in support, in whole or in part, of a claim, order or remedy sought by one of the parties and is made before the closure of the written procedure (unless the Court of First Instance or the Court of Appeal should order otherwise).[1454]

A limited number of members of the patent community proposed to add a Rule on *amicus briefs*.[1455] The Rule stated that in cases involving legal questions of general importance the Court of First Instance or the Court of Appeal could invite

---

1454. Rule 313.2.
1455. Old Rule 318.

any person or legal entity concerned by that legal question to a file a brief as *amicus curiae*. After discussions between the experts (inviting US judges to explain the advantages and disadvantages of the briefs) the drafting committee deleted Rule 318. The reason for deleting this Rule was that this would unnecessarily complicate proceedings. The Drafting Committee found that if a person has a legal interest in the result of an action submitted to the Court, he can make use of the mentioned Application to intervene.

6. Re-establishment of Rights (Rules 320)

Flowchart: Application for re-establishment of rights (R. 320)

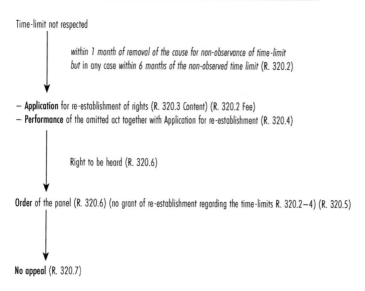

In the event a time limit for an appeal was not observed by a party or by the Court for a cause which was outside his control and the non-observance of this time limit has had the direct consequence of causing the party to lose a right or means of redress, the relevant panel of the Court can, upon the request of that party, re-establish the right or means of redress.

G. (CHAPTER 7) MISCELLANEOUS PROVISIONS ON LANGUAGES (RULES 321–324)

1. Change of language in general

Change of language of proceedings (at first instance and appeal level) seems only possible into the language in which the patent was granted.

Part Three – The Rules of Procedure of the Unified Patent Court

Flowchart: Change of language of the proceedings (R. 321 – R. 324)

1. Court of First Instance (Rule 14)

Language of proceedings
- Central Division: Language in which the patent was granted
- Local and Regional Division: Designated language by Contracting Member State

Change possible (R. 321 – R. 324) (see also flowchart hereunder)
- Central Division: no change possible
- Local and Regional Division: change of language of proceedings to the language in which the patent was granted

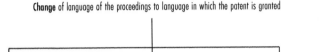

Application by both parties (R. 321)   **Proposal by Judge-Rapporteur** (R. 322)   **Application by one party** (R. 323)

2. Court of Appeal (R. 227)

Language of proceedings
- Language of the proceedings before the Court of First Instance (R. 227.1)
- Note: Bifurcated Case: language of the proceedings of the main action (infringement) (mentioned on the UPC website (FAQ) but not in the Rules) or language of the proceedings of the first decision appealed)

Change possible (R. 227) (see also flowchart hereunder)
- Into language in which the patent was granted by agreement of the parties (R. 227.1(b) *juncto* Art. 55(2) UPCA)
- Into any language of a Contracting Member State subject to agreement by the parties (R. 227.1(a) *juncto* Art. 55(3) UPCA)

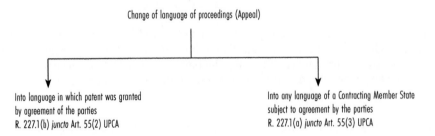

The UPCA states only one possibility where a language can be changed to another official language of a Contracting Member State. It is the Court of Appeal who can make use of this possibility but only subject to agreement by the parties[1456]

1456. Rule 227.1(a) *juncto* Article 50(3) UPCA.

Chapter VIII – (Part 5) General Provisions

and this even in the event a bifurcated case (making use of two different languages of proceedings) has been brought before the appellate court.

The next flowchart provides an overview of the general language regime.

2. **Application by both parties to use the language in which the patent was granted as language of the proceedings (Rule 321)**

Flowchart: Application by both parties to use of the language in which the patent was granted as language of the proceedings (R. 321)

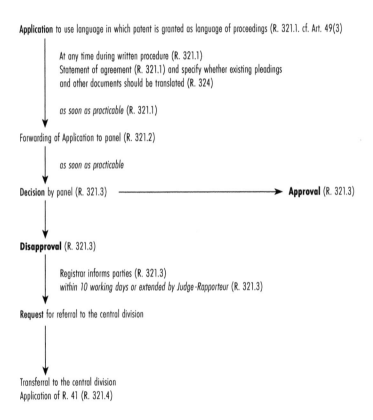

3. **Proposal from the Judge-Rapporteur to use of the language in which the patent was granted as language of the proceedings (Rule 322)**

At any time during the written and interim procedure, the Judge-Rapporteur may, of his own motion or on a request by a party after consulting the panel, propose to the parties to change the language of the proceedings (Rule 14.2) to the language in which the patent was granted (in accordance with Article 49(4)). Upon agreement of the parties and panel, the language of the proceedings will be changed.

4. Application by one party to use the language in which the patent was granted as language of the proceedings (Rule 323)

Flowchart: Application by one party to use the language in which the patent was granted as language of the proceedings (R. 323)

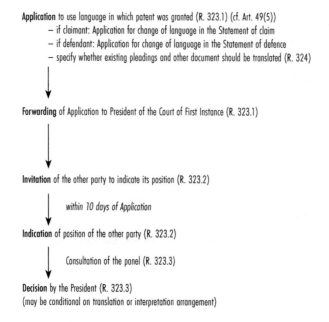

5. Consequences where the language of the proceedings is changed in the course of the proceedings (Rule 324)

An Application under Rule 321.1 or Rule 323.1 should specify whether existing pleadings and other documents should be translated and at whose cost. If the parties cannot agree the Judge-Rapporteur or the President of the Court of First Instance, as the case may be, shall decide in accordance with Rule 323.3.

H. (CHAPTER 8) CASE MANAGEMENT (RULES 331–340)

1. Responsibility for case management (Rule 331)

During the written and the interim procedure the Judge-Rapporteur is responsible for the case management.[1457] He may refer a proposed order to the panel.[1458] After the

---

1457. Rule 331.1.
1458. Rule 331.2.

Chapter VIII - (Part 5) General Provisions

closure of the interim conference, case management is transferred to the presiding judge in consultation with the Judge-Rapporteur.[1459]

The Registry needs to serve any case management orders on the parties *as soon as practicable* upon the decision of the Judge-Rapporteur, presiding judge or panel.[1460]

2. General principles of case management (Rule 332)

Active case management consists of:

(a) encouraging the parties to co-operate with each other during the proceedings;
(b) identifying the issues at an early stage;
(c) deciding promptly which issues need full investigation and disposing summarily of other issues;
(d) deciding the order in which issues are to be resolved;
(e) encouraging the parties to make use of the Patent Mediation and Arbitration Centre and facilitating the use of the Centre;
(f) helping the parties to settle the whole or part of the action;
(g) fixing timetables or otherwise controlling the progress of the action;
(h) considering whether the likely benefits of taking a particular step justify the cost of taking it;
(i) dealing with as many aspects of the action as the Court can on the same occasion;
(j) dealing with the action without the parties needing to attend in person;
(k) making use of available technical means; and
(l) giving directions to ensure that the hearing of the action proceeds quickly and efficiently.

3. Review of case management orders (Rule 333)

Flowchart: Review of case management orders (R. 333)

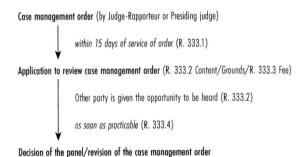

Case management order (by Judge-Rapporteur or Presiding judge)

within 15 days of service of order (R. 333.1)

Application to review case management order (R. 333.2 Content/Grounds/R. 333.3 Fee)

Other party is given the opportunity to be heard (R. 333.2)

as soon as practicable (R. 333.4)

Decision of the panel/revision of the case management order
(R. 333.5 *juncto* R. 220.2 – procedural decision open for appeal)

1459. Rule 331.3.
1460. Rule 331.4.

4. Case management powers (Rule 334)

In order to perform these actions the case manager (be it the Judge-Rapporteur, the presiding judge or the panel) and except where the UPCA, the Statute, or the Rules provide otherwise, may:[1461]

- (a) extend or shorten the period for compliance with any rule, practice, direction or order;
- (b) adjourn or bring forward the interim conference or the oral hearing;
- (c) communicate with the parties to instruct them about wishes or requirements of the Court;
- (d) direct a separate hearing of any issue;
- (e) decide the order in which issues are to be decided;
- (f) exclude an issue from consideration;
- (g) dismiss or decide on a claim after a decision on a preliminary issue makes a decision on further issues irrelevant to the outcome of the action;
- (h) dismiss a pleading summarily if it has no prospect of succeeding;
- (i) consolidate any matter or issue or order them to be heard together;
- (j) make any order pursuant to Rules 103 to 109.

5. Varying or revoking orders (Rule 335)

A power of the Court to make a case management order includes a power to vary or revoke such order.

6. Exercise of managing powers (Rule 336)

The Court may exercise its case management powers on the application by a party or of its own motion, unless otherwise provided.

7. Orders of the Court's own motion (Rule 337)

Where the Court proposes to make an order of its own motion, it may do so but only after hearing the parties.

8. Connection – Joinder (Rule 340)

In the interests of the proper administration of justice and of avoiding inconsistent decisions, where more than one action concerning the same patent (whether or not between the same parties) is pending before different panels (either in the Court of First Instance or in the Court of Appeal) the panels may by agreement, at any time, after hearing the parties, order that two or more actions shall, on account of the

---

1461. Rule 334.

connection between them, be heard together.¹⁴⁶² When joining the cases Article 33 should be respected.

Joined cases should have the same patent in common. The proceedings mentioned in Rule 340 do not apply if the action concerns different patents.¹⁴⁶³

The cases may subsequently be disjoined.¹⁴⁶⁴

I. (CHAPTER 9) RULES RELATING TO THE ORGANISATION OF THE COURT (RULES 341-346)

1. Precedence (Rule 341)

With the exception of the President of the Court of Appeal and the President of the Court of First Instance, the judges rank in precedence according to their seniority in office.¹⁴⁶⁵ Where there is an equal seniority in office, precedence shall be determined by age.¹⁴⁶⁶ Retiring judges who are reappointed shall retain their former precedence.¹⁴⁶⁷

The Presidium may determine the presiding judge of a panel. In the absence of such a determination by the Presidium and unless otherwise agreed by the panel, the most senior judge will act as presiding judge.¹⁴⁶⁸ The Rule entails that the Court focuses on the experience of the presiding judges and not necessarily on a judge's seniority.

2. Dates, times and place of the sittings of the Court (Rule 342)

Judicial vacations shall be fixed by the President of the Court of Appeal, on a proposal from the Presidium. The dates and times of the sittings (the date of the hearings) of the Court shall be decided by the presiding judge on the panel in question.¹⁴⁶⁹

The Court may choose to hold one or more particular sittings (hearings) in a place other than that in which it has its seat. Subject to any rules agreed by the relevant Contracting Member State¹⁴⁷⁰ where an action is pending before a regional division, the Judge-Rapporteur or the presiding judge shall designate the place within the region for each hearing. In taking such decision the Judge-Rapporteur or the presiding judge will take into regard: the residence or place of business of the defendant(s) and all other relevant circumstances such as the facilities available, the financial means of the parties and the place of actual or threatened infringement.¹⁴⁷¹

1462. Rule 340.1.
1463. Rule 340.1.
1464. Rule 340.2.
1465. Rule 341.1.
1466. Rule 341.2.
1467. Rule 341.3.
1468. Rule 341.4.
1469. Rule 342.1.
1470. Pursuant to Article 7(5) UPCA.
1471. Rule 342.2.

3. Order in which actions are to be dealt with (Rule 343)

Actions are dealt with in the order they become ready for hearing.[1472] The presiding judge on a panel[1473] may after hearing the parties:[1474]

(a) direct that a particular action be given priority and that time limits provided for in these Rules be shortened; or
(b) defer an action to be dealt with later.[1475]

4. Deliberations (Rule 344)

Deliberations, presided over by the presiding judge, are held in closed sessions between the judges that were present at the oral hearing and this as soon as possible after the closure of the oral hearing.

5. Composition of panels and assignment of actions[1476] (Rule 345)

The President of the Court of First Instance or a judge to whom he has delegated this task in a division, the seat of the central division or one of its sections shall allocate the judges to the panels of the local and regional divisions, the seat of the central division and its sections.[1477] The allocation of the legally qualified judges shall be in conformity with Article 8 UPCA.[1478]

Pending actions in the division, the seat of the central division or one of its sections shall be assigned to the panels by the Registrar following an action-distribution scheme established by the presiding judge of each local or regional division, the seat of the central division and its sections (being the judge appointed by the Presidium as the presiding judge) for the duration of one calendar year, preferably distributing the actions according to the date of receipt of the actions at the division or section.[1479]

Each panel may delegate to one or more judges on the panel:[1480]

(a) the function of acting as a single judge; or
(b) the function of acting for the panel in the procedures of Part 1 Chapter 4 (Procedure for the Determination of Damages and Compensation, including the procedure for the laying open of books) and Chapter 5 (Procedure for

---

1472. Rule 343.1.
1473. By giving this power to the presiding judge on the panel, interference by the presiding judge of the division or section is limited. This Rule evidences the independence of the judges on the panel. The same principle can be found in Rule 342.1 where it is up to the presiding judge on the panel to set the dates and times of the sittings of his panel.
1474. Reference is made is to Rule 264.
1475. Rule 343.2 with reference to facilitating an amicable settlement of the dispute.
1476. The rules mentioned hereunder under Rule 345.1 through 6 apply also for the Court of Appeal (Rule 345.8). President of the Court of First Instance should be read as President of the Court of Appeal.
1477. Rule 345.1 and 2 states that the allocation should be in conformity with Article 8.
1478. Rule 345.2.
1479. Rule 345.3.
1480. Rule 345.4.

Cost Orders). These functions may be delegated to the Judge-Rapporteur who has prepared the action for the oral hearing.

The President of the Court of First Instance or a judge to whom he has delegated this task in a division, the seat of the central division or one of its sections shall designate the judges assigned to each division as a standing judge for urgent actions. The assignment may be limited to certain periods of time.[1481]

If all parties agree to having the action heard by a single judge, the presiding judge on the panel to which the action is allocated shall assign the action to a legally qualified judge on the panel.[1482]

The President of the Court of First Instance may of his own motion review all decisions described in this Rule 345 made by the presiding judge of the seat of the central division or one of its sections.[1483]

Rule 345.1 through 346.6. apply *mutatis mutandis* to the Court of Appeal. The President of the Court of Appeal will exercise the respective functions.[1484]

6. Application of Article 7 Statute[1485][1486] (Rule 346)

Article 7 of the Statute deals with the principle of impartiality and the procedure to be followed when a party or a judge considers that he cannot take part in the judgment or examination.

A judge who considers that he should not take part in the judgment or examination of a particular case, shall inform his President (either the President of the

---

1481. Rule 345.5.
1482. Rule 345.6.
1483. Rule 345.7.
1484. Rule 345.8.
1485. Article 7 Statute: Impartiality (only articles referred to are cited hereunder):
    (1) Immediately after taking their oath, judges shall sign a declaration by which they solemnly undertake that, both during and after their term of office, they shall respect the obligations arising there from, in particular the duty to behave with integrity and discretion as regards the acceptance, after they have ceased to hold office, of certain appointments or benefits.
    (2) Judges may not take part in the proceedings of a case in which they:
    (a) have taken part as adviser;
    (b) have been a party or have acted for one of the parties;
    (c) have been called upon to pronounce as a member of a court, tribunal, board of appeal, arbitration or mediation panel, a commission of inquiry or in any other capacity;
    (d) have a personal or financial interest in the case or in relation to one of the parties; or
    (e) are related to one of the parties or the representatives of the parties by family ties.
    (3) ...
    (4) Any party to an action may object to a judge taking part in the proceedings on any of the grounds listed in paragraph 2 or where the judge is suspected, with good reason, of partiality.
    (5) ...
1486. Rule 346.1 and 2 apply to a judge of the Court of Appeal. The President of the Court of Appeal performs the functions attributed in the Rules to the President of the Court of First Instance (Rule 346.3).

Part Three – The Rules of Procedure of the Unified Patent Court

Flowchart: Application of Art. 7 Statute (R. 346)

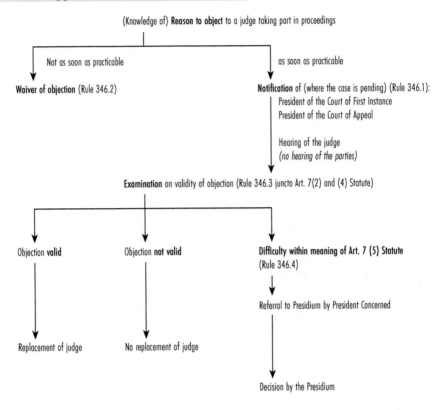

Flowchart: Application of Art. 7.3. and 7.5. Statute ('Own motion by judge')

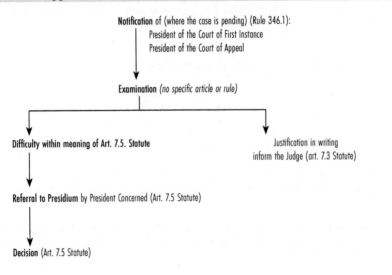

Court of Appeal either the President of the Court of First Instance) thereof.[1487] If the President considers that the judge should not sit or make submissions in a particular case, he shall justify this in writing and notify the judge concerned accordingly. As the President should justify his decision in writing, this means that the judge should inform his President of the particulars of the issue of impartiality.[1488]

A party may object to a judge taking part in proceedings pursuant to Article 7(4) of the Statute. This procedure has been subject to a major amendment as adopted by the Administrative Committee on 8 July 2022 (Amendment 31 (to Rule 346)) and this to avoid objections on tactical grounds. The accompanying flowchart graphically clarifies the procedure.

It is important to note that Rule 346.6 states that, in order to provide flexibility,[1489] the panel assigned to the proceedings may decide to continue with the proceedings or to stay the proceedings pending the final decision of the President concerned or the Presidium (see flowchart). Furthermore, this rule provides that the President concerned or the Presidium may give instructions in the final decision as to the future conduct of the proceedings.

J. (CHAPTER 10) DECISIONS AND ORDERS (RULES 350–354)

1. Decisions (Rule 350)

Any decision should contain:[1490]

(a) the statement that it is a decision of the Court;
(b) the date of its delivery;
(c) the names of the presiding judge, the Judge-Rapporteur and other judges taking part in it;
(d) the names of the parties and of the parties' representatives;
(e) an indication of the claim, order or remedy sought by the parties;
(f) a summary of the facts; and
(g) the grounds for the decision.

An order of the Court consequential upon the decision (other than costs) including any order giving immediate effect to an injunction, needs to be appended to the decision.[1491]

The possibility of dissenting opinions is foreseen in the Rules. Such dissenting opinions should be part of the Court's decision.[1492]

1487. Article 7(3) Statute.
1488. The principle applied in some countries where it is acceptable that a judge can withdraw from the case on his own motion without stating the reasons, seems not to apply.
1489. As clarified in the explanatory notes to Amendment 31 (to Rule 346) as adopted by the Administrative Committee on 8 July 2022.
1490. Rule 350.1.
1491. Rule 350.2.
1492. Rule 350.3.

The decision of the Court of First Instance needs to contain a summary of the requests and facts submitted by the parties and a statement of the facts and arguments on which the Court bases its decision.[1493] The decisions are recorded in the Register.[1494]

2. Orders (Rule 351)

Every order should contain:[1495]

(a) the statement that it is an order of the Judge-Rapporteur, of the presiding judge, of a President of the Court or of the Court;
(b) the date of its adoption;
(c) the names of any judge taking part in its adoption;
(d) the names of the parties and of the parties' representatives; and
(e) the operative part of the order.

Where the Court grants leave to appeal, the order should additionally contain:[1496]

(a) a statement of the forms of order sought by the parties;
(b) a summary of the facts; and
(c) the grounds for the order.

All orders shall be recorded in Register.[1497]

3. Binding effect of decisions or orders subject to security (Rule 352)

Decisions and orders may be subject to rendering of a security by a party (by deposit or bank guarantee or otherwise) to the other party for legal costs and other expenses and compensation for any damage incurred or likely to be incurred by the other party (or parties) if the decisions and orders are subsequently revoked.[1498] The security may, upon the application of a party, be released by the Court by means of an order.[1499]

4. Rectification of decisions and orders (Rule 353)

Clerical mistakes, errors in calculation and obvious slips in the decision or order may be rectified by way of order by the Court, of its own motion or on application by a party made within one month of service of the decision or order to be rectified.[1500]

1493. Rule 350.4.
1494. Rule 350.5.
1495. Rule 351.1.
1496. Rule 351.2.
1497. Rule 351.3.
1498. Such security may be rendered by deposit or bank guarantee or otherwise. The Rules remain silent as to what is meant by *"otherwise"* and whether it is the Court that may decide in which form the security is rendered.
1499. Rule 352.2.
1500. Rule 353.

5. Enforcement (Rule 354)

Decisions and orders of the Court are *directly* enforceable from their date of service in each Contracting Member State. Enforcement shall take place in accordance with the enforcement procedures and conditions governed by the law of the particular Contracting Member State where enforcement takes place.[1501]

Regarding the enforceability, Rule 118.8 is of importance. This Rule provides that orders are only enforceable on the defendant after:[1502]

(i) the claimant has notified the Court which part of the order he intends to enforce;
(ii) a certified translation of the orders in accordance with Rule 7.2, where applicable in the official language of the Contracting Member State in which the enforcement shall take place, has been provided by the claimant; and
(iii) where applicable, a certified translation has been served on the defendant by the Registry.[1503]

Further, the enforceability may be subject to the rendering of a security.

Where during an action an enforceable decision or order of the Court is subsequently varied or revoked, the Court may order the party which has enforced such decision or order, upon the request of the party against whom the decision or order has been enforced, to provide appropriate compensation for any injury caused by the enforcement.[1504] Rule 125 shall apply *mutatis mutandis*. Where an enforceable decision or order has been made pursuant to a finding of infringement of a patent and (following the conclusion of the action) the patent is amended or revoked, the Court may order (upon the request of the party against whom the decision or order would be enforceable) that the decision or order ceases to be enforceable.

Decisions and orders may provide for periodic penalty payments payable to the Court in the event that a party fails to comply with the terms of the order or an earlier order. It would be opportune for the Court when ordering such periodic payments to set a maximum. The value of such payments shall be set by the Court having regard to the importance of the order in question.[1505]

If it is alleged that a party has failed to comply with the terms of the order of the Court, the first instance panel of the division in question may decide on penalty payments provided for in the order upon the request of the other party or of its own motion after having heard both parties.[1506] The issued order under this rule may be subject to an appeal.[1507]

1501. Rule 354.1.
1502. Rule 352.
1503. For an exception to this Rule see Rule 196.3 where the drafters used the word "*immediately*".
1504. Rule 354.2.
1505. Rule 354.3.
1506. Reference is made to Rule 264 (An opportunity to be heard).
1507. Pursuant to Rule 220.2.

The payment to the Court differs from the system in most Contracting Member States where the periodic penalty payment should be paid to the party requesting the enforcement.

K. (CHAPTER 11) DECISION BY DEFAULT (RULES 355–357)

1. Court of First Instance (Rules 355–356)

Upon request, a decision of default may be given against a party where:[1508]

- the Rules[1509] so provide if a party fails to take a step within the time limit foreseen in the Rules or set by the Court;
- a party (duly summoned) fails to appear at an oral hearing (without prejudice to Rules 116-117).

A decision by default against the defendant of the claim or counterclaim may only be given where the facts put forward by the claimant justify the remedy sought and the procedural conduct of the defendant does not preclude to give such decision,[1510] and where the time limits for the defence to the claim or counterclaim have expired (and it is established that the service of the claim or counterclaim was effected in sufficient time to enable the defendant to enter a defence).[1511]

Although a decision by default is enforceable, the Court may grant a stay of enforcement until it has given its decision regarding an Application to set aside the decision by default or grant a stay of enforcement subject to the provision of security.[1512] In the latter case the security will be released if no Application to set aside the decision by default is made or such Application would fail.

The Application to set aside a decision by default should be lodged within one month of the service of the decision.[1513] In its Application to set aside the decision by default the party should put forward an explanation for the default and pay the fee.[1514] If the decision by default is because of the failure to take a step, the Application to set aside the decision by default should be accompanied by this step.[1515]

If the provisions of Rule 356.2 are met, the Application to set aside a decision by default shall be allowed unless a party has been put on notice in an earlier decision that a further decision by default shall be final.[1516] The notice in an earlier decision that a further decision may be final, is included to prevent abuse of the

---

1508. Rule 355.1.
1509. See Rules 16.4 and 16.5, 27.3 and 27.4, 89.3 and 89.4, 103.1, 158.4 and 158.5, 229.3 and 229.4, 232.1 and 232.2.
1510. Rule 355.2 as amended by the Administrative Committee on 8 July 2022 (Amendment 31a (to Rule 355)).
1511. Rule 355.3 as amended by the Administrative Committee on 8 July 2022 (Amendment 31a (to Rule 355)).
1512. Rule 355.4.
1513. Rule 356.1.
1514. Rule 356.2.
1515. Rule 356.2 *juncto* Rule 355.1(a).
1516. Rule 356.3.

Chapter VIII – (Part 5) General Provisions

Flowchart: Decision by default (Court of First Instance) (R. 355)

Request for Decision by default

    if failure to take step within time limit (R. 355.1(a) *juncto* R. 16.5, 27.4, 89.4, 103.2, 229.2 and 232.2)
    if failure to appear at an oral hearing (R. 355.1(b))

Decision by default

    awarded when the facts justify the remedy *and* the procedural conduct of the defendant does not preclude to give such decision (R. 355.2)
    awarded when the time limits of the defence to the claim or counterclaim have been expired and thus, it is established that the service of claim or counterclaim was effected in sufficient time to enable the defendant to enter a defence (R. 355.3)

    Enforceable except if (R. 355.4):
    – Court grants a stay of enforcement until it has given its decision on any Application under R. 356
    – Court makes enforcement subject to the provision of security which is released if no Application is made or if the Application fails

    Within one month of service of the decision (R. 356.1)

Application to set aside a decision (R. 356.1, R. 356.2 Content and Fee)

If the provisions of R. 356.2 are met the Application shall be allowed unless a party has been put on notice in an earlier decision that a further decision by default shall be final. If the Application is allowed, a note of allowance shall be included in any publication of the decision by default.

---

possibility to introduce an Application to set aside a decision by default in order to delay proceedings.

If the Application to set aside a decision by default is allowed, a note of allowance shall be included in any publication of the decision by default.[1517]

The following example provides an overview of the means to correct possible deficiencies and/or pay the requested fee[1518] to avoid a decision by default in application of Rule 355 *juncto* Rule 16.4 and 16.5:

- the claimant who has been unable to lodge a proper Statement of claim and pay the fee will first get an opportunity to correct deficiencies (Rule 16.3), together with a warning that a decision by default may be given (Rule 16.4);
- if the deficiencies are not corrected, the judge of the division shall be informed and may reject the action as inadmissible by a decision by default (Rule 16.5). The judge may give the claimant an opportunity to be heard;
- if the claimant cannot agree with a decision by default, he may introduce an Application to set aside the decision by default (Rule 356.1);
- if the claimant is able to set out *"explanations for the default"* (Rule 356.2) and pay a fee and correct the deficiency in the Statement of claim, his Application will be allowed (Rule 356.3);

1517. Rule 356.3.
1518. During the drafting process questions were raised as to whether such a system is in line with Article 37 UPCA.

- in the event the Application to set aside the decision by default is rejected, the claimant may lodge an appeal against this rejection.

2. Court of Appeal (Rule 357)

The above Rules also apply where a respondent on whom a Statement of appeal and a Statement of the grounds of appeal have been duly served, fails to lodge a Statement of response or where a party fails to file a Reply to a statement of cross-appeal or translations ordered by the Judge-Rapporteur.[1519] When considering whether to give a decision by default, the Court of Appeal may consider the merits of the appeal.[1520]

L. (CHAPTER 12) ACTIONS BOUND TO FAIL OR MANIFESTLY INADMISSIBLE (RULES 360–363)

1. No need to adjudicate (Rule 360)

If the Court finds that an action has become devoid of purpose and that there is no longer any need to adjudicate on it, it may at any time, of its own motion, after giving the parties an opportunity to be heard, dispose of the action by way of order.

2. Action manifestly bound to fail (Rule 361)

Where it is clear that the Court has no jurisdiction to take knowledge of an action or where the action or defence is, in whole or in part, manifestly inadmissible or manifestly lacking any foundation in law, the Court may, after giving the parties an opportunity to be heard, give a decision by way of order.

3. Absolute bar to proceeding with an action (Rule 362)

The Court may at any time, of its own motion, after giving the parties an opportunity to be heard, decide that there exists an absolute bar to proceed with an action, for example because of the application of the principle of *res judicata*.

4. Orders dismissing manifestly inadmissible claims (Rule 363)

Orders under Rules 360, 361 and 362 need to be taken by the panel upon the recommendation of the Judge-Rapporteur. Where the decision is taken by the Court of First Instance, pursuant to Rules 360, 361 and 362, it is a final decision within the meaning of Rule 220.1(a).

[1519]. Rule 357.1.
[1520]. Rule 357.2.

M. (CHAPTER 13) SETTLEMENT (RULE 365)

If a settlement is reached, the Judge-Rapporteur should be informed. The settlement may, at the request of the parties, be confirmed by decision of the Court.[1521] This decision will be enforceable as a final decision by the Court. At the request of the parties the Court may order that details of the settlement are confidential[1522] and enter the decision in the Register.[1523] The Judge-Rapporteur shall give a decision as to costs either in accordance with the terms of the settlement or, if not agreed upon in the settlement, at his discretion.[1524]

1521. Rule 365.1 *juncto* Rule 11.2.
1522. Rule 365.2.
1523. Rule 365.3.
1524. Rule 365.4.

Chapter IX

(Part 6) Fees and Legal Aid (Rules 370–382)

A. COURT FEES (RULES 370–372)

When the 18th (and final) draft of the Rules of Procedure was published on 19 October 2015, the Preparatory Committee stressed that Rule 370 and all other Rules providing a fixed or variable Court fee were still subject to further negotiations. This had everything to do with the fact that the Preparatory Committee had held a public consultation regarding court fees and recoverable costs. The public consultation was launched on 8 May 2014. The consultation document Rules on Court fees and recoverable costs provided two options for a revised Rule 370, a table of fees, a scale of ceilings for recoverable costs and an explanatory note.[1525]

Eventually, the Preparatory Committee agreed at its 14th meeting of 24/25 February 2016 in Brussels on the Rules on Court fees and recoverable costs for the Unified Patent Court as prepared by the Legal and Finance Working Groups, which were laid down in a separate document, alongside an explanatory note. By decision of 8 July 2022 the Court fees were approved entering into force on 1 September 2022 including some amendments made to the initial draft.

Hereafter, we shall discuss the court fees and the principles for determining the Court fees. At the same time, the Preparatory Committee published Guidelines for the determination of Court fees and the ceiling of recoverable costs of the successful party.[1526]

For the explanation of the recoverable costs, we refer to Part Two, Chapter VII F.13, *supra*.

1. Court fees (Rule 370)

a. *General*

This Rule contains the provisions that shall apply to the levy of the Court fees and the tables with the fees (to be) adopted by the Administrative Committee in accordance with Article 36(3) UPCA. Article 36(3) UPCA provides inter alia that the Court fees shall be fixed by the Administrative Committee, and shall consist of a fixed fee, combined with a value-based fee above a pre-defined ceiling. The level of the

---

1525. The consultation document was published on the Unified Patent Court website (www.unified-patent-court.org).
1526. www.unified-patent-court.org/news/guidelines-determination-court-fees-and-ceiling-recoverable-costs.

Court fees shall be reviewed periodically by the Administrative Committee. Targeted support measures for small and medium-sized enterprises and micro entities may be considered.

b. No opt-out fee

Something which immediately caught every one's attention at the date of publication of the Rules on Court fees and recoverable costs (hereinafter "Rules on Court Fees"), was that there is no fee provided for the Application to opt-out or the Withdrawal of an opt-out. The explanatory note to the Rules on Court Fees explains that one of the few areas of clear consensus in consultation responses was that the opt-out fee should be removed or lowered to reflect the commitment made by the Preparatory Committee that the fees for both the opt-out and its withdrawal are set to reclaim administrative costs only and that the Court would not profit from either of these. The comments during the consultation process were of course understandable. However, we notice that no opt-out fee is a double-edged sword. On the one hand it is certainly defendable not having a fee to opt-out since at the time most patent proprietors acquired their European Patent, they did not and could not know that one day the Court would have jurisdiction over their European Patents. On the other hand, the removal of the opt-out fee could result in an even slower start of the Court than practitioners already expect today. Not having a fee to opt-out shall be an extra incentive for proprietors of a European Patent to opt-out. Therefore, the Court could miss out on its economic purpose, i.e. lowering the costs of a European-wide enforcement of patent rights and providing quality case law with a high degree of predictability. The explanatory note sets out the reasons why the Preparatory Committee finally decided to remove the opt-out fee:

> "We now know much more detail as to how the proposed opt-out process will work and that the administration burden rests almost entirely with the applicant. We also know that any cost to the Court associated with the opt-out is related to processing the fee. There is no additional cost for the Case Management System to process opt-out requests if there is no fee. Requiring people to make payment generates costs for the court which would not be needed if there were no fee. So, removing the fee removes the cost; it also eliminates the problem of how to process payments particularly during provisional application and honours the commitment already made to only reclaim administrative costs for the opt-out."

c. Fixed Fees

The following fixed fees shall be applicable for the following actions at the Court of First Instance (table I):

Procedures/actions	Fixed fee
Infringement action (Rule 15)	EUR 11,000
Counterclaim for infringement (Rule 53)	EUR 11,000
Action for declaration of non-infringement (Rule 68)	EUR 11,000

Chapter IX – (Part 6) Fees and Legal Aid (Rules 370–382)

Procedures/actions	Fixed fee
Action for compensation for license of right (Rule 80.3)	EUR 11,000
Application to determine damages (Rule 132)	EUR 3,000

As can be seen, the Member States did not distinguish between the fixed fees for the different actions. Only the separate procedure to determine the damages has its own (lower) fee. This is logical since a lot of cases are settled after a decision on the infringement/revocation action, so that a determination of damages is no longer necessary.

During the final assessment of the Court fees, the fee for other counterclaims, described in Article 32(1)(a) UPCA as "other defences", has been deleted. The Preparatory Committee explained that during the consultation it was noted that it is unclear as to exactly what the fee related and so when it would be incurred. Therefore it was deleted from the list of fees.

d. Value-based fees

Rule 370.3 provides the value-based fees that shall be due for actions at the Court of First Instance which exceed a value of EUR 500,000. The value-based fees have, on the whole, been slightly increased from the previously proposed levels. Two more values of action, i.e. "up to and including € 50 million" and "more than € 50 million", have been added to the scale.

The value-based fees are the following (table II):

Value of action	Additional value-based fee
Up to and including EUR 500,000	EUR 0
Up to and including EUR 750,000	EUR 2,500
Up to and including EUR 1,000,000	EUR 4,000
Up to and including EUR 1,500,000	EUR 8,000
Up to and including EUR 2,000,000	EUR 13,000
Up to and including EUR 3,000,000	EUR 20,000
Up to and including EUR 4,000,000	EUR 26,000
Up to and including EUR 5,000,000	EUR 32,000
Up to and including EUR 6,000,000	EUR 39,000
Up to and including EUR 7,000,000	EUR 46,000
Up to and including EUR 8,000,000	EUR 52,000
Up to and including EUR 9,000,000	EUR 58,000
Up to and including EUR 10,000,000	EUR 65,000
Up to and including EUR 15,000,000	EUR 75,000
Up to and including EUR 20,000,000	EUR 100,000
Up to and including EUR 25,000,000	EUR 125,000

Value of action	Additional value-based fee
Up to and including EUR 30,000,000	EUR 150,000
Up to and including EUR 50,000,000	EUR 250,000
More than EUR 50,000,000	EUR 325,000

e. **Fixed fees for other actions**

For the following procedures and actions at the Court of First Instance, Rule 370.3 provides the following fixed fees (table III):

Procedures/actions	Fixed Fee
Revocation action (Rule 47)	EUR 20,000
Counterclaim for revocation (Rule 26) same fee as the infringement action subject to a fee limit of	EUR 20,000
Application for provisional measures (Rule 206.5)	EUR 11,000
Action against a decision of the EPO (Rule 88.3 and 97.2)	EUR 1,000
Application to preserve evidence (Rule 192.5)	EUR 350
Application for an order for inspection (Rule 199.2)	EUR 350
Application for an order to freeze assets (Rule 200.2)	EUR 1,000
Filing a Protective letter (Rule 207.3)	EUR 200
Application to prolong the period of a Protective letter kept on the Register for Unitary Patent Protection (Rule 207.8)	EUR 100
Application for re-establishment of rights (Rule 320.2)	EUR 350
Application to review a case management order (Rule 333.3)	EUR 300
Application to set aside decision by default (Rule 356.2)	EUR 1,000

The fixed fee of EUR 20,000 for a revocation action and the fee cap of EUR 20,000 for a counterclaim for revocation seem reasonable. If you defend yourself through a counterclaim it seems reasonable that you do not pay a higher court fee than the fee paid by the initial claimant. The level of the fixed fee for standalone revocation actions shall be *"competitive"* compared to EPO opposition proceedings. Therefore, it could be possible that – combined with the ambition of the Court to provide its decisions within a year – this could incentivise third parties to attack weak European Patents before the Court instead of before the EPO opposition divisions, certainly if the European Patent only designates Unified Patent Court Member States.

The fees for applications to preserve evidence (EUR 350), for applications for an order for inspection (EUR 350) or an application for an order to freeze assets (EUR 1,000) are low. Therefore, the success of the *"saisie-contrefaçon"* shall most likely remain in the Court arena, or may even increase because of the new possibilities of cross-border measures.

Filing Protective letters is very cheap (EUR 200). Given the low cost and the possibly large impact of cross-border orders for inspection or freezing orders, one

Chapter IX – (Part 6) Fees and Legal Aid (Rules 370–382)

can expect there to be a large number of Protective letters on the Register for Unitary Patent Protection.

f. Court of Appeal fees

Rule 370.5 provides the Court fees payable at the Court of Appeal. The Court fees for the appeal proceedings shall to a large extent be the same as those at first instance. Therefore, the previously proposed fixed fee of EUR 16,000 for appeals as to an application for provisional measures was decreased in final text from EUR 16,000 to EUR 11,000, in order to make it equal to the Court fee at first instance.

Appeals / applications	Fee
Appeal pursuant to Rule 220.1(a) and (b) (Rule 228) as to an infringement action (Rule 15)	EUR 11,000 + additional value-based fee according to table II
Appeal pursuant to Rule 220.1(a) and (b) (Rule 228) as to a counterclaim for infringement (Rule 53)	EUR 11,000 + additional value-based fee according to table II
Appeal pursuant to Rule 220.1(a) and (b) (Rule 228) as to a revocation action (Rule 47)	EUR 20,000
Appeal pursuant to Rule 220.1(a) and (b) (Rule 228) as to a counterclaim for revocation (Rule 26)	Fee paid in the first instance
Appeal pursuant to Rule 220.1(a) and (b) (Rule 228) as to an action for declaration of non-infringement (Rule 68)	EUR 11,000 + additional value-based fee according to table II
Appeal pursuant to Rule 220.1(a) and (b) (Rule 228) as to an action for compensation for licence of right (Rule 80.3)	EUR 11,000 + additional value-based fee according to table II
Appeal pursuant to Rule 220.1(a) and (b) (Rule 228) as to an Application to determine damages (Rule 132)	EUR 3,000 + additional value-based fee according to table II
Appeal pursuant to Rule 220.1(c) (Rule 228) as to an application for provisional measures (Art. 62 UPCA, Rule 206.5)	EUR 11,000
Appeal pursuant to Rule 220.1(b) (Rule 228) as to an application for orders referred to in Articles 49(5), 59, 60, 61 or 67 UPCA	EUR 3,000
Application for rehearing (Rule 250)	EUR 2,500
Appeal pursuant to Rule 220.1(a) and (b) (Rule 228) as to an action against a decision of the EPO (Rule 88.3, 97.2)	EUR 1,000

Appeals / applications	Fee
Appeal pursuant to Rule 220.2 (Rule 228) for which leave of appeal has been granted by the Court of First Instance (Rule 220.2) or which has been allowed by the Court of Appeal (Rule 220.4)	EUR 1,500
Request for discretionary review to the Court of Appeal (Rule 220.3). The fee does not arise if the appeal is not allowed.	EUR 350
Appeal against cost decision pursuant to Rule 221.4 (Rule 228)	EUR 3,000
Application for leave to appeal against cost decisions (Rules 221, 228) The fee does not arise if the appeal is not allowed.	EUR 1,500
Application for re-establishment of rights (Rule 320.2)	EUR 350
Application to review a case management order (Rule 333.3)	EUR 300
Application to set aside decision by default (Rule 356.2)	EUR 1,000

g. Guidelines for assessment of the value of the action

Rule 370.6 provides that the assessment of the value of the relevant action – important for determination of the value based fee – shall reflect the *"objective interest pursued by the filing party at the time of filing the action"*. In deciding on the value, the Court may (and shall) in particular take into account the guidelines laid down in the decision of the Administrative Committee for this purpose. The Preparatory Committee agreed in February 2016 on draft Guidelines for Valuation. These Guidelines for Valuation are not only important for the determination of value based Court fees, but also for the ceilings for the recoverable costs for the representatives of the successful party.

The Guidelines for Valuation state that a method of determining a value-based fee should be as simple as practically possible. The most practicable method, in most cases, will be a valuation based on an appropriate licence fee. A valuation based on the claimant's loss of profits or the defendant's profits gained may also be applied, where appropriate, but will normally be too complex to be determined at the beginning of proceedings, resulting in a mini-trial.[1527]

The valuation should relate to the summed values of the main remedies claimed (injunction for the future, damages for the past), not excluding, where appropriate, the value of other remedies claimed.[1528] Where the parties agree on a valuation the Court should in principle base its valuation on their estimate.[1529]

1527. Point I.1 of the Guidelines for Valuation.
1528. Point I.2 of the Guidelines for Valuation.
1529. Point I.3 of the Guidelines for Valuation.

Under Title II of the Guidelines for Valuation, the Preparatory Committee has suggested approaches for the valuation of infringement actions, revocation actions or counterclaims for revocation, declarations of non-infringement and actions for compensation for licence of right.

The Guidelines suggest that the calculation of the value of the injunction claim and the damage claim in infringement actions should be based on a royalty calculation as follows:

(1) The defendant's turnover in the alleged infringing product for the future up to the expiry of the patent (injunction claim) and for the past (damage claim) should be calculated based upon the known existing turnover of the defendant or, if not known or not yet existent, the market share the defendant has taken and/or may reasonably be assumed to take.
(2) A royalty rate should be applied to (1) based upon:
   (i) the existing royalty rate for the same invention charged by the claimant, or
   (ii) the generally accepted industry rate for the type of invention in question, or
   (iii) a royalty rate determined by the Court after hearing the parities.
(3) Where a damage claim:
   (i) is limited to awarding damages in principle, the value of that claim (pursuant to (1)) should be reduced by 50%;
   (ii) specifies the amount of damages, the value should correspond to the amount claimed.
(4) The value of an Application for the determination of damages including any Request to lay open books should correspond to the amount of damages specified in the Application or if no such sum is specified the value as calculated in accordance with (1) and (2).
(5) If the action is based on more than one patent and/or if the action is directed against more than one party the value should be calculated in accordance with (1) and (2) on the basis of a combined licence for all patents and all defendants across all territories covered by the patents.

The same valuation is suggested for declarations of non-infringement and actions for compensation for a licence of right.

h.   *Multiple claimants or defendants*

Rule 370.7 provides that if an action has more than one claimant and/or more than one defendant or if an action concerns a plurality of patents, only one fixed fee and, if applicable, one value based fee shall apply. For this reason, Rule 304 was deleted by the Preparatory Committee after agreeing on the Court fees. Rule 304 provided that multiple parties were only regarded as one party if they were represented by one and the same representative.

Rule 370.7 can be favourable for parties which all have the same interest in revoking a patent. The fixed fee for the revocation action can be shared between the claimants, while the fee for the patent proprietor for its counterclaims for infringement shall be much higher and shall have to borne by the proprietor alone.

i. Small and micro-enterprises

Rule 370.8 further implements Article 36(3) UPCA as this Article provides that the Court fees shall be fixed at such a level as to ensure a right balance between the principle of fair access to justice, in particular for small and medium-sized enterprises, micro-entities, natural persons, non-profit organisations, universities and public research organisations, and an adequate contribution of the parties for the costs incurred by the Court, recognising the economic benefits to the parties involved, and the objective of a self-financing Court with balanced finances.

Rule 370.8 provides that small enterprises and micro-enterprises are entitled to pay only 60% of the regular fees.

In the Statement of claim or counterclaim or in the Application for a procedure or an appeal the applicant shall lodge with the Registry a notification in an electronic form in the language of the proceedings. In this notification the applicant shall provide an affirmation that he fulfils either the criteria of a "small enterprise" or a "micro-enterprise" as defined in Title I of Annex of the Recommendation of the European Commission No. 2003/361 of 6 May 2003. If the requirements referred to above have not been met, Rule 16 regarding the examination as to formal requirements of the Statement of claim applies *mutatis mutandis*.

To counter the criticism that measures for small or micro-enterprises could in reality favour NPEs (patent trolls), Rule 370.8 contains a number of security measures for abuse of the 40% discount. The Court, of its own motion, may order the applicant to supply further documentation including any document linked to its financial resources. The application shall be dealt with by the Court without delay.

The Court may, at any time, of its own motion, and after having heard the applicant, order payment of:

(1) the remainder of the regular fee, in case payment of just 60% of the regular fees is manifestly disproportionate and unreasonable in respect of the financial capacity of the applicant; or
(2) the remainder of the regular fee plus an additional 50%, if the affirmation given by the applicant is found to be wholly or partially incorrect.

An order of an additional fee pursuant to paragraphs (1) and (2) above shall state the reasons on which it is based and may be appealed to the Court of Appeal in accordance with Rule 220.2.

If the additional fee is not paid within the time limit given by the Court, a decision by default against the applicant will be given by the Court pursuant to Rule 355.

j. Reimbursement of Court fees

Rule 370.9 covers the situations in which parties are entitled to a reimbursement of fixed and value-based fees.

If the action is heard by a single judge (Rule 345.6) the party liable for the Court fees will be reimbursed by 25%.[1530]

1530. Rule 370.9(a).

In case of the Withdrawal of an action (Rule 265) the party liable for the Court fees will be reimbursed by:[1531]

- 60% if the action is withdrawn before the conclusion of the written procedure;
- 40% if the action is withdrawn before the conclusion of the interim procedure;
- 20% if the action is withdrawn before the conclusion of the oral procedure.

If the parties have concluded their action by way of settlement the party liable for the Court fees will be reimbursed by:[1532]

- 60% if the action is settled before the conclusion of the written procedure;
- 40% if the action is settled before the conclusion of the interim procedure;
- 20% if the action is settled before the conclusion of the oral procedure.

Only one of the possible reimbursements will apply per action and party. Where more than one reimbursement is applicable, the larger will be applied for each party.[1533]

In exceptional cases, having regard, in particular, to the stage of the proceedings and the procedural behaviour of the party, the Court may decide to deny or decrease the reimbursement for withdrawal of action or for settlement.[1534]

Rule 370.10 includes the ultimate fall-back position for the Court, when the payment of the Court fees by a legal entity threatens the economic existence of a party. If the amount of payable Court fees threatens the economic existence of a party who is not a natural person, and has presented reasonably available and plausible evidence to support that the amount of Court fees threatens its economic existence, the Court may upon request by that party, wholly or partially reimburse the fixed and value-based fee. The request shall be dealt with by the Court without delay. In reaching a decision the Court shall reflect on all circumstances of the case including the procedural behaviour of the party. Before making such a decision the Court may give the other party an opportunity to be heard. A party who is adversely affected by the order may bring an appeal pursuant to Rule 220.

Natural persons can get legal aid to cover the Court fees (cf. *infra*).

2. Time period for paying fees (Rule 371)

The *fixed fees* should be paid at the time of lodging the relevant pleading or application (cf. Rules 5, 15.1, 26, 46, 53, 70, 132, 192.5, 206.5, 207.4, 228)[1535] and this to one of the bank accounts indicated by the Court. The payment needs to indicate the paying party (or its representative) together with the number of the patent (or patents) involved. Proof of payment should be provided together with the relevant pleading.[1536] In cases of urgency, where a payment in advance is not possible, the representative of the party in question can pay the fixed fee within the period set by the Court and the Court may order that the relevant pleading or application shall be

---

1531. Rule 370.9(b).
1532. Rule 370.9(c).
1533. Rule 370.9(d).
1534. Rule 370.9(e).
1535. Rule 371.1 *juncto* Rules 5, 15.1, 26, 46, 53, 70, 132, 192.5, 206.5, 207.3 and 228.
1536. Rule 371.2.

deemed lodged and effective when received by the Registry if payment of the fixed fee is made within such period.[1537]

The *value-based fees* should be paid within ten working days of service of the order determining the value of the dispute.[1538]

During the public consultation, this Rule provoked a lot of questions and comments. Who shall initially determine the value of the case? Which order was meant here? The explanatory note that accompanied the Rules on Court fees and recoverable costs provides that the expert panel recommended that claimants should make their own value assessment and pay the value-based fee based on that initial assessment at the same time as the fixed fee, that is when lodging the relevant application. If there is any contention over the assessment this will be rectified by the Court at the interim conference. The Fees Sub-Group of the Preparatory Committee agreed that this was the most simple and efficient process and so accepted the recommendation. As a result, it appears that Rule 371.4 does not have to be read with the meaning that the Court shall always service an order for determining the value. On the contrary, it will be up to the claimant to make its own value assessment and pay the value-based fee based on its own assessment when lodging its application. Only in case of contention will there be an assessment of the correctness of the Court fees during the interim conference.

There appears to be no sanction when downplaying the value of an action, apart from a contention by the other party. Moreover, it is not clear if downplaying the value of an action has an impact on the ceiling for recoverable costs. Since this ceiling will only become important at the end of the proceedings, it is possible that the Court assesses the value of the proceedings to determine the ceiling for recoverable costs, irrespective of the earlier paid Court fees. And even if the assessment by the claimant influences the ceiling for recoverable costs, this will take place at a stage when it is unclear who will ultimately be successful and whether that low ceiling is actually of benefit or a detriment.

Should an Application for legal aid been lodged,[1539] the Rules on the obligation to pay the fixed fees under Rule 371.1 shall not apply.[1540]

B. LEGAL AID (RULES 375–382)

1. Aim and scope (Rule 375)

The Court may grant legal aid to a party[1541] in order to ensure effective access to justice. Such legal aid may be granted in respect of any proceedings before the Court.

1537. Rule 371.3.
1538. Rule 371.4 *juncto* Rules 22, 31, 59, 60, 74, 104(i) and 133.
1539. In accordance with Rule 377 (laying out the conditions for granting legal aid).
1540. Rule 371.5.
1541. In earlier drafts of the Rules this was limited to a natural party.

Chapter IX – (Part 6) Fees and Legal Aid (Rules 370-382)

Flowchart: Examination application for legal aid (R. 375 – R. 382)

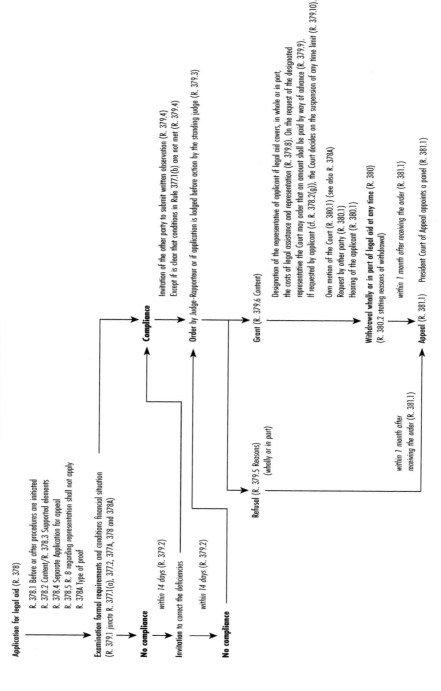

401

2. Costs eligible for legal aid (Rule 376)

Subject to Article 71(3) UPCA,[1542] legal aid may cover, besides the costs awarded to the successful party in the event the applicant loses the action,[1543] in whole or in part, the following costs:

(a) Court fees;
(b) costs of legal assistance and representation regarding:
   (i) pre-litigation advice with a view to reaching a settlement prior to commencing legal proceedings;
   (ii) commencing and maintaining proceedings before the Court;
   (iii) all costs relating to proceedings including the application for legal aid;
   (iv) enforcement of decisions;
(c) other necessary costs related to the proceedings to be borne by a party, including costs of witnesses, experts, interpreters and translators, and necessary travel, accommodation and subsistence costs of the applicant and his representative.

3. Maximum amount to be paid for representation (Rule 376A)

For the costs of representation[1544] the maximum level of legal aid that may be granted by the Court is the maximum amount of recoverable costs laid down in the decision of the Administrative Committee pursuant to Article 69(1) UPCA and Rule 152.2.[1545] [1546]

The Administrative Committee may define thresholds below the level set in Rule 376A.1 for the maximum level of legal aid for representation[1547] taking into account necessary costs for legal representation in the Contracting Member States and the need to guarantee adequate access to justice.[1548]

4. Conditions for granting legal aid (Rule 377)

Any natural person who is a citizen of the European Union or a third country national residing lawfully in a Member State of the European Union shall be entitled to legal aid where:[1549]

(a) owing to his economic situation, he is wholly or partly unable to meet the costs referred to in Rule 376; and

---

1542. The Article states that the level of legal aid as well as the rules on bearing the costs shall be set by the Administrative Committee on proposal from the Court.
1543. Rule 372.2.
1544. Pursuant to Rule 376.1(b).
1545. Rule 152.2 provides that the Administrative Committee shall adopt a scale of recoverable costs which shall set a ceiling for such costs by reference to the value of the dispute.
1546. Rule 376A.1.
1547. Pursuant to Rule 376.1(b).
1548. Rule 376A.2.
1549. Rule 377.1.

(b) the action in respect of which the application for legal aid is made has a reasonable prospect of success, considering the applicant's procedural position; and

(c) the claimant applying for legal aid is entitled to bring actions under Article 47.

The Administrative Committee defines thresholds above which legal aid applicants are deemed wholly or partly able to bear the costs of proceedings set out in Rule 376. These thresholds may not prevent applicants whose economic situation is above the thresholds from being granted legal aid if they prove that they are in fact unable to pay the costs of the proceedings referred to in Rule 376 as a result of the high level of the cost of living in the Contracting Member State of domicile or habitual residence.[1550]

When deciding on the granting of legal aid the Court shall, without prejudice to Rule 377.1(a) consider the importance of the action to the applicant but may also take into account the nature of the action when the application concerns a claim arising directly out of the applicant's trade or self-employed profession.[1551]

5. Conditions regarding the financial situation of the applicant (Rule 377A)

When assessing a party's financial situation his income and assets must be taken into account.[1552] *Income* should be understood to include all earnings in money or equivalent value after deducting all costs required by the applicant and dependent persons in order to cover their reasonable living expenses (disposable income).[1553] It is up to the Administrative Committee to define the deductions from income and assets to be taken into account when assessing the applicant's financial situation. The Administrative Committee shall also define levels of monthly instalments to be paid by the applicant. All thresholds set by the Administrative Committee shall be adapted regularly to price and income indices.[1554]

The application for legal aid should be drafted in the language of a Contracting Member State.[1555]

If the Court orders another party to pay the costs of the applicant for legal aid, that other party shall be required to refund to the Court any sums advanced by way of legal aid.[1556] In the event of a shortfall between the costs so ordered and the sums advanced by way of legal aid the applicant may be required to meet such shortfall from any damages or compensation awarded by the Court or from any sum received by way of settlement. In the event of withdrawal of legal aid under Rule 380, the applicant may be required to refund to the Court any sums advanced by way of legal aid.[1557]

1550. Rule 377.2.
1551. Rule 377.3.
1552. Rule 377A.1.
1553. Rule 377A.2.
1554. Rule 377A.3.
1555. Rule 378.2.
1556. Rule 382.1.
1557. Rule 382.2.

6. Appeal

Amendment 33 (to Rules 379 and 381) as adopted by the Administrative Committee on 8 July 2022 introduced Rule 382.2. Where Rule 382.1 deals with the appeal against the order of the Court of First Instance refusing or withdrawing legal aid (see final part of Flowchart: Examination application for legal aid), Rule 382.2 deals with legal aid *itself* for an appeal against a decision of the Court of First Instance and clarifies that according to Rule 375.2 and Rule 378.4 it is possible to apply for legal aid in order to appeal a decision of the Court of First instance.

The explanatory notes to this amendment further clarify that since a new application has to be filed (Rule 378.4), such application has to meet the requirements of Rules 377 to 379. Furthermore, since Rule 224 applies only to the appeal against the decision of the Court of First instance itself, Rule 381.2 clarifies that the application for legal aid has to be filed where possible within the same time limit provided for the appeal itself and should be accompanied by this appeal itself. Such application will be assigned according to Rule 345.8.

Index

A

Accession, 33, 34, 236, 237
Action, 380, 381
   action against decision by the EPO with regard to Article 9 of Regulation (EU) 1257/2012, 294
   action for compensation for licences on basis of Article 8 of Unitary Patent Regulation, 293
   action for declaration of non-infringement, 289, 292
   action within Article 33(5) and (6) UPCA, 292, 293
   actions bound to fail/manifestly inadmissible, 388
   actions pursuant to Article 22 UPCA, 355
   distribution of actions between the seats of the Central Division, 280, 281, 282, 283
   infringement action, 163, 164, 283, 285, 287, 289
   revocation action, 289
Administrative Committee, 110, 111, 229
   Administrative Committee of the Patent Mediation and Arbitration Centre, 113, 114, 125, 126
   Administrative Committee of the Unified Patent Court, 97, 98, 100
Advisory Committee, 111, 112
Alternative dispute resolution (ADR), 113
Appeal proceedings
   appeal, 218–220
      decision of, 221
      effects of, 220, 221
Appealable decisions, 333, 335, 336
Application
   Application by both parties to use the language in which the patent was granted as language of the proceedings, 375
   Application by one party to use the language in which the patent was granted as language of the proceedings, 376
   Application for leave of appeal against cost orders, 336, 337
   Application for legal aid, 401
   Application for preserving/to preserve evidence, 319, 322
   Application for re-establishment of rights, 373, 394, 396
   Application for rehearing, 346, 348
   Application for rehearing by panel, 347, 348
   Application for suspensive effect, 338
   Application for the determination of damages and compensation, 307
   Application of Article 7 Statute, 381–383
   Application to intervene, 372
   Application to opt-out, 261
   Application to review case management order, 377
   Application to withdraw, 263
   entry into force and, Unitary Patent, 79, 80
   provisional application, 241
   reimbursement of translation cost, 81, 82, 83, 84, 85
Appropriate qualifications, 186, 187, 188, 189
Arbitral award, 123–125, 272
Arbitrator, 110, 113, 117, 119–121, 126
Attorney–Client privilege. *See* Representation/representatives
Award of damages
   determination of damages, 210, 211
   period of limitation, 212

B

Bifurcation, 166–168
Brexit, 34
Budget, 227
Budget Committee, 111, 119, 228, 230
Budgetary and Financial Rules (BFR), 77, 78, 79
Burden of proof, 198, 199

C

Case management. *See also* Judges
  connection-joinder, 378, 379
  exercise of managing powers, 378
  orders, 378
  powers of, 378
  principles of, 377
  responsibility for, 376, 377
  review of orders, 377
  varying/revoking orders, 378
Case Management System (CMS), 243
Ceiling, 30, 81, 84, 212–217, 282, 312, 391, 396, 400
Central division, 380, 381
CJEU/Court of Justice of the European Union
  preliminary rulings of, 94
  primacy of Union law, 92, 93
  Union law
    liability for infringements, 95–97
Communicate information, 319
Community Patent, 5, 6
  Council Regulation, 6, 7
Community Patent Convention (CPC), 5, 6
Compensation, 82
  amount of, 84, 85
  procedure for, 83
  revision of decision to grant, 84
  transfer, 83
Competition law, 49
Composition of panels, 380, 381
Compulsory licences, 56
Confidential information, 352, 353
Conflicts of jurisdiction, 165, 166
Connection–Joinder, 378, 379
Corrective measures, 207, 208
Costs, 81–85
  security for costs, 312
Court experts, 317
Court fees, 217, 218

Court of Appeal, 105
  appealable decisions, 333, 335, 336
  application for leave, 336
  application for suspensive effect, 338
  decision, 388
  decisions and effect of decisions, 345
  full court, 104
  interim procedure, 343
  language of proceedings, 196
  President, 104
  procedure for application for rehearing, 346, 347, 348
  subject matter before, the, 337
  written procedure, 338, 339, 342, 343
Court of First Instance
  birds' eye view, 271, 272, 275, 277–283
  central division, 100, 101
  damages and compensation, 307–309
  decision, 386–388
  discontinuance, 104
  interim procedure. *See* Interim procedure
  language of proceedings
    central divisions, 194
    general exception, 195
    local divisions, 192, 193
    regional divisions, 194
  local division, 101, 102
  oral procedure. *See* Oral procedure
  President, 99
  procedure for cost orders, 311, 312
  regional division, 103
  security for costs, 312
  written procedure. *See* Written procedure
Court of Justice
  preliminary rulings, 105, 106

D

Damages, 48, 49
Date
  date of application, 86
  date of effect, 44, 45
  date of pleadings, 349
Decision
  basis for decisions, 222
  binding effect of, 384
  compensation, to grant, 84
  court of appeal, 388

Index

court of first instance, 386–388
decisions by default, 223
dissenting opinions, 222, 223
effect of, 345
enforcement of, 225, 226, 385, 386
EPO, 209, 210
formal requirements, 222
publication of decisions, 224
rectification of, 384
rehearing, 224, 225
settlement decisions, 224
validity of patent, 208, 209
Delegate, 380
Deliberations, 380
Discontinuance, 103, 104
Dissenting opinions, 223
  decision making process, 222, 223
Distribution of actions between the seats of the Central Division. See Action

E

Effect
  consequences included in Unitary Patent Regulation, 45–47
  damages, 48, 49
  Participating Member States, 47, 48
Enforcement, 385, 386
  decisions and orders, of, 225, 226
Enhanced cooperation, 11–13, 33, 34
  opposition, to, 13–17
Entry into force, 87, 88, 238, 239
  Unitary Patent, 79, 80
Equal claims, 41, 42
EU Patent
  communication, 7, 8
  community patent, 5–7
  community patent convention, 5, 6
  enhanced cooperation, 11–17
  language regime, 9–11
  Swedish presidency, 8, 9
European Patent Bulletin, 83
European Patent Convention (EPC), 5
European Patent Litigation Certificate, 186–189
European Patent Office (EPO), 1, 2, 9, 10, 22, 24, 27–31, 35–42, 44, 49–87, 100, 106, 130, 132, 135, 136, 153, 154, 162, 167, 168, 170, 183–186, 188, 189, 192–194, 209, 210, 220, 224, 233, 256, 257, 259, 260, 266, 271, 279, 289,

293–296, 305, 306, 327, 362, 365, 366, 394, 395
  publication by, 87
  renewal fees, 73–76
  Unitary Patent, role of, 60, 61
European Patent System
  communication, 7, 8
European Patents
  transitional regime and opt-out, 231–233
Evidence, 313
  duty to produce, 314
  experiments ordered by court, 325
  judicial cooperation, 314
  means of evidence, 198, 199
  offering of, 313, 314
  order to freeze assets, 324, 325
  order to preserve evidence, 319–324
  order to produce evidence, 318
Exhaustion
  unfair competition and competition law, 49
Expert committee, 86
Experts, 317
  experts of parties, 314–316

F

Fees
  assessment of value of action, 396, 397
  court fees, 391, 392
  Court of Appeal fees, 395, 396
  fixed fees, 392–395
  multiple claimants/defendants, 397
  opt-out fees, 392
  reimbursement of court fees, 398, 399
  small and micro-enterprises, 398
  time period for paying fees, 399, 400
  value-based fees, 279–282, 393
Financial Regulations, 228, 229
Financing, 227, 228
Formal requirements, 39, 40
Formal requirements/examination, 272, 274, 275, 277
Forum-shopping, 105
Freezing orders, 202

I

Independent revocation action, 168, 169
Information purposes, 87

407

Infringement
  corrective measures, 207, 208
  permanent injunctions, 206, 207
  unitary patent regulation, 22
Infringement actions, 163, 164
Inspection
  order for inspection, 319–324
Intellectual Property Judges Association (IPJA), 45
Interim procedure, 198, 298, 299, 301
International jurisdiction, 157–161
International Patent Classification, 100
Interpretation arrangements, 197
Intervention, 370–373

J
Judges, 135
  Administrative Committee, 137–139
  disciplinary measures, 143, 144
  end of duties, 152
  full time and part-time judges, 141
  immunity, 151, 152
  judicial independence and impartiality, 144–151
  leave, 143
  legally qualified judges, 139, 140
  Pool of Judges, 153
  Preparatory Committee, 136, 137
  remuneration, allowances and reimbursement of expenses, 142
  social security benefits, 143
  staff and judicial vacations, 155
  technically qualified judges, 129, 135, 147
  training framework for, 153–155
  working conditions, 140
Judgment
  translation regulation, 27–31
  unitary patent regulation, 22–27

L
Language
  Application by both parties to use the language in which the patent was granted as language of the proceedings, 375
  Application by one party to use the language in which the patent was granted as language of the proceedings, 376
  change of language of proceedings, 373, 374
  Consequences where the language of the proceedings is changed in the course of the proceedings, 376
  regime, 9–11, 81–85, 255–258
Language regime, 255–258
Languages
  authentic languages, 238
Lapse, 44, 49, 50, 58, 67, 68, 75, 76, 84, 86, 202, 212, 324
  Unitary Patent, 60
Leave to change claim/amend case, 353
Legal aid, 218
  aim and scope of, 400
  appeal, 404
  conditions for granting, 402, 403
  conditions regarding financial situation of applicant, 403
  cost eligible for, 402
  maximum amount to be paid for representation, 402
Legal status, 35–37
  CJEU, 91
  EU Member States, 91
  legal capacity of court, 98
  Unified Patent Court, 97, 98
Licence statements, 54, 55

M
Multinational composition
  Court of Appeal, 131–133
  Court of First Instance
    central division, 130
    judges, 130, 131
    local division, 127, 128
    panels, 131
    regional division, 128
    technically qualified judge, 129

N
National judges, 94, 98, 105, 116, 127, 128, 130, 135, 142, 235
National proceedings
  transitional regime and opt-out, 233–236
Non-infringement actions, 169
Non-profit organisations, 81, 82

Index

O

Object of property
  applicable law, 52, 53
  compulsory licences, 56
  procedure, 56–58
  renewal fee reduction, 53–55
Opportunity to be heard, 353
Opt-out
  transitional regime, and
    European Patents, 231–233
    national proceedings, 233–236
Oral procedure, 198, 301, 303–307
Oral proceedings, 66, 67
Order, 380
  binding effect of, 384
  enforcement of, 385, 386
  inspection of premises, 200–202
  order for inspection, 319–324
  order to communicate information, 319
  order to freeze assets, 202, 324, 325
  order to preserve evidence, 200–202, 319–324
  order to produce evidence, 204, 318
  rectification of, 384
Orders, 384

P

Panel, 379–381
Participating Member States, 47, 48
Parties, 183
  change in, 369
  death/demise of, 369
  insolvency of, 369, 370
  intervention, 370–373
  plurality of claimants/patents, 367, 368
  plurality of defendants, 368
  re-establishment of rights, 373
  transfer of patent, 370
  witnesses and experts of, 314–316
Patent Mediation and Arbitration Centre, 113, 114, 125, 126
  issues, 121
    competence of centre, 122
    enforceability of settlements, 123–125
    revoking and limiting patents, 125
    one-stop shop dispute resolution system, 114, 115
  rules of operation
    Administrative Committee, 119
    auditors, 119
    Budget Committee, 119
    case managerial assistance, 120
    director, 118–120
    Expert Committee, 119, 120
    finances, 118
    framework in, 115, 116
    languages, 118
    list of arbitrators and mediators, 120, 121
    name, status, seat and aims, 116–118
    secretarial assistance, 120
    start of operations, 121
Patent Protection
  layer of, 37, 38
Permanent injunctions, 206, 207
Place of business, 81, 82
Powers
  to order communication of information, 205, 206
Powers of court
  award of damages, 210–217
  court experts, 204, 205
  decisions of EPO, 209, 210
  freezing orders, 202
  general powers, 200
  inspection of premises, 200–202
  order to preserve evidence, 200–202
  protective measures, 202, 203
  provisional measures, 202, 203
  recoverable legal costs, 212–217
Preliminary Objection, 277–279
Preliminary references to CJEU, 354
Preparatory Committee, 107, 108
  facilities, 110
  financial regulations, 109
  human resources and training, 110
  IT system, 110
  legal framework group, 108, 109
Presidium, 100, 104, 106, 107, 111–113, 131, 132, 141, 143, 144, 146, 148, 150–152, 154, 155, 228–230, 241, 343, 379, 380, 383
  Unified Patent Court, of, 100
Procedural principles, 182, 183
Procedure, 40
  EPO, 38–41

for acquiring compensation, 83
for cost orders, 311, 312
for the award/determination of damages, 307
object of property, 56–58
procedure for application for rehearing, 346–348
Statute and the Rules of, 181, 182
Proprietorship
Unified patent, 259, 260
Protective letter, 329–331
Protective measures, 164, 165
Provisional measures, 164, 165
Provisional protection, 164, 165
Public access to Register, 350–352
Publication
decision, of, 224
Unitary Patent, 58, 59

R

Ratification, 236, 237
Recoverable legal costs, 212–217
Re-establishment of rights, 67, 68, 373
Referral back, 221
Register for Unitary Patent Protection, 49–52, 83
Registry, 106, 107
Deputy-Registrar, 254
examination by, 349
Registrar, 254
RegistryRegistrar, 380
Rehearing, 224, 225, 346, 347, 348
Reimbursement
translation cost, of, 81–85
Renewal fees
administration by EPO, 73–76
appropriate consideration, 54
distribution of, 71–73
in general, 68
level of, 68–71
offer of licences, 53, 54
registration of licence statements, 54, 55
rules relating to fees for Unitary Patent Protection, 76, 77
withdrawal of, 54
Representation
code of conduct, 189–192
in general, 184–186

Rules on the European Patent Litigation Certificate and other appropriate qualifications, 186–189
Representation/Representatives
Attorney-client privilege, 361, 362
certificate, 361
change of, 364
duties, 360
exclusion from proceedings, 363
litigation privilege, 362
powers of attorney, 361
powers of court, 363
privileges, immunities and facilities, 363
removal from register, 364
right of audience, 364
Request for unitary effect, 83
Residence, 81, 82
Rules of Procedure
application of, 253
framework, 247
language regime, 255–258
legal history of, 247–249
lodging of documents, 254, 255
opt-out and withdrawal, 261, 264–268
powers of court, 260, 261
Preamble to, 251, 252
Registry/Registrar and Deputy-Registrar, 254
service and supply of orders, 255
supplementary protection certificates, 254
templates and guidances, 249, 250

S

saisie. See Order to preserve evidence
Security for costs. See Costs
Select committee, 61–63
Service
change of electronic address, 360
Service by an alternative method, 358, 359
Service of decision, 359, 360
Service of orders, 255, 359, 360
Service of written pleadings, 359, 360
Service outside the Contracting Member States, 358
Service within the Contracting Member States/by agreement, 355–358

Settlement, 389
SME, 81–84, 86
Sources of law, 173–175
Stay of proceedings
   accelerated proceedings before EPO, 366
   duration and effects of, 366
   resumption of proceedings, 366
   situations, 365, 366
Substantive competence
   Court, actions for, 162, 163
   patents, 161
Substantive patent law, 175
   direct use of invention, 175
   exhaustion, 179
   indirect use of invention, 176
   limitations of, 176–178
   prior use, 178
   supplementary protection certificates, 179
Substantive requirements, 39, 40
Supplementary Protection Certificates (SPC), 179, 254

T

Territorial competence
   conflicts of jurisdiction, 165, 166
   counterclaim for revocation, 166–168
   general exception, 170
   independent revocation action, 168, 169
   infringement actions of, 163, 164
   licences of Unitary Patent, 165
   non-infringement actions, 169
   provisional and protective measures, 164, 165
   Unitary Patent, 170
Time periods
   automatic extension of periods, 367
   calculation, 366, 367
Transfer, 83
Transitional period, 85–87
Transitional regime, 86, 87, 234, 236, 249, 264
   opt-out, and
      European Patents, 231–233
      immediate and exclusive jurisdiction for Unitary Patents, 231
      national proceedings, 233–236

Translation arrangements, 197
Translation cost
   reimbursement of, 81–85
Translation Regulation, 21, 22, 27
   autonomy of EU law, 31
   consequence of dismissals, 31
   lack of legal basis for Article 4, 29, 30
   legal certainty, 30, 31
   Meroni judgment, 29
   non-discrimination on ground of language, 27, 28

U

Unfair competition, 49
Unified Patent Court Agreement (UPCA), 2
   legal status. *See* Legal status
Union law
   liability for infringements, 95–97
   primacy of, 92, 93
Unitary character, 42
   impact of opposition, 44
   revocation/limitation of, 43
   scope of, 43
   transfer/licence, 43, 44
Unitary Patent
   date of effect, 44, 45
   decision of Unified Patent Court, 59
   effect, 45–49
   entry into force, 79, 80
   equal claims, 41, 42
   exhaustion, 49
   Implementing Rules of EPC, 63–66
   language regime, 81–85
   lapse, 60
   layer of patent protection, 37, 38
   legal status of, 35–37
   object of property, 52–58
   oral proceedings, 66, 67
   procedure, 38–41
   publications, 58, 59
   re-establishment of rights, 67, 68
   Register for Unitary Patent Protection, 49–52
   renewal fees, 68–77
   role of EPO, 60, 61
   rules relating to Unitary Patent Protection, 63
   select committee, 61–63
   unitary character, 42–44

Unitary Patent Protection, 19, 49–52
    Implementing Rules of EPC applying *mutatis mutandis*, to, 63–66
    renewal fees, rules relating to, 76, 77
    rules relating, to, 63
Unitary Patent Regulation, 21, 22
    autonomy and uniformity of EU law, 25–27
    consequence of dismissals, 31
    effect and consequences included in, 45–47
    infringement of Article 2D1(2) TFEU, 24
    infringement of rule of law, 22
    legal basis, for, 23
    legal status of, 35–37
    misuse of powers, 23

W

Withdrawal, 354
    opt-out, 261, 264–268

Witnesses, 314–316
Written procedure, 198
    action for compensation for licences on basis of Article 8 of Unitary Patent Regulation, 293
    action for declaration of non-infringement, 289, 292
    action within Article 33(5) and (6) UPCA, 292, 293
    Actions against decision by the EPO with regard to Article 9 of Regulation (EU) 1257/2012, 294
    Actions against decision of the EPO in carrying out the tasks referred to in Article 9 of Unitary Patent Regulation, 296
    infringement action, 283, 285, 287, 289
    revocation action, 289